Ulick Joseph Bourke

The College Irish Grammar

Compiled Chiefly with a View to Aid the Students of St. Patrick's College. Third Edition

Ulick Joseph Bourke

The College Irish Grammar
Compiled Chiefly with a View to Aid the Students of St. Patrick's College. Third Edition

ISBN/EAN: 9783337117641

Printed in Europe, USA, Canada, Australia, Japan

Cover: Foto ©Paul-Georg Meister /pixelio.de

More available books at **www.hansebooks.com**

THE
COLLEGE IRISH GRAMMAR,

COMPILED CHIEFLY WITH A VIEW TO AID

THE STUDENTS OF ST. PATRICK'S COLLEGE, MAYNOOTH,

AND OF

THE CATHOLIC UNIVERSITY OF IRELAND,

IN THE STUDY OF

THE NATIONAL LANGUAGE.

BY

THE REV. ULICK J. BOURKE,

Professor of Logic, Natural Philosophy, and Languages, St. Jarlath's College, Tuam.

"Ah! the pleasant Tongue, whose accents were music to the ear!
Ah! the magic Tongue, that round us wove its spell so soft and dear!
Ah! the glorious Tongue, whose murmur could each Celtic heart enthral!
Ah! the rushing Tongue, that sounded like the swollen torrent's fall!"
Rev. M. M.—Ballads of Ireland, Edited by Edward Hayes.

"Éire! O Éire! tá le saoġaltaiḃ faoi tsáċ,
'Nuair éalóċar a g-cliú-ran beiḋ do ċaiṫréim faoi bláṫ."
Irish Melodies, p. 19.

𝔗𝔥𝔦𝔯𝔡 𝔈𝔡𝔦𝔱𝔦𝔬𝔫—𝔗𝔥𝔦𝔯𝔡 𝔗𝔥𝔬𝔲𝔰𝔞𝔫𝔡.

DUBLIN:
JOHN MULLANY, 1 PARLIAMENT-STREET.
T. JONES, PATERNOSTER-ROW, LONDON.
AND SOLD BY ALL BOOKSELLERS.
1865.

TO

THE IRISH STUDENTS,

AT HOME AND ABROAD,

WHO LOVE THE PRESERVATION OF

THE NATIONAL LANGUAGE,

THE COLLEGE IRISH GRAMMAR—

WRITTEN CHIEFLY WITH A VIEW

TO TEACH THE YOUTHS OF IRELAND

SOMETHING ABOUT THEIR MOTHER TONGUE

Is most respectfully Dedicated,

BY THEIR HUMBLE AND MOST OBEDIENT SERVANT,

THE AUTHOR.

"Sweet Tongue of our druids and bards of past ages!
Sweet Tongue of our monarchs, our saints, and our sages!
Sweet Tongue of our heroes and free-born sires!
When we cease to preserve thee, our glory expires."

Anon.

PREFACE TO THE SECOND EDITION.

SINCE this edition has been put to press, one of the greatest Irish Scholars of the present or any former century has passed away—the learned and the lamented John O'Donovan, LL.D. A cycle of years will not repay to the cause of Celtic literature the loss it has sustained in his death. May his memory be ever dear to every lover of ancient lore and real learning.

His was the master-hand which first moulded into philological and philosophical form and fullness the chaotic mass into which persecution for ages past, and consequent inability of Irishmen at home to attend to its preservation, much less to its literary cultivation, had reduced their mother-tongue; a tongue which has been pronounced by a linguistic lover to be as clear as Latin, flexible and harmonious as Greek, stately as Spanish, soft as Italian, fluent as French, and expressive as German. Dr. O'Donovan's work infused into the written speech of the Gael spirit and life, which length of time alone can extinguish.

Although he did much, yet—no wonder—he left much undone; and though he laboured for the cause of the people's language, the many had not been enabled to profit by his labours.

The College Irish Grammar was written and published for the sake of the many, and to improve, as best one could, the literary character of the vernacular speech. On its first appearance the work was favourably noticed by the learned. Being now entirely re-cast, the present edition—embracing the results of observations made during the last six years throughout the provinces on the spoken dialects, and in works published and unpublished on the written speech—cannot fail to be of much additional service to the student and the *savant*.

To lament, like hireling mourners, the loss of the language of the past, and at the same time, to neglect or decry the living, spoken language of the present, bespeaks insincerity at heart, and proves such flippant eulogists of the Gaelic to be actuated for its preservation or advancement only by that kind of regard for which step-mothers are proverbial. Good wishes without practice are like flowers without fruit.

St. Jarlath's College, Tuam,
Feast of SS. Philip and James, 1862.

CONTENTS.

PART I.

	Page
PREFACE	1
INTRODUCTION	3
Penal process exercised even lately on children speaking Irish	4
Letter of the Most Rev. Dr. O'Connor, Bishop of Saldes, on the way to teach Irish to the rising generation	5
What the Irish societies have done and are doing for the language	5
What the National Schools are not doing	6
The Catholic University—note thereon	6
What the language of a nation symbolizes	7
This is a grammar of the Irish language as it is at present spoken and written	8
Dr. O'Donovan's grammar—its merits	9
Why the present work had been commenced by the writer while a student of Maynooth	10
Grammar in its general and special acceptation	11
Grammar an art and a science	11
Irish grammar	11
ORTHOGRAPHY.—A word	12

CHAPTER I.

THE LETTERS—THEIR CLASSIFICATION AND SOUNDS.

Section.		Page
1.—*The Elements of Words—Letters*		12
h, a mere aspirate—authorities on this		12
The Irish alphabet—names, sound, pronunciation of the letters		13
The original character of the Irish letters—not borrowed—proofs		13
Peculiar sound of *s* (i.e., *sh*) before or after the vowels e, í		14
Sound of ɼ same as if ɑɼ—reason thereof by Henry Leo		14
Vowels defined—consonants		14
2.—The vowels—how sounded—how classified		15
How the Irish sounds given to the vowels accord with the view of philosophers on phonetics		15
O'Donovan shows how natives of Munster and Connaught differ in the way they sound some vowels. This is the source of the difference in pronunciation where it exists		15
The length of a vowel regulated by its position with respect to the accent—this shown on philosophical principles		16
Classification of the vowels into broad (ɑ, o, u), and slender (e, í)		16
Rule cɑol le cɑol, ɑʒuɼ leɑtɑn le leɑtɑn		16
3.—AUTHORITIES FOR AND AGAINST THE RULE		16-17
The opinion that appears most reasonable		18
4.—PHILOSOPHIC REASONS IN SUPPORT OF THE RULE		18-19
5.—Each consonant has a two-fold sound		20

CONTENTS.

Sect.		Page
6.—Broad and slender sounds of the consonants		20
C Gaelic always sounds *k*		20
The two consonants ng represent only a single sound		21
7.—Mutes, Liquids		22
8.—Gemination, or doubling the same letter		22
9.—Immutables, Mutables		23
10.—A Syllable		23
11.—DIPHTHONGS.—True or perfect, imperfect; long, short, number of		23
12.—The long diphthongs—sound of the six long diphthongs		24
13.—Observations on the long diphthongs		24
Long diphthongs ought not to be marked with the accent		24
Each vowel in a diphthong should be distinctly enunciated		24
Correct sound of "ɪᴀ"—difference between the sound of ɪᴀ and ᴀo		24
Remarkable sound of "co"—is like *yeo*, or *eogh* in *Keogh*		25
14.—Sounds of the variable diphthongs—when a variable diphthong is long, the accent is placed over the lengthened vowel—when short, it is omitted		25
The sound of *ou* in *house*, though not found as a diphthong, is in use, in the form ᴀb, ᴀm, a vowel and consonant combined		26
Uniform spelling of "eu" adopted in this work for the long diphthongal sound of éᴀ		26
Speaking the language and hearing it spoken, is the only way, after all, to learn correctness of pronunciation		26
Pronunciation appertains to phonetics, and therefore, like a tune in music, or the air of a song, is best learned by ear		26
15.—Triphthongs—five in number—remember, each vowel is sounded		26
Difference between the sounds of the triphthongs and the diphthongs from which they are formed		26
ɪᴀɪ (pr. *ee-yee* in one); ɪᴀ (pr. *ee-a* in one)		26

CHAPTER II.
OF THE CONSONANTS.

16.—*The natural sound of the consonants changed by aspiration*		27
17.—Aspiration—what is it?		27
Consonants divided into four classes, named after the organs of speech which chiefly contribute to their articulation		27
Table of		27
By aspiration, the organic class-division of the consonant is not changed; the sound alone becomes modified		28
18.—SYNOPSIS OR TABLE OF ASPIRATES AND THEIR SOUNDS		28
19.—Sounds of the aspirated consonants fully explained		28-29
20.—Aspiration is founded on a principle of phonetics, or on the laws of sound, and is not the result, as Davies and Pinkerton would make it appear, of barbarity		31
The universal law of phonetics is, that vowels and consonants blend better in united sound with letters of their own genus, than with any others. Hence after vowels, the aspirated, i.e., the softer or affected sound of the consonant, is heard		27-33
Men regard this or that sound as polished or barbarous, according as it agrees with or differs from the sounds to which they have been accustomed from infancy		31

CONTENTS.

Sect. | Page
21.—Sounds of ᴀò eᴀó, and of uᴊ́ᴀó at the end of a word .. 31
22.—Similarity between aspiration in Greek and aspiration in Irish .. 32
23.—The custom of aspirating by the letter *h* ought not to be followed—
the aspirate mark (') preferable 33
The aspirate form is secondary, and not primary—no aspirated consonant commences a word in its natural state—the word must follow or depend upon another in some way .. 33
O'Mahony's views on the use of *h* 34
24.—Rules for aspiration 34-39
25.—Eclipsis—what is it? 39
Table of the cognate consonants 39
26.—Table of eclipses 39
27.—Rules for eclipsing 40-42
28.—Advantages of eclipsing compared with the changeable system of the Welsh 42
29.—The combinations ʒɲ and nʒ 42
The combinations cɲ, ɩb, ɩʒ, ɩm, ɲb, nʒ, ɲɲ 42

CHAPTER III.
ON SPELLING AND WRITING IN IRISH.

30.—*Spelling* 43
31.—A few practical hints on the spelling of the Irish language .. 43-45
32.—That it is easy to learn the spelling of Irish or Gaelic .. 46
33.—An example, showing at one view the number of words that can be formed from a single root of one syllable 47
34.—Of writing Irish in the Irish character 47
35.—Exercises 48

PART II.—ETYMOLOGY.

36.—Etymology defined—its subdivisions—parts of speech .. 49

CHAPTER I.

37.—The article 50
38.—The various initial changes which the *article* causes, when governed or when not governed by a preposition 50

CHAPTER II.
NOUNS.

39.—Definition of a noun 51
40.—Gender—rules by which the gender of every class of nouns in Gaelic can become known 52
41.—Number 55
42.—Person 55
43.—Case 55
44.—Number of cases 55
45.—Reasons why there are only four cases—reasons why the first oblique case is called *genitive* and not *possessive*—other cases 55-56
46.—Declension 56

CONTENTS.

Sect.		Page
47.—Number of declensions		56
48.—First declension		57
49.—Second declension		59
50.—Third declension		61
51.—Primitive nouns of one or more syllables, of which some end in a slender vowel		62
52.—Fourth declension		63
53.—Fifth declension		64
54.—A list of all the nouns belonging to the fifth declension		65
55.—Reasons for retaining the fifth as a special declension		65
56.—Rules for the formation of the several cases, singular and plural, of the five declensions		66
First declension—genitive singular		66
57.—The distinguishing mark of the first declension		66-67
58.—Second declension—the formation of the genitive singular		68
59.—Third declension—the formation of the genitive singular		68
60.—The dative case		69
61.—The vocative		70
62.—The vocative singular of nouns of the fourth or of the fifth declension		70
63.—The genitive plural of nouns in the different declensions		71
64.—The formation of the dative plural		71
65.—How the plural of nouns is formed		71
66.—General rule, regarding the parasyllabic class		72
67.—Formation of the plural of nouns of the fourth declension ending in l, m, n, ɲ, r, followed by a vowel		73
The endings ɲaɪò, laɪò, have a collective meaning, rather than a plural one		74
68.—Formation of the plural of the imparasyllabic class		74
69.—Irregular nouns		75

CHAPTER III.
OF THE ADJECTIVE.

70.—Properties of adjectives		76
Their position is after the noun—they change with the changes of the noun		76-77
71.—How adjectives are declined—four classes		78-79
72.—Adjectives terminating in the liquid letters l, m, n, ɲ, or r, eliminate the vowel in the change of case. This is a law of phonetics, and therefore not peculiar to Gaelic, but common to all languages		79
73.—Monosyllables spelled with the diphthongs, ea, eu, ɪa, ɪo		80
74.—Adjectives declined with nouns		80
75.—An exercise containing many adjectives		81
76.—Degrees of comparison: there are three degrees—reasons for this		82
The superlative a degree of comparison		82
77.—Comparison of equality		82
78.—Comparison of superiority and of inferiority		83
Many examples—meaning of njor, and ar, or fr		83
79.—Peculiar idiom—use of " oe," *of it,* after an adjective in the comparative degree		84
The true view of this idiom opposed to Stewart and Haliday		84

CONTENTS.

vii

Sect.		Page
80.—The relative superlative		84
81.—The formation of the superlative absolute		85
Adjectives of the same meaning—some always precede, others are made to follow the noun		85
82.—Irregular comparison		85
A list of all adjectives which do not follow the regular manner of comparison		86
83.—Numeral adjectives		86-87
84.—"ᴅeuᵹ," from "ᴅeᴊċ," same as English teen, from ten		88
Observations		88
85.—Numerals applied to persons only		88
86.—Various examples of numeral adjectives with nouns		89
Table showing the names of the numerals in six primitive languages		89

CHAPTER IV.
THE PRONOUN.

87.—Definition—classification of pronouns		90
88.—The personal pronouns		90
89.—Declension of the personal pronouns		91
90.—Affinity between the personal pronouns in Gaelic, Cornish, and Welsh		92
91.—The emphatic forms of the personal pronouns		92
92.—The emphatic suffixes, ꞃᴀ, ꞃe, ꞃᴀɲ		92
93.—The old emphatic form of the plural ꞃɪɲɲ, ɪɲɲ		92
94.—The emphatic suffixes follow whenever the possessive pronouns are employed		93
95.—Why the emphatic suffixes are annexed		93
96.—Are personal pronouns inflected in Gaelic?		94
Prichard's view shown to be erroneous		94
97.—Gaelic personal pronouns, the original forms of the pronouns in the Indo-European group		95
98.—The personal pronouns compounded with prepositious		95
Analysis		95-97
99.—On the spelling of ᴅᴀɪɲ		98
100.—Seᴀċ, *besides*, in the compounded form		99
101.—Possessive pronouns		99-100
102.—On ɱo ꞃ o, &c., ꞃéɪɲ		100
103.—Relative pronouns		101
104.—Interrogative pronouns		101
105.—Demonstrative pronouns		101
106.—Indefinite pronouns		102

CHAPTER V.
THE VERB.

107.—Definition of—nature of		102
108.—Moods and tenses		103
109.—Number of moods		103
110.—Meaning of the different moods		103
111.—The subjunctive mood not specifically different from the form of the indicative		103
112.—Tense		104

viii   CONTENTS

Sect.		Page
113.—Number, person, inflection of verbs		105
114.—Conjugation—are there two in Gaelic?		105-106
115.—Synoptical conjugation of the substantive verb ɓo ɓeιṫ, *to be*		106-107
116.—Conjugation of the verb ɓo ɓeιṫ, *to be*, in full		108-113
117.—Analytic conjugation		113
Some observations on the verb ɓo ɓeιṫ		114
118.—No verb like *have* (English), signifying *to possess*—idioms		114-115
Spelling of the plural endings of the perfect tense		115
119.—Analogy between bιò and the forms of the substantive verb in other languages		116
120.—On the difference in meaning between ṫᴀιɱ and bιòιɱ		116

CHAPTER VI.

REGULAR VERBS—FIRST CONJUGATION.

121.—Analogy between Hebrew and Irish verbs		117
122.—Ending of the first person plural imperative		117
123.—Table showing at one view the personal endings of all the tenses and moods of verbs of the first conjugation		118-119
Example of a verb of the first conjugation having in the root the final vowel broad		120
124.—Uniformity in spelling the verbal inflections desirable—endings of the first person plural		121
125.—A change—cᴀol le cᴀol not to be always applied		122
126.—Future of the first conjugation, ꜰᴀò		123
127.—Example in which the last vowel of the verbal root is slender		124
128.—Second conjugation—the final syllable, uιġ		126
Spelling of the future tense		128
129.—Particular rules for the formation of the tenses of the second conjugation		129
130.—A list of verbs of the second conjugation		129-132
131.—Substantival character of the infinitive mood		132
132.—The most common endings of the infinitive		132-133
133.—Passive voice		134
134.—Table of the personal endings of verbs of the second conjugation		136
135.—The analytic form of the passive voice		137
136.—When ṫᴀ (or ṫɛ) of the past participle is aspirated, and when not		137
Rules		138
ṫ, in the past participle, is not aspirated in the Erse		139
137.—Participles		139
138.—Division of participles		139
139.—The active participle		139
140.—The passive participle		140
141.—The formation of the passive participle		140

CHAPTER VII.

CONJUGATION OF THE IRREGULAR VERBS.

142.—Irregular verbs		140
143.—Conjugation of the ten irregular verbs		141-143
144.—Passive voice of the irregular verbs		143

CONTENTS.

Sect.		Page
145.—How far these verbs are irregular—"the whole scheme of language is analogical"		144
146.—Remarks on the irregular verbs—on beıɲɩɲ, *I bear*		144
147.—On beıɲɩɲ, *I give*		145
148.—The verb cluɩɲ		146
149.—The infinitve cloɾ and its cognate terms		146
150.—The verb béʌn		147
151.—The verb beɩɲ		147
152.—The verb ꝼaṡ		147
153.—The verb ꝼeɩc		148
154.—The verb ıṫṡ		148
155.—The verb céɩʋ		148
156.—The verb cıṡɩɲ		149
157.—The verb ɩċ		149
158.—Number of irregular verbs in French and in Irish contrasted		150
159.—Defective verbs		150
160.—Obsolete verbs		151
161.—Impersonal verbs		152
162.—Pure impersonals—few		152

CHAPTER VIII.
ADVERBS.

163.—Definition of an adverb		152
164.—Adverbs of two kinds		153
165.—Adverbs formed from adjectives		153
166.—Meaning of "ꝛo"		153
167.—Power of "ꝛo"		153
Ode chanted at the battle of Harlow		153-155
168.—Clauses of sentences		155
Adverbs of this class		155-160
169.—Adverbial prefixes		160

CHAPTER IX.
PREPOSITIONS, CONJUNCTIONS, INTERJECTIONS

170.—Definition of a preposition		161
171.—Simple prepositions		161
172.—Compound prepositions		161-165
173.—Definition of a conjunction		165
174.—Definition of an interjection		168
175.—Interjectional sentences		169

CHAPTER X.
DERIVATION AND COMPOSITION.

176.—Importance of this subject		170
177.—Division of		170
178.—The stem of a word		170
179.—Simples, derivative, compounds		170
180.—Prefixes		171
181.—Three parts of speech chiefly are subject to derivation or composition		171

CONTENTS.

Sect.		Page
182.—Nouns—various classes of		171
183.—Nouns ending in ᚐn, ɪn		171
184.—Derivations from the root cᚐn, or cᚐɪn		172
185.—Nouns in bᚐn		172
186.—Adjectives, derived		172
187.—Ꭺṁᚐɪl, *like*		172
188.—Ꮇᚐn		173
189.—Ꭺċ		173
190.—Derivation of adjectives ending in "ᚐċ"		173
191.—Patronymics		173
192.—Other nouns in "ᚐċ" and lᚐċ		174
193.—Derivative verbs		174
194.—Of the formation of Irish compound terms		174
195.—Substantives in the nominative case compounded with other substantives in the same case		175
196.—Names found in Cæsar, such as Dumnorix—how derived		176
197.—Form of compound substantives		176
198.—Other nouns of Keltic origin		177
199.—Nouns with an adjective prefixed		177
200.—Nouns with a verb prefixed		179
201.—Adjectives with a noun prefixed		179
202.—Adjectives having adjectives prefixed		180
203.—Adjectives with a verb prefixed		180
204.—Verbs, or participles, with a substantive prefixed		180
205.—Verbs, or participles, with an adjective prefixed		180
206.—Words with a preposition prefixed		181
207.—Second class of compound terms		181-191
208.—Primary and secondary signification of words		191
209.—An example of		191

PART III.—SYNTAX.

CHAPTER I.

SYNTAX OF THE ARTICLE.

210.—Definition of		192
211.—The three great principles on which Syntax rests		192
212.—A sentence		192
213.—Order followed in this treatise		193
214.—The article—eleven rules—an idiom		193-196
215.—What some grammarians think of this idiom		197
216.—English indefinite article		197
217.—An idiom		197
218.—The defining office of the article		197
219.—Exceptions		200
220.—Agreement of the article with its noun		200
221.—Influence of this agreement		200

CHAPTER II.

SYNTAX OF THE NOUN.

222.—Apposition		201
223.—A Gaelic idiom regarding nouns in apposition		201

CONTENTS.

Sect		page
224.—Government of the genitive case		202
225.—The Saxon genitive—the Gaelic genitive		203
226.—How to translate English compound substantives into Gaelic		204
227.—The several meanings of the preposition *of*		
228.—A most peculiar idiom		205
229.—Ownership—how expressed		206
230.—O, or ua, a *descendant*, mac, a *son*, govern the genitive		226
231.—Aspiration of the genitive of proper names		207
232.—Nouns which convey a plural idea		208

CHAPTER III.
SYNTAX OF THE ADJECTIVE.

233.—Division of this subject—position of the adjective—as a predicate it suffers no change ..		208-210
234.—Agreement of the adjective with the noun		210
235.—It agrees with the latter of two nouns		211
236.—Governing power of the adjective		211
237.—Use of oe, *of*		212
238.—" De" for oe é, *of it*		212
239.—Idioms		213
240.—Sentences of the form, *he is six feet high*		213
241.—Adjectives affected like nouns		213
242.—General rule on this subject		214
243.—Idiomatic use of " oa," *two*		214
Da, *two*, has the form of a dual number		214

CHAPTER IV.
THE PRONOUNS.

244.—*Personal Pronouns*		214
245.—Their position in relation with the verb		214
246.—Compound personal pronouns		215
247.—Idioms in the use of the pronouns		215
248.—The possessive pronouns		215
249.—Relative pronouns		216
An instance of amphibology		216
250.—Mixed compound form of the relative		217
251.—" He who," an cé.		217
252.—The relative is omitted in familiar language		217
253.—Whether the use of the preposition in Irish, as in English, at the end of a sentence, is an error or an idiom?		217
Mine, thine, his, her, theirs, whose—how translated		218
254.—The demonstratives		218

CHAPTER V.
VERBS.

255.—The verb and nominative case		219
256.—The synthetic form		219
257.—The place which a verb holds in a Gaelic sentence		220
258.—Philosophical analysis of the Irish and English methods of placing the predicate		220-221

CONTENTS.

Sect.		Page
259.—The copula ɪſ, *is*		221
260.—Active verbs		222
261.—Idioms of the infinitive and participles of active verbs		222
262.—The active participle		222
263.—Passive verbs		223
264.—Secondary form of the personal pronoun after verbs passive		223
265.—Thesis—the nominative, and not the accusative case of the personal pronouns follows verbs passive		224
266.—*Do, did, may, can, will, shall,* how to be translated		225
267.—Example, *I am* striking—meaning of—translation of		225
268.—Relative dependence of verbs		225
269.—The sign of the infinitive mood occasionally omitted		226
270.—A *purpose* or *end* expressed in Irish by le, *with*		226
271.—Substantive character of the infinitive mood		226
272.—The case absolute—how translated		226

CHAPTER VI.
ADVERBS.

273.—Their position		227
274.—Adverbs beginning with a vowel		227
275.—Peculiar use of the *negative* adverb in Irish		227

CHAPTER VII.
PREPOSITIONS, CONJUNCTIONS, INTERJECTIONS.

276.—Simple prepositions		227
277.—Compound prepositions		227
278.—Ꙍnn or ɪn, signifying *towards*		228
279.—Conjunctions		228
280.—Interjections		229

PART IV.—PROSODY.

CHAPTER I.

281.—Definition of		229
282.—Division of		229
283.—Orthoepy		229
284.—Pronunciation		229
285.—Accent		229
286.—Quantity		230
287.—A syllable is long when		230
288.—A syllable is short when		230

CHAPTER II.
VERSIFICATION.

289.—Defined		230
290.—A verse		230
291.—Rhyme		230

CONTENTS. xiii

Sect. Page
292.—Rhythm 230
293.—Metre—how *rhyme*, and *rhythm*, and *metre* differ .. 231
294.—Measure 231
295.—Other definitions 231
296.—*Certain esssential properties of verse* 231
297.—Alliteration 231
298.—Assonance 231
 Showy writers over-fond of alliteration 231
299.—Various kinds of accented metre 232
300.—Nomenclature of modern metre 232
301.—Proposition : *The metrical system founded on accent differs widely from that founded on quantity* 233
302.—The Irish language a flexible medium in plastic hands for conveying all the modifications of the poetic spirit 233
 Examples (translations).—(*a*) *Go where glory waits thee*, by His Grace the Most Rev. Dr. MacHale. (*b*) *The harp that once*, by His Grace the Most Rev. Dr. MacHale. (*c*) *Proudly the note*, by a Maynooth Student. (*d*) *Remember the Glories of Brien the Brave*, Dr. MacHale. (*d*) *The Exile of Erin*, by Rev. James Casey 233-236
303.—*Jesu dulcis memoria*—translated 236
 An example of accented heroic metre from the Irish Iliad by Dr. MacHale 237
304.—Lord Macaulay's view of poetry—Gerald Griffin's—conclusion to be drawn therefrom—Irish in *accented metre* is as rhythmical and euphonious as English, French, or Italian .. 237

CHAPTER III.
VERSIFICATION AS PRACTISED BY THE IRISH BARDS.

305.—A summary of the essential characteristics of poetry in the different languages of ancient and modern Europe and of Asia 239
306.—Requisites of Irish verse—composition 239
307.—These requisites fully explained—first requisite 240
308.—Uaim, *i.e.*, alliteration 240
309.—Comanba, *i.e.*, assonance 241
310.—Classification of assonant consonants by Irish bards .. 241
311.—Rhyme—perfect, imperfect 242
312.—Uaitne—union, symphony, parallelism .. 242-243
313.—Other requisites, Rinn 243
314.—Ceann 244
315.—Amur 244

CHAPTER IV.

316.—Dán óirneac, its various kinds 244
318.—Oglacar—example of 245
318.—brulingace 245
319.—Cnoigneac 245
 Example.—The characteristics of the four provinces in four stanzas 246-247
320.—Conaclon—very remarkable 247

xiv CONTENTS.

Sect.	Page
321.—Several other kinds of metre	247
322.—The Saracens were not the first to introduce rhyme into Europe	247
323.—Analysis of a stanza—applicatian of the requisites..	248
Examples I. II. III.	251
324.—Example IV.—Ϝorʒ ʒuıll Ɑ)ac Ɑ)oղղa	251
325.—Deductions to be drawn from the foregoing	251

CHAPTER V.

VERSIFICATION OF LATIN HYMNS.

326.—Latin hymns..	251
327.—Their metrical character..	252
328.—How account for the Keltic form in which they are composed?	252
329.—*Latin* hymnologists	252
330.—The (Latin) hymns written by Irishmen	252
331.—The hymns written by St. Ambrose	252
332.—Those by St. Augustine, St. Paulinus	253
333.—These the prototypes of future copies	253
334.—Examples—(*a*) by Sedulius	253
(*b*) by St. Columbanus	254
(*c*) St. Secundinus	255
(*d*) by St. Augustine	255
(*e*) by St. Ambrose	256
(*f*) by St. Aldhelm	256
(*g*) by St. Thomas Aquinas	257
(*h*) by the author of the *Stabat Mater*	257
(*i*) *Dies iræ* ..	257

APPENDIX I.

Specimens of the Irish language from the fifth century to the seventeenth	258-274

APPENDIX II.

Irish proverbs	274-302
POETRY—*The Celtic Tongue*, by the Rev. Michael Mullin	302-304

PREFACE.

The first motive that induced me to write an Irish Grammar was, to supply a want under which my fellow-students in Maynooth College have laboured in the study of their mother-tongue. They, and all who have studied here, know how much a work of this kind has been required. And if it be useful to the students of Maynooth—as it is confidently expected it will—must it not be equally useful to the students of Ireland's Catholic University, who, in facilities for acquiring a knowledge of the Irish tongue, have not been more fortunate than the clerical sons of our own Alma Mater?

I have for a long time desired to see some one with sufficient talent and learning for the task, undertake to bring the language to a settled form of Orthography, and not to have even the simple words of our beautiful Celtic tossed into numberless shapes by every one who wished to deal with their spelling as he might think proper. This desire has led me just to introduce the matter in a short dissertation on the use of the old rule "caol le caol," which is looked upon, and justly, as the key to the spelling of the Irish language I have also in several parts of the work touched on the same subject, in a discursive way.

The subject of writing in Irish, has not, though contrary to custom, been omitted.

Nearly all the grammars on our language that have been written before this were, practically at least, of very little use, except to those who knew already how to speak Irish, and who just merely required to become acquainted with it as a written dialect. The Author has avoided this mistake, as may be seen from the heading notices of each declension.

The learner can now, nearly in every case, know, from the termination of the nominative alone, to what gender, and to what declension, every noun belongs, without waiting, as some writers require, to learn first how it forms the genitive or possessive case.

In the conjugation of verbs, I go more minutely into detail than has been done by any other.

In Syntax, many rules are given that were never printed before.

In the Prosody, I show the capabilities of the Irish language for all the purposes of melody and song, and how easy it is to distil through it the sweetest effusions of the Grecian or Roman muse, in measures of the same kind as those in which the great masters of old scattered the poetic fire; and how gently it will rise and fall with the *accented* measure of English or Continental poetry, preserving not only the rhythm and melody of the verse, but also its graces of cadence and beauties of rhyme.

The work is, then, I trust, made suitable to the wants and requirements of the present time and present improved taste, containing a little of what is pleasing with a great deal of what is useful. Fashioned in some measure after the improved editions of those elementary works that treat of the fashionable languages of the Continent of Europe, it is, perhaps, in style and arrangement not inferior to many of them.

St. Patrick's College, Maynooth,
May 1. 1856.

INTRODUCTION.

No nation supposes her sons and daughters to be educated who have not learned their mother-tongue. It would be considered incongruous in a German not to know the German language; in a native of Italy not to know the sweet Tuscan; in an Englishman not to know English. A Frenchman unable to understand the language in which a Bossuet or a Chateaubriand wrote—in which a Massillon preached, a Mirabeau thundered—in which Napoleon I. dictated laws to Europe—would be an anomaly in his own land: and, strange to say, an Irishman without knowing Irish is nothing incongruous; a native of Eire without knowing his own ⁊eanga míp mílır, máᴀapóa, is no anomaly among his people; and he has his education finished while he has yet learned nought of that language in which his own St. Patrick preached to our heathen sires, Cormac Uulfhada[1] composed his famous laws, and in which Brian fired that heroism that blazed for the freedom of Ireland at the battle of Clontarf. Are we a paradox among the nations!

If one were to visit Spain or Portugal, with the desire of learning the Spanish or Portuguese languages, and should find on entering those kingdoms that very few, comparatively, of the natives could speak to him in the dialect of their country, what, I ask, would be his surprise? Let us reverse the case, and suppose that a Spaniard, or any

---

[1] "The most accomplished of all the Milesian princes, whether as a legislator, soldier, or scholar, was Cormac Ulfhada."—Moore's *History of Ireland*. vol. i. chap. 7. "Cormac surpassed in knowledge all his predecessors on the Irish throne; he composed many very useful laws which are still preserved in works on Irish jurisprudence."—Keating, as quoted in *Cambrensis Eversus* edited, with translation and notes, by the late Rev. Matthew Kelly, D.D., St Patrick's College, Maynooth, vol. i. n. 481."

foreigner, landed amongst us, with the desire of learning the Irish language, how many, I ask, would be found capable of teaching him—of satisfying his desire for Irish philological knowledge? Comparatively few indeed.

To what, then, is this lack of knowledge of their mother-tongue among our people to be attributed? We love the land of our birth; we love the Celtic soil which the sons of Milesius first planted; government, besides, is not illiberal in the patronage it has extended to Irish literature. The age of persecution too has passed. The children of Ireland are no longer, as of old, flogged[1] for lisping in the broad Celtic of their fathers. To what, then, is this decay, which at present is fast eating up all that remains of our language, to be ascribed? Chiefly to that desire which the humbler classes of our people naturally have, of speaking the language spoken by their more enlightened countrymen; and to that total exclusion of everything relating to the Irish language from our *national* schools; to the want also of elementary treatises, written with philological taste, in a style at once simple, pleasing, and attractive, published withal at a moderate price, so that they might become readily accessible to the great majority of the reading public. These are some of the causes that are fast promoting the decay of our dear old tongue. How shall the evil be remedied?

The proverb, " Remove the cause and the effect will cease," is well known to all. Hence the removal of the foregoing causes would greatly tend to aid the advancement of Hiberno-Celtic literature.

[1] There are hundreds of persons still living who, "in boyhood's days," had suspended from the neck "scores" or tablets, the number of incisions on which showed how often the prohibition to speak Irish had been violated, and for which the schoolmaster inflicted on the delinquent a proportionate number of stripes. Verily that was beating the language out of the country with the vengeance! yet depart it would not, till the lash of fashion and corruption was employed against it.

INTRODUCTION. 5

It is true a reaction in its favour is of late, indeed, fast gaining ground among the higher and more enlightened classes of our countrymen. Hence the baneful effects produced by that blighting spirit of false shame[1] to speak their mother-tongue, which was fast sucking out of the hearts of the peasantry the very life-spring of their venerable old Gaoḋailge, will soon, it is hoped, be undone. " *The Irish Archæological and Celtic Society;*" " *The Kilkenny and South-East of Ireland Archæological Society;*" and the " *Ossianic Society,*" are living proofs of this favourable movement. The few publications in Irish that are now and again

---

[1] The following words, which I quote from an autograph letter of an Irish prelate, Most Rev. Daniel O'Connor, Bishop of Saldes, aptly accord with the opinions expressed above. The letter has been received since the *Introduction* was written.

"Oh! would that our copious, melodious, soul-inspiring, and heart-moving language were revived and had become universal. And why should it not? Should it not be our pride and our boast to have such a language, whilst other countries rejoice in their jargon—in their compound of various languages?

"Are not Scotland and Wales to be admired for their patriotism in this respect? and are they not a reproach to us? But why do their languages prevail among them? Because they are used as the common language of the country; because they are taught in their elementary schools and encouraged by the nobility and gentry, instead of being ashamed of their mother-tongue—as I am sorry to say we are generally found to be of ours—or rather, are sought to be made so, by those who are interested in suppressing it as a mark of our nationality.

"Unless this shame of the language of our ancestors cease to exist, and a kindred feeling be cultivated generally, and especially among the middle classes of our countrymen, in vain do you labour. . . .

"If I could take the liberty, I would recommend that in every parish in Ireland there should be an Irish teacher, and that as the ear governs the tongue, it may be familiarized by hearing the language spoken as much as possible, at school, at home and abroad; if it were only thus to employ some poor men and women to speak nothing but Irish in the hearing of the children, who, in a short time, would acquire a facility in speaking it in a commonplace, colloquial way."

issuing from the press tend to show the same. And so does the general tone or feeling about the *Irish language,* and about Irish literature, that is at present getting up among the learned at home and abroad, indicate, that there is a spirit summoned to awaken from the slumber of neglect and decay our dying-mother tongue. Hence we hear her mellow notes rise again on the breeze of fashionable life; her guttural Celtic tones may then, perchance, soon grow popular— for fashion is the first step to popularity.

The Board of *National Education* in Ireland could do much for the language of Ireland. In fact, without their co-operation or that of the Christian Brothers, it will, it is to be feared, soon become a dead language; for it never can be *nationally* revived unless nursed again in the *national* cradle —the schools of Ireland.[1]

But yet does not the opening of the Catholic University of Ireland bid us fairly hope? It looks like the dawn of returning day for Ireland, her history, and her language. And under the bright and warm sun of collegiate and university intelligence, this fading old Celtic tree may yet revive and bloom again, in some way, as it did in days of old.[2]

But, it may be asked, what use is there in studying this much neglected language! It can be answered, there is much use every way. It is useful to the philologist; it is useful to the antiquarian.[3] To them a knowledge of the

---

[1] In his speech delivered in favour of the rights of the "holy Apostolic See, and in sympathy and sustainment of our Most Holy Father Pope Pius IX.," his Grace the Archbishop of Tuam calls the National Schools "the graves of the National Language."—*The Voice of the West,* p. 7.

[2] So we thought when we wrote these lines. But it is a vain hope. We have yet to learn that any scholar taught to speak and write the old language of fatherland has come forth from the halls of our Irish Catholic University!

[3] *Vide* O'Donovan's *Irish Grammar, Introduction,* Section 3. Zeüss, preface to his "*Grammatica Celtica,*" published at Leipsic, 1853. See also

Irish—admittedly the best preserved branch of the great Celtic stock—is absolutely necessary. But to the children of Ireland ought it not be a precious inheritance? We glory in the name of *Celt*, and why not then hold the *Celtic* language dear? With it are interwoven a thousand national recollections which we fondly cherish; with it is wound up the history of our glory, of our triumphs, of our fame. It ought to be fostered even for its own sake. For if age bring with it respect, and if length of years should command esteem, surely our Celtic tongue, which has outlived three thousand years—years of glory, years of tribulation—and yet flourishes, young, fresh, and vigorous, as when it flourished in the schools of Bangor, Mayo, Clonmacnois, and Glendalough, ought to be esteemed and cherished.

If we do not cherish the language for its own sake, why let us do it for our own. We know the language of a nation is the exponent of a people's antiquity—the index of their refinement—the mouth-piece of their history—the type of their freedom—the echo of a nation's greatness and fame; shall we, then, let our language die?

Every nation cherishes its own language; it cherishes it even in death. The Greeks loved their language the more, the more it was banned by the Turkish foe. From the ashes of thraldom they have brought it forth—though bearing another name[1]—fresh and youthful as the phœnix rising in its newly created power, after a literary slumber through ages of woe. The Jew in his exile loves, as did his captive

the preface to the work of Mons. Adolphe Pictet (pp. viii. ix.), " De l'affinité des langues Celtiques avec la Sanscrit." The same is confirmed by many other writers: see Vallancey, " Essay on the Celtic language," p. 3; in which he quotes Ussher's words in praise of the elegance and copiousness of our venerable old tongue.

[1] See the "KAPTEPIA," and other journals published at Athens. The *Romaic* in which they are written differs very little from the *Greek* of Xenophon, of Aristotle, or of St. Luke.

sires of old, to sing out, in his own sweet Hebrew, his sorrows in a strange land. And shall Irishmen, in the land of their birth, neglect to cultivate what has been justly called " the language of song—the language of the heart—the sweet, mellow language of Eiṅe ꝢO bṙaṫ ?"

To help, then, in some measure, the young student who wishes to learn something of the Irish language, and to contribute to the supply of suitable elementary treatises, has been the chief object of the Author in compiling the following Grammar. His principal wish was, to convey as much knowledge as he could, in the shortest and simplest form; to disentangle the rudiments of the Irish language from the maze of mystic explanation in which, not unfrequently, some grammarians have involved them. The Author, on commencing this portion of philological study, was strangely puzzled by the variety of forms, in which the treatises that he was obliged to consult explained the simple, elementary portions of Grammar. Hence, on sitting down to write this volume, he was acquainted with all these difficulties that usually beset the pathway of beginners, on their first entering the road of Celtic literature. He has endeavoured, therefore, to remove them as much as possible, by simplifying all that appeared any way knotty or abstruse; explaining all that required explanation; leaving out all that he thought useless and redundant. He has made no assertion, he has given no rule, without showing some right foundation for the assertion—some genuine reason or some valid proof for the rule.

This is chiefly a grammar of the living language—of the Irish language as it is at present spoken and written. Hence these pages are not over-crowded with extracts from ancient authors. For all people do not wish to become antiquarians; and even those amongst us who feel inclined, would do well to learn first the *living* Irish language, and after that they can more readily become acquainted with those phrases and terms that are more ancient or more recondite; just like one who, by knowing modern English well, can with greater ease learn the quaint idioms of Chaucer and Gower.

In learning any language, we should as much as possible aim at acquiring the most correct pronunciation; then the different dialects in use amongst the people who speak that language will, if the learner has a taste for them, very soon be mastered by him. So in learning Irish: if he learn that which is admitted by all Irish writers to be the most correctly spoken dialect, he can, at pleasure, afterwards learn the others. Hence the Author has adhered principally to the Connaught dialect, because "it has," says the proverb, "the accent and the propriety," tá ceart agus blas aig an g-Connactac.

It must not however be inferred, that this is not, therefore, a true grammar of the other dialects. Such an inference would be entirely erroneous—just as erroneous as if one should infer, from the absence of any disquisition on the flat gibberish of a Lancashire peasant, and the glib chattering of the Kentshire workman; or on the difference between the polite slang of the Dublin and the quaint cant of the London cabmen, in O'Sullivan's Grammar, that it is therefore faulty and imperfect. The reason is, the written language of every country differs much from the spoken dialects. The written language is generally one, uniform, not varying with place, though it may with time, not provincial, northern or southern, nor cockney, nor cant, nor slang—though it may avail itself of all these; but, like the sea, is one wide, changeless whole, as far as it goes, receiving the waters of many tributaries, yet never varying, by their influx, its native and essential hue.

This Grammar, it is true, is not so large nor so copious as Dr. O'Donovan's. If it were, it would not have answered the ends intended by the Author, those of popularizing the language and facilitating its study for his own fellow-students Although the learned Doctor's work is now twelve years published, few copies indeed, with the exception of those given as premiums, have found their way into our College, partly owing, in all probability, to its price. To him who wishes to learn, not only the modern, but also the ancient Irish, as spoken ten centuries ago by our fathers; to the antiquarian, and to every one who desires to unlock the hidden lore which our Manuscripts contain, Dr. O'Donovan's will be found a "Thesaurus," and as such will hold its place. He has, in a great measure, done for Ireland's language what the learned Lancellot and his distinguished associates of Port Royal did for the classic language of Greece. Still, notwithstanding the just claims of his Grammar to praise and patronage, it must be confessed a cheaper or more practical Grammar, written in a popular way, was needed in our colleges and schools. Whether that want has been removed by the present work, it remains for our Irish students and the Irish public to declare.

Those who are acquainted with the labours of a divinity student in Maynooth—the strictness with which college discipline is enforced and observed—the want of accommodation, at least for students, for any literary task, will not be slow to believe that nothing but a desire to facilitate the study of our national language—which *alone* was ours when all Europe looked upon our country as the "hive of wisdom and the cradle of sanctity"—and to dispel any existing apathy regarding it, could have induced the Author, in the midst of grave and essentially important studies, and surrounded with circumstances so disadvantageous, to write and publish the present treatise.

IRISH GRAMMAR.

GRAMMAR, taken in a general sense, treats of the best method of employing language as a medium of communicating thought with simplicity and clearness to the minds of those whom we address. As a science, it teaches how to speak and write correctly; and as a special art, it shows the relation of words in a sentence, and reduces to rules the speech of a nation.

Although it is true, as Scaliger* remarks, that correctness in writing is the ally and the result of correctness in thinking and speaking, yet grammar being at once an art and a science, it becomes the duty of a grammarian to treat of writing, which experience has proved to be the means best calculated to learn how words in a sentence are connected, and of the rules by which their relations are guided.

Grammar, in this two-fold acceptation, teaches us to know what is called the philosophy of language, as well as to speak and write with propriety.

Irish grammar should therefore point out the principles on which correctness in speaking the Irish language is founded, and should furnish rules by which propriety in writing, as well as in speaking, can be readily acquired.

In the present treatise we purpose accordingly to treat of the philosophical principles from which the leading as well as the peculiar features of our mother-tongue are developed, and to deduce from them rules calculated to insure to the learner a knowledge of its general and idiomatic correctness, as it is at present spoken and written.

The divisions of grammar are four—Orthography, Etymology, Syntax, and Prosody.

PART I.—ORTHOGRAPHY.

Orthography, as its name imports, teaches how to write a language according to a fixed standard, founded on the

---

* "Grammatica igitur unus finis est, recte loqui . . . neque aliter scribere debemus, quam loquimur."—*De Causis Linguæ Latinæ*, l. i. c. 1.

philosophy of the language, and agreed upon by the learned amongst the people who speak it.

At present orthography denotes the art of spelling. In order to learn how to spell correctly we must know the elements that constitute spelling, which are words, syllables, letters.

A word, according to Aristotle,* is a sound, or its sign, significative of itself, of which no part is, of itself, significative.

CHAPTER I.

THE LETTERS—THEIR CLASSIFICATION AND SOUNDS.

SECTION I.—*The Elements of Words—Letters*—The elements of words are letters. A letter† is correctly defined to be a simple mark in written language, standing for a simple sound in spoken language.

There are in Irish only seventeen letters; some authors have given another, h, which in Irish, as in Greek and Italian, never performs the functions of a letter, and cannot therefore strictly be ranked as such.‡

---

* Φωνὴ σημαντικὴ, ἧς μέρος οὐδέν ἐστι καθ' αὑτὸ σημάντικον.—*De Poetica*, c. xx.

† "Litera igitur est pars dictionis indivisibilis."—*Scaliger de Causa Linguæ Latinæ*, l. i., c. 1
Φωνῆς στοιχεῖα ἐξ ὧν συνκειται ἡ φωνή. καὶ εἰς ἃ' διαιρεῖται ἐσχατα. Ἐκεῖνα δὲ μηκέτ' εἰς ἄλλας φωνὰς ἑτέρας τῷ εἴδει ἀυτων.— *Metaph.* 5, c. iii. "The elements of speech are those of which voice is composed, and into which, as its last remains, it is divided, they themselves being no longer divided into other voices differing in species from them."

‡ "It is to be observed that *h* never stands as the initial of a word in Erse in the primitive form, or is never in fact an independent radical letter. It is merely a secondary form or representative of some other initial, viz., *f* or *s*."—*Eastern Origin of the Celtic Nations*, by Dr. Prichard, edited by R. G. Latham, M.A., p. 165.

Edward Lhuyd observes that *h* is never the proper or primitive initial of any word in Gaelic—that wherever found it is the aspirated form of ꝼ, ꞃ, or ꞇ, and hence infers, with much probability, "that cognate words beginning with h in other languages lost their proper initials;" that thus the Greek numerals ἕξ, *six*, and ἑπτά, *seven*, must, at some early period, have been written, as in Latin, *sex* and *septem*.

"Other nations (besides the Greeks) distinguish the *spiritus asper* by a peculiar letter—for example *h*—but have no mark for the *lenis*."—*Influence of Physical Causes on Languages, Mythology, &c.* (*Atlantis*, p. 62.)

"The letter *h* is no articulate sound, but only a breathing."—*The English Language*, by Latham (3rd ed. p. 144).

THE IRISH ALPHABET.*

Cap.	Smal.	PRONUNCIATION.	Names.	
A	a	a French, or aw English	Ailm,	Alm
B	b		Beiṫ,	Beh
C	c	c hard, or k; never at all pronounced like s or ch soft	Coll,	Kull
D	d	dh	Dair,	Dhair
E	e	e (as é in *there*)	Eoḋa,	Aya
F	f	f	Feaṙn	Farn
G	g	g hard, as g in *get*; never sounded soft, like g in *gin*.	Goṙt,	Gurth
I	i	i French, ee English.	Ioḋa,	Eeya
L	l	l generally as the first l in *William*	Luiṙ,	Lush
M	m	m	Muin,	Muin
N	n	n	Nuin,	Nuin
O	o	o	Oiṙ,	Oir
P	p	p	Peiṫ,	Peh
R	r	r	Ruiṙ,	Rush
S	s	s	Suil,	Suil
T	t	t Italian, or th English.	Teine,	Thené
U	u	u Italian, oo English, or u in *bull*; never sounded as u (*you*) in *tune*.	Uṙ,	Oor

The *name* of the Irish letters should not be mistaken for the *pronunciation*. The *name* teaches us to *know*, the *pronunciation* gives us the *sound* of the letter. The pronunciation is that which alone helps us to spell the word; the name serves to distinguish the letters one from the other, as the Greek *Alpha, Beta, Gamma*, &c. From the three first in the last column are formed the word aibéitiṙ, the Irish word for *alphabet*, as the latter has its rise from the names of the two first Greek letters, A, B (Alpha, Beta).

---

* "It follows, therefore, that as there was no prototype to copy them (the Irish alphabet) from, they must be original."—*Harris's Ware*, c. iii.

Hyde Clarke, in his "Grammar of the English Tongue," says that the Anglo-Saxon alphabet "is likewise found in some Irish books, the Irish having taken this alphabet from our English forefathers." "The very contrary," says Mr. Keane, in his *Handbook of the History of the English Language*, "we venture to say was the case. To the Irish his English forefathers were indebted for all the literature and learning they possessed, and

Every letter in Irish retains its own full sound, and never usurps, as letters in English and Latin words do, the place which other letters by right of sound should hold; thus, in English we find, for instance, in the word "pronunciation" *c* and *t*, before *i*, to have the sound of *sh*; not so with the Irish letters—each always retains its own sound; c has always the sound of *k*, and c of *t*, never changing their sound, no matter where they are placed.

S = *sh* before and after e, ɪ :

Sɪn-nc, *we*, - - - -	pronounced	*shinnee.*
Seʌn (ʀ before e) - - - -	,,	*shean.*
Sʌn (*not* before e or ɪ) - - -	,,	*san.*
Cʊʀ, *a foot* (ʀ after the broad vowel o)	,,	*kos.*
Coɪʀ, *of a foot* (ʀ after ɪ), - - -	,,	*ko-ish.*

In reading the language the learner should therefore bear in mind that ʀ before or after e or ɪ is *always* sounded like *sh* English; and in spelling an Irish word, that wherever the sound of *sh* is heard, e or ɪ is invariably before or after ʀ. Iʀ, *is*, is an exception; so is ʀo, *this*, which is in parts of Connaught pronounced as if written ʀeo. This strong sibilant sound it appears to have at first received from the influence of a slender vowel in the syllable going before ʀo, and then gradually became in some districts a common form.

The reason why ɪʀ is pronounced as if written ʌʀ appears to be given by Henry Leo, in his commentary on the hymn by the Bishop of Sletty in praise of St. Patrick: "Tertia singularis verbi 'esse,' modo ʌʀ, modo ɪʀ (nostro tempore ɪʀ) scribitur."—*Commentatio de Carmine Vetusto Hibernico in S. Patricii laudem, ab Henrico Leo, Ordinis Phil. II. T. Decon. Halis Saxonum*, 1845.

These seventeen letters are divided into vowels and consonants; the vowels are ʌ, e, ɪ, o, u; the consonants, b, c, ᴅ, ꜰ, ᵹ, l, m, n, p, ʀ, ʀ, c.

A *vowel* is a mark which of itself represents a full, perfect sound. A *consonant*, so called because sounded not of itself, but *with a vowel's* aid, is a mark which represents a sound not perfect nor full of itself.

---

the Irish, two hundred years before the Anglo-Saxons knew how to read or write, employed this very alphabet, not in *some*, but in all of their books, whether in Latin or in the vernacular." Mr. Keane may rest assured he has "ventured" with all safety and truth to refute so gross a misstatement. Mr. Keane further adds the observation made by Alban Butler in his life of St. Austin: "The Saxons were a barbarous race, unacquainted even with the art of writing previous to their arrival in England, where they adopted their alphabet from the Irish" (p. 18).

"ᴀ beɪn *Spencer* ᵹun ab ó Cɪnɪonncaɪb ꜰuʌnʌɒʌn nʌ Sʌᵹʀʌnʌɪᵹ ʌɪbᵹɪceʌn ʌɪn ɒ-cuʀ, ʌᵹuʀ ɒʌ neɪn ʀɪn, nɪ nʌɪb ꜰɪoʀ lɪceʌnɒʌécʌ ʌn bɪc ʌᵹ nʌ Sʌᵹʀʌnʌɪᵹɪb ᵹo b-ꜰuʌnʌɒʌn ó Cɪnɪonncaɪb ꜰ."—*Keating.*

§ 2—*The Vowels—how Sounded; how Classified.*— The vowels have two principal sounds, the one long, the other short: ᴀ long, as *a* in the word *war*—example, ᴀᴩᴅ, *high*, pronounced *awrd*, answering to the *broad* sound of *a* in English; ᴀ short, as *a* in *fat*—example, ᴀɴᴀᴍ, *a soul*.

There is a third sound of ᴀ, very common in the West and South of Ireland, just the same as the short sound of broad *a* in English, as *a* in *what, quadrant*; example, bᴀll, *a member;* bᴩᴀᴛ, *a cloak, garment;* cᴀᴩᴀᴅ, *a friend;* mᴀᴩᴛ, *a beef;* ᴛᴀᴩᴛ, *thirst*.

é, long,	*e* in *where;*	cᴩé, *clay;* ᴊᴏ, *a goose.*
e, short,	*e* in *when;*	bᴀᴊlᴇ, *a town.*
í, long,	*ee,* or *i* in *pique;*	mín, *fine*
i, short,	*i* in *pick;*	mɪn, *meal.*
ó, long,	*o* in *told;*	ól, *drinking.*
o, short,	*o* in *other;*	coɴɴ, *a crane.*
ú, long,	*u* in *rule:*	úɴ, *fresh;* ᴅᴜɴ, *a stronghold.*
u, short,	*u* in *fur;*	ᴜcᴛ, *breast;* uɴᴩᴀ, *a jamb, a support.*

The vowels u and o before ᴍ, ll, nᴊ, are incorrectly pronounced in Munster like the German diphthong *au*, or the English *ou* in *pounce;* as, ᴀᴍ, *time (owm);* bᴀll, *a member, a limb (bowll);* cᴩoᴍ, *bent, stooped (crowm);* poll, *a pit, a hole (powl).* O before ó and ᵹ is sounded long; as, ᴩoᵹᴍᴀɴ, *harvest;* ᴩoᵹlᴀᴍ, *learning;* but in the words ɴoᵹᴀ, *choice;* ᴛoᵹᴀ, *selection,* oᵹ are pronounced like *ow—rhow-a, thow-a*.

" It may be remarked here," says Dr. O'Donovan, in his " Irish Grammar," p. 13, " that the principal difference between the Munster and the other dialects of the Irish language consists in the diphthongal sounds of the vowels here pointed out."

" In the modern Irish orthography the vowel e never appears alone in the body of a word or syllable, but is always accompanied by other vowels."— *Id.* p. 11.

In Gælic, e at the end of a word is not silent, as it is in English; example, mɪɴᴇ is pronounced in two syllables—*meen-ne,* and not *mine,* like the English possessive pronoun; so mᴊlᴇ is pronounced *mee-la,* and not *mile;* as, ccuᴅ mᴊlᴇ ᴩᴀᴊlᴛᴇ.

That the sounds which the vowel letters in Irish receive are correct, and that they are exactly in accordance with the phonographic scale of pure vowel intonation, will be seen by any orthoepist skilled in phonetics, who knows the proper sound of each vowel. " The pure vowel sound of *a* exists in English in the *a* in *far;* of *o* in most words in which that letter occurs. But the letters *e, i, u* (in English) do not represent perfect vowel sounds, but mixed ones, and we have accordingly to look for the true simple vowel sounds under others; thus, *e* will be found to be best represented by the *a* in *name; i* by the *e* in *theme;* while *u* is expressed by the *oo* in *cool*."— *Atlantis,* No. 1, p. 61.

" In English e long has evidently lost it original sound, it being now pronounced *ee,* like *i* long in all ancient and most modern languages.

. . . E still keeps its ancient long sound in a few words, as *where, there, ere,* &c., in which words it exactly corresponds with é long in Irish."— *O'Donovan's Irish Grammar,* p. 11.

No vowel is ever doubled in the *same* syllable.

Vowels have two principal sounds, the accented and the non-accented.

That each vowel has at least two special sounds is plain, for the vowel in any word of one syllable, when pronounced freely and fully, as in the words, *ward, able* (English), or in the word, ᴀɴ̨ᴀɪʟ (Irish), becomes short, when in composition the emphasis is shifted to another syllable; as, *ward, seaward, lee-ward; able, bearăble;* ᴀɴ̨ᴀɪʟ, ᴄᴇᴀɴ-ᴀɴ̨ᴀɪʟ, ꜰᴇᴀɴᴀɴ̨ᴀɪʟ. In English the *a* long in *able* becomes short in *ability;* the *e* in *precéde* is shortened in *precĕdent.* In like manner *i.* which is long in the word *impose,* is short in *imposition,* on account of the shifting of the accent or emphatic syllable.

The reader cannot fail to remark that the vowel sound immediately after the accented syllable is generally pronounced very curtly. From this fact, sounds of ᴀ, o, u, e arise, in which the ear cannot distinguish one from the other, as that of final ᴀ, e, in the participles ᴄᴇᴀɴᴄᴀ, ʙᴜᴀɪʟᴄᴇ. On this account a third sound called the *obscure* is given by some grammarians.

The principal here explained is common to all language. On it especially is founded the system of Masoretic (or variable vowel) points in the Hebrew language.

The vowels are classified into *broad* and *slender;* ᴀ, o, u, are called *broad;* e, ɪ, *slender.* The *broad* vowels are not always long; nor are the *slender* vowels always short. Both *broad* and *slender* are to be sounded long when marked with the grave (´) accent, which corresponds in form to the acute of the Greeks.

This division of the vowels into *broad* and *slender* should not be lightly noticed by the student; for the spelling of all the words in the language depends much, nearly entirely, on the position which the slender and broad vowels hold with regard to the consonants. There is an old Gaelic rule which directs that a consonant or consonants should, in every written word, lie between either two *slender* or two *broad* vowels; and consequently, that a *broad* vowel, such as ᴀ, o, or u, could not correctly go before, while a slender vowel (either e or ɪ) comes immediately after a consonant; but that if a broad vowel preceded, so should a broad one follow; if a slender vowel preceded, so should a slender one immediately follow the said consonant or consonants. This rule, called " ᴄᴀoʟ ʟᴇ ᴄᴀoʟ, ᴀᴢᴜʀ ʟᴇᴀᴛᴀɴ ʟᴇ ʟᴇᴀᴛᴀɴ"— *" slender with slender, and broad with broad,"* has been praised by some grammarians, rejected by others. Colonel Charles Vallancey, Dr. John O'Brien, Bishop of Cloyne, Halliday, P. MacElligott (*Observations on the Gaelic Language,* in the first vol. of the *Transactions of the Gaelic Society*). Rev. Jonathan Furlong, condemn the rule. O'Molloy, Hugh Boy M'Curtin, Rev. A. Donlevy, Dr. O'Donovan, O'Daly, and other distinguished Irish scholars, recommend its use. The authority of the latter seems to me stronger, and therefore preferable to that of the former.

§ 3.—AUTHORITIES FOR AND AGAINST THE RULE.

Dr. O'Brien says. " A rule devised in like manner by our bards or rhymers—I mean that which is called ᴄᴀoʟ ʟᴇ ᴄᴀoʟ, ᴀᴢᴜʀ ʟᴇᴀᴛᴀɴ ʟᴇ ʟᴇᴀᴛᴀɴ—

has been woefully destructive to the original and radical purity of the language."—*Dr. O'Brien's Irish-English Dictionary*, 2nd ed., p. 52; *Dublin*, 1832.

Vallancey's words are to the same effect: " This rule (of inserting consonants between vowels), together with that of substituting small or broad vowels in the latter syllables, to correspond with the vowel immediately following the consonant in the preceding syllable, has been very destructive to the original and radical purity of the Irish language."—*A Grammar of the Irish Language*, p. 19; *Dublin*, 1782.

" Grammarians," says P. MacElligot, "have so often found the inconvenience arising from this rule that it should be entirely exploded."—*Transactions of the Gaelic Society*, vol. i., note, p. 25.

Rev. J. Furlong, after quoting the words of Dr. O'Brien, Stewart, MacElligott, decides against this canon : " Sanctioned," says he, " by those grave authorities, with whom my own experience and observation perfectly coincide, I have preferred certainly *the more simple*, and, according to the above authorities, the more correct mode of orthography, in the rejection of the rule in question."

It is remarkable that these writers merely disclaim against the rule, without giving a single reason worthy of notice to show that it is either wrong or of no use. Rev. J. Furlong's plea of *simplifying* the language would, if fully carried out, render the most polished language—say the French—a written jargon. Phonographists might well be glad, and bad spellers rejoice.

Haliday and Stewart are the only two who have given anything like reasoning for the partial rejection of this much disputed rule. Haliday, on the ground that its disuse is more in conformity with the spelling found in ancient manuscripts. This is true, but not entirely so, for there are even in ancient manuscripts numerous instances in which the canon is applied, in others not applied, by the same writer. All that can be thence inferred is that its application was not very general. And this is all we want to claim for it, even at present, as we shall immediately show. And in fact this is all that Stewart too claims ; for it is "to the *extensive application*, and the rigid observance of this rule," that he ascribes all the inconveniences that arise from it.

Those who recommend its use are:

O'Molloy, who wrote in the seventeenth century, and who says: " Rursus observa in vocalis polisyllabis quibuscunque saltem ordinarie servari debere regulam Hibernis tritam, tùm in scripturâ tùm in sono, quæ dicitur cáol le cáol ᴀᵹur, leatan le leatan."—*Grammatica Latino-Hibernica*, p. 50 ; Romae, 1677.

Hugh Boy M'Curtin, in the Grammar (pp. 680, 681) attached to his English-Irish Dictionary, published at Paris, 1732, speaks of this " canon of Gaelic orthography" as of something absolutely necessary for a learner of Irish to know, and about the propriety and usefulness of which there is no doubt.

Dr. Donlevy, to whom the language in its spoken and written state was perfectly known, says, " It is a sure guide in writing, and even in reading and pronouncing."—*Christian Doctrine*, 3rd ed., p. 442.

O'Donovan gives the canon as a useful and necessary help for every one who wishes to know the spelling of Irish : " This influence of the vowels over the consonants, which exists to some extent in every language, has given rise to a general rule or canon of orthography which distinguishes the Irish from all the European languages." And again he says: "It is certain that it is not always strictly adhered to in the ancient Irish manuscripts, but the principle on which it is founded is observable in the *oldest* fragments of Irish composition remaining to us."—*Irish Grammar*, pp. 3, 4.

O'Daly, writing on this rule (*Self-Instruction*, &c., p. 22, ed. 1846). says: "It enables the learner to come at the proper pronunciation of the language with greater facility than he could otherwise attain." And again, "There is a natural, euphonious, and graceful pronunciation, marked by the use of it."

The author's opinion is that the rule *ought to be used*, yet *with a certain limitation*. Its application in every instance ought not to be insisted on as necessary.

I say "*ought to be used*"—first, because there are very many instances in which both the gender and inflection of nouns and conjugations of verbs require its application; as, nom. sing., coṟ; nom. plu., coṟa (*cosa*), and not coṟe (*coshe*), which sounds like the genitive singular coiṟe (*coshé*); ꜱɴáḃuiꜱ̇, *love*; ꜱɴáḃúꜱ̇aḋ, *to love*; and not ꜱɴáḃuiꜱ̇aḋ, &c. &c.

Secondly—Because most of the modernly-printed Irish books have the spelling very nearly altogether in accordance with this rule, and therefore the students who read them should get some easy way of knowing the spelling adopted by their respective authors.

Thirdly—The natural tone of the language, which can, in most instances, be learned from the physiological sounds of the vernacular, as spoken by the country Irish-speaking people, requires the collation of "slender with slender and broad with broad." "Regulam," says O'Molloy, "Hibernis tritam, tum in scriptura, tum in *sono*," p. 50.—*Vide infra*, § 4.

Fourthly—Its adoption prevents that confusion which arises from the same words being spelled differently by different writers.

I say, "*yet with a certain limitation*." It is manifestly incorrect to alter the radical spelling, for instance, of a prefix, for the sake of conforming to this canon. ḃeaꜱ̇, *good;* ḃcaɴḃ, *real;* ḃo, *bad, ill* (see *Etymology*, chapter ix.) should not be changed into ḃeiꜱ̇, ḃeiɴḃ, ḃoi, whenever the first vowel of the word with which it becomes compounded is e or i; example, ḃeaꜱ̇-ḃeaɴꞇa, *well done*, should be spelled as if ḃeaꜱ̇ were compounded with the word ḃáɴ, *a poem;* ḃeaꜱ̇-ḃéaɴꞇa, and not ḃeiꜱ̇-ḃéaɴꞇa, as some, adhering too strictly to the rule, write it. This manner of spelling is, in compound terms especially, carrying the thing to excess, and it is in this excess, or as Stewart says, "the extensive application of the rule," that its entire fault lies. "Dixi ordinarie," says O'Molloy, "nam exceptio datur de quibusdam paucissimis."—See chapter iii., *infra, Spelling in Irish*.

§ 4.—PHILOSOPHIC REASONS IN SUPPORT OF THE RULE.

The work from which the following extract is taken, appears to be the only one in which this subject of *vowel assimilation* in Irish has been treated from a philosophic point of view:

"'The reason of such a division is quite philosophic, for every vowel sound is produced 'by the passage of the air through the opening of the glottis;' and thus all intonated vowel sounds 'partake somewhat of the character of musical notes, while, at the same time, they constitute the elements of speech.' In the musical octave each successive note, from the highest to the lowest, is sounded with a volume of voice deeper than that of the note preceding; and conversely the preceding is sounded with a higher, that is, a more *slender* (we shall so call it) volume of voice than its succeeding note. The two highest are, therefore, the two which may properly be called *slender*, when compared to those which, lower in the scale, are pronounced deep, or *broad*. In this manner intonated vowel sounds, as far as they partake of this musical character, are some slender, some broad. Let us arrange them then in the philosophic order (See *Atlantis*, vol. i., pp. 60, 65), 'from the highest to the deepest; thus, ɪ, e, ʌ, o, u.' And in this arrangement, which is that made by philologists and philosophers, native and foreign, we find ɪ, e, to rank highest, that is, to constitute the class called cᴀol, or *slender*, and ʌ, o, u, lowest, that is, to constitute the class called leᴀtᴀn, *broad*, or deep Thus we see that the classification of vowels made by Irish grammarians accords exactly with that which the investigations of philosophy point out as correct. There are in Gælic, therefore, two classes of vowels clearly and philosophically distinguishable. Do they differ in their influence and in their effects? We shall see:

"Vowels and consonants constitute the one grand, universal family of letters. Consonants derive their name from being *sounded along with*, or by the aid of the vowels. When articulated, they partake, therefore, of the sound of that vowel by the aid of which they are enunciated. Irish vowel sounds are, as we have seen, of a twofold character, *broad* or *slender*; each consonant must, accordingly, partake of a twofold articulation, *broad* or *slender*, according to the broad or slender intonation of the vowel by the aid of which it is sounded. This twofold articulation can, in some measure, be applied with truth to consonants in any language; but, with the exception of the Keltic dialects, and particularly Irish, we know of none in which this phonetic distinction in the articulation of consonants, has retained its radically distinctive philosophic character.

"The influence of a twofold sound of the vowels thus acting on the consonants, and causing them to participate in it, is so fused into our national language that it has stamped its pronunciation and orthography with a complexion and individuality quite different from everything English. To Irish-speaking natives this individuality appears quite easy and natural, and, like accent, with which it is essentially blended, is naturally acquired and practised by them without knowing or adverting to the existence of the principle from which it springs; yet, to those who do not speak the language, it appears at once strange and difficult.

"As the language is spoken and written, the effects of the influence exercised by the two-fold division of vowel sounds extend to both departments—the written and spoken Gælic. These effects may well, therefore, be called *articulate*, or phonetic, and *orthographic*.

"The *articulate* regards the sound of each consonant when it is intonated with a broad or a slender vowel. The *orthographic* regards the laws of spelling."—*Easy Lessons; or, Self-Instruction in Irish*, part iii., pp. 200, 201; Dublin, Mullany, publisher.

It springs from a principle of euphony, according to Latham:

"The Irish Gaelic, above most other languages, illustrates a euphonic principle that modifies the vowels of a word. The vowels *a, o, u*, are full, whilst *i, e*, are small. Now if to a syllable containing a small vowel; as, *buail*, there be added a syllable containing a broad one; as, *am*, a change takes place. Either the first syllable is accommodated to the second, or the second to the first, so that the vowels respectively contained in them are either both full or both small. Hence arises, in respect to the word quoted, either the form *buatam*, or else the form *buailim*."—*Latham on the English Language*, 3rd ed., § 228, p. 158.

And from a principle of harmony, according to Professor W. K. Sullivan:

"The Irish rule of 'slender to slender, and broad to broad—caol le caol, agur leatan le leatan,' is very similar to the law of vocal harmony (in the Finnic-Tartarian, or nothern family of languages).—*Atlantis*, p. 77.

§ 5. EACH CONSONANT HAS A TWO-FOLD SOUND.

The term phonetic means, relating to articulate sound. From what has been explained in the foregoing section it is clear that the Gaelic canon, caol le caol, agur leatan le leatan, or the principle on which it rests, is ordinarily observed in the spoken language. The student, then, who wishes to acquire a facility in speaking Gaelic should keep the principle in mind. This is quite sufficient; for it is practice with the ear and tongue, in listening to and speaking the language, that can at any time make a person master of the spoken elegance of a nation's speech.

A consonant partakes of the sound of the vowel by aid of which it is articulated. As some vowels are broad and others slender, the same consonant is necessarily pronounced at one time broad, at another time slender—*broad*, when sounded in union with a, o, or u; *slender*, when sounded in union with e, ı.

The *slender* sound of a consonant in Gaelic becomes to an English student distinct and perceptible, in the fullest manner, by blending the sound of *y* with the common consonantal articulation.

§ 6.—BROAD AND SLENDER SOUNDS OF THE CONSONANTS.

C.—c broad sounds like *c* in *could*, as capað, *a friend*. C slender, like *k* in *king*, as ceann (pronounced *kyean*, in one syllable), *a head*.

In page 13 it is observed that c Gaelic is always sounded like *k*. It was thus the Latins pronounced it—as the Greeks pronounced κ (*koppa*). The Germans of the present day retain the hard sound (*k*), and will not admit any other. The learned at home and throughout Great Britain are so sure of this philological phonetic fact, that in defiance of usage and pronunciation they have commenced—and rightly too, in order to force the adoption of the correct sound—to write Cæsar, *Kæsar*; Celtic, *Keltic*. O'Molloy, writing on this error, as he calls it, of giving the sibilant sound of *s* to *c*, remarks— "Imo olim apud Latinos litera *c* non solum in locum sed in sonum literæ *k* plane plenèque substituatur, nec assertione res eget. Quis enim grammaticorum unquam aliter tradidit ante hæc tempora? Hoc est nisi quod hodie eó inoleverit usus, seu potius error, an pravus anne pertinax quis non videat? Latini inquam, recentiores duplicem ei sonum dant; alterum ut debent; alterum ut volunt."—*Grammaticâ Latino-Hibernica*, p. 13.

D.—d broad, like *dh* English, as dun (*dhun*), *a fort*; dán (*dhawn*), *a poem*. D slender, like *d* in *dew*, *d* in radiant, in guard*ian*; as, dılır, *fond, dear*; dıan, (*dhyee-an*, in one syllable), *vehement*.

The assimilating influence of the liquid letters l, n, r, over d, is observable in the following instances, in which the sound of d is lost: codlað, *sleep*, pronounced as if written collað; fodla, an ancient name of Ireland, pronounced róllᴀ; céᴀbnᴀ, *same*, pronounced as if ceᴀnnᴀ, as ᴀn lᴀ ccᴀbnᴀ, *the same day;* mᴀıbne, gen. case of mᴀıbın, *morning*, pronounced as if mᴀınne, as unnᴀıᵹe nᴀ mᴀıbne (mᴀınne), *prayers of the morning;* Ruᴀbıɾı, *Roderick*, pronounced Ruᴀnɾıı. In ancient MSS., the use of b after n is very common. In modern Irish double (nn) is commonly adopted instead.

A similar homologous assimilation arises when the liquids l and n come together.

Ᵹ.—ᵹ broad, like *g* in *gun;* as, ᵹᴀn (*gun*) cıɾce, ıɾ ꝼuᴀɾı ᴀn clıu, *without wealth fame is cold.* ᵹ slender, like *g* in *get* (*gyet*), as ᵹeᴀn (*gyean*) mo cɾoıbe ċu, *thou art my heart's affection.*

l.—l broad, like *ll* in *mill,* as coll, *a wood.* l slender, like *l* in va*l*iant. l, followed by b or n, assimilates their articulate value to its own, as colnᴀ, *of the body,* gen. case of colᴀn, is pronounced *colla:* and muılneoıɾ, *a miller* (from muılın, *a mill*), pronounced *muilleoir.*

N.—n broad has a thick sound, " pronounced by inserting the tip of the tongue between the teeth." The sound of *nh* is very like it, as nóɾ, *a custom* (pronounced *nhos*). N slender, like *n* in *new.*

Double (nn), when intonated with the slender vowels, has a nasal sound like *n* prolonged, or *nh,* differing very little from that of *ng* in *sing,* as bınn (*binh*), *melodious;* cınn (*kinh*), *heads;* ɾınn (*shinh*), *we, us.*

The difficulty of articulating the combinations cn, ᵹn, mn, is overcome by inserting a short vowel sound between n and the preceding consonant, as cnoc, *a hill,* is pronounced *kinock,* Anglicè *knock;* ᵹnıom (*an act*), *giniov;* mnᴀ (*women*), *minaw.* The sound of *ı* in these instances is only slightly heard. Many of the Irish-speaking people overcome the difficulty by changing the sound of n, after c and after m, into that of ɾ, as cnoc, *kruck;* mnᴀ, *mraw.* The learner need not be told that in such combinations in the English language, the sound of *n* assumes a dominant influence, leaving the helping consonant quiescent, as *g*naw, *k*night, *m*nemonics, words in which *g, k, m,* are not at all heard.

Nᵹ.—These two letters, called in Irish ᵹneċᴀl, represent only a simple, single sound. Its broad and slender sounds are heard, says Dr. O'Donovan in the English word *longing,* as ceᴀnᵹᴀ, *a tongue* (*theang-a*); ɾeᴀnᵹ, *lean, thin* (*sheang*).

Robert Gordon Latham speaks of this combination in his remarkable work, " The English Language," in the following words:

" *Ng.*—The sound of *ng* in *sing, king, throng*—when at

the end of a word, or of *singer, ringing, &c.*—in the middle of a word, is not the natural sound of the combination n and g, each letter retaining its natural power and sound ; but a single, simple sound, of which the combination *ng* is a conventional mode of expressing."—*Section* 207, p. 148, 3rd edition.

R—ꞃ broad, like *r* in any simple English word, as ꞃuɴ, *a secret ;* ꞃuaᵭ, *red.* Slender, like *r* in *carrion* ; as ꞃɪ₅ (*ree*), *a king* ; ꞃɪɴɴ (*rhin*), *a headland, a promontory ;* in *poetry, harmony, termination.*

S.—ꞅ, see p. 14.

T.—т always like *th*. т, at the end of words, has an explosive sound, as if *h* were added, as cат, *a cat*, is pronounced *hath*.

In pronouncing *cat* in English, the tongue is kept inside the upper teeth; in articulating the same word in Irish, the tongue must be protruded between the teeth.

In the consonants, b, ꝼ, m, p, and ṗ aspirated (*i.e., f*), the effects of this principle of slender and broad vowel assimilation, and its influence, are not noticeable to any great degree.

The consonants in their natural state are articulated according to the foregoing notation.

Their sounds in their affected or aspirated form shall be presented after the subject of diphthongs and triphthongs, which immediately follow, pp. 23, 27.

§ 7. *Mutes, Liquids*.—The usual division of the consonants is into liquids—l, m, ɴ, ꞃ—and mutes—b, c, ᵭ, ꝼ, ᵹ, p, ꞅ, т. The former are called liquids because they flow readily, or combine with any other consonant in the same syllable after which they chance to be placed.

The term *mute* is here employed in a wide sense, and is not intended to come against the strict division made by Scaliger, who expends a chapter in proving that ꝼ is not a mute, but a semivowel. (*De Causis Linguæ Latinæ, liber* i.)

§ 8. *Gemination, or Doubling of Consonants.*—Three of the liquids, l, ɴ, ꞃ, admit of being doubled at the end of a word, and are therefore called, with some seeming impropriety, *double-letters*, as ll, ɴɴ, ꞃꞃ, in ᵹeall, *a promise;* ceaɴɴ, *a head, an individual;* baꞃꞃ, *the top, summit, crop, produce*.

" The reduplication of the consonants is, in English and the generality of languages, a conventional mode of expressing upon paper the shortness (dependence) of the vowel that precedes."—*Professor Latham on the English Language*, sec. 221, p. 155.

The other consonants do not admit of being doubled at the end of a word.

In Gaelic there is no double or compound letter, such as *x*, *z*, or the Greek χ (*chee*), φ (*phee*).

§ 9. *Immutables, Mutables.*—ℓ, ꞃ, ꞅ, never change their primitive sound, and are for this reason termed *immutables*. The eight mutes and the liquid ᴍ change the primitive sound, and hence receive the name *mutables*.

§ 10. *A Syllable.*—A consonant and one vowel or more sounded together in the same breath constitutes a syllable. In a wider and more general sense, a syllable is a word or part of a word.

DIPHTHONGS.

§ 11. *True or Perfect, Imperfect; Long, Short, Number of.*—A diphthong is the fusion of two different vowel sounds in the same syllable: a triphthong is the fusion of three.

"If we arrange the vowels in the order from the highest to the deepest thus, *i, e, a, o, u*, it will be found that the passage from the middle vowel, *a*, towards *i* on one side and *u* on the other—that is, the combination of a flowing or initial with a fixed or final vowel alone, produces a true diphthong. . . . . There can consequently be only six true diphthongs, *ai, au, ei, eu, oi, ou.*"—*Atlantis*, vol. i. p. 65.

A diphthong is true or perfect when the fusion of the two vowel sounds is perfect; false or imperfect, when not.

A diphthong is long or short according as the time taken to pronounce it is long or short.

A diphthong is therefore said to be long or short in regard to its duration of sound; perfect or true in regard to its fullness of sound.

In Irish there are thirteen diphthongs; five triphthongs. There are six of these naturally long; seven short. The latter are sometimes long. This change is noted by the presence of the grave accent (`) over the vowel that receives the dominant sound.

§ 12. *The Long Diphthongs.*—The long are ae, ao, eo eu, ia, ua.

SOUNDS OF THE SIX LONG DIPHTHONGS.

Diphthong.	Sound.	Example.
ae	æ in *Musæ*	ɴae, *yesterday*
ao	ao in *gaol*	ɒaoɲ, *dear;* ɼaoɲ, *cheap*
eo	eo in *Keon, yeoman*	ceol, *music**
eu	ai in *wail*	beul, *mouth;* ɼȝeul, *story*
ia	ia *filia*	pıaɲ, *pain*
ua	ua in *truant*	ɼuaɲ, *rest*

§ 13.—OBSERVATIONS ON THE LONG DIPHTHONGS.

ᴀe; ᴀo.—The diphthong ᴀe is seldom employed in modern Irish orthography. It is found commonly in manuscripts and books of our ancient language. The diphthong ᴀo is at present generally employed in its stead. Hence it is that ᴀo receives very properly the sound of é long, or *ao* in *gaol;* but in Connaught it is usually pronounced *ee*.

eo.—eo and ıu ought to be ranked amongst the class of diphthongs called long, since they are short only in a few words.

Long diphthongs ought not to be accented.

It is unnecessary to note as long, by means of the accent, the diphthongs éo, éu, ía, úa, or even íu, since they are by nature already long. This mistake is not uncommon.

Each vowel in a diphthong should be distinctly enunciated.

In enunciating the long diphthongs eo, eu, ıa, ua, ıu, and the naturally short diphthongs when they become accented, the two vowels composing the digraph should be each distinctly heard; thus, beul, *a mouth*, is pronounced *be-ul*, as if an English word of two syllables; and ɼuaɲ, *cold*, as if written *fuo-ar*, like *ua* in *truant*, as noted in the paradigm. So, ıa is pronounced *ee-a*, as pıaɲ, (*pain*), *pee-an*, and so of the rest.

It was in this manner the ancients of Rome and Greece pronounced the diphthongs. The word Zευs, *Jupiter*, was pronounced by the latter as if written Ze-us, and ευγε, as if ε-ύγε; and by the former the diphthong *eu* or *eo* is so enunciated, appearing, as it were, cut in twain, as in the exclamation *Deus meus,* "my God," and *Deo meo.*

This peculiarity, so un-English in character, in the sound of Irish diphthongs should be remembered by the learner.

Difference in Sound between ᴀo *and* ıa.—The difference between ᴀo and ıa is best shown by an example, as mıaɲ, *a wish*, is pronounced *meean;* maoɲ, *wealth*, pronounced *mueen;*

---

* eo is short in the following words: eocaıɲ, *a key;* ɒeoc, *a drink;* Cocaıb, *a man's name;* reo, *this;* ɼeoc, *beside, by, apart.* This latter is now usually spelled ɼeac.

whilst ᴀoᵢ in ᴍᴀoᵢᴅ, *of wealth*, is pronounced *muee-in* (in one syl.)

Eo.—Remember that eo is pronounced like *eo* in *yeo*, or *eogh* in *Keogh*, see " Easy Lessons in Irish," pp. 8, 9.

§ 14. *Sounds of the Variable Diphthongs.*—The variable diphthongs become long by placing the grave (`) accent over the emphatic vowel.

The sound of the *accented* vowel predominates.

The learner should note well the sound of the diphthong ᴀᵢ in Irish, which to an English speaker is so very uncommon, and so unlike the sound of the same diphthong in English, the language with which his ear is so familiar.

Diphthong		Sound.	Example.
Aᵢ.— àᵢ		*awi* in *sawing*	cáᵢl, *fame*; fáᵢl, *fate*
	ᴀᵢ	*ai* in *wassail*; *taille* (French)	cᴀᵢll, *loss*; fᴀᵢll, *a sty*
Eᴀ.—êᴀ		*ea* in *bear, rear*	bêᴀn, *do, make*
	eᴀ	*ea* in *heart*	meᴀſ, *respect*
	eᴀ { accent on ᴀ }	*a* in *father*	ɜeᴀᵢɼɼ, *short, to cut*
	éᵢ	*ei* in *deign*	céᵢl, *sense*
	eᵢ	*e* in *den*	ceᵢll, *conceal*
Io.— ío		*ee* in *green*	fíon, *wine*
	ᵢo	*i* in *grin*	fᵢoɴɴ, *white*
Iu.— íu		*ieu* (French) or *ew* in *chew*	ríuɼ, *a kinswoman, a sister*
	ᵢu	*oo* in *flood*	flᵢuċ (pr. *flyuch*), *wet*
Oᵢ.— óᵢ		*o* and *i* blended into one	cóᵢɼ, *justice*
	oᵢ	*ui* (short) in *quill*	coᵢɼ (pr. *coirh*), *a crime*
	oᵢ { accent on ᵢ }	*uee* in *queer*	cɼoᵢbe, *heart*, as ɼτóᵢɼ mo cɼoᵢbe (*sthore mo chree*), *my heart's treasure.**
Uᵢ.— úᵢ		*ui* in *fruit*	rúᵢl, *eye*
	uᵢ	*ui* in *guilt*	fuᵢl, *blood*
	uᵢ { accent on ᵢ }	like *oᵢ* above	buᵢbe (*bwee*), *yellow*

* In the word oᵢbe (*e-dhe*), *a teacher, a professor*, oᵢ = *e* in *great*

The diphthongs *au* and *ou*, belonging to the class called perfect or true, are not found in modern Gaelic orthography; their sounds, however, are quite usual, as in the words, ᴛᴀʙᴀɪʀ (*thow-erh*), *give;* ᴄᴀʙᴀɪʀ (*cow-erh*), *help*, in which the digraph ᴀʙ receives the sound of *ou* in *house*.

Conformably with the authority of O'Molloy and MacFirbis, and following the instructions conveyed in "Easy Lessons," the spelling eu, and not eu, for the long diphthong, shall be observed in these pages.

"In Tipperary, Waterford, and Kilkenny, the diphthongs eu, ɪo, and sometimes ɪu, on coming before ll, m, nn, n, are incorrectly pronounced *ow*, as ᴢʟeᴀɴ, *a valley*, is pronounced *glown;* so ꜰɪoɴɴ, *fair*, is pronounced *fown*." ("Easy Lessons,"part 1. p. 15, second edition.) Their correct pronunciation is pointed out in the preceding page.

Though the foregoing list gives the sounds of the diphthongs as correctly as can well be given through the medium of English letters, still it must be said that the proper sound is acquired best by ear. A person learns to speak French much more correctly by conversing with natives of France than he could ever acquire through the rules given by writers of French grammar; so it is with him who wishes to speak *Irish* correctly. He must listen to and converse with those who know and speak the language.

§ 15.—TRIPHTHONGS.

The triphthongs, five in number, are formed from the long diphthongs that end in a *broad vowel*—eu excepted—by inserting ɪ after the second vowel; as, from ᴀo is formed ᴀoɪ; from eo, eoɪ; from ɪᴀ, ɪᴀɪ; from ɪu, ɪuɪ; from uᴀ, uᴀɪ. These are all *long*. It is not necessary, then, to note their sounds, or to employ the accent (´) to show they are long.

In some printed books, ɪ, both in diphthongs and triphthongs, is found subscribed for the sake of brevity. Unlike the Greek ɩ (*iota*), in such positions it is always sounded. Indeed, whenever there is a union of two or three vowels in any *Irish* word, each vowel retains its own distinct sound, fused, however, into the melody, so to speak, of the others that accompany it, so that all the vowels in that syllable will form only *one full sound*, as mᴀoɴ, (*mween*), *wealth;* mᴀoɪɴ (*mwee-in*), *of wealth;* the two vowels in the one case, and the three in the other, are in each word sounded in one voice, yet each vowel gives its own share to the entire volume of sound.

"The sound of each triphthong differs from that of the diphthong from which it is derived in two points—first, in a slight prolongation of the diphthongal sound; secondly, in imparting to the consonant immediately following, on account of its proximity to the slender vowel ɪ, a liquid or slender sound, which otherwise it would not receive."

ᴀoɪ, like *uee* in *queen*, as ꜰᴀoɪ, *under*, pronounced, not *fee*, but *fwee*.

ɪᴀɪ, *ee*, like the sound of the diphthong ɪᴀ, from which it is formed, yet imparting to the consonant which follows the second ꞁ a slender sound.

Juꞁ, *eeyu*, as cꞁuꞁꞃ (pronounced *keeyuin*, in one syllable).

The triphthong uaꞁ is sounded quickly and curtly in the prepositional pronouns, uaꞁm (*wem*), *from me;* uaꞁт (*weyth*), *from thee;* uaꞁðe (*wy-ya*), *from him;* uaꞁꞃꞃ, *from us;* uaꞁb, *from you.*

CHAPTER II.

OF THE CONSONANTS.

, § 16. *The Natural Sound of the Consonants changed by Aspiration.*—The natural or primitive sounds of the consonants—l, n, ɲ, excepted—become, under certain governing influences which shall be presently pointed out, changed into others of homorganic articulation. By the term homorganic is conveyed the idea of being sounded by the same organ of speech, such as the tongue, teeth. This change in the sound and form of the consonants is called Aspiration.

§ 17. Aspiration is nothing more than a rough breathing or sibilant utterance affecting the primitive or natural sounds of certain consonants, so as to modify those sounds, or change them into others of cognate value.

Any one who takes the trouble of noting how he articulates each consonant, cannot but perceive that the lips, the palate, throat, teeth, tongue, through the agency of which articulate sound is produced, very largely contribute, each in turn, to mould the distinctive sound of each consonant. On this account consonants are classed into *labial* or lip-letters, *palatal, guttural* or throat-letters, *dental* or teeth-letters, and *lingual*. They are classed as follows:

Labial.	Dental.	Palatal.
...	ꞃ	...
ꝼ, ḟ or ꝼh	ṙ or ꞃh	...
...	l	ɴ
m, ṁ or mh	ɴ	ŋ
		Guttural.
b	ð	ᵹ
p	t	c
ḃ or bh	ḋ or dh	ġ or gh
ṗ or ph	ṫ or th	ċ or ch

A consonant affected by aspiration remains still of the same class of cognate letters to which it belonged in its primitive state. For instance, the *labial* p remains, when aspirated (ṗ or ph), a *labial*, and is not changed into the class *dental* or *palatal*.

"From this principle of similarity of sound in letters of the same organ, and of their retaining still a similarity in their aspirated forms, a table of the aspirable consonants, and of their aspirate sounds, as represented by Roman letters, can be formed."

§ 18.—SYNOPSIS OF ASPIRATES AND THEIR SOUNDS.

[This synopsis should be referred to till the aspirate sounds are known by the learner.]

⁎ The notation for the aspirate sounds is a dot (˙) or h.

Plain or Primitive Form.		Aspirated or Secondary Form, as Spelled.	Pronunciation, or Secondary Form as Articulated.	
Labials	p	ṗ, or ph	F	
	b	ḃ, or bh	V, or W	
	ᴍ	ṁ or mh	V, or W	
	f	ḟ, or fh	H	
Palatals	c	ċ, or ch	Guttural	KH, or χ
	ᵹ	g᷂, or gh		GH, Y
Dentals	d	ḋ, or dh	DH, Y	
	t	ṫ, or th	H	
Sibilant	s	ṡ, or sh	H	

§ 19.—SOUNDS OF THE ASPIRATED CONSONANTS.

Ph or ṗ = *ph* or *f*.

Bh or ḃ and mh or ṁ = *w* or *v*; of *w* when placed between two of the broad vowels, a, o, u; of *v* when placed before or after a slender vowel, e, ɪ. The reason is that already given in section 4, p. 19—that the consonants, as well aspirated as primitive, partake of the nature of that vowel-sound by the aid of which it has been enunciated. In Munster, b (asp.) is commonly pronounced like *v*. B (slender) has exactly the sound of *v* through all parts of Ireland. In the dative and ablative or prepositional cases of nouns b is consequently sounded like *v*. In the end of a word, as in gaḃ (*gav*), *seize, get, conceive*, it has usually the like sound.

Mh (asp.) is slightly nasal, as cuṁa, *grief*, pronounced

much like *coonga;* and coṁṗa, *a coffin,* like *conrha;* coṅ-ṅaṁtóiṗ, *a helper,* as if coaṅ₅tóiṗ, changing the syllables.

"The only difference between the sounds of ṁ and ḃ (both aspirated) is that the ṁ is somewhat nasal."—*Dr. O'Donovan's Irish Grammar,* p. 52.

"The sounds of some letters (as m, n) cannot be produced without the intervention of the nose; indeed the former (m) passes into b, if we attempt to sound it by the mouth alone."—*Atlantis,* p. 70.

Ḟh or ḟ is silent; it has the sound of *h* in some words, as ḟeiṅ, *self;* ḋo m' ḟéiṅ (*dhom he-en*), *to myself.**

Ch or ċ has the guttural sound of the German *ch* (*i.e.,* of *gh* in the word *lough*) when it comes before or after any of the broad vowels, a, o, u; as mo ċaṗa (*mo khawrah*), *my friend;* caṗċanaċ (*kharhanach*), *friendly;* but when it precedes or follows the slender vowels e, i, it has the less guttural sound of the Greek χ (*chee*); as mo ċeaṅṅ (*mo χean*), *my head;* a ċiṅe (*a χiné*), *his people.*

There is no sound in English like that of ċ (asp.); for when it is said that ċ aspirated sounds like *gh* in *lough,* very few take up that sound, for few in these countries, except Irish-speaking people alone, pronounce that digraph with a guttural tone. To pronounce it correctly add to the sound of *k* (or Irish c) a little rough breathing from the throat, as oċ (*och !*).

Ġh or ġ (asp.) = *gh,* guttural, in the beginning of a word, if before the vowels a, o, u; before the vowels e, i, it has the less guttural sound of *y;* as mo ġean (*mo yean*), *my affection.* But in the end and middle of words it has no other power than that of lengthening the sound of the preceding vowel, and fixing the spelling, just as *gh* in the English words *high, highness, nigh, neighbour, thought, thoughtful, thoughtfulness,* tends to lengthen the vowel *i,* or the diphthongs *ei, ou,* and to aid in forming a correct orthography.

Example—riġ, *a king,* pronounced as if written rī (*rhee*); riġeaċt (*rhee-acht*), *a kingdom;* riġ-aṁail (*rheeawail*), *kingly.*

Soġ, *happiness, prosperity,* pronounced *só;* soġ-aṁail, *pleasant, prosperous;* soġ-aṁlaċt, *pleasantness.*

---

* "The same words which begin with S or F as their primitive initial in the Erse, taking h in their secondary form, have, in Welsh, h as their primary."—*Prichard's Eastern Origin of the Celtic Nations,* p. 165.

In the middle of proper names of men, ᵹa or ᵹu is pronounced like *uee* or *yee;* as Feaṅᵹur, *Fergus.*

Ḋh or ḋ has a thick, guttural sound, very like that of ᵹ (*gh*) whenever it precedes any of the broad vowels; as, mo ḋólar (*mo ghòlas*). In the beginning of a word, ḋ has, before e or i, the sound exactly of *y* in the English word *yearn*, as mo Ḋia (*mo Yia*), *my God.* In the *middle* or *end* of words ḋ (asp.) is the same in all respects as ᵹ aspirated—*i.e.,* it only lengthens the sound of the preceding vowel or diphthong.

"There is another sound peculiar to ᵹ and ḋ when following the vowels a or o, in the first or second syllable of a word, which deserves particular attention. The two letters aᵹ, or aḋ, sound like *i* in *ire*, or *ey* in *eye*, *eyre;* as aḋain (*ey-en*), *aspen;* aḋairt (*ey-arth*), *a bolster;* aḋan, *a cauldron*, a large pot in which wool is dyed; aḋarc (*eye-ark*), *a horn*, aḋlacaḋ, (*ey-luch-oo*), *burial;* aḋraim, *I adore;* aḋrtar, *a halter;* ealaḋan, *a science*, ᵹaḋair, *a beagle;* paḋarc, *sight;* Taḋᵹ, *Thaig*, laᵹaḋ, *fewness;* aᵹaiḋ, *face, against;* laᵹair, *a finger, toe, prong, fork.* (Sleaᵹan, *a turf spade,* and Seaᵹan, *John*, are exceptions.) The exceptions are generally marked with the grave accent, as àḋbar, *a cause;* àḋmuḋ, *timber;* aḋ, *luch.*"—*Easy Lessons,* p. 20.

"This rule holds good throughout the southern half of Ireland; but it must be varied for the pronunciation of the North and West. In Connaught, aḋ and aᵹ, when followed by a vowel, have the sound laid down in the text; but when followed by l, m, n, r, they are pronounced like a long, as aḋraḋ, *adoration;* aḋlacaḋ, *burial;* aḋmuḋ, *timber,* which words are pronounced as if written ànraḋ, àlacaḋ, ànmuḋ. . . . . It is highly probable that it (the true sound) was originally pronounced a long, as it is in some instances in Connaught at present."—*Dr. O'Donovan's Irish Grammar,* p. 9.

Ṫh or ṫ   =   h ⎫ The aspirate alone is heard in
Ṡh or ṡ   =   h ⎭ these consonants.

"The addition of *h* to the primitive consonants serves only to render it obtrusive, or, in other instances, to obliterate it."—*Prichard's Eastern Origin of the Celtic Nations,* p. 168.

"*Súil,* an eye. 1st form, *súil.* 2nd form, *a húil,* his eye. *Sláinte,* health. 2nd form, *do hlainte,* your health."—*Ibid.,* 168.

"In these instances the initial *s*, though converted into an aspirate in pronunciation, is sometimes retained in orthography, either with a dot over it, or followed by *h*. But in either case the sibilant is entirely lost."—*Note by Dr. Latham.*

S.—ꞃ, before the consonants b, c, ᴅ, ꜰ, ᵹ, m, p, ᴛ—*i.e.*, all except l, n, ꞃ—is never aspirated, nor when closing a word or syllable; mo ᵹꞁobol, *my barn;* ᴅo ꞃᵹꞃꞁob me leꞁ-ᴛꞁꞃ, *I wrote a letter.*

§ 20.—The charge made by Davies and Pinkerton—that the change in the radical sound of the consonants is the result of barbarity—is ably refuted by Dr. O'Donovan This change is common with the Semitic languages, and those of the Indo-European family. It existed in the old Saxon, and is found in German. And in French, the most polished language in Europe, this suppression and change of consonantal sounds exists to a degree far beyond anything of the kind in all the Keltic dialects. He adds: "The English people, in whose polished language, spoken and written, no trace of a guttural sound is now to be found, abhor the rough sound of *gh* in the broad Scotch, but much more the Irish guttural sibilant sounds of ċ, ḋ, ġ; although in reality their own *y, c, ch,* and *g* soft, are equally sibilant, and as much aspirations as the Irish ċ, ḋ, ġ. The fact is, men will regard this or that sound as polished or barbarous, according as it agrees with or differs from the sounds to which they have been themselves accustomed from infancy."—*Irish Grammar by Dr. O'Donovan,* p. 41.

§ 21. *Sounds of* aḋ (eaḋ) *and of* uᵹaḋ *at the end of a word.*—Any new form of words could not make this subject plainer than it is in those here presented to the learner taken from "Easy Lessons."

"As *a general rule,* aḋ final, in words of *two or more* syllables, is pronounced, in Munster, like a unaccented; in Connaught and Ulster, like *oo* (English), or u (long) Irish. This peculiar pronunciation the learner should remember, as aḋ final occurs almost in every sentence of Irish, read or spoken.

"With regard to words of *one* syllable, and their compound forms, the Munster pronunciation of aḋ final is adopted not only in the South, but in the West and North of Ireland: example—aḋ (*aw*), *luck;* mꞁ-aḋ (*me-aw*), *bad luck, misfortune;* bꞁaḋ, *food* (pronounced as if bꞁa, *beea*); blaḋ, *blow, fame, renown;* cꞁaḋ, *a ditch* (formerly spelled cluꞁ); cꞃaḋ (*craw*), *anguish;* ᵹeuꞃ-cꞃaḋ, *piercing anguish;*

buan-cṅaḋ, *lasting anguish;* buaḋ, *labour, toil;* ꞃeaḋ (pr. *fah—a* short), *length, duration;* aiꞃ ꞃeaḋ, *for the length, during;* aiꞃ ꞃeaḋ laeṫe uile do beaṫa, *during all the days of thy life* (Gen. iii. 14); ꞁleaḋ (*fleh*), *a feast;* ꞡaḋ, *peril;* ꞡꞃaḋ, *love;* dian-ꞡꞃaḋ, *intense love;* ṫiꞃ-ꞡꞃaḋ, *patriotism;* ꞁaḋ, *speaking* (Gr. ῥεω, *I speak*); coṁ-ꞁaḋ, *speaking together, a chat;* cuiꞁꞁ-ꞁaḋ (from cuiꞁꞡ, *a bond;* and ꞁaḋ), *a covenant;* ꞁoiṁ-ꞁaḋ, *a preface, a prologue;* ꞃeaḋ, (*shah;* for iꞃ é), *yes;* and its compound, maiꞃeaḋ (ma, *if;* iꞃ, *is;* ꞃe, *it), well then.*

"Obs.—In verbs, participles, and verbal nouns, the ending uꞡaḋ is pronounced *oo—i.e.*, uꞡ, as if aḋ were not in the syllable, aḋ being like *ent* in French verbs, not sounded. This pronunciation of uꞡaḋ is common throughout Ireland. It is a termination, like "*tion*" in English, peculiar to a vast number of words, as beaꞃꞅuꞡaḋ (*bannoo*), *a benediction,* from beaꞃꞅuiꞡ, *bless thou;* cꞃuṫuꞡaḋ (*kruhoo*), *creating, creation, proof,* from cꞃuṫuiꞡ, *create thou, prove thou;* ꞡꞃaḋuꞡaḋ (*grawoo*), *loving,* from ꞡꞃaḋuiꞡ, *love thou;* ꞁlaꞃuꞡaḋ (*slawnoo*), *salvation,* from ꞁlaꞃuiꞡ, *save thou.*

"In Munster and in the south of Connaught—in parts of the counties of Galway and Roscommon—the ending aḋ of the third person singular, imperative, and of the imperfect tense, indicative, is sometimes incorrectly—at least contrary to general usage—pronounced with a guttural accent, like *agh;* as, ꞡlaꞃaḋ (*glonagh,* instead of *glonoo*) ꞃe, *let him cleanse;* ꞡlaꞃaḋ (*ylanagh,* instead of *ylonoo*) ꞃe, *he used to cleanse;* bioeaḋ (*beeyagh,* instead of *beyoo*) ꞃe, *let him be.*"

"The original pronunciation of aḋ and aꞡ (at the end of words) was, in all probability like *agh,* guttural, which is still partially preserved in the mountainous districts of the counties of Londonderry and Tyrone.—*Dr. O'Donovan's Irish Grammar,* p. 10.

§ 22 *Similarity between Aspiration in Greek and Aspiration in Irish.—* ṗ (aspirated) is the best illustration of the almost perfect similarity that exists between aspiration in Greek and that in Irish. ꞁ in Irish and π in Greek are perfectly the same; aspirate both, and you have ṗ from the one, and φ from the other, each of which is sounded like *f* or *ph* in English; Ιωσεφ, Scorep, *Joseph.*

C also is a good illustration; c is the κ (*koppa*) of the Greeks; κ aspirated becomes χ; and ċ (aspirated) assumes the sound of χ. What more plain? It may be said the other letters, when aspirated, do not bear out this similarity so well. True, at first sight they do not—but let us see.

Besides the usual division of consonants into mutes and semivowels, or liquids, there is that other (sec. 17, p. 27) which points out those that are allied in organic sound; b, ꝼ, m, p, are called labials; c, ꒑, palatals or gutturals; ꝺ, l, n, ꞃ, r, ꞅ, dentals or linguals. Now b and p are therefore, being of the same organ, sounded nearly by the same opening of the mouth. The one is often in old MSS used for the other, as béꞇꞃ for péꞇꞃ. The Greeks wrote λειβσω for λειπσω; βικρον for πικρον: the Latins, *pleps* sometimes for *plebs*; *suppono* for *subpono*—so closely are the two letters p and b allied in sound. Hence when b becomes aspirated, its sound should be very like the aspirate sound of p—and so it is. For the sound of ṗ (asp.) is *ph* or *f*; the sound of ḃ (asp.) *v* or *w*. Now *v* and *f* are letters of the same organ, and are so closely allied that in some MSS. or books the one is found sometimes written for the other as ꞃꞇꝼ for ꞃꞇḃ: *w* in German sounds like *v* (English), and *v* nearly like *f*. And what more common than to hear unlettered persons pronounce *what*, *fot*, thus showing in the very mistake how nearly identical these letters are in sound. In li*f*e, lives; wi*f*e, wives, *f* is changed into *v*.

ṁ, too, is of the class called *labials*; hence, for the same reason it has, when aspirated, the sound of *v* or *w*.

In the same manner ꒑ and c—which also are often used one for the other, both being of the same organic class, called *palatals*—become, when aspirated, gutturals—ċ (*ch* guttural); ġ (*gh*): example—mo ċabaꞃꞃ, *mo chowerh* (*my help*); mo ġabaꞃꞃ, *mo ghowerh* (*my goat*). (See *Zeuss*, p. 85, *et passim*.)

The other aspirable consonants, ꝺ, ꝼ, ꞃ, ꞅ, when influenced by aspiration, either lose their natural sound, or retain that of the aspirate only, as we see by the table of aspirates.

Hence aspiration supplies in Irish the want of those letters which other languages possess. And it is owing in some measure to the vast number of different euphonious combinations of sound, brought by its use into requisition, that our language is so musical and so copious.

§ 23.—*The Custom of placing an* h *after a Consonant, for the purpose of Aspirating, ought not to be adopted in writing Irish.*

In Latin and in English and the Romance languages, *h* is the only mark employed to note the presence of aspiration. But *h* assumes in them, to some extent, the character of an independent letter. In Irish its addition to the consonant "serves only," as Pritchard remarks, "to obliterate it." Its presence, therefore, in Irish after consonants leads the eye and ear of most readers astray. Few indeed think of the force or value of h in Gaelic— that it is only a mere aspirate—nay, that in many instances it obliterates the consonantal sound. Hence they are quite at sea—completely puzzled at the number of consonants found in an ordinary Irish word in English dress.* This custom of adding *h* for the aspirate notation should be avoided as much as possible. Yet it is adopted in some works written in the Irish character— *e. g.*, " Hardiman's Minstrelsy."

The aspirated form is not the primary—it is only the secondary or accidental form of the consonant. No aspirated consonant therefore, in its primary or natural form, commences a word :

---

* " In the spelling of these aspirate sounds by means of the English, we are hampered by the circumstance of *th* and *ph* being already used in a different sense."—*Latham*, p. 156.

Primary Form.	Affected Form.
ᚱlᚂᚉ, *slath (a rod)*.	(mo) ḟlᚂᚉ, *hlat (my rod)*.
ᚱlᚂinᚉe, *sláinthe (health)*.	(mo) ḟlᚂinᚉe, *hlainte (my health)*.

"The use of the adventitious *h* after silent or aspirated consonants has been considered objectionable. It has been repeatedly found that the insertion of this parasite character in positions where it is not employed in modern European languages, and where in Irish the change of sound is merely expressed by a dot (·) placed over the consonant so affected, does but prevent one who can read only English from any attempt at the pronunciation of those words in which it is found; or if such person should make any attempt to pronounce them, the result is as unlike the real Irish sounds as it is possible to conceive."—*Keating's History of Ireland by O'Mahony—Translator's Preface*, p. 14. New York, Haverty, 1857.

§ 24.—RULES FOR ASPIRATION.

1. All the possessive pronouns singular, mo, *my*; ᚇo, *thy*; ᚐ, *his* (ᚐ, *her*, is excepted), cause, in every case, the initial (that is, the first) mute letter of a word before which they are placed to suffer aspiration; as,

ᚌrᚐḋ, *love*	Ṁo ġrᚐḋ. *my love*; ᚇo mo ġrᚐḋ, *to my love.*
Ṁeur, *finger, toe.*	Ḋo ṁeur, *thy finger*; ᚇo ṁeurᚐ, *thy fingers.*
Slᚐnuiġᚉeoir, *Saviour.*	Ꭺ Ṡlᚐnuiġᚉeoir, *his Saviour*; ó n-ᚐ Ṡlᚐnuiġᚉeoir, *from his Saviour.*

The initial ᚌ of ġrᚐḋ, m of ṁeur, ᚱ of Slᚐnuiġᚉeoir, which in their primitive state were unaffected, become, under the influence of the pronouns singular, mo, ᚇo, ᚐ, affected by aspiration.

Ꭺ, *her*, is excepted, as ᚐ meur, *her finger*; ᚐ ġrᚐḋ, *her love*; ᚐ Slᚐnuiġᚉeoir, *her Saviour.*

2. The vocative or nominative case of address; as, Slᚐnuiġᚉeoir, *Saviour*; ᚐ Ṡlᚐnuiġᚉeoir, *oh, Saviour!* ġrᚐḋ, *love*; ᚐ ġrᚐḋ, *oh, love!*

S of Slᚐnuiġᚉeoir, and ᚌ of ġrᚐḋ are aspirated in the vocative.

3. The initial consonant, if mutable, of all words that form in composition the second part of a compound term; as,

Simple Form.	Compound Form.
oiġ, *a virgin*; beᚐn, *a woman*.	oiġ-ḃeᚐn, *a maiden*.
luᚐᚉ, *swift*; cor, *foot*.	luᚐċ-ċor, *swift-foot*.
ᚱo (*a particle betokening ease*); ᚇéᚐnᚉᚐ, *done.*	ᚱo-ḋéᚐnᚉᚐ, *easily done, feasible*.

See, in Etymology, the chapter on *Prefixes*.

IRISH GRAMMAR. 35

Exception 1.—Words beginning with any of the dental consonants, ᴅ, ᴛ, s, when the preceding part of the compound ends in ᴅ, ᴛ, s, l, n.

Simple.	Compound.
ard, *high;* tigearna, *Lord.*	ard-tigearna, *sovereign Lord.*
brat, *a covering;* taire, *a ghost.*	brat-taire, *a winding sheet.*
bean, *a woman, a female;* ridhe, *a sprite.*	bean-ridhe, *a fairy woman.*
ceann, *a head;* tír, *a country.*	ceann-tír, *headland.*
buan, *lasting, enduring;* saoghal, *life;* saoghalach, *living, in life.*	buan-shaoghalach, *long-lived.*

" Go m-buḋ faḋa, buan-ṡaoġalaċ a ḃeiḋeas tu beo."
" May it be long; life-enduring you may exist."
Hardiman's Irish Minstrelsy, vol. i. p. 24.

fios, *knowledge;* duine, *a person.* fios-duine, *a seer.*

Exceptions 2.—Sometimes, for euphony's sake, the aspirate is omitted in other words, besides those that begin with ᴅ, ᴛ, s; as,

Simple.	Compound.
breug, *a lie, false;* fáiḋ, *a prophet.*	breug-fáiḋ, *a false prophet.*
fear, *a man;* bolg, *a quiver, a pouch.*	fear-bolg, *a Belgian.*

This is particularly true in compound words, of which the latter part is governed in the genitive case·

Simple.	Compound.
cnoc, *a hill;* gréine, *of the sun.*	cnoc-gréine, *sunny hill.*
fear, *a man;* feasa, *of knowledge,* gen. case of fios.	fear-feasa, *a man of knowledge, a seer.*
fear, *a man;* tíġe, *of a house.*	fear-tíġe, *a householder*
fear, . ceoil, *of music.*	fear-ceoil, *a man-of-music, a musician.*

"Tá páirt foġur agam féin leat;
. Is mo go mór tú 'na Cnoc Ġréine—
Is airde ruar tú 'na na spéura."
" I have a close relationship myself with thee;
Thou art by far higher than Knock Greine—
Thou art higher than the skies above."
Hardiman's Minstrelsy, vol. i. p. 152.

Rule 3 and its exceptions the learner should endeavour to remember, for their application is common, not only to all compound words, but to adjectives and nouns coming together in concord, and to the aspiration of the final syllable te or ta in past participles.

4. All the simple prepositions, except aig, *at;* go, *to;* le, *with;* os, *over, above;* along with gan, *without;* and ain, *on* (sometimes), cause, if aspirable, the first consonant of a noun, not having the article (an, *the*) going before, to be aspirated; as,

brón, *grief* } tré brón agus tre gáb, *through grief and*
gáb, *danger* } *through danger.*

Tá aige an bann ó feanaib agus ó mnaib am feile—"He has the palm of superiority from men and from women for generosity." In those instances, b of brón, g of gáb, f of feanaib, m of mnaib, are aspirated by the prepositions tre, *through;* ó, *from.*

Or, *over;* as or cjonn, *over-head, above;* or comain, *at the presence, on before;* gan rjun gan bratain, *without sister or brother;* ain talam, *of earth;* ain báll, *on (the) spot;* ain meirge, *in (a state of) inebriety, drunk;* "Agus d' ol re ne 'n b-fjon agus do bi re ain meirge—And he drank of the wine, and he became inebriated."—*Gen.* ix. 21.

We see in the foregoing examples that c of cjonn, r of rjun, b of bratain, m of meirge, are not aspirated. Final r, n, or n of these prepositions blend with sufficient euphony with the sounds of consonants that follow, without the aid of aspiration.

The preposition ann for cum, *towards,* does not aspirate; as, na baoine a cuireab ann báir—"the people who were put to death;"

"Saon mé, noin me ful ann bealaig."
"Forgive me, before I go on the road (to eternity)."

Dies Iræ, 12th stanza, 3rd line.

This rule regards nouns governed by prepositions when the article is not expressed. Under the heading *eclipsis* shall be shown how nouns preceded by the article and preposition together, are affected.

5. Do, *to* (a preposition); do, *thine* (poss. pronoun); do, *to,* a particle preceding the infinitive mood; *do,* an emphatic particle going before the perfect tense active, causes aspiration, as,

do, (prep.); Seoirsa, *George.*   do Seoirsa, *to George.*
do, *thy;* gnáb, *love* (see Rule 1, p. 34).   do gnáb, *thy love.*
do, *to;* gnábugáb, *loving.*   do gnábugáb (inf.) *to love.*
    „   gnábuig, *love thou.*   do gnábuig re, (perf. tense), *he loved.*
    „   gnábuig, *love thou.*   do gnábocainn, *I would love.*

The infinitive mood, the perfect, and conditional tenses, are commonly aspirated, even when the particle do is not expressed.

Ro in ancient writings, and in many modern printed works, is found to precede the perfect and conditional tenses in instances in which modern writers and speakers employ do.

Ro is incorporated with many particles of interrogation, negation, supposition; as,

                                            For the Past Tense.

an, *whether.*   an, *whether,* compounded of an and ro.
ma, *if.*   man, *if,* „ „ ma „ ro.
nac, } *whether not.*   nar, } *whether not,* compounded of nac
nac, }   nacan, } and ro.
muna, *if not* (na, *if,* and na, *not*).   munan, *if not,* compounded of muna and ro.
ní, *not.*   níor, *not,* compounded of ní and ro.

Examples.

	Past Tense.
an maiṫ tu? *are you good?*	an ṁaiṫ tu? *were you good?*
má tiocfaiḋ re, *if he shall come.*	man táinic re, *if he have come.*
muna d-tiocfaiḋ re, *if he will not come.*	munan táinic re, *if he have not come.*
ní maiṫ an lá é, *it is not a good day.*	níor ṁaiṫ an lá é, *it was not a good day.*

Ro is not an augment, as a writer in a late periodical would fain make it. An augment in Greek causes a syllable to be prefixed to a verb commencing with a consonant; as, ἔτυπτον, τετυφα, from τυπτω, *tupto*. In German it prefixes the syllable *ge*; as, from *sehen*, "to see," is formed the past participle *gesehen*, "seen"; from *haben*, "to have," the participle *gehabt*. But neither in Greek nor in German is the prefixed syllable separated from the verb. It is not so in Gaelic; the particle ro is quite disjoined from the verb, except in three instances—raib, *was*; and rainic, *reached*; rug, *brought*; to which may be added dubairt, *said*. (See Irregular Verbs.)

The vowels e, o, before another vowel are elided, as is usual for euphony's sake; as, "d' aitin Dia do Ṡ]aoire—God commanded Moses;" d' innir re an rgeul—"he told the story;"

"do ṁair re d' a ṗún; agur d' eug re d' a ċríé."
"He lived for his love; for his country he died."

Moore's Melodies.

Before the article an, *the*, it is the vowel a of the article, and not that of the preposition, which suffers elision; as, glóir do 'n aṫair, agur do 'n ṁac agur do 'n Spionad Naoṁ—"Glory be the Father, and to the Son, and to the Holy Ghost."

6. After the past tense, buḋ, or ba, and contractedly b', *was*, of the assertive form of the verb beiṫ, *to be*, the first letter of the adjective, if a labial—that is, b, f, m, p—is aspirated: if not a labial, it is not; as,

buḋ ḃreaġ é, *he (or it) was fine, grand, elegant.*
buḋ ḟada an lá é, *it was a long day.*
buḋ ṁaiṫ é, *he was good.*
ba ṗriainneaċ leir é, *it was specially estimable with him.*

Not Labials.

ba rlán é, *he was safe (sound, well).*
ba dilir é, *he was dear.*
ba trom é, *it was heavy.*

An Example of both.

"buḋ ṁall 'r buḋ trom bí teaċt an tra."
Literally—Slow and heavy was the coming of the time.
"The last sad hour of freedom's dream;
And valor's task mov'd slowly by."
"*Moore's Melodies*"—Song, *After the Battle.*

7. The genitive singular of nouns masculine, the nomi-

native and accusative of nouns feminine, declined with the article, are aspirated; as,

Nom. Sing.—an bard, *m.*, *the bard.* Gen. Sing.—an baird, *of the bard.*
„ an cearc, *f.*, *the hen.* „ na circe, *of the hen.*
Acc. Sing.—an cearc, *the hen.*

Exception 1.—S, instead of being aspirated in these cases, is eclipsed by t—only, however, when it is immediately followed by any of the vowels, or of the liquids, l, n, r; for r, when followed immediately by any of the mutes, undergoes no change; as,

Nom. Sing.—an t-slat, *f. the rod.* Gen.—na slaite, *of the rod.*
„ an sagart, *the priest.* „ an t-sagairt, *of the priest.*

Thus, instead of being aspirated S, r is preceded by t, a dental letter:

Nominative.	Genitive.
an sgiobol, *the barn.*	an sgioboil, *of the barn.*
an sparan, *the purse.*	an sparain, *of the purse.*

In those instances, the initial r suffers no change, because it is followed by a letter which is not a vowel or a liquid.

Exception 2.—Nouns of which the first letter is d or t are not aspirated; as, nom. sing.—an talam, *f., the earth;* an dair, *the oak;* ta an talam tirim, *the land is dry;* ta an dair sean, *the oak is old.* Gen. sing.—an Tigearna, *of the Lord;* an domain, *of the world;* as, la an Tigearna, *the Lord's Day;* do mnaib deasa an domain', *of all the fair women of th world.*

The reason of this latter exception is the concurrence of the final n of the article and the initials d or t of the noun, both linguals, is quite harmonious without the aid of aspiration.

8. All nouns, both of the mas. and fem. gender, of which the initial letter is a vowel, always take, when declined with the article, the aspirate h after na, to prevent the hiatus which would be occasioned by the concurrence of two distinct vowel sounds, as na h-inghine (gen. sing.), *of the daughter;* na h-aithreaca, *the fathers.*

Exception.—The gen. case plural, which takes n, and not "h." Ex.—na n-aithreach, *of the fathers.*

9. The numeral adjectives, aon, *one,* do, *two;* and their compounds, aon-deug, *eleven;* do-deug, *twelve,* cause aspiration. (See Numeral Adjectives.)

10. The relative pronouns, a, noc, in the *nominative* case, cause aspiration. (See Pronouns, in Etymology and Syntax.)

11. Adjectives are affected like nouns, and suffer aspiration from the same causes. Their exceptions are like those which occur among nouns—exceptions for the sake of euphony.

All the foregoing changes arise from a principle of euphony. To it may also be ascribed another peculiar trait of Irish consonants—Eclipsis.

§ 25.—*Eclipsis* is the suppression of the sound of the initial mute consonant for that of another cognate letter, which in the written language is prefixed to that consonant or which the sound is silenced.

"This element, though in its present form peculiar to Gaelic alone, is not foreign to other languages. The learned who write of the Sanscrit tongue say that Gaelic, in the phonetic laws that regulate its consonantal changes, is analogous to those of *Shandi*, or conjunction, by which consonants at the end, and sometimes at the beginning of words in that language, have their sounds suppressed for those of cognate letters. In Greek, Latin, German, this change of consonants is chiefly confined to words united by composition, and is seldom observed in words that remain distinct, or form the constituent parts of sentences."—*Easy Lessons in Irish*, p. 98.

TABLE OF THE COGNATE CONSONANTS.

₊ The Cognate are in the perpendicular columns.

	Labial.	Dental.	Palatal.
Sibilants ...		ſ	...
Aspirants ...	ꝼ, ḟ (h)	ṙ (*h*)	...
Liquids { *oral*	...	l	n
{ *nasal*	m ṁ	n	ṅṅ
			Guttural.
Mutes ⎧ *soft*	b	d	ᵹ
⎨ *hard*	p	t	c
⎨ *soft*	b (*i.e.*, v or w)	ḋ (*y*)	ġ (*gh* Eng., or *y*)
⎩ *hard*	ṗ (*ph* or *f*)	ṫ (*h*)	ċ (χ, *chi*, Gr., or ċ in oċ.)

§ 26.—TABLE OF ECLIPSES.

	Eclipsed by.	Example.	Pronounced as if written.
Labials.			
b	m	buɼ m-bᴀɼd, *your bard*	buɼ mᴀɼd
ꝼ	b	buɼ b-ꝼɩle, *your poet*	buɼ bɩle
p	b	buɼ b-pobᴀl, *your people*	buɼ bobᴀl
Gutturals.			
c	ᵹ	buɼ ᵹ-cᴀpᴀl, *your horse*	buɼ ᵹᴀpᴀl
ᵹ	n	buɼ nᵹᴀɼɼe, *your laugh*	
Dentals.			
d	n	buɼ n-duɩne, *your person*	buɼ nuɩne
t	d	buɼ d-tɩɼ, *your country*	buɼ dɩɼ
ſ	t	ᴀn t-ſlᴀt, *the rod*	ᴀn tlᴀt

ᴢ, preceded by n, is not eclipsed or silenced; but η and ᴢ together form one simple sound. It is for this reason there is no hyphen mark placed between them (see p. 21). O'Molloy says of the ηᴢ: "Hoc habet speciale, quod *g* non penitus taceatur sed aliqualiter uno tractu simul cum *n* efferatur, ut ᴀη ηᴢοηc latine *nostra seges*."—*Grammatica*, p. 63.

From this table it is seen that no consonant is eclipsed by any other than by a cognate; and again, that all the hard mutes, p, c, τ, and f, are eclipsed by those sounded soft; and the soft consonants themselves, b, ᴢ, ᴅ, are eclipsed by the liquid letters. For instance, b, a soft mute, is silenced by m, a liquid, and thus in the expression, bun m-bᴀηᴅ (*nu: márd*), the flow of the consonants, m after n runs freely and softly. This phonetic law directs the eclipsing influence of the other consonants after a similar articulate process.

In eclipsis it is the first letter that is sounded, the second only shows the radical structure of the word.

There is a form of eclipsis adopted not uncommonly, of doubling the consonants c, f, p, τ; thus—

cc like ᴢ, as ᴀη ccᴀpᴀl, *our horse;* pronounced ᴀη ᴢᴀpᴀl.
ff „ b, „ bun ffjlc, *your poet;* „ bun bjlc.
pp „ b, „ ᴀ ppobᴀl, *their people.* „ ᴀ bobᴀl.
ττ „ ᴅ, „ ᴀ ττjη, *their country;* „ ᴀ ᴅjη.

This form of eclipsis is not much in use amongst modern writers—and so much the better.

"But this (manner of eclipsing) is not to be recommended, as the prefixed consonant could not be then said to eclipse the one which follows it, but both combined to assume the sound of a consonant different from either—a system which would neither be philosophically correct nor convenient."—*Dr. O'Donovan's Irish Grammar*, p. 64.

§ 27.—RULES FOR ECLIPSING.

1. All the plural possessive pronouns, ᴀη, *our;* bun, *your;* ᴀ, *their;* as, ᴀη m-bᴀᴅ, *our boat;* bun m-boηᴅ, *your table;* ᴀ m-bo, *their cow.*

2. The prepositions ᴀ, *in;* jᴀη, *after;* ηjᴀ, *before.*

3. The genitive *plural* of nouns declined with the article (ᴀη, *the*), as bᴀηη "*ηᴀ*" ᴅ-τοηη, *the surface "of the" waves;* rljᴀb "*ηᴀ*" m-bᴀη, *the women's mountain;* ᴀ rcᴀηc "*ηᴀ*" ᴢ-cuηᴀη, *O thou love "of the" affections.*

4. The dative singular, articulated form. (ᴀη)—a "ᴀη ᴀη' m-bᴀηη, *on the top;* "ᴀjᴢ ᴀη" m-buη, *at the foundation;* "ο'η" ᴢ-cηoηᴅc, *from "the" heart;* "fᴀο' η" ᴢ-coηr, *under the foot*—is eclipsed.

Except, first, words beginning with ᴅ, τ. For, since the eclipsing cognate of ᴅ is η, the final η of the article (ᴀη, *the*) is quite sufficient; as, ᴀη ᴀη ᴅοηᴀη, *on the world.* τ, being much like ᴅ in sound, is for the same reason not eclipsed by ŋ; as, "ɠo ná|b uɪɾɟéè ná oɪleán áɪɾɪ áŋ tá-lám—*That the waters of the flood were on the earth.*"—*Gen.* vii. 10.

Except, secondly, nouns which are governed by the prepositions ꝺe, *of;* ꝺo, *to;* ɠán, *without;* eɪꝺɪɾ, *between.* The prepositions ꝺe, ꝺo, ordinarily cause aspiration and not eclipsis—see Syntax, rule 70, and Dr. O'Donovan's "Irish Grammar," pp. 393-4-5-6.

This exception is particularly true when the initial consonant of the noun is one of the labial class, ꝼ, b, p.

Any of the other simple prepositions may, if euphony or clearness require it. cause aspiration instead of eclipsis; as, o' ŋ b-ꝼuɪl, *from the blood;* in this sentence, b-ꝼuɪl, *blood*, has the same appearance to the eye as b-ꝼuɪl, *is*, are, and it would appear therefore more correct not to eclipse ꝼ in such a case; as, o' ŋ ꝼuɪl, and not o' ŋ b-ꝼuɪl.

Initial *S.*—ꞅ is usually eclipsed by t after the preposition when the article is expressed; as o' ŋ t-ꞅáɠáɪꞅ, *from the priest;* o' ŋ t-ꞅléɪb, *from the mountain;* áꞃ áŋ t-ꞅꞃáɪꝺ, *on the street.*

5. Whenever a question is asked, whether the interrogatory begin with ᴀ (for áŋ), áŋ, *whether;* cá, *where;* ŋáċ, *whether not;* as, á b-táɪŋɪc ꞅé, *has he come?* ŋáċ ŋɠꞃá-ꞅuɪɠeáŋŋ me, *do I not love?* cá b-ꝼuɪl tu Áꝺáɪm, *where art thou Adam?* after ɠo, *that;* as, ɠo m-beáŋŋuɪɠe Ɖɪá ꝺuɪt, *God save you;* after ꝺá, *if, suppose that;* as, ꝺá m-buáɪlꝼɪŋŋ é, *if I should beat him;* muŋá, *if not;* as, muŋá m-buáɪlꝼɪŋŋ e, *if I should not have beaten him.*

6. The relative pronoun (á), governed by a preposition expressed or understood, commonly causes the initial mutable of the succeeding verb to suffer *eclipsis;* as, ꝺ'euɠ Joꞅá leɪꞅ "á" m-bꞃoŋtáꞃ beátá oꞃáɪŋŋ—"*Jesus died, by whom life is bestowed on us.*"

Should the preposition be left understood, eclipsis, notwithstanding, ensues; and hence á for áŋŋ á *in which (place or time), i.e., where* or *hen*, causes eclipsis.

Except, however, those instances in which the particles ꝺo, ꞃo, signs of the perfect tense, come between the relative á and the verb—then ꞃo or ꝺo, assumes a dominant influence, and therefore causes aspiration and not eclipsis as, áŋ tó áɪꞃ (for áɪꞃ á ꞃo) tuɪt áŋ cꞃáŋ—"he on whom the lot fe (See Dr. O'Donovan's "Irish Grammar," p. 397.

For the several meanings and powers of á, see "Easy Lessons," part ii., p. 115.

7. The numerals ꞅeáċt, *seven;* oċt, *eight;* ŋáoɪ *nire;* ꝺeɪċ, *ten,* eclipse consonants liable to such suppression.

8. Initial vowels have ŋ prefixed in every case in which initial consonants are eclipsed; as, áꞃ ŋ-átáɪꞃ, *our father;* áꞅꞃ áŋ áꝺbáꞃ ꞅɪŋ, *for that reason.*

From the last example it is seen that ɲ of the article preceding a noun of this class answers all the requirements of euphony without the insertion of a second ɲ.

OBS.—Between the possessive pronoun a, *her*, and the initial vowel of the noun following it, an aspirate h is employed; as, a h-aċaɪɲ, *her father;* a h-aɪɲm, *her name;* a h-oɲouġaḋ, *her order.*

N is inserted between the prepositions terminating in a vowel (ꝼaoɪ, *under;* le, ɲe, *with;* ó, *from;* ꞇꞅe, *through*) and the possessive pronouns a, *his;* a, *her;* a, *their;* as,

    ó ɲ-a ġnaḋ, *from his love.*
    ó ɲ-a ꞅnaḋ, *from her love.*
    ó ɲ-a nġnaḋ, *from their love.*

§ 28. Some writers have remarked that it is better to omit the eclipsed consonant, as in Welsh; but this would, in Irish, lead to endless confusion, as the radical letter of the word would, in almost every instance, be disguised; and though this is unavoidably the case in the spoken language, yet it has been thought advisable to preserve in the written language the radical consonant in every instance, even at the risk of giving the words a crowded and awkward appearance. "On this subject," says Dr. O'Donovan (Grammar, p. 59), O'Molloy remarks: "'Adverte ex dictis nunquam sequi, quod in scriptione liceat literam mergendam omitti esto omittatur in sono; alias foret magna confusio, et ignoraretur dictio, seu sensus voculae ejusque tum proprietas, tum natura.'"—*Grammatica,* p. 66.

By means of eclipsis and aspiration in Irish, the varying sounds of the mutable consonants are clearly noted, while, at the same time, the radical, unvarying spelling of each word is preserved. From the non use of this system of notation for the variable consonants, the Welsh have in changing the consonant with every successive mutation of sound, sadly destroyed the orthography of their language, and rendered etymology a puzzle.

The difference in the manner of notation is best seen from the following example:

Irish.	Welsh.	English.
Caɲ ꝼoġuꞅ	Câr agos	A near kinsman or friend
A ċaɪɲ	Ei gâr	His friend
A caɪɲ	Ei châr	Her friend
Mo ċaɪɲ	Vy nghâr	My friend
Aɲ ġ-caɪɲ	..	Our friend

"The radical initial is four times changed in Welsh; in Irish it is preserved unchanged; its various permutations in sound being noted by means of aspiration and eclipsis."—*Note in "Easy Lessons."* p. 116.

§ 29.—The combination ġn differs from nġ. The latter is sounded like *no* in *wrangling;* the former is articulated by the aid of a short vowel-sound inserted between ġ and ɲ; thus ġnaċ is pronounced *günaw*—so cɲoc *künock;* ɲɲa, *müna.* (See p. 21, under letter N.)

It is in this manner the combinations cɲ, lḃ, lġ, lɲ, ɲb, ɲḃ, ɲġ, ɲɲ, are pronounced—viz., by the aid of a short vowel between the consonants:

	Pronounced.
cn—cnoc, *a hill,*	*kŭnock.*
lb—balb, *dumb,*	*balŭv.*
lʒ—realʒ, *a hunting,*	*sealŭy.*
lm—colm, *a pigeon,*	*colŭm.*
rb—borb, *fierce, violent,*	*borŭh.*
rb—rearb, *bitter piercing,*	*searŭv.*
nb—leanb, *a child,*	*leanŭv.*
nʒ—reanʒ, *anger,*	*fearŭy.*
nn—cann, *a heap,*	*carŭn.*

There is no difficulty attending the pronunciation of these combinations in Irish. The liquid letters, l, n, r, unite with other consonants in every language; as, in English, *warm (warŭm), alarm (alarŭm), film (filŭm).*

CHAPTER III.

ON SPELLING AND WRITING IN IRISH.

§ 30. *Spelling.*—Irish, like every other independent language, has, or ought to have, a fixed orthography. Some words are, however, written differently by different writers. This is really not so much to be wondered at, for Irish has been for centuries a persecuted language, and the nation could not furnish an improved standard of orthography which all alike should be bound to follow. Even French, a language that has been so highly cultivated—the language of court, the language of fashion—has, for the last half-century, undergone material improvements. English too, after ages of cultivation, from the days of Chaucer to the days of Macauley, is not yet incapable of being made more perfect. What wonder then that a language like ours, banned for centuries and trodden under foot, should require to have its orthography improved, or rather regulated.

"Every language," says Dr. Johnson, "has its improprieties and absurdities, which it is the duty of the lexicographer to correct or proscribe."

§ 31.—A FEW PRACTICAL HINTS ON THE SPELLING OF THE IRISH LANGUAGE.

It will be admitted that the same word in the same circumstances—that is, that a word in one place, under the same governing influence that regulates it in another, ought to be spelled in both always the same way. This axiom, simple as it is, has, for all that, not been conformed to by Irish writers.

The spelling of Gaelic or Irish is easy if the learner attend to the following points which can by any one be readily perceived and easily remembered.

The first is the principle of vowel assimilation so peculiar to Irish, and expressed practically in the rule, caol le caol—which has been already explained in section 3, and 4, pp. 17, 18, 19.

The second is, proper attention to the prefixes and suffixes which are to be annexed to the roots.

The third is, to aspirate the parts according to the principle explained in section 24, rule 3 and its exceptions, pp. 34-5.

Prefixes and suffixes, or affixes, are common to every language. Prefixes are particles going before, yet annexed to the root; suffixes, those that come after it. Affix is a term used for prefix or suffix.

Every word is simple or compound; simple when it has no root to which it can be traced but is itself an unmixed, underived term. It is called a root or stem if other words spring from it. A compound word is made up of two or more simples, or of a simple and a broken form of a simple term; the former may be called a pure compound; as, bó-ṗuıl. *cow-eye;* beaṅ-tiġearna (*woman-lord*), *lady;* tıṗ-ġráḋ, *country-love, patriotism;* ánd-ṗagánt, *a high-priest;* the latter, derivative; as, ragaṗtaċt, *priesthood;* ġráḋ-aṁail, *lovable;* ġráḋṁaṗ, *loving;* ġráḋṁaṗaċt, *lovingness.* Derivative implies, flowing from—and hence is only a relative term, implying that there is another from which it proceeds, and to which is given the name primitive. Thus, the word ġráḋṁaṗ is primitive when compared with ġráḋṁaṗaċt, which is formed from it, while it is itself a derivative from the word ġráḋ. All words then may be classed into simple and compound; or, in their relation of derivation, into primitive, derivative, and purely compound.

1. Every simple primitive word, either of one or two syllables, has, as must be admitted, a fixed spelling which, generally speaking, no individual caprice can or ought to change; as, cṗut, *form* or *shape;* ḟeaṗ, *a man;* duıṗe, *a person.*

2. Derivatives are either of two, three, or more syllables. Now the first part of the derivative must certainly be spelled like the root from which it has sprung; and the second part, according to that termination indicated by the part of speech under which the new word may be classed. Ex.— from cṗut is formed the verb cṗutuıġ, *create (thou);* cṗutuıġım, *I create;* by annexing to the root the verbal termination uıġ for the imperative; uıġım for the indic. present, first person, an affix which the learner, after knowing how to conjugate the verbs, will be able to spell. The whole word is in this ready way spelled correctly. In like manner, if from this verb a derivative noun or adjective be formed, the noun or adjective will retain the radical form of its parent stock; as, from cṗutuıġ is formed cṗutuıġṫeoıṗ, *creator,* and cṗutuıġṫeaċ, *creative;* by adding to the root tóıṗ or óıṗ (Latin, *or,* as creator) for the noun; and ṫeaċ for the adjective. Again, we have cṗutuıġaḋ, *a proof,* or *creation;* ro-ċṗutuıġṫe, *easily proved;* do-ċṗutuıġṫe, *hard to be proved*—retaining all through the spelling of cṗut, the parent root—annexing the affixes, but at the same time directing their connexion by the rule caol le caol, in order to carry out the principle of vowel-likeness in each consecutive syllable.

"In writing rlánuıȝée, and such other words as present many indistinct vowels, a fixed orthography should be preserved, and the form of the word to be adopted should be decided upon by observing the root and proper grammatical inflections or branches springing from it; thus, from the root rlán, *safe*, is formed rlánuȝáo, *salvation*; and the u in this form should be retained in the passive participle rlánuıȝée, and in all other derivatives springing from it; as, rlánuıȝéeoıp, *a saviour*; rlánuıȝéeaċ, *sanative.*"— *Dr. O'Donovan's Irish Grammar*, p. 6.

3. A compound term is composed of two simple words, or of a primitive and a derivative word. Hence, if we know how to spell its component parts, we must necessarily know how to spell the word itself. Ex.—ὁeaȝ, *good*, and cpuċ, *form*, make when joined together the compound word ὁeaȝ-cpuċ, *a graceful form*. All the derivatives of cpuċ, compounded with ὁeaȝ, can be spelled in the same manner, as, ὁeaȝ-cpuċuıȝ, ὁeaȝ-cpuıȝċuıċeaċ, ὁeaȝ-cpuċuıȝċeoıp. In like manner, ὁıap-ȝpáò, ὁıap-ȝpáòuıȝ, ὁıap-ȝpáòuıȝ-ċeoıp. These prefixes should be spelled always the same way, and not, either for the sake of rule or sound, be spelled differently when put before different words; as, ὁeaȝ-ὁuıpe, *a good person*; ὁeaȝ-ḟeap, *a good man*; the a in ὁeaȝ should be preserved, even when prefixed to a word whose first vowel is slender. Ex.—ὁeaȝ-ḟeap, and not ὁeıȝ-ḟeap, as some authors write it. They write in the same manner the words po|-ὁéaıṫċa, ıp-ὁéaıṫċa, instead of po-ὁéaıṫċa and joṅ-ὁéaıṫċa. This kind of false spelling is calculated to lead the learner astray, or give him a distaste for the language altogether. Besides, as the prefixes aṅ, *very*; ápò, *high*; aċ, *back, re*; ὁeaȝ, *good, upright*; ὁıaṅ, *vehement*; ὁo, *difficult*; ὁpoċ, *bad*; ὁuṫ, *black*; joṅ, *fit*; leaṫ, *half, one of two*; ṅeaıṅ, *not*; pó, *easy*; cpom, *heavy*—and the rest, have a fixed meaning, they should likewise have a fixed spelling. If not the learner may reasonably suppose that a difference in spelling indicates a difference of meaning, whilst in reality there is none. (See "Self-Instruction," parts iii., iv, lessons 37, 38, 39, 40, 41.)

Ceuò-láoȝ bó, ceuò-uaṅ caopaċ, ceuò-ṁıoṅáṅ ȝabaıp—"the first calf of a cow, the first lamb of a sheep, the first kid of a goat." (*Numbers*, xviii. 17.) Ceuò, before ṁıoṅaṅ, is correctly written by Dr. Macliale ceuò, not céıò.

§ 32.—*That it is easy to learn the Spelling of Irish or Gaelic.*

By a little attention to what has just been explained any person, after knowing the declension of nouns and adjectives and the conjugations of verbs, could readily spell any word in the language. A little practice in reading Irish or Gaelic would teach him the correct spelling of most of the roots. For a collection of simple Gaelic terms see "Self-Instruction," part i.

All derivative words have certain endings according to the different parts of speech to which they belong, or the different ideas they express. These endings, than the spelling of which nothing can be simpler, affixed to the root give the derivative word or words spelled correctly. For instance, personal nouns end in ⱥɩɩɼe, ⱥɩò or uɩò, derived from other nouns; óɩɼ (derived from the verbs), ⱥċ; as,

Root.	Derivative.
ceⱥlʒ, *deceit, a trick.*	ceⱥlʒⱥɩɼe, *a trickster.*
ɼeⱥlʒ, *to hunt.*	ɼeⱥlʒⱥɩɼe, *a hunter.*
ceⱥɲɲuɩʒ, *buy, purchase.*	ceⱥɲɲuɩòe, *a merchant.*
ɼlⱥɲ, *safe,* ɼlⱥɲuɩʒ, *save, v.*	ɼlⱥɲuɩʒceoɩɼ, *saviour.*
mol, *praise.*	molcóɩɼ, *a praiser.*
bⱥc, *lame.*	bⱥċⱥċ, *a lame person.*

Abstract nouns, derived commonly from adjectives or other nouns, end in ⱥɼ, or cⱥɼ, ⱥċc; as,

ceⱥlʒ, *deceit.*	ceⱥlʒⱥɼ, *deception.*
mⱥɩċ, *good.*	mⱥɩċcⱥɼ, *goodness.*
olc, *bad.*	olcⱥɼ, *badness.*
ɼeⱥlʒⱥɩɼe,, *a hunter*	ɼeⱥlʒⱥɩɼeⱥċc, *hunting.*

Other abstract nouns derived from adjectives end in e, and are in form like the genitive singular, feminine:

ɼɩoɲɲ, *fair, white.*	ɼɩɲɲe, *fairness*
ⱥɼò, *high.*	ⱥɩɼòe, *height.*

Derivatives in ɩɲ or ⱥɲ.

ⱥɼò, *high.*	ⱥɼòⱥɲ, *a hillock.*
leⱥbⱥɼ, *a book.*	leⱥbⱥɼɩɲ, *a little book.*

Derivative adjectives end in ⱥṁⱥɩl, mⱥɼ, ⱥċ, ɩò, òⱥ, or òⱥ and cⱥ; as,

cuɼⱥɩɲ, *care, attention.*	cuɼⱥmⱥṁⱥɩl, *careful.*
cɩʒeⱥɼɲⱥ, *lord.*	cɩʒeⱥɼɲⱥṁⱥɩl, *lordly.*

flaṫ, *a prince.*   flaiṫamail, *princely.*
feile, *a feast day;* feilte, feilteamail, *happening at*
  (plural).   *each recurring festival.*

Tagann ro go feilteamail, *he comes surely—i.e., as sure y as each recurring festival.*

feoil, *flesh.*   feoilṁar, *fleshy.*
firinne, *truth.*   firinneaċ, *truthful.*
fireun, *one of the faithful.* fireunta, *righteous.*

Verbs terminate in iġim, uiġim, im, or aim, for the first person, singular. On learning the conjugations, the endings of the other tenses and persons of the verbs will become plain and easy.

Read what Webster says of the speech of the Anglo-Saxon: "Such is the state of our written (English) language that our citizens never become masters of orthography without great difficulty and labor; and a great part of them never learn to spell words with correctness."—*Webster.*

§ 33.—*An Example, showing at one view the number of words that can be formed from a single root of one syllable.*

Nouns—*from* grád, *love.*—An-grád, ceud-grád, caoṁ-grád, oil-grád, dian-grád, fíor-grád, maoṫ-grád, mear-grád, mí-grád, mór-grád, sean-grád, searc-grád, síor-grád, tear-grád, tír-grád. Grádaigṫeoir (from grádaig, *love thou*)—Caoṁ-grádaigṫeoir, dian-grádaigṫeoir, ... fíor-grádaigṫeoir, tír-grádaigṫeoir.

Adjectives—*from* grádaċ, *loving.*—An-grádaċ, caoṁ-grádaċ, oil-grádaċ, dian-grádaċ, fíor-grádaċ, ... tír-grádaċ. Grádṁar—an-grádṁar, .. as before. Grád-ṁaraċt, *fondness, lovingness.* Grádaigṫe, *beloved*—An-grádaigṫe, in-grádaigṫe, do-grádaigṫe, so-grádaigṫe. . Grádaṁail, *lovable.*—An-grádaṁail. . . .

Verbs.—Grádaigim, with all its tenses and persons, and the tenses and persons of its compound forms; grádugad, *loving.*

§ 34. *Of Writing.*—To write Greek in the characters of any foreign language is to destroy half its worth. It becomes bound in literal bands that take away all its natural grace and native grandeur. True, Greece has never really suffered the disgrace of having her national language thus paraded in alien costume. Ireland has. Her written language has been tortured into a thousand ignoble shapes, which have made it appear to the eyes of some the penciled jargon of slaves. It is to be hoped there will be no more of this. It has been too long practised. More full of aspirates than the Greek, the Irish language has been unmercifully mangled in endeavouring to make it look neat in its foreign, anti-national dress. English letters and English accent, however grand they may appear to some, are, to say the least, quite *un-Keltic,* and therefore most unfit to display the natural grace and energy of the Irish language. Hence no *Irishman* ought to write his native tongue in any other than in Irish or Keltic characters.

How then, it will be asked, are these characters written? The manner in which Irish chirography is now practised shall be pointed out. If the language revive, this form of writing will, it is probable, become more improved Even as it is at present written a person could with a little practice learn to write it as quickly as he would the Roman style of penmanship. The Irish characters do not differ much in shape from the German; and the Germans have, in one century, made their language the admiration of Europe.

In some of the written and printed books a few inaccuracies occur which it would be well to avoid.

When a preposition, such as ꞇ ꞅ n n, goes before a noun in Irish, it is not right to join, as some writers do, the preposition and the noun, so as to form of both but one written word. Ex.—ꞇ ꞅ n n ꝺ ꝋ ꞃ ꞓ ꞇ ꞇ ꞅ ꞃ, *in darkness* ("Imitation," [Irish], chap. i., book 1); the preposition ꞇ ꞅ n n going before ꝺ ꝋ ꞃ ꞓ ꞇ ꞇ ꞅ ꞃ is incorporated with it; and the young learner looks in vain into an Irish dictionary to find the word.

Again, when the aspirate h precedes a word beginning with a vowel, it should not be joined to the initial of that word; nor should o of the possessive pronouns mo, ꞇ o, when going before a word beginning with a vowel, be dropped, and the bereft consonant m or ꞇ united with the first letter of that word, without as much as an apostrophe (') to mark the omission of the o—nay, more, ꞇ is often, by some careless writers, changed into ꞇ, a letter of the same organ; as, ꝺ o ꜰ n ꜱ m, *thy soul,* dropping o becomes ꝺ'ꜰ n ꜱ m, and by changing ꞇ into ꞇ and omitting the apostrophe, ꞇ ꜰ n ꜱ m. Now, a person who beforehand had not been well acquainted with the language could never make out what the term ꞇ ꜰ n ꜱ m means. And to what is all this owing? To a want of proper attention in writing the language. Hence, then, whenever a word is elided, eclipsed, or aspirated, the change should be noted by its proper sign, and not thus be putting unnecessary difficulties in the way of those who wish to advance in the paths of Keltic literature.

§ 35.—EXERCISES.

One of the best methods a person can adopt to acquire a perfect knowledge of the idioms, as well as of the grammatical construction of any language is to take up some prose author—say, the most approved, in that language which he wishes to learn; to translate therefrom a few sentences into the vernacular, or into that tongue with which the learner may be best acquainted; then, after a day or two, to take up his pen and retranslate the translation as well as he can into the original; next, to compare what he has thus retranslated with the text of the author. The learner can, as he becomes better acquainted with the language which he is thus learning, enlarge this exercise according to his taste and leisure. By this method a person is enabled to see how far he is deficient in ability to write with correctness and propriety in the language he is endeavouring to acquire. He will thus perceive at once, even without a master's aid, the appropriate words he should have used, the peculiar turn he should have given the sentence—the pithy, idiomatic manner in which a native writer would have expressed the same idea.

.n this Grammar there are consequently no exercises given.

The need of such aids is at present less felt than when the first edition of the College Grammar had been published, as a new work, containing exercises to be translated from Irish to English and from English to Irish, with proper explanations of the grammatical changes and idiomatic forms in each lesson, has been given to the public who still cherish a taste for the Gaelic tongue.

Those who wish to learn the language by the exercise of *translating*, would do well to translate a few ds daily from any correctly written Irish book,* and to retranslate the same at their leisure; when more fully acquainted with its grammar to translate sentences, and to retranslate them again into the original. By this means they will find that in a very short time they shall have acquired a wonderful knowledge of the language as it is spoken and written. In fact, the idioms of a dialect cannot be learned so well by any other means. That other method—not unfrequently adopted by young ladies at boarding-schools, and by mere jabberers in French and in Italian—of committing idioms to memory, is at once tedious and slavish.

PART II.—ETYMOLOGY.

§ 36. Etymology, as a division of grammar, shows the correct relation of words in the same language with one another.

The inflections or changes which words undergo in their endings point out this relation.

Etymology, in a wider sense, shows how words spring from their stem or root; and general etymology shows how words in different languages spring from a common stock.

Words are classed under nine heads, called parts of speech—namely, the Article, Noun, Adjective, Pronoun, Verb, Adverb, Preposition, Cunjunction, and Interjection.

---

* There are many works in Irish which the reader could study with profit, *v. g.*, the volumes i., ii., iii., iv., v., of the *Ossianic Society Transactions* (Dublin, John O'Daly, Anglesea-street, publisher). The Irish in these volumes is very correct, and much in the style of the spoken language. The works published by His Grace the Archbishop of Tuam—the "Pentateuch," or five books of Moses, the Catechism, the Iliad, the Melodies. Keating's "History of Ireland" is an admirable text-book. The author was the Livy of Ireland. Rev. A. Donlevy's Catechism is really very good for its splendid English version and Irish text on corresponding pages.

Dr. Gallagher's *Seventeen Irish Sermons* are admirable. Their style is so natural, so easy, so purely idiomatic, that no person having a knowledge of the language can read them without being affected. (Dublin, O'Daly.)

CHAPTER I.
THE ARTICLE.

§ 37. The article, so called because it adheres to the noun, always precedes it, and often points out its gender and number.

There is only one article in Irish, the definite, and it is thus declined:

	Singular.		Plural.
	Masc.	Fem.	Masc. and Fem.
Nom. and Acc.,	ᴀɲ, *the.*	ᴀɲ, *the.*	ɲᴀ, *the.*
Gen.	ᴀɲ, *of the.*	ɲᴀ, *of the.*	ɲᴀ, *the.*
Dat.	(ᴏo) 'ɲ, *to the.*	(ᴏo) 'ɲ, *to the.*	ᴏo ɲᴀ, *to the.*

Thus we see the article in the singular number is the same in all cases, except the genitive feminine; and that in the plural it is the same (ɲᴀ) in both genders.

The ᴀ, or vowel of the article in the singular number is sometimes elided when preceded by a preposition ending with a vowel; as, ó ᴀɲ is written ó'ɲ. This omission should always be noted by an apostrophe (').

In the spoken language ɲ of the article ᴀɲ, *the,* is not always heard whenever the speaker articulates quickly. Some writers omit, on this account, ɲ of the article in writing. But this habit is faulty, and would finally lead to the corruption of the language.

Those initial changes which the noun declined with the article undergoes have already been noticed under the heads, "Eclipsis" and "Aspiration."

Yet it may be well here, for the learner's advantage, to give a very brief summary of those changes which the article causes in the initial or first letter of all kinds of nouns, as well when governed as when not governed by a simple preposition.

§ 38. Firstly: when not governed by a simple preposition, then the first letter of the noun is either a *consonant* or a *vowel*. If a *consonant*, it is one of the three immutables, l, ɲ, ʀ; or one of the remaining nine consonants, called *mutables*. If one of the three—l, ɲ, ʀ—no change takes place by prefixing the article; if any other consonant than l, ɲ, ʀ, then a change takes place—yet in different cases, according to the gender and number of the noun. The noun, if masculine, becomes, on the article being prefixed, affected in the *genitive* case, singular, by the aspirate; as, ᴀɲ ꜰɪʀ, *m.* (gen. singular), *of the man;* ᴀɲᴀɲ ᴀɲ ꜰɪʀ, *the soul of the man;* if feminine, in the nominative and accusative singular—ᴀɲ ʙᴇᴀɲ, *the woman.*

Exception—1. In the singular number nouns beginning with ʙ or ᴄ.

2. Nouns whose initial letter is ꜱ take, in these very same cases in which *aspiration* would be produced, *eclipsis* in its stead by prefixing ᴛ; as, ᴀɲ ᴛ-ꜱʀᴀɪʙ (f. nom.), *the street;* ʙʀɪꜱ ꜱé ᴀɲ ᴛ-ꜱʟᴀᴛ (f. acc.), *he broke the rod,* ʟᴇᴀʙᴀʀ ᴀɲ ᴛ-ꜱᴀɢᴀɪʀᴛ (gen.), *the priest's book.*

Secondly: when governed by a simple preposition—then the noun, no matter of what gender, commonly undergoes eclipsis (see exceptions, after the prepositions ꞅe, *of;* ꝺo, *to*), if its initial consonant be of the eclipsible class. S in this instance ordinarily follows the common rule; as, leiꞅ ᴀn b-ꝼeᴀꞅt, *with the man;* o'n t-ꞅꞅᴀiꝺ, *from the street;* leiꞅ ᴀn t-ꞅlᴀic, *with the rod.* " In manuscripts of considerable antiquity, ꞅ is eclipsed by t after all the simple prepositions when the article is expressed." (Dr. O'Donovan's " Irish Grammar," pp. 396-7.) But ꝺ and t do not not conform to this rule; as, ᴀnnꞅ ᴀn ꝺomᴀn, *in the world;* for reasons see pp. 40-1. " And when the noun begins with ꝺ or t, it never suffers any change, in these counties (Kilkenny, Tipperary), in the articulated dative." (*Ibid.*, p. 396.)

Thirdly : if the noun begin with a vowel and the article be prefixed—the noun if masculine takes, in the nominative and accusative, singular, t before it; as, ᴀn t-ᴀéᴀꞅ. If feminine, it takes the aspirate h in the genitive; as, bᴀoiꞅ nᴀ h-óiʒe, *the folly of youth.*

NOTE.—The euphonic t, before masculine nouns beginning with a vowel, should not be joined to it. To do so is erroneous in principle and fact, and calculated to puzzle young students. Ex.—ᴀn tᴀꞅᴀl (for ᴀn t-ᴀꞅᴀl), *the ass* (*Isaias,* i. 3, Protestant version); ᴀn tᴀꞅᴀn, *the bread.* For ᴀn t-ᴀꞅᴀn see Etymology, p. 48.

In the plural the genitive case only of all eclipsible nouns is eclipsed. And those nouns of which the initial letter is a vowel take n; in the other cases take h after nᴀ.

O'Donovan says (" Irish Grammar," p. 65), " that in every situation where an initial consonant is eclipsed, an initial vowel takes n; as, ᴀn n-ᴀꞅᴀn, *our bread.*" Yet—as the same author himself observes in p. 115 of the same Grammar—" when the noun begins with a vowel, and is preceded by a preposition with the article, the n is not prefixed to the noun, because n of the article is enough to answer the sound; as, leiꞅ ᴀn ᴀꞅᴀn, *with the bread.*

There is no indefinite article in Gaelic. The absence of the definite answers its purpose quite as well.

Obs.—If the article be not expressed these initial changes here pointed out will not arise. (See Syntax, rules, 1, 2, 3, 4, 5, 6, &c.)

The initial changes following the article are the effects of euphony, and, contrary to the teaching of the Rev. Paul O'Brien, have nothing to do with inflection, which regards the changes that arise in the endings of nouns and verbs.

CHAPTER II.

NOUNS.

§ 39. Noun, from the Latin word *nomen*, is the name of anything that exists, or may be conceived to exist. Nouns are distinguished by the grammatical qualities of gender, number, person, case.

§ 40. Gender is a real or conventional quality by which nouns, like living beings, are classified into two great orders—masculine and feminine; and in certain languages into three—masculine, feminine, and neuter—that is, neither one nor the other. Like French and Italian, the Irish language admits only of two genders.

In English grammar sex and gender are confounded; yet they differ widely. Sex is a natural distinction; gender a grammatical one. Sex appertains to things—nay, to living things; gender to names of things. Sex is limited in its extent; gender extends to all classes of nouns. Sex is, however, a sure sign by which the gender of certain nouns becomes known. These nouns we shall immediately point out.

Things are endowed with life, or are not. Those endowed with life are called animate; those not so endowed, inanimate. The names of these two classes are as easily distinguishable as the objects they represent—names of things animate, and names of things inanimate. The gender of all nouns of the former class is regulated according to the sex of the object.

Rule 1. If the object be male, its name—that is, the noun—is masculine; if female, feminine. The word aċaıṙ, *father*, is masculine; maċaıṙ, *a mother*, is feminine; ınġeaın, *a daughter*, feminine.*

To this rule there is an exception given by the Rev. Paul O'Brien, copied and approved by Dr. O'Donovan—that the noun "cáılın, *a girl*, is masculine." The reason, it would seem, for this opinion is that in the nominative and accusative cases cáılın does not suffer, as nouns feminine do, aspiration on coming after the article.

The word cáılın is, for all that, a feminine noun —

1. Because the mere accident of not being aspirated can never of itself change the gender of a noun.

2. From Latin and Greek examples we have analogy in favour of this deviation. Nouns of the first declension, ending in *a* in the singular number, are in Latin feminine as a class; yet the noun *nauta* and others are masculine, on account of the ideas conveyed to the mind by these words. Greek nouns ending in *os* are masculine; still ὁδός (*odos*) and its compounds are feminine. Cannot, after the same manner, a term in Irish be declined like a oun masculine, while it is in reality feminine?

3. But, taking Hugh Boy MacCurtin's sixth rule for finding the gender of Irish nouns—"that those which agree with the pronoun é (*he*) are masculine; those with í (*she*) are feminine"—as the test on this occasion for proving the gender of the noun cáılın, we cannot but find that the noun is of the feminine gender. Who ever heard this form of expression—ıṙ bṙeaġ an cáılın é, *he is a fine girl*. In this form at least the noun cáılın claims the gender peculiar to nouns expressive of that sex to which the being denoted by the word belongs.

It may be interesting to show the probable reason why the noun cáılın is aspirated after the manner of masculine nouns. Derivative nouns, it is

---

* "In omnibus linguis Celticis," says Zeus, in his "*Grammatica Celtica*," (vol. i., p. 228, 1st ed., published at Leipsic, 1853)—"Hodiernis non nisi duo nominis genera distinguuntur genus masculinum et femininum, sed patet è vetustis nostris glossis Hibernicis, et e pronominis demonstrativi Cambrici formis, fuisse, ut in omnibus aliis linguis hujus affinitatis, etiam in vetere Celtica, tria genera, non solum pronominum sed etiam substantivorum et adjectivorum, et deleto serius discrimine grammaticali inter masculinum et neutrum commixta esse hæc duo genera in unum, eodem modo ut in lingua hodierna Gallica-romana."

known, follow the nature of those from which they are derived. Cáilín is derived from caile, which originally denoted any person—man or woman—who wore the cála, or hood worn by the Keltic Gauls and early Irish. Even at present cáile means a *virago*, a woman devoid of feminine comeliness.

It is plain, from what has been shown in the foregoing paragraph, that the general rule is true—that the names of all males are masculine, and of all females, feminine.

Rule 2.—The names of offices, employments, and the like, peculiar to men, are masculine; as, Fuarzaltóir, a *Redeemer*; clazaire, a *coward*; manac, a *monk*; zaduize, a *thief*; file, a *poet*; ceolraidhe, a *songster*. Hence almost all nouns ending in óir, aire, ac, aid, oid, uid, uig, are of the masculine gender.

The term coinpura, *a neighbour*, is feminine; because its derivative, ursa, *the jamb or support of a door*, is feminine; and derivatives, as a rule, follow the nature of their primitives.

Trianóid, *Trinity*, is feminine on account of its termination.

Leanán (from lean, *to follow*), one who is always hanging on, or constantly tracking the steps of another—a pet, an elf, a harlot. The noun is masculine on account partly of its termination, and partly because the primary idea conveyed is a *pursuer:* ceile (as it were cia, eile, *another*), a *companion, a husband or wife, a spouse*, is masculine and feminine.

How is the gender of nouns which are the names of inanimate objects known? From their termination, which in every language, except English, is the guide to gender.

Rules for knowing the Gender of those Irish Nouns which are the names of Inanimate Objects.

[The Exceptions are in the opposite column.]

MASCULINE NOUNS.

Rule 1.—All nouns generally, whether primitive or derivative, that end in a single or double consonant, immediately preceded by one of the three broad vowels, a, o, u, are masculine; as, rac, a sack; bád, a boat; loc, a lough; lúb, a button; fód, a sod; nór, a manner; cúr, a tower; canb,

FEMININE NOUNS.

Exception 1.—All derivative abstract nouns that end in acc* (or acd); as, ceanracc, mildness—from ceanra, mild; dánacc, boldness—from bán, bold; milreacc, sweetness—from milir, sweet (root nil); raonracc, freedom—from raon, free; ruigeacc, a kingdom.

---

* The spelling acc is to be preferred to that of acd. "Two or more mutes of different degrees of sharpness and flatness are incapable of coming together in the same syllable. . . . . *Spelt* indeed they may be; but attempts at pronunciation end in a *change* of the combination. . . . . . The combinations *abt* and *agt*, to be pronounced, must become either *apt* or *abd*, or else *akt* or *agd*."—*Latham*, "*The English Language*," p 152, sec. 215, 3rd ed.

MASCULINE NOUNS.

a chariot, a coach, a litter, a basket; ronar, happiness, prosperity; bonar, ill-luck, misery—the one derived from the adjective rona, happy, prosperous; the other from bona, unhappy, bad, evil.

Rule 2.—All verbal nouns ending in ugaḋ, aḋ, eaḋ, or having any of the broad vowels immediately preceding the final consonant or consonants; as, beannugaḋ, blessing; graḋugaḋ, loving; dunaḋ, shutting; ríneaḋ, stretching.

Exception 1.—Nouns ending in óir, aire, aiḋ, uiḋ, aiḋe, which although common to males and females, imply offices peculiar to men. See Rule 2, above, which refers to nouns of this class—the names, commonly, of animate objects.

Exception 2.—Diminutives ending in ín are of that gender to which the nouns from which they are formed belong; as, cnoicín, m., a little hill—from cnoc, m., and cnocainín, a very little hill—from cnocán, a hillock; leaḃairín, m., a little book, a pamphlet—from leaḃar, m., a book.

Exception.—Nouns derived from adjectives in the *nominative* case are masculine or feminine according to the termination; if the ending is broad, the noun is masculine; if slender, it is feminine; as, an t-olc, m., evil; an t-ruaire, f., the sweet; ir beag eiḋir an t-olc a'r an maiṫ, little (difference) exists between the good and bad; maiṫ is fem. according to Rule 3; olc is mas. according to Rule 1.

FEMININE NOUNS.

Exception 2.—Diminutives ending in óg (young); as, cianóg, a chafer; onḋóg, a thumb.

Exception 3.—Some words of one syllable, a knowledge of which can only by study be acquired; as, grian, the sun; cor, a foot; lam, a hand; neaṁ, heaven; pian, pain; rliaḃ, a mountain; treaḃ, a tribe.

Exception.—Verbal nouns ending with a slender termination—as, fuargaile, redemption; foicrinc, vision, sight—are feminine.

Rule 3.—All nouns generally, whether primitive or derivative, that end in a single or double consonant, preceded immediately by one of the two slender vowels e or i, are feminine; as, tír, a country; onóir, honour; uair, an hour; uaill, howling; laraiṁ, a flame—from lar, ignite; coircéim, a footstep.

Rule 4.—Abstract nouns formed from the possessive case, singular, *feminine* of adjectives, are, like the stock from which they spring, of the feminine gender; as, ailne, beauty—from ailne, for aluiṁe, more beautiful, poss. case, sing. fem. of aluiṁ, beautiful; airḋe, height—from airḋe, more high, poss. case, sing. fem., of arḋ, high; binne, melody, sweetness of sound—from binn, melodious, nior binne, more melodious; finne, fairness—from fion, fair; gile, whiteness — from geal, uairle, nobility — from uaral, noble.—*Easy Lessons*, part ii.

§ 41. *Number.*—All nouns are either of the singular or plural number. A noun is of the singular number if it denote one object; plural, if more than one.

For the manner of forming the plural see section after the five declensions.

§ 42. Nouns are of the first, second, or third person, according as they represent the speaker, the person or thing spoken to, and that spoken of.

§ 43. Case, from the Latin *cadere*, " to fall," is a certain change which nouns, pronouns, and adjectives undergo in their termination, expressive of a correlative change in their signification.

§ 44. *Number of Cases.*—Nouns in Gaelic undergo, in the singular and plural, three final inflections from the nominative, or the direct form. There are then three oblique cases and one direct, which, because it differs in its suffix from the root, or because it betokens a certain determinate state of the noun, may well be regarded as a case. These are—

1. { Nominative.
   { Accusative; in English grammar, objective.
2. Genitive; in English grammar, possessive.
3. Dative; or objective governed by a preposition.
4. Vocative; or nominative case of address.

§ 45. In regard to the cases, their names and their number, it may be well to propose here a few questions, and to answer them, for the satisfaction of the learned and enlightened student.

Why are the nominative and accusative ranked as one case? Because, according to the definition of case, they have only one or the same inflection. Why then retain the term accusative? Because it expresses an idea different, either in fact, in mode, or in grammatical relation, from those conveyed by the direct or nominative case. Dative alone is a name given, in this edition, to the third case, just to lessen the number of cases, and because this practice—of calling the third case by the term dative—has the sanction of Greek grammarians in the grammars they have written of that ancient tongue. Why is the term *possessive*, as in English grammar, not employed instead of genitive? Because less suitable and less truthful to express the meaning of the first oblique case. Let us see what the words possessive and genitive mean, and how far that meaning is applicable to this case.

The term genitive conveys the idea of *generation, origin, birth, source, first cause,* and indirectly, that of *possession, control, relation;* as, the father's son (generation, birth); this boy is Patrick's son (birth, possession); that is George's gun (possession); father's land (possession); James's arm (connexion, source, origin); the ship's side (same, by analogy). The term possessive conveys only the secondary meaning of the first oblique case—

namely, possession, and does not express that of generation, origin, birth, source, while the term genitive does fully convey those ideas along with that of possession. Which term, then, is to be preferred? Certainly that of genitive.

Again, in English there are two kinds of possessive cases—the real and the false, or the Anglo-Saxon and the Norman:

The Real—Anglo-Saxon.	False—Norman.
Peter's side.	The side of Peter.
The hill's foot.	The foot of the hill.

We cannot say, the hill's foot; because the possessive, hill's, would denote a possessor, and a hill cannot possess. The false possessive (*of*) then must be used in those instances where no real possession is implied. The real and the false English possessives have only one *real* corresponding case in Gaelic, the genitive. It expresses, as in Latin and in Greek, real or analogical origin, cause, connexion, procession, possession.

In Syntax it shall be shown that in translating the false possessive cases (or possessive with *of*) into Gaelic, the words, *of the*, are expressed by the genitive case of the article ᴀɴ, *the;* and *of* simply by the genitive case of the noun; as,

The foot *of the* child.	Cor "ᴀɴ" leɪnɛ.
The top *of the* foot.	Baɴɴ "ɴᴀ" coɪrc (fem.)
The side *of* Peter.	Taob Peadaɪr (gen. of Peadar).
The top *of* a mountain.	Baɴɴ sleɪbe.

The vocative singular and plural has in many instances inflections different from the nominative, and is on this account properly called by another name than that of "nominative case of address."

§ 46. DECLENSION.

Declension, viewed generally, is the formation of case-endings. Viewing the manner in which case-endings of Irish nouns are fashioned, by idiom or grammatical government, grammarians are at present agreed that there are five special classes or groups—that is, there are five declensions.

§ 47. The number of declensions adopted by Irish grammarians was, till lately, quite unsettled. The different writers who treated the subject have adopted various systems, according as they thought they could best show the peculiar changes of all classes of Irish nouns. Haliday adopts seven; Connellan, six; Neilson, four; Zeuss classifies the nouns into two groups—those that end in vowels and those that end in consonants, and thus admits two declensions. Stewart likewise makes two declensions, classifying the nouns into two great divisions—those that end in a broad vowel, and those that end in a slender vowel. Armstrong has followed Stewart in this division; and the compilers of the Gaelic Dictionary, who wrote for the Highland Society, run in the same beaten path.

In this treatise are adopted the number and order of declensions as laid down by Dr. O'Donovan; first, because the division adopted by him appears to be the most philosophically correct; and, secondly, in order to have uniformity in the number of declensions in the language, and not to have Irish grammar a changing, unsettled thing.

Nouns of a certain class follow one form of inflection; those of another, a form quite different. There are five such classes, and therefore five declensions. This number embraces the several forms of inflection, and, at the same time, secures uniformity amongst Irish grammarians.

OBS.—Every noun ends either in a vowel or in a consonant. (1) If in a consonant, the noun is of the first, the second, or third declension, excepting derivatives ending in ɪu, which are of the fourth. Nouns *masculine* alone, having a broad vowel before the final consonant, are of the first; nouns *feminine* alone, whether they have the slender vowel ɪ before the final consonant or have it not, are of the second declension; and the third declension embraces all personal nouns in óɪɪ, abstract nouns in ᴀċᴛ, verbal, and some derivatives. (2) If in a vowel, the noun belongs to the fourth or to the fifth declension.

The final vowel is called the characteristic, because when the gender is known, it shows whether the noun is of the first, second, or third declension.

"The fact is," says Dr. O'Donovan, "that the declension cannot be discovered until the gender is first known, and that even then the characteristic vowel of the nominative is no absolutely certain guide. It is no doubt a help to suggest what declension the noun may be of—but cannot, in many instances, be relied on; and the learner will discover that, as in Latin, Greek, and other ancient languages—so in Irish, he must learn the gender and genitive case singular of most nouns by reading or the help of a dictionary."—*Irish Grammar*, p. 78.

The learner is aware the vowels e, ɪ, are called cᴀol, *slender*. The term "attenuation," cᴀolυɡᴀò, which is employed by grammarians (Haliday, p. 22; O'Donovan, "Irish Grammar," p. 78), means making slender (cᴀol). It consists in annexing the slender vowel, ɪ, to the characteristic broad vowel. Making broad, leᴀᴛnυɡᴀò, is the opposite process, and consists in omitting the slender vowel, or reducing it to a broad.

Thus, ᴀ and ᴀo attenuated become ᴀɪ, ᴀoɪ; and conversely ᴀo, ᴀoɪ, on being made broad, become ᴀ, ᴀo.

§ 48. FIRST DECLENSION.

The first declension comprises all nouns *masculine* which have, in the nominative case singular, the characteristic, or key-vowel, *broad*.

This declension is distinguished by attenuation in the genitive case singular and nominative plural. In these cases ı is inserted after the key-vowel.

EXAMPLES.

Boċtáṅ, *a poor person.*

Primary form, without the article, and therefore not affected by aspiration or eclipsis.

	Singular.	Plural.
Nominative } Accusative }	boċtán.	boċtaın.
Genitive	boċtaın.	boċtán.
Dative	boċtán.	boċtanaıḃ.
Vocative	boċtaıṅ.	ḃoċtana.

NOTE.—The vocative case is always aspirated whenever the initial consonant admits it.

Eaċ, *m., a steed.*

	Singular.	Plural.
Nom. } Acc. }	eaċ, *a steed.*	eıċ, *steeds.*
Gen.	eıċ, *of a steed.*	eaċ, *of steeds.*
Dat.	eaċ, *to a steed.*	eaċaıḃ, *to steeds.*
Voc.	eıċ, *oh! steed.*	eaċa, *steeds.*

Eıċ, pl. of eaċ; eaċṗaıṫ, cavalry, is a noun of multitude.

In this manner is declined every noun masculine of one or more syllables ending in c (unaspirated). And in the same manner are declined all nouns of *one* syllable ending in ċ (aspirated). But if more than one syllable and that ċ final be aspirated, then it is changed, in the genitive case, into the softer guttural ġ; as,

Marcaċ, *a rider.**

	Singular.	Plural.
Nom. } Acc. }	marcaċ.	marcaıġe.
Gen.	marcaıġ.	marcaċ.
Dat.	marcaċ.	marcaıġıḃ.
Voc.	marcaıġ.	marcaċa.

" In all printed books, and in most manuscripts of the four last centuries, final ċ becomes ġ when attenuation takes place; as, bealaċ, *a way, a road;* gen. bealaıġ. But in very ancient Irish manuscripts, and in all printed

---

* From marc, an old Keltic term for *horse.*

books in the Erse or Scotch Gaelic, the ċ (asp.) is retained."—*Dr. O'Donovan's Irish Grammar*, p 80.

"In Munster the ϛ is unaccented and pronounced hard. . . The fact is that ϛ in this inflection is so distinctly pronounced with its radical sound in Munster that a native of that province would look upon the substitution of ċ in its place as a very strange innovation." And again: "The pronunciation of ϛ in this inflection is one of the strongest characteristics of the Munster dialect."—*Ibid*.

Boṗo, *m.*, *a table* (declined with the article ᴀɴ).

Articulated Form.

	Singular.	Plural.
Nom. Acc.	ᴀɴ boṗo, *the table.*	ɴᴀ boṗṗo, *the tables.*
Gen.	ᴀɴ boṗṗo, *of the table*	ɴᴀ m boṗo, *of the tables.*
Dat.	oo'ɴ m-boṗo, *to the table.*	ᴏᴏ ɴᴀ boṗoᴀɪḃ, *to the tables.*

From the last example it is seen that boṗo in the genitive case (boṗṗo) is aspirated after the article; and in the dative singular and genitive plural it is eclipsed (See Rules for Aspiration and Eclipsis, pp 37, 38, 40, 51).

§ 49. SECOND DECLENSION.

The second declension comprises (1) all nouns *feminine*, of which the characteristic is *slender*—the vowel ɪ; (2) nouns *feminine* of one or more syllables, of which the characteristic is broad.

The second declension is distinguished from the first by taking, in the genitive case singular, an additional syllable, e, called by grammarians—because e is a slender vowel—the slender increase.

Examples.

Suɪl, *eye* (pr. *soo-il*, in one syllable).

	Singular.	Plural.
Nom. Acc.	ꞅuɪl.	ꞅuɪle (pr *sooil-le*).
Gen.	ꞅuɪle.	ꞅul.
Dat.	ꞅuɪl.	ꞅuɪlɪḃ.
Voc.	ḟuɪl.	ḟuɪle.

All nouns of *this class* ending in a consonant, preceded by the slender vowel ɪ, are declined chiefly like the foregoing:

A noun feminine, of which the characteristic is broad, cor, *f.*, *a foot.*

	Singular.	Plural.
Nom. } Acc. }	cor, *kos.*	cora, *kossa.*
Gen.	coire, *koshé.**	cor.
Dat.	coir, *kosh.*	coraib.
Voc.	choir, *khosh.*	chora.

Derivative nouns feminine, terminating in óg, are of this class.

	Singular.	Plural.
Nom. } Acc. }	reampóg.	reampóga.
Gen.	reampóige.	reampóg.
Dat.	reampoig.	reampógaib.
Voc.	a reampoig.	reampóga.

Nouns feminine of one syllable, terminating in c (asp.)—as críc, *a country;* gen., críce, *of a country;* cloc, *a stone;* gen., cloice, *of a stone;* cuac, *cuckoo;* gen., cuaice—are declined like the foregoing, but feminine nouns of more than one syllable in c (asp.), are declined like the following:

Geallac, *f., the moon,* from geall, *bright, luminous, silver-colored.*

Articulated Form.

	Singular.	Plural.
Nom. } Acc. }	an geallac, *the moon.*	na geallaca, *the moons.*
Gen.	na geallaige, *of the moon.*	na ngeallac, *of the moons.*
Dat.	do 'n ngeallaig, *to the moon*	do na geallacaib, *to the moons.*
Voc.	a geallaig, *oh! moon.*	a geallaca, *oh! moons.*

Owing to the presence of the article, the noun geallac, being fem., is aspirated in the nom. and accusative singular, and like other nouns is eclipsed in the dative sing. and gen. plural (See Rules for Aspirating and Eclipsing, pp. 26, 29, 38, 40).

Obs.—Nouns masculine in c final are of the first declension; nouns feminine in c final are of the second. Observe how they differ in the formation of the genitive and dative singular, and nominative plural.

Deoc, *f., a drink,* makes dige, and dat. dig; teac, *m., a house,* gen. tige, dat. tig; plu., tigte, *houses.*

---

* S before or after e or i, the slender vowels, is sounded like *sh* English. This should be remembered (See p. 14).

§ 50.—THIRD DECLENSION.

Neither key-vowel nor gender serves to point out the class of nouns that belong to this declension, and to distinguish them from those of the first and second. The meaning alone and certain peculiar endings serve for this purpose. These are—

(1) Personal nouns in óıp; (2) abstract nouns in act; (3) verbal nouns in uġaḋ, aḋ, eaḋ, act, aıl; (4) certain primitive nouns of one syllable or more. The genitive singular takes a broad increase (a).

Examples of each.

(1) Of Nouns ending in óıp.

Slánuıġteoıp, *a Saviour* (with the article).

	Singular.	Plural.
Nom. }	an Slánuıġteoıp, *the*	na Slánuıġteoıpḋ, *the*
Acc. }	*Saviour.*	*Saviours.*
Gen.	an t-Slánuıġteopa.	na Slánuıġteoıp.
Dat.	ó 'n t-Slánuıġteoıp.	ó na Slánuıġteoıpḃ.
Voc.	a Slánuıġteoıp.	a Ṡlánuıġteoıpḋ.

(2) Of Nouns feminine ending in act.

Caıllḋeact, *qualification, virtue.*

	Singular.	Plural.
Nom.	an caıllḋeact.	na caıllḋeacta.
Gen.	na caıllḋeacta.	na g-caıllḋeact.
Dat.	ó 'n g-caıllḋeact.	ó na caıllḋeactaıḃ.
Voc.	a caıllḋeact.	a caıllḋeacta.

Most nouns terminating in act, expressing, as they do, an abstract idea, have no plural. A few—as caıllḋeact, *virtue;* mallact, *a curse*—admit a plural.

Derivative abstract nouns terminating in ar or car are of the first rather than of the third declension, as well because (1) they are uniformly masculine; and (2) form the genitive singular by attenuation—inserting ı after a; as, nom. ronar, *good luck;* gen. ronaır, *of good luck:* or changing ea into ı; as, flaıtear, *heaven, a kingdom;* gen. flaıtır, *of a kingdom.* A few, and only a few, are found declined like nouns of the first and third; as, maıtear, *goodness,* from maıt, *good;* gen. maıtır and maıteara; ruaımnear, *ease, quiet;* ruaımnır and ruaımneara; aoıḃnear, *delight;* gen. aoıḃnır and aoıḃneara.

(3) A verbal noun (without the article).

Ꮇolaꙍ, *praise.*

	Singular.	Plural.
Nom. Acc.	ꙧolaꙍ, *praise.*	ꙧolta, *praises.*
Gen.	ꙧolta.	ꙧolaꙍ.
Dat.	ꙧolaꙍ.	ꙧoltaiḃ.
Voc.	ṁolaꙍ.	ꙧolta.

In the same manner are declined all verbal nouns; as,

Verbal Noun.	Genitive.	Past Participle of Verb.
beannuġaꙍ, *a blessing.*	beannuiġte, *of a blessing.*	beannuiġte, *blest.*
ġnaꙍuġaꙍ, *act of loving.*	ġnaꙍuiġte, *of loving.*	ġnaꙍuiġte, *loved.*
miniuġaꙍ, *explanation.*	miniġte, *of an explanation.*	miniġte, *explained.*
rlanuġaꙍ, *salvation.*	rlanuiġte, *of salvation.*	rlanuiġte, *saved.*
ruarġailt, *redeeming.*	ruarġalta, *of redeeming.*	ruarġalta, *redeemed.*
ꝼeicrint, *seeing, vision.*	ꝼeicrinte, *of vision.*	ꝼeicrinte, *seen.*

As a general rule a noun derived from the active participle assumes, in the genitive singular, the form of the past participle.

To this general rule are exceptions—nouns formed from verbs terminating in act, ail, aṁain; as,

	Genitive.	Past Participle.
ġabail, *taking.*	ġabala (formed regularly).	ġabta.
ġealaṁain, *promising.*	ġealaiṁana, (formed regularly).	ġealta.
teact, *coming.*	teacta, (formed regularly)	wanting, being an intransitive verb.

As the vowel that comes between mute and liquid letters, or between two liquids, is by syncope taken away, so words thus contracted are lengthened again by inserting between the same two consonants the elided vowel; as, aꙍnaꙍ, *adoration;* gen. aꙍanta, *of adoration:* coꙉlaꙍ, *sleep;* gen. coꙉalta, *of sleep:* cornaꙍ, *defence;* gen. coranta: connaꙍ, *a covenant;* gen. connanta.

Occasionally one meets a participial noun (in aꙍ, eaꙍ) declined after the form of the first declension by attenuation; as, bruġaꙍ, *breaking, crushing;* croiꙍ-bruġaꙍ, *heart-breaking, contrition;* gen. croiꙍ-bruġaiꙍ, *of contrition;* as, ġnioṁ croiꙍ-bruġaiꙍ, *an act of contrition.*

§ 51. (4) Primitive nouns of one or more syllables, of which some end in a slender vowel; as,

Nominative.	Genitive.
coir, *f., justice.*	cora.
ꝼeoil, *f., meat.*	ꝼeola.
treoir, *f., a guide, troop, strength.*	treora.

Others in a broad vowel:

Nominative.	Genitive.
act, *m.*, *an act, decree.*	acta.
craob, *m.*, *a branch.*	craoba.
fíon, *f.*, *wine.*	fíona.
foġ, *m.*, *booty.*	foġa.
leun, *m.*, *a swamp.*	leuna.
lionn. *m.*, *beer.*	leanna.
róġ, *m., felicity, happy state.*	roġa.
cpeur, *m., a battle.*	cpeura.

With regard to monosyllabic nouns of this declension, and some feminines of the second of which the key-vowel is broad, the learner must conform to the advice of Dr. O'Donovan—"that as in Latin, Greek, and other languages, so in Irish he must learn the gender and genitive case singular of most nouns by reading or the help of a dictionary."

The observation of the learned Doctor regards this class especially. For their gender, and consequently their form of declension, is not settled amongst speakers as well as writers of the Gaelic tongue. Thus there are in Irish some words of one syllable, feminine, which are found to be masculine in Erse or Scotch Gaelic:

Erse.	Irish.
meud, *m., size, extent, price.*	méid, *f.*; gen. méide.
speur, *m., the sky, firmament.*	spéir, *f.*; gen. spéire.

Thus the gender regulates the form of declension and the spelling.

A peculiarity in pronunciation, which a people or a province may give to some words, directs the gender and consequently, their form of inflection and spelling. This is plain to any one who thinks over what has been written in section 4, p. 19.

§ 52.—FOURTH DECLENSION.

The great body of nouns terminating with a consonant belong to the first, second, and third declension; those that terminate with a vowel or aspirated mute consonant, are of the fourth and fifth.

(1) Personal nouns, therefore, of which the termination is aire, ire, or aide, uide, aiġe (spelled now aid, uid, aiġ); (2) those that end in a, o, e, i, of either gender—abstract nouns formed from the genitive feminine of adjectives; (3) diminutives in ín and proper names not declined, are of the fourth declension.

It is distinguished from any of the others by having no inflection or change in the singular number.

Example.

Tiġearna, *Lord.*

	Singular.	Plural.
Nom.	⎫	tiġearnaḋ, *the lords.*
Acc.	⎪	
Gen.	⎬ tiġearna, tiġearnaḋ,
Dat.	⎪	tiġearnaiḃ.
Voc.	⎭	tiġearnaḋ.

In the vocative singular aspirate t of tiġearna.

For a long list of nouns of this declension see "Easy Lessons; or, Self-Instruction in Irish," part iv., forty-fourth lesson—Dublin, Mullany.

§ 53.—FIFTH DECLENSION.

This declension, like the fourth, comprises nouns that end in a vowel (a, e), with a few in ain. They are, with a few exceptions, of the feminine gender.

This declension is distinguished from the former by a peculiar inflection (n or nn) in the genitive singular.

Example.

Pearsa, *f., a person* (with the article).

	Singular.	Plural.
Nom.	⎱ an pearsa.	na pearsana.
Acc.	⎰	
Gen.	na pearsan.	na b-pearsan.
Dat.	do 'n b-pearsain.	do na pearsanaiḃ.
Voc.	a pearsa.	a pearsana.

The ending of the genitive case is the only means by which a person can know whether a noun terminating in a vowel is of the fifth declension. If a noun of this class undergoes no inflection, it is then of the fourth. Any difficulty on this head is removed by the accompanying list of all the nouns in the language belonging to the fifth declension.

§ 54.—NOUNS BELONGING TO THE FIFTH DECLENSION.

Ára, f., kidney.
Alba, f., Scotland.
Alinja, f., Allen, in Kildare.
Ára, f, the Island of Arran; plu. ainne.
bo, a cow; gen. bo; dat. boin; nom. plu. ba (dat. plu. buaiḃ).

breiteaṁ, a judge; gen. breiteaṁan; it is also of the first declension, breiteiri.
bro, f., a quern, a handmill; gen. bron; dat. broin; plu. brointe.
bru, or bruinn, f., a womb; gen. bronn; as, beannuiġte toraḋ do

bnonn, blessed is the fruit of thy womb; dat. bnoinn; nom. plu. bnonna.

Ceatnama, f., a quarter, from ceatan, *four*.

Comunra, f., a neighbour, from coim and unra, a jamb, a support.

Cu, f., a hound; gen. sing. con, (pronounced *kŭn*, short); dat. coin; nom. plu. coin.

Cuirle, f., a vein.

Dailcaim, a cup-bearer; bail, a festive gathering.

Dearna, f., the palm of the hand.

Dile, f., a flood.

Duileam, the Creator; from buil, an element.

Earcu, f., an eel; gen. earcon; from ear, water, and cu, a hound. See cu, above.

Ealaba, f. (pr. *al-y-ah*), a science.

Ealba; gen. ealban; plu. ealbana; "Prioim-geince b' ealban—The first fruits of thy herds."—*Deuteronomy*, xii. 18, *Irish Bible by Dr. MacHale*, p. 345.

Eine, Ireland; gen. Eineann; dat. Eininn.

Goba, m., a smith.

Guala, f., a shoulder.

Fealram, a philosopher, like bneiteam, is of the fifth and first.

Feicean, m., a debtor.

Fionn-guala, f., a woman's name. *Fionguala* (fair shoulder.)

Ionga, f., nail (of the finger).

Laca, f., a duck; makes the gen. sing. and gen. plu. lacan, and lacain in the nom. plu.

Lanama, f., a married couple.

Leaca, m., a cheek.

Loigeann, f., Leinster; Cuige Loigeann, province of Leinster.

Lunga, f., the shin.

Muma. f., Munster; gen. Muman; as Cuige Muman, the province of Munster. Dear-Muman, South-Munster—Desmond; Tuab-Muman, North-Munster—Thomond; Oir-Muman, East-Munster—Ormond.

Meanma, f., the mind; urnaige na meanman, mental prayer, meditation.

Peanra, f., a person.

Sacrain, f., England; gen. Sacran; as, talam Sacran, land of England.

Seanga, f., a cormorant.

Raoine, Reelion, in the county Kildare.

Tailte, f.. Teltown, in Meath.

Teanga, f., a tongue; plu. teangta.

Teora, m., border, boundary, limit; Latin, *terminus*.

Uille, f., an elbow; Latin *ulna*; *ell*, a measure.

Ulca, f., beard.

Ursa, the jamb of a door.

Braga, shoulder, mas. and fem; gen. bragab.

Cara, m., a friend, makes gen. carab, and dat. carab, plu. caraba, or caraibe, and contractedly cairbe. Cairbe is the usual form. Carab, a friend, in the nom. case, is not unusual. It is then of the first declension; pl. carain.

Caora, f., a sheep, makes the gen. sing. and pl. caorach; nom. pl. caoraig, sheep.

Talam, f., land, earth, makes gen.; talman, contractedly for talaman, dat. talaim; plu. talmana and tailte.

Those are the only nouns in the language that belong to the fifth declension.

§ 55. Are not the foregoing fifty nouns too few to constitute a declension? It must be answered they should constitute a declension virtually or formally—virtually, by being exceptions to the fourth; formally, as in the text. The latter way is preferable for the sake of clearness and classification. In the famous Eton Latin grammar, and in all the Latin grammars, that have been modeled on it, the fifth declension is retained, although the number of nouns in Latin belonging to it are, it is probable, fewer than forty.

Some adept in Irish, seeing that certain nouns of the third declension form the genitive in ᴀċ, may object and say, why not classify that family also into a separate declension? The reason is obvious, they are too few. Again, the inflection ᴀċ in the genitive singular is in some, as ḃᴀɪɴ, *an oak*, a corrupt form.

Rules for the formation of the several cases, singular and plural, of the five declensions.

§ 56. FIRST DECLENSION—GENITIVE SINGULAR.

The genitive singular is formed from the nominative by attenuating the key-vowel.

With the article the initial mute consonant is aspirated, or (if the letter ŗ) eclipsed by ᴛ (See p. 38).

Words of one syllable follow this rule; as, nom ᴀɴ cɴᴀɴɴ, *the tree;* gen. ᴀɴ cɴᴀɪɴɴ, *of the tree.*

The improper attenuation consists in changing or omitting the key-vowel when ɪ is inserted, as, coɴp, *a body;* gen. cuɴp. It is time to reject this improper attenuation. The genitive of coɴp should therefore be coɪɴp, and not cuɪɴp; and the substitution of u for o in this and in other instances arises manifestly from a tendency to make phonetic curtness, rather than correct orthography, our guide in spelling.

§ 57. The distinguishing mark of the first declension, as has been already noticed, is the taking, in the genitive, of ɪ after the final *broad* vowel. Some words of one syllable, however, seem to be exceptions to this rule, for, although of the first declension, still they assume quite a different form, in the genitive, from other nouns of the same inflection. Nevertheless the rule is true of them also, for instance, cᴇᴀɴᴛ, *justice,* should, correctly speaking, form, in the genitive, cᴇᴀɪɴᴛ, but it is found to be cᴇɪɴᴛ and cɪɴᴛ. How is this? The ɪ, which it gets by *attenuation,* must, in order to show the case in which it is, be freely sounded, and this sounding of the ɪ assumes such a dominant influence over the other two accompanying vowels that the value either of one or of both is entirely lost to the ear. Hence, then, for the sake of brevity, it has been written cᴇɪɴᴛ or cɪɴᴛ, since the sound, if quickly enunciated, is still the same as if written cᴇᴀɪɴᴛ.

Hence monosyllables of the first declension, spelled with the diphthongs eᴀ or eu, change eu or eᴀ (when ċ is accented) into éɪ (*ē* long) in the genitive—when short or unaccented, into eɪ, and sometimes into ɪ alone; as,

Irregular Attenuation.

	Nominative.	Genitive.
(*a*)—Eᴀ, long or eu	éᴀɴ, *m., a bird.*	éɪɴ, *of a bird.*
	ɾᴇuɴ, *m., grass.*	ɾᴇɪɴ, *of grass.*
	neul, *m., a cloud.*	néɪl, *of a cloud.*

IRISH GRAMMAR.

	Nominative.	Genitive.
(b)—Ꞃa, short, into ꞇi, in nouns of the first and second declensions; as,	beać, m., a bee.	beić, a bee's.
	ceaꞃꞇ, m., justice, right.	ceiꞃꞇ, of justice.
	cꞃeaꞅ, f., cliff, crag.	cꞃeiꞅe, cliff's, of a cliff.
	ꞃeaꞃꞅ, f., anger.	ꞃeiꞃꞅe, of anger.
	leaꞃb, m., a child.	leiꞃb, of a child.
	ꞃeaꞃ, f. (2nd dec.), heaven.	ꞃeiꞃé, of heaven.
	ꞃeaꞃꞇ, m., strength.	ꞃeiꞃꞇ, of strength.
	ꞇꞃeaꞃ, f. (sec. dec.), a battle.	ꞇꞃeiꞃe, of a battle.
And into ɩ; as,	bꞃeac, m., a trout, a speckled thing.	bꞃic, of a trout.
	ceaꞃꞃ, m., head.	ciꞃꞃ, of a head.
	ceaꞃc, f. (2nd dec.), a hen.	ciꞃce, of a hen.
	ꞃeaꞃꞃ, m., a man.	ꞃiꞃ, of a man.
	iꞃǵeaꞃ, f. (2nd dec.), a daughter.	iꞃǵiꞃe, of a daughter.
	peaꞃꞃ, m., a pen.	piꞃꞃ, of a pen.
	ꞃiꞃꞃeaꞃ, m., progenitor.	ꞃiꞃꞃiꞃ, progenitors.

Also derivatives in eaꞃ, commonly; as,

ꞃlaiꞇeaꞃ, m. (fláihas), heaven.   ꞃlaiꞇeiꞃ (fláihish), of heaven.
ꞃuaꞃiꞃꞃeaꞃ, m., rest.   ꞃuaꞃiꞃꞃiꞃ, of rest.
ꞇiꞃꞃeaꞃ, m., sickness.   ꞇiꞃꞃiꞃ, of sickness.

> " Aiꞃ baꞃ ꞃa cꞃeiꞅe aꞃoiꞅ 'ꞃꞃa luiꞃe
> Ceiꞃ ꞅe ćum ' 'ꞃuaꞃiꞃꞃiꞃ' a'ꞅ ćum ꞃꞅiċ."
> On the top of the cliff now lying
> He seeks to enjoy tranquillity and rest.

" On the bold cliff's bosom cast,
Tranquil now he sleeps at last."

SONG—*By that lake whose gloomy shore.*

mac, m., a son, makes mic, of a son.
mac mic, the son of a son, grandson.
ꞃeać, an individual, is not declined.

Co.—In ⌐ouns of one syllable or more, characterized by eo, the genitive singular is regular (coi), except ceo. *a fog*, makes ceoć; ꞅleo, ꞅliaiꞇ.

Ia.—Monosyllables in ia are not regular. In forming the genitive case singular ia is changed—*not* into iai, but into éi, in nouns of the second as well as those of the first declension; as, iaꞅꞅ, m., *a fish*; gen., éiꞅꞅ.

Nominative.	Genitive.
iall, f., a latchet, a thong.	éille.
ꞅꞃiaꞃ, f., the sun.	ꞅꞃéiꞃe.
ꞅꞅiać, f., a shield.	ꞅꞅeiće.
ꞅliab, f., a mountain.	ꞅléibe.

" Aꞅuꞅ ꞃeaꞅꞃaiꞅ ꞇu liom-ꞅa aiꞃ mullać ꞃa 'ꞅleibe.'
And you will stand with me on the summit *of the* mountain."

Irish Bible, by Dr. MacHale, p. 169.

Exceptions.—In the first declension, bnian, *Brien*, forms the gen. regular bniain; fiaż, *a deer*, fiaiż; Oia, *God*, makes Dé; biaó, *food*, bió.

"A catað bió man oaoinc, no 'ʒ ól ffon'."
"Using food like to mortals, or drinking wine."
Irish Homer, book v. l. 427.

Nouns of one syllable or more, spelled with ıo, as the characteristic syllable change, in the genitive singular, ıo into ı (the sound of o in the nominative case is almost quiescent); as,

Nominative.	Genitive.
lıon, *m.*, *a net*.	lın.
ríol, *seed, race*.	ríl.
ainʒıoo, *silver*.	ainʒıb.
cíon, *f.*, *a comb*.	cíne.
cnıoć, *f.* (2nd dec.), *an end*.	cnıce.
oojlżjor, *grief, sorrow*.	oojlżır.
faıcéjor, *fear, dread*.	faıcéır.

. *By adopting the regular attenuation all the foregoing rules can be dispensed with.*

§ 58. *Second Declension.*—The genitive singular is formed, as in the examples, by annexing e to the final syllable. The final syllable must be attenuated. (See § 49, pp. 59, 60.)

Attenuation is regular or irregular—regular (see § 56), when ı is inserted before the final consonant; irregular, when the final broad vowel is changed for sound's sake—*e. g.*, a into o, and o into u; as,

Nominative.	Genitive.
clan, *f.*, *children*.	cloınne for claınne.
lonʒ, *f.*, *a ship*.	luınʒe for loınʒe.

And in the first declension—

conp, *m.*, *a body*.	coınp. (See p. 66, section 56.)

In most printed Irish works and in manuscripts the irregular attenuation prevails. The regular has been with good reason adopted by late writers.

In nouns of this declension the diphthongs ea, eu, ıa, ıo, in the final syllable, are changed in the genitive case into eı or ı, as has been shown, *supra*, § 57.

§ 59. *Third Declension.*—(1) The genitive takes a broad increase (a); (2) ı final is omitted for correct spelling.

(3) Nouns classed by some grammarians under a special declension terminate in ać in the genitive. They are only few in number:

Nominative.	Genitive.
beoın, *f.*, *beer*.	beonać.
cataın, *f.*, *a city*.	catanać, contractedly caenać.
conoın, *f.*, *a crown*.	cononać, and contractedly cnonać.
Feoın, *f.*, *the river Nore*.	Feonać.
laın, *f.*, *a mare*.	lanać.
laraın, *f.*, *flame*.	larnać.
Ceamaın, *f.*, *Tara*.	Ceamnać.

(4) The following, ending in ın, generally omit the increase (a), peculiar to this declension:

IRISH GRAMMAR. 69

Nominative.	Genitive.
atair, m., father.	atar.
mátair, f., mother.	mátar.
bráitair, m., brother, friar.	brátar.
briatar, m., a word, an expression.	briatar.

(5) Many monosyllables of the masculine gender are of this declension; as,

Nominative.	Nominative.
át, a ford.	gul, crying.
blát, a blossom.	gut, a voice.
bot, a tent, a cot.	lur, an herb.
cát, a battle.	nát, luck.
cruit, form.	scot, a flower.
druct, dew.	sruit, a stream.
gráb, love.	uct, the breast.
gnut, curds.	unblát, a fresh blossom, a bud.

Many of these, in forming the genitive, change the final vowel; as, cruit, gen. crota; gul, crying; gen. gola. It would accord better with the principles of orthography to have no such change.

(6) Monosyllables spelled with io (or i) change it, in the genitive singular, into ea; as,

Nominative.	Genitive.
bion, a spit.	beana.
bie and biot, life.	beata.
bliott, butter-milk.	bleacta.
ciot and cit, a shower.	ceata.
fior, knowledge.	feara.
lionn, beer, ale.	leanna.
lior, a fort.	leara.
rioc, frost.	reaca.
rliott, prosterity.	rleacta.

(7) Fuil, blood, makes fola; toil, the will, tola; muir, the sea, mana.

*** The genitive case of the fourth and fifth declensions has nothing peculiar.

§ 60. The dative case, in each of the four first declensions, is like the nominative. In the second declension, however, when the noun takes attenuation along with the slender increase, the dative is formed from the genitive by dropping the final é; as,

Genitive.	Dative.
coire, of a foot.	coir.
lairne, of a hand.	lairn.
reamnóige, of shamrock.	reamnóig.
clairrige, of a harp.	clairrig.
gréinne, of the sun.	gréin.
maigoine, of a virgin—from maig dean.	maigoin.
rléibe, of a mountain.	rléib.
neime, of heaven.	neim.

Nouns of the second declension spelled with ea or ia in the final syllable

of the nominative case—as, ᵹnᴊan, neaṁ, rḷab—taking ı̇ in the genitive, form, according to rule, the dative from the genitive; as,
"De na torạıḃ beınceaṅ anṡaċ leır an 'ᵹnéın' aᵹur leır an ᵹealḷaıṡ—of the fruits brought forth by the sun and by the moon."—*Deuteronomy*, xxxiii. 14—*Irish Bible by Dr. MacHale*.
"An n-aṫaır a ta aın 'neıṁ—Our Father, who art in heaven." 'Neıṁ is the dative or prepositional case.

Yet it must be said that amongst the Irish speaking people the sound given to the prepositional case in these instances is that of the nominative; as, an n-aṫaır a ta aın "neaṁ" (pronounced *nawv*, and not *nēyv*). It is written in this way by some of the best Irish writers; as,
"'Nuaır do ċrıoċnuıᵹ ṙe a ċoṁraḋ leır aın 'Sḷıab' Sınaı euᵹ an Tıᵹearna do Ṁaoıre—And the Lord, when he had ended these words on Mount Sinai, gave to Moses."—*Exodus*, xxxi. 18.
"Aᵹur ṫan éır ṫeaċṫ a nuar de 'n 'ṫ-ṙḷıab' ḋó, do leanaḋan cuıdeaċṫa ṁór é—And when He was come down from the mountain, great multitudes followed Him."—*Matt.* viii. 1 (*Protestant Version, by Dr. William O'Donnell*).

*** In the fifth declension the dative is formed from the genitive singular by inserting ı before the final consonant.

§ 61. *Vocative.*—The vocative singular is attenuated. In the first declension the vocative is like the genitive; as,

Nominative.	Genitive.	Vocative.
boṙd.	boıṙd.	boıṙd.
caṙan.	caṙaın.	caṙaın (*chos-aw-in*; pronounce *awin* in one syllable).

Seaᵹan (*Shawn*), *John*; a Ṡeaᵹaın! (*a haw-in*), *O John!* Seamur (*Shemus*), *James*; a Ṡeamuır! (*a heamuish*), *O James!*

In the second declension it is like the dative, because it has the slender vowel ı before the final consonant; as,

	Vocative.
fuıl (nom. and dat. are the same).	a fuıl (*a hoo-il*).
coır, nom.; coıṙ (*koish*), dat.	a ċoıṙ (*a cho-ish*).
ṫeaċ, m., nom.; ṫıᵹ, dat.	a ṫıᵹ; as, a ṫıᵹ oṙda, *house of gold*.

Nouns terminating in aċ, of which the great majority are masculine, form, when of the first declension, the vocative like the genitive—in ıᵹ; as, a ṁaṙcaıᵹ! *O horseman!* a foıṙṫıᵹ rpıonaḋalṫa (from foıṙṫeaċ, *a vessel*), *spiritual vessel;* a foıṙṫıᵹ onóṙaıᵹ, *honorable vessel*. If of the second declension they should, conformably to rule, be like the dative, and, therefore, should end in ıᵹ. But this is not the case. To distinguish them from nouns masculine of the same ending, they form the vocative singular like the nominative; as, a ċaılleaċ! *you hay!* a ᵹıonnṙaċ, *you lass!*

§ 62. In nouns of the fourth and fifth declension the vocative singular is like the nominative. It is not unusual to see the word Eıre, *Ireland*, apostrophised, Éirin; as, "Eirin, the tear and the smile in thine eye." Although this use of the name is very common, yet it is not grammatically correct. We should say, Éire 50 bráṫ, and not Éirin 50 bráṫ.

§ 63. The genitive plural is, as a general rule, like the nominative singular in all nouns of the first declension. This rule is more or less general in the four remaining declensions.

In nouns of the second declension it is the same as the nominative singular. If, however, the nominative singular end in ı, it is usually omitted in the genitive plural; as, nom. sing. ruıl; gen. plu. na rul.

Obs.—In all the declensions it is worthy of notice that the genitive plural terminates in a broad vowel, if possible. This is true of nouns of the first and of the second, as has been shown; of the third also, for commonly personal nouns terminate in aċ. Those that form the nominative plural in anna form the genitive by dropping a; and if they form the plural in ṫe, whether of the second, third, or fourth, the genitive plural terminates in eaḋ; as,

	Plural.	Genitive.
coıll, *f.*, *a wood* (2nd dec.)	coıllṫe.	coıllṫeaḋ.
ṫaın, *a flock*, *a territory* (3rd dec.)	ṫaınṫe.	ṫaınṫeaḋ.
baıle, *a town* (4th dec.)	baılṫe.	baılṫeaḋ.
ṫeıne, *f.*, *a fire* (4th dec.)	ṫeınṫe.	ṫeıneaḋ.

Personal nouns ending in óır, and others, form the genitive plural often like the nominative plural; as, agallaıṁ na reanóırıḋ, *the dialogue of the sages*; Keating would have written it, agallaıṁ na reanóraċ—or, according to the general rule, agallaıṁ na reanóır.

"Le h-aır na 'ṫonṫa' glórać, ǵeıṁeaċ, ganǵ."—*Homer's Iliad, by Dr. MacHale.*

In nouns of the fifth declension, the genitives plural and singular are alike.

§ 64. The dative plural is, as a general rule, formed from the nominative plural by changing the vowel e into ıḃ; as, nom. plu. ruıle, *eyes*; dat. plu. ruılıḃ: coıll, *f.*, *a wood*; nom. plu. coıllṫe, *woods*; dat. plu. coıllṫıḃ: or if the plural end in a, by annexing ıḃ; as, cora, coraıḃ; if in ıó, by changing the digraph (ıó) into ıḃ. In nouns of the first declension the dative plural is formed from the nominative singular (and not from the nominative plural) by annexing aıḃ.

In colloquial language the termination ıḃ is seldom heard, nor is it much known. In the written language, however, it is quite common.

☞ The vocative plural is like the nominative plural. In the first declension it receives an increase which the nominative has not.

§ 65.—HOW THE PLURAL OF NOUNS IS FORMED.

Now that the learner has got through the several declensions, and has seen how in each the noun is inflected, the formation of the plural is to him a matter of no difficulty. It is on this account that the way in which Gaelic nouns form the plural has not been presented to the learner at an earlier stage. (See section 41, p. 55.)

On examining the several classes of nouns it is seen that some have the same number of syllables in the plural as in the singular. These are called *parasyllabic*—that is, equal in number of syllables. Others form the plural from the singular by annexing an additional syllable. These are *im*parasyllabic, or unequal in the number of syllables in the singular and plural.

The parasyllabic include all nouns of the first declension, and some of the fourth; the *im*parasyllabic, all those of the remaining declensions.

§ 66. *General Rule.*—All nouns of the first declension form the nominative plural like the genitive singular.

Nom. Singular.	Gen. Singular.	Nom. Plural.
ball, *m.*, *a limb.*	baill.	baill.
bopb, *m.*, *a table.*	boipib.	boipib.
eac, *m.*, *a horse.*	eic.	eic.
bpeac, *m.*, *a trout.*	bpic.	bpic.
pinpcap, *a progenitor.*	pinpip.	pinpip.
cleipeac, *m.*, *a cleric.*	cleipig.	cleipige (e is annexed.)
mullac, *m.*, *summit*	mullaig.	mullaige.

Nouns in ia.

giall, *m.*, *a cheek.*	geill.	geill.
iarg, *m.*, *a fish.*	eirg.	eirg.

Some have two forms; as,

feap, *a man.*	fip.	fip and feapa.
mac, *a son.*	mic.	mic and maca.

It is worth remarking that the class of nouns of this declension having a two-fold form in the plural are those which end in any of the liquid letters, l, n, p, or happen to have a liquid letter in the final syllable; as,

In l.

aingeal, *an angel.*	aingil.	aingeala, contractedly aingle—and not aingla.
ubal, *an apple.*	ubail.	ubala, contractedly ubla.

In n

meacan, *a carrot, a parsnip—any top-rooted plant.*	meacain.	meacain and meacana—contractedly meacna.
uan, *a lamb.*	uain.	uana.

R *final.*

Nom. Singular.	Gen. Singular.	Nom. Plural
leabar, *a book.*	leabair.	leabair, leabara, leabra.

R *in last syllable.*

| doruf, *a door.* | doruif. | doruif and dorura, contract. doirfe. |

S *final has this liquid trait—*

| eigear, *a learned man.* | eigif. | eigeara, eigra; but to conform to the rule, caol le caol— eigre. |

A few nouns of the first declension, ending in l, n, r, take c before the annexed vowel; as,

ceol, *music.*	ceoil.	ceolta.
neul, *a cloud.*	neil.	neulta.
rgeul, *a story.*	rgeil.	rgeula, rgeulta.
cogad, *war.*	cogaid.	cogaid, cogta.
mur, *a wall,*	muir.	mura.
clar, *a board, a plain, a level.*	clair.	clair, clarada.

The termination ada for nouns of this class is a corrupt form.

§ 67. Nouns of the fourth declension, ending in l, n, m, r, r, followed by a vowel, form the plural from the singular commonly by inserting c before the final vowel; as,

In l.

Nom. Singular.	Nom. Plural.
baile, *a town.*	bailte and bailteada.
cuille, *a staff.*	cuillte.
muille, *a mule.*	muillte.

In n.

cuaine, *a corner.*	cuainte.
leine, *a shirt, a tunic.*	leinte, leinteada.
ceine, *fire.*	ceinte, ceinteada.

C is *commonly* inserted before the final vowel—but not always, as the following show:

4

Nom. Singular.	Nom. Plural.
ᵹile, *a poet.*	ᵹiliᵹ (*filee*), and not ᵹilte.
ᵹainne, *a ring.*	ᵹainniᵹ, and not ᵹainte.
aiṫne, *a command.*	aiṫeanta.
buine, *a person.*	baoine (*dheeny*).
cirbe, *a treasure.*	cirbi, or cirbiᵹ.
peire, *a pair.*	peiri, or peiriᵹ.
peirce, *a perch.*	peirciᵹ

Personal nouns in aire, and a few others, are imparasyllabic; as,

| clabaire, *a babbler.* | clabairiᵹ. |
| tiᵹearna, *lord.* | tiᵹeannaiᵹ |

Note.—The endings iᵹ, iᵹ, or i, are pronounced like *ee* English, or *i* French; as, cirbi, ceirbiᵹ, *treasures* (*kish-dee*); tiᵹeanniᵹ, *lords* (*thee-urnee*).

"Stewart is justly of opinion," says O'Donovan, "that the termination naiᵹ or tiᵹ, added to nouns, has a collective (not a plural) import—like the termination *rie* in the French words *cavalerie, infanterie*, and *ry* in the English words *cavalry, infantry, yeomanry*; as, laocnaiᵹ, *a band of heroes.*" That such words as laocnaiᵹ, macnaiᵹ, cacnaiᵹ, are collective nouns, and not plurals of laoc, mac, cac, appears from the examples cited by him from *Keating, Cormac's Glossary*, and the *Dinnsenchus*. The word cunlaiṫ, *birds*, also is a collective noun, and not the plural of cun, *a bird*.

§ 68. The imparasyllabic class forms the plural from the nominative case singular by annexing e or a to the final syllable—e when the preceding vowel is slender; a when broad; as,

Nouns of the second declension.

Nom. Singular.	Gen. Singular.	Nom. Plural.
buil, *an element, a wish.*	buile.	buille.
lub, *a plait, a fold.*	luibe.	luba.
luc, *a mouse.*	luice.	luca.
inᵹean, *a daughter.*	inᵹine.	inᵹeana.
ᵹeallac, *the moon.*	ᵹeallaiᵹe.	ᵹeallaca.
ᵹuineoᵹ, *a window.*	ᵹuincoiᵹe.	ᵹuineoᵹa.
ciar, *a comb.*	ceire.	ciara.

Of the third declension.

mallact, *a curse.*	mallacta.	mallacta.
meab-ail, *subtlety.*	-ala.	-ala.
lior, *a fort.*	eara.	leara.

Nouns in óɪɼ; as,

Nom. Singular.	Gen. Singular.	Nom. Plural.
ʒɲoróɪɼ, *a frying-pan.*	-oɼɑ.	-óɪɲó.
ɑċɑɪɼ, *father.*	-ɑɼ.	ɑɪċɼe, ɑɪċɼeɑċɑ.
mɑċɑɪɼ, *mother.*	-ɑɼ.	mɑɪċɼe, mɑɪċɼeɑċɑ.

Of participles, the plural is the same as the genitive singular.

Of the fourth declension,

Nom. Singular.	Nom. Plural.
Nouns in ɪɲ, into	ɪó.
ɪʒe, or ɑɪóe, by changing e into	ce
ɼɑoɪ, *a learned man.*	ɼɑoɪċe.

Of the fifth declension,

Nouns change ɑ into ɑɲɲɑ; as,

peɑɼɼɑ.   peɑɼɼɑɲɲɑ.

Some nouns—as, luɪb, *an herb;* beɪl, *a lathe* (of the second declension); ʒɾeɪm, *a morsel* (of the third)—form the nom. plural in ɑɲɲɑ. This plural ending, "which is like the Saxon termination *en* (as in *oxen*) is more general" than the slender increase, because more distinct and forcible.

The termination ɑċɑ, in nouns of the second and third declensions, adds strength to the term. However, the form seems corrupt.

Nom. Singular.	Gen. Singular.	Nom. Plural.
ɼlɑc.	ɼlɑɪce.	ɼlɑcɑ, ɼlɑcɑċɑ.
clɑɪɼ.	clɑɪɼe.	clɑɪɼe and clɑɪɼeɑċɑ.
ɼcɑɪɼɪc, *lights (Exodus,* xxix. 8).	ɾʒɑɪɼce.	ɾʒɑɼcɑċɑ.

§ 69. IRREGULAR NOUNS.

Nom. Singular.	Gen. Singular.	Dat. Singular.
beɑɲ, *f., a woman.*	mɲɑ.	mɲɑoɪ.
ceo, *m., a fog.*	cɪɑċ, ceoɪʒ.	ceo.
cɲo, *f., a nut.*	cɲuɪ.	cɲu.
cɼé, *f., the earth.*	cɼɪɑó.	cɼé.
cɼó, *m., a sty or fold.*	cɼoɪ.	cɼó.
Ðɪɑ, *God.*	Ðé.	Ðɪɑ, vocative Ðé, and Ðɪɑ.

Nom. Singular.	Gen. Singular.	Dat. Singular.
ᵹᴀ, *m.*, *a ray or javelin*	ᵹᴀe, ᵹᴀɪ.	ᵹᴀ, ᵹᴀɪ.
ᵹé, *f.*, *a goose*.	ᵹeᴀᴆ.	ᵹeɪᴆ.
lᴀ, *m.*, *a day*.	lᴀe.	lᴀ, lō.
mɪ̄, *f.*, *a month*.	mɪoɼᴀ, mɪɼ.	mɪ.
o, or uᴀ, *m.*, *a grandson or descendant*.	uɪ, uᴀ, or o.	

	Plural.	
mɴᴀ, *women*.	bᴀɴ.	mɴᴀɪᴃ.
cɪᴀᴆ, *fogs*.	ceo.	ceocᴀɪᴃ.
cɴó, cɴoċᴀ, *nuts*.	cɴoᴆ.	cɴoċᴀɪᴃ or cɴoɪᴃ.
cɼéᴆeᴀɴᴀ, *earths*.	cɼɪᴀᴆ.	cɼéᴆeᴀɴᴀɪᴃ.
cɼóɪċe. *folds*.	cɴó.	cɼóċᴀɪᴃ.
cuɪɴ, *hounds*.	coɴ.	coɴᴀɪᴃ.
Ðée or Ðéɪċe, *Gods*.	Ðɪᴀ.	Ðéɪċɪᴃ.
ᵹᴀċċe or ᵹᴀɪ, *rays or javelins*.	ᵹᴀċ or ᵹᴀeċᴀᴆ.	ᵹᴀɪᴃ, ᵹᴀċċɪᴃ.
ᵹéᴀᴆɪ̄ or ᵹéᴀɴᴀ, *geese*.	ᵹéᴀᴆ.	ᵹéᴀᴆɪᴃ, ᵹéᴀɴᴀɪᴃ.
lᴀċċe, *days*.	lᴀ or lᴀeċᴀᴆ.	lᴀeċɪᴃ.
mɪoɼᴀ, *months*.	mɪoɼ.	mɪoɼᴀɪᴃ.
uɪ, *grandsons*, &c.	uᴀ.	uɪᴃ, Voc. uɪ.

CHAPTER III.
OF THE ADJECTIVE.

§ 70. *Properties of Adjectives.*—In Gaelic, adjectives are declined.

Their position is *after*, not before the noun with which they agree; as, ғeᴀɼ "ᵹeᴀɴᴀṁᴀɪl," *a friendly man*—like the French *homme aimable*, literally "a man amiable." (See "Syntax," c. ii.)

"In English, adjectives remain unchanged in their terminations. The word *good*, for instance, undergoes no change in gender, number, or case, in the following—*a good man* (m.); *a good woman* (f.); *a good house* (n.); *I see a good man* (obj.); *I see good men* (plu. obj.); *a good man's* (poss.) *house*; *good men's* (plu. poss.) *houses*.

The slightest acquaintance with any foreign language will show the mere English student that the adjective is inflected like the noun with which it agrees. In French and in Italian, for example, it varies in gender and number.

	French.	Italian.
Sing.	*bon*, m.; *bonne*, f.. *good*.	*bono*, m.; *bona*, f.
Plu.	*bons*, m.; *bonnes*, f.	*boni*, m.; *bone*, f."

In other languages—say, Latin, Greek, German—it varies in gender number, and case:

	Latin.	Greek.	German.	
Nom.	bonus.	αγαθος.	guter.	good (man).
Gen.	boni.	αγαθου.	gutes.	of a good (man).
Dat.	bono.	αγαθω.	gutem.	to a good (man).
Acc.	bonum.	αγαθον	guten.	good (man.)
Ab.	bono.	αγαθω.	gutem.	with a good (man).

In the singular number, masculine gender, the adjective undergoes several inflections as is seen by the foregoing.

These remarks are in some measure necessary for the young student, who is accustomed to look upon the adjective in English as invariable. They will serve to render clear what is going to be said on the declension of adjectives in Gaelic.

Take an example of a noun and adjective:

Feaṅ móṅ, *a big man.*

	Singular.	Plural.
Nom. } Acc.	an feaṅ móṅ.	na fiṅ móṅa.
Gen.	an fiṅ móiṅ.	na b-feaṅ móṅ.
Dat.	do 'n feaṅ móṅ.	do na feaṅaib móṅa.

In this example, móṅ, the nominative singular, masculine, becomes móiṅ in the genitive singular, and móṅa in the nominative plural:

bean móṅ. *the big woman.*

	Singular.	Plural.
Nom. } Acc.	an bean móṅ.	na mna móṅa (*mōra*).
Gen.	na mna móiṅe (*moirhye*)	na m-ban móṅ.
Dat.	do 'n mnaoi móiṅ.	do na mnaib móṅa.

Agreeing with a noun of the feminine gender, móṅ becomes, in the genitive singular, móiṅe, and in the dative móiṅ; nom. plu. móṅa, masculine and feminine"—*Easy Lessons; or, Self-Instruction in Irish,* part iv.; forty-fourth lesson. (Dublin—Mullany, Publisher.)

Another example—one in which the final vowel of the adjective is slender:

Snátad míṅ, *the fine needle.*

	Singular.	Plural.
Nom. } Acc.	an snátad míṅ.	na snátaib míṅe.
Gen.	an t-snátaib míṅ.	na snátad míṅ.
Dat.	do n' t-snátad míṅ.	do na snátadaib míṅe.

Obs.—Míṅ is not changed in the genitive masculine, because the peculiar effect of that case is to assume a slender vowel. Now, as the vowel is already slender, the genitive cannot assume another, and therefore undergoes no change.

§ 71. *How Adjectives are Declined.*—Adjectives in Gaelic

follow the form of inflection peculiar to nouns of the same gender and of the like termination.

(*a*) Adjectives with a broad characteristic—as, ᴀʀᴅ, *high;* móʀ, *large, great;* ᴄᴀoʟ, *slender;* ᴊʀᴀᴅᴀċ, *loving;* ᴛʀom, *heavy*—are declined after the form of the first and second declension.

(*b*) Adjectives with a slender characteristic—as, ʙɪɴɴ. *harmonious;* mɪɴ, *fine;* mɪʟɪʀ, *sweet;* ᴛᴀɪʀ (tha*sh*), *soft, moist*—are declined after the form of the fourth and first declension.

(*c*) Adjectives ending in ᴀmᴀɪʟ, after the form of the third declension.

(*d*) Adjectives ending in vowels are *in*declinable.

Examples of each in their simple or unaspirated form.

(*a*)—Cᴀoʟ, *slender.**

	Singular.		Plural.
	Masc.	Fem.	Masc. & Fem.
Nom. Acc. }	ᴄᴀoʟ.	ᴄᴀoʟ.	ᴄᴀoʟᴀ.
Gen.	ᴄᴀoɪʟ.	ᴄᴀoɪʟᴇ.	ᴄᴀoʟ.
Dat.	ᴄᴀoʟ.	ᴄᴀoɪʟ.	ᴄᴀoʟᴀ.
Voc.	ċᴀoɪʟ.	ċᴀoɪʟ.	ċᴀoʟᴀ.

ᴊʀᴀᴅᴀċ, *loving.*

	Singular.		Plural.
	Masc.	Fem.	Masc. & Fem.
Nom. Acc. }	ᴊʀᴀᴅᴀċ.	ᴊʀᴀᴅᴀċ.	ᴊʀᴀᴅᴀċᴀ.
Gen.	ᴊʀᴀᴅᴀɪᴊ.	ᴊʀᴀᴅᴀɪᴊᴇ.	ᴊʀᴀᴅᴀċ.
Dat.	ᴊʀᴀᴅᴀċ.	ᴊʀᴀᴅᴀɪᴊ.	ᴊʀᴀᴅᴀċᴀ.
Voc.	ᴊʀᴀᴅᴀɪᴊ.	ᴊʀᴀᴅᴀċ.	ᴊʀᴀᴅᴀċᴀ.

(*b*)—Ɑ)ɪɴ, *fine, smooth.*

	Singular.		Plural.
	Masc.	Fem.	Masc. & Fem.
Nom. Acc. }	mɪɴ.	mɪɴ.	mɪɴᴇ.
Gen.	mɪɴ.	mɪɴᴇ.	mɪɴ.
Dat.	mɪɴ.	mɪɴ.	mɪɴᴇ.

Ꞇᴇɪᴛ, *hot,* makes ᴄᴇo in the genitive singular and nominative plural.

---

* Pronounced *kael*—see sound of diphthong ᴀo, p. 24, section 12.

IRISH GRAMMAR. 79

(c)—Flaıċaṁaıl, *princely, generous.*

	Singular.	Plural.
Nom.	} flaıċaṁaıl.	flaıċaṁla
Acc.		
Voc.		
Gen.	flaıċaṁla.	flaıċaṁaıl.
Dat.	flaıċaṁaıl.	flaıċaṁla.

The spelling of the root flaıċ, *a prince*, is preserved even though the suffix aṁaıl (same as raṁaıl—Latin *simile*)—beginning with a broad vowel a—is annexed.

(d)—Sona, *lucky*; dona, *bad, unlucky*; aoṛda, *aged.*

Singular & Plural.

Nom. ⎫
Acc. ⎪
Voc. ⎬ rona.
Gen. ⎪
Dat. ⎭

Beo, *living,* makes gen. bı; plur. beoda; as, Ⰰac De bı, *the Son of the living God.*

§ 72. Adjectives terminating in the liquid letters l, m, n, ṅ, or r, are like nouns syncopated (see section 66, p. 72); as,

Nom. Masc.—Sing.	Gen. Fem.—Sing		Plural.
(a) umal, *humble.*	uṁaıle;	contractedly, uıṁle.	uṁla.
uaral, *noble*	uaraıle;	„	uaırle.	uarla.
neaṁan, *fat.*	neaṁaıne;	„	neıṁne.	neaṁna.
(b) aluın, *charming.*	aluıne;	„	aılne.	aılne.
aoıbbın, *delightful.*	aoıbbıne;	„	aoıbbne.	aoıbbne.
bılır, *fond.*	bılıre;	„	bılre.	bılre.
mılır, *sweet.*	mılıre.	„	mılre.	mılre.
(c) ʒcanaṁaıl.	ʒcanaṁla;	„	ʒcanaṁla.	ʒcanaṁla.

It is the nature of the liquid letters to unite with the consonants to which they are in proximity, and thus elide the vowels. This is a law of phonetics, and therefore not peculiar to any language.

Obs.—The termination aṁaıl is contracted in Scotch Gaelic into aıl and eıl; as, feanaṁaıl, *manly;* Scotch Gaelic, feanaıl: flaıċaṁaıl, *princely;* flaıċeıl: cuaċaṁaıl (from cuaċ, *the left hand, the north,* the country as opposed to the word *town), ominous, sinister, left-handed, awkward, clownish, rustic;* Scotch Gaelic, cuaċaıl. In some few Irish works this contracted form has been adopted. What a strong affinity the termination aıl has to the English *ly*—man*ly* (man-*like*), prince*ly* (prince-*like*).

§ 73. Monosyllables spelled with the diphthongs ꟾa, ꟾu, ia, io, follow in, every particular, the analogy of the declension of nouns; as,

Nom. ⎱ ᵹeuṗ, *sharp.*
Acc. ⎰
Gen.   ᵹéiṗ; fem. ᵹéiṗe.
Dat.   ᵹeuṗ; fem. ᵹéiṗ.

"Peunla an cuil cnaoḃaiᵹ" (gen. case, masculine, of cnaoḃaċ agreeing with the noun cuil, *m., back,* gen. case of cul)—"the pearl of the branching tresses."—*Ancient Music of Ireland,* vol. i., p. 184.

"Do laḃair, 'r do tuᵹ rí Mars amaċ ar ḃrut
Na h-ianᵹail' ceiṅ' da faᵹail aiṁ ḃruaċ rruċ'
Sᵹamanḃaiṁ ruiṓce."
     Homer, book v. lines 39, 40.

Literally—"She spoke, and led Mars forth from the din of the fierce strife, Leaving him seated on the bank of Scamander's stream."

The adjective ceiṅ' (from cear, *stern*), in the second line, is gen. singular, feminine, for ceiṅe, agreeing with ianᵹail' (for ianᵹaile).

"Ca naḃair anoir a ċailín ḃiᵹ—Where have you been, my little girl.' (*Ancient Music of Ireland,* vol. i., p. 66.) ḃiᵹ, in this line, is the vocative case of beaᵹ.

§ 74. *Adjectives declined with Nouns.*—Adjectives beginning with mutable consonants are aspirated like nouns with which they agree. (See Rule 11, p. 38.)

The learner knows, from what has been stated in p. 37, that (1) nouns feminine, having the initial consonant mutable, are aspirated in the nominative and accusative singular—so are adjectives feminine; and (2) nouns masculine in the genitive—so are adjectives masculine. The vocative, like the vocative of nouns, is aspirated. The consonants not aspirated are the same—viz., ḋ, ċ, r, after ḋ, ċ, r, l, n; as, a ċailín ḋear, *O fair maid!*

An fear ᵹeal, *the white man.*

    Singular.   Plural.

Nom. ⎱ an fear ᵹeal.   na fir ᵹeala.
Acc. ⎰
Gen. an fir ᵹil.   na ḃ-fear nᵹeal.
Dat. do'n fear ᵹeal. do na fearaiḃ ᵹeala.
Voc. a fir ᵹil.   a feara ᵹeala.

(For other examples, see p. 77).

Note.—The nominative plural of adjectives masculine are commonly aspirated in the initial mutable, when the noun going before it ends in a consonant, as in the foregoing example. But if the noun terminate in a vowel, or in a consonant of the same class as the initial of the adjective—or in b, c, f, when the preceding consonant is b, c, r, l, or n, see p. 35—aspiration is not produced; as, na ceolta binne, *the harmonious melodies;* na carain dírgeácha, *the straight paths;* na báid trioma, *the heavy boats.*

OBS.—The initial mutable of adjectives is sometimes eclipsed, as in the foregoing examples—na b-fean n-geal; also in the following—"De bairr na fean fliab, agur de topaib na g-cnoc 'm-buan'—Of the tops of the ancient mountains, of the fruits of the everlasting hills." (*Deuteronomy,* xxxi. 5, *Irish Bible by Dr. MacHale.*)

"And when the adjective begins with a vowel, it has n prefixed; as, na b-fean n-aluin, *of the fair men.*"

The following examples show how nouns and adjectives beginning with a vowel are declined:

Example 1—óganac árd, *a tall young man.*

	Singular.	Plural.
Nom. Acc.	an t-óganac árd.	na h-óganaig árda.
Gen.	an óganaig áird.	na n-óganac n-árd.
Dat.	do'n óganac árd.	do na h-óganaigib árda.
Voc.	a óganaig áird.	a óganaca árda.

Example 2—óig aluin, *a beautiful virgin.*

	Singular.	Plural.
Nom. Acc.	an óig aluin.	na h-óige aluine.
Gen.	na h-óige aluine.	na n-óig n-aluin.
Dat.	do'n óig aluin.	do na h-óigib aluine.

*** In the dative singular the initial mutable of the adjective is not eclipsed, although that of the noun with which it agrees is. Aspiration, in this case, at present generally prevails. (See "Syntax.")

☞ In modern Irish the dative plural of nouns terminates in ib; that of adjectives does not, except those employed like nouns; as, "Air beodaib agur air marbaib—On the living and the dead." (*Apostles' Creed.*)

OBS. 2.—The plural of adjectives is formed according to the rules given for the formation of the plural of nouns.

§ 75.—*An Exercise containing many Adjectives.*

"Cé aluin tu, a ingín finn, ibir corr, ceann agur cnut,
Do beirim mo briatar féin nac b-fuil ionnta act cnjab dub.
Na déan díomar, na déan tnut; air deilb duine dán cum Dia.
Na bí baot-glórac na boinb; cuinnig do conn a'r do ciall.
Bí d'aontoil ir de téill cóir, na bnir do moide tar gac ní b,
Na bí guairmean, na bí gang; bí go macanta, mall, min.
Ní bí bog, a'r na bí cruaib; na bnir a'r na déan uaill arab féin.
Mo teagarg da ngeabair uaim, ir fada rracfar do cliu a g-céin."

"Though beautiful thou art, O fair daughter, in body, head, and form,
I give my own word that these are nothing but black clay.
Conceive not pride, then, nor jealousy on account of the figure of a body God has framed.
Be not vain-glorious, nor haughty; be mindful of your (being gifted with) reason and sense.
Be of one will and of right understanding; do not, above all, break thy vow.
Be not courting danger; be not rough; be becoming, retiring, gentle.
Be not soft, and be not hard; do not provoke boasting, nor express it yourself.
My advice should you accept from me, far shall thy fame spread—even to the remotest time."

Coṁaįnle Doįnģjoŋ.*

§ 76.—DEGREES OF COMPARISON.

Adjectives express the qualities of things. An adjective may have a certain quality—say (1), whiteness, as something differing from blackness or redness—and so far indicates a state or degree, which it can in some sense be called; or, viewing it in relation to some other definite object, it may have the quality (2) in a higher or lower degree; or (3) in relation to all other things of the same kind, it may possess the quality in a state which no other object possesses, and therefore in the highest or utmost degree. There are, then, three states, called degrees, which an adjective represents—(1) the positive, (2) comparative, and (3) superlative. They are termed degrees of comparison, for, even in the superlative, there is a comparison between the quality found in the special subject spoken of, and the like quality as it abides in all other things, taking each singly. This view of the superlative degree is correctly expressed in Gaelic by the form of words employed."—*Easy Lessons; or, Self-Instruction in Irish*, lesson 46—Dublin, published by John Mullany, 1, Parliament-street.

(a) The positive is the simple form of the adjective; as, caol, *slender;* ₅eanainaįl, *amiable.*

(b) The comparative expresses an increase or decrease of the quality, form, or number of one thing in respect to those that abide in some other.

(c) The superlative shows them to exist in the highest state, either absolutely or relatively.

§ 77. Comparison of equality, ċo; as, {le, *as, (with);* aȝuṛ, *as, (and).*

OBS.—Le, *with,* means *as* when the comparison of equality is drawn between two things; as, cá Seaġan "ċo" ano "le" Seaṁuṛ—John is as tall as James; "co" ṛean "le" Mạcuṛalem—as old as Mathusalem.

Aȝuṛ, *and,* means *as* when the comparison is drawn between two actual or possible states of the same or kindred things; as, cá Dįa "ċo" lạįoįṛ ann įuḃ "a'ṛ" bį ṛe ann né—God is *as* strong to-day *as* He was yesterday. Cá an ṛcolaįṛe "ċo" ṁaįc ann įuḃ "a'ṛ" bį ṛe bḷaȝaįn o ṛįn—the

---

* Composed by Angus O'Daly Fįoṇṇ, A.D. 1570, and copied from a MS. belonging to Dr. Murphy, late Bishop of Cork.

scholar is *as* good to-day *as* he was a year ago. Tá an t-oide "eo" foṡlamṫa "a'r" béiṡ re a ċoiḃċe—the professor is *as* learned *as* he ever will be.

§ 78. Comparison of superiority and of inferiority is the same as the genitive singular feminine followed by the conjunction 'ná or ioná; as,

Nominative.	Gen. Sing. Fem.	Comparative
trom, *heavy.*	troime.	troime, *more heavy.*

Is "troime" ór "'ná" airgiod—
Gold is heavier than silver.

Ní "troime" ór 'ná airgiod—
Gold is not heavier than silver.

An troime ór 'ná airgiod?—
Is gold heavier than silver?

In plain discourse níor is employed before the comparative, and 'ná, *than,* after; as,

Tá ór níor troime 'ná airgiod—
Gold is heavier than silver.

"In all perfect sentences the comparative is usually followed by ioná, *than;* and when preceded in the sentence by any verb, except the assertive verb is, it has níor prefixed.

"When the assertive verb is or as begins the sentence, níor cannot be used; as, is feárr mé ioná tu—I am better than thou."—*O'Donovan.*

Níor is a contraction of ní or níḋ, *a thing,* and the assertive verb is. "It is often," says O'Donovan, "found written in two words in very ancient manuscripts." In the past tense níor becomes ní buḋ (or ba):

"Trí h-aicmeaḋa iomarra, be treun feararṡ bo bí a g-coimairrin ann Eirinn, agus ní raiḃ rompa, no ó rin a leiṫ be macaiḃ Miḷeaḋ "ba mo," agur "ba annacta," "ba croḋa," agur "ba calma, ba clirbe" a g-cleararḃ goile agur gairgiḋ 'ná iab—There were three tribes or orders of champions at the same time in Ireland; and before them, nor since, there were not of the descendants of Milesius any set of men *taller,* more *manly,* more *courageous, stronger,* or more *expert* in feats of valour and bravery than they."—*Keating,* vol. i., p. 398. (Dublin, edited by William Haliday.)

"Gaiḃ mo teagarg, a inġin finn, ná beán bán ar bo ḃeilḃ.
Níor b' ailne tu a folt man ór, ná Uġna inġion Deirg;
Níor b'ailne tu a g-cruṫ raoin, 'ná Deirbre fa caoṁ cnuiṫ.

"Receive my instructions, O fair daughter; claim not superiority on account of thy frame.
Thou art not fairer in golden tresses than Una, the daughter of Dearg;
Thou art not fairer in a free frame than Deirdre of the gentle form."

From a MS. by Aøgus O'Daly Fionn (A.D. 1570).

§ 79. Sometimes ᴅe, for ᴅe é, *of it*, is annexed to the comparative so as to form a "synthetic union" with it; as, ꜰeáꞃꞃnᴅe, *better of;* ʒɩłeᴅe, *whiter of;* τꞃoꞃmꞃᴅe, *heavier of;* mꞃꞃᴅe for meáꞃáᴅe, *worse of;* ꞃꞃ ꜰeáꞃꞃnᴅe τu ꞃꞃn, *you are the better of that;* nꞃ mꞃꞃᴅe τu ꞃꞃn, *you are not the worse of that*—a form of expression quite common amongst the people whenever they give one anything that is likely to serve him. Nꞃ mꞃꞃᴅe τu ꞃꞃn is resolved to this form—nꞃ meáꞃá τu ᴅe ꞃꞃn, *thou (art) not the worse of that*. That ᴅe is a prepositional pronoun is certain (a) from authority: (1) "This should not be considered a second form of the comparative, as Stewart and, from him, Haliday have stated, but a mere idiomatic junction of ᴅe, i.e., *of*. ᴅe é."—*O'Donovan's Irish Grammar*, p. 121.

(2) "Post comparitivum frequens est particula ᴅe quæ videtur respóndere Latiné, eo"—*Zeuss—Grammatica Celtica*, vol. i., p. 283.

(b) Any person who speaks the language, and knows its structure, must of necessity agree with the two learned authorities just cited.

(c) No valid reason is given by Stewart, Haliday, nor by a certain late writer, in support of their views.

₊ The repetition of the positive is used—after the manner of the Italians—as a superlative absolute, by the peasantry: Ex.—τꞃom τꞃom, *heavy heavy;* móꞃ móꞃ, *great g eat;* cꞃoꞃn cꞃoꞃn, *crooked crooked*.

§ 80. The relative superlative, like the comparative, is the same in form as the genitive singular, feminine.

How then is it distinguished from the comparative? In three ways— first, by the use of the article before the noun, as in French and Italian; as,

Se Lonᴅon "án" báꞃle ꞃꞃ céꞃmáꞃláᴅe ᴅe báꞃłcꞃᴅ án ᴅomáꞃn—London is *the* most famous city of the cities of the world. *French*.—Londres est *la* plus fameuse de toutes les villes du monde.

Sꞃ án τ-Scánáꞃn án ábáꞃn ꞃꞃ ꜰáꞃᴅe ánn Cꞃꞃꞃꞃnn—The Shannon is the longest river in Ireland. *French*.—La Shannon est *la* plus longue de toutes les rivieres d'Irlande.

☞ The article precedes the *noun* in Irish; In English, French, Italian, the adjective. The article (án) is often left understood; as, ꞃe Seáʒán ꞃꞃ ʒeánáꞃmlá, *John is the friendliest;* án τe, *the person;* án neác, *the individual*, can be supplied—ꞃꞃ ꞃe Seáʒán án τe ꞃꞃ ʒeánáꞃmlá.

Secondly, the comparative degree is always followed by 'ná, *than;* the superlative is not.

Thirdly, with the comparative there are only two things contrasted, with the superlative, three or more are either expressed or understood.

NOTE.—This form of phrase—cꞃá ácá ꞃꞃ ꞃꞃnne; cꞃá ácá ꞃꞃ oꞃʒe, can certainly be translated by a comparative or superlative—Which of them is the *older;* which of them is the *younger:* or, Which of them is the *oldest;* which of them is the *youngest*. But in sentences of this formation the context is sufficient guide; for the question put, regards two or more than two— if the former, ꞃꞃ ꞃꞃnne and ꞃꞃ oꞃʒe are the comparative degree; if the latter, they are each the superlative.

Whenever it happens that the meaning in such phrases is ambiguous, it is well to supply such expressions as will destroy the ambiguity. For this reason some Irish grammarians have thought it necessary to add to the relative superlative form in such instances, the words ᴀɪɼ bɩċ, *at all;* ɼᴀn ḃoṁᴀn, *in the world,* and the like.

Adjectives in the comparative or superlative degree are not declined.

§ 81. The superlative absolute is formed by prefixing—as in French, *bien, tres, fort;* Italian, *molto, piu;* English, *far, much, very, by far, too*—to the positive, the following:

ᴀn, *very, as.*   ᴀn ṁᴀɩċ, *very good.*
ꝼɪoɼ, *true.*   ꝼɪoɼ-ṁᴀɩċ, *truly good.*
ᵹlė, *pure.*   ᵹlėᵹeᴀl, *purely white.*
ɼó, *very, excessively.*   ɼo ṁᴀɩċ, *excessively good, too good.*
ɼᴀɼɩ, *exceedingly* (German, *sehr*). ɼᴀɼɩ ṁᴀɩċ, *exceedingly good.*
úɼɩ, *very,* (in the depressing sense). úɼɩ-íɼɩol, *very lowly;* úɼɩ-ᵹɼᴀnᴀ, *very ugly.*

There are many primitive adjectives in Irish, such as cᴀoɩn, *kind;* bɩl, *fond;* onoċ, *bad;* oɩᴀn, *strong;* mċn, *great,* and the like, which—like φιλος, *fond;* κακος, *bad;* μεγὰς, *great;* ὠκυς, *swift*—unite with nouns, verbs, and other adjectives. In this case, of course, they precede the noun.

Uɩle, signifying *all,* follows its noun; in the sense of *every* it precedes it. Ex.—Ⱥn ḃomᴀn uɩle, *all the world;* nᴀ ḃᴀoɩne uɩle, *all the people;* ᴀn uɩle ḃuɩne, *every body.*

Ḋeᴀᵹ, *good;* onoċ, *bad;* ꝼɩonn, *white;* nuᴀḋ, *new;* ɼeᴀn, *old,* go before the noun.
Ṁᴀɩċ, *good;* olc, *bad;* bᴀn, ᵹeᴀl, *white, bright;* uɼ, *new, fresh;* ᴀoɼtᴀ, *old,* follow the noun.

§ 82. *Irregular Comparison.*—The following adjectives, which are, it is remarkable, irregular in most languages, are irregular in Gaelic. They do not form the comparative and superlative like to the genitive case singular, feminine.

beᴀᵹ, *little.*   nɪoɼ luᵹᴀ.   ɩɼ luᵹᴀ.
beᴀᵹ, *good.*   „ ḃeᴀċ.   „ ḃeᴀċ.
ꝼᴀḃᴀ, *long.*   „ ꝼᴀɩḃe.   „ ꝼᴀɩḃe.
                     „ { ꝼoɩᵹɼe, or   „ { ꝼoɩᵹɼe.
ꝼoᵹuɼ, *near.*   { ꝼoɩɼᵹe.   { ꝼoɩɼᵹe.
                       { neᴀɼᴀ.   { neᴀɼᴀ.

ꝼuꞃuꞃ, } easy.   ꝋꞃ ꝼuꞃꞃ, uꞃꞃ.   ꞁꞃ ꝼuꞃꞃ, uꞃꞃ.
uꞃuꞃ,

ꝛꞏꞃ, *near (of place).*   „ ꝛꞏꞃꞃꞁ.   „ ꝛꞏꞃꞃꞁꞁ, irreg. increase, ꝛꞏꞃꞃꞁ.

ꝛꞏꞃꞃꞁ, *near (of time).*   „ { ꝛꞏꞃꞃꞁꞁ.   „ { ꝛꞏꞃꞃꞁꞁ.
                             { ꞁeꞃꞃ.   { ꞁeꞃꞃ.
                             { ꞇuꞃꞃꞁ.   { ꞇuꞃꞃꞁ.

ꝛeꞃꞃꞁ, *short.*   „ ꝛꞏꞃꞃꞁꞁ.   „ ꝛꞏꞃꞃꞁꞁ.

uꞃ, *quick.*   { ꞁuꞃꞃꞁꞁ, *regularly.*   { ꞁuꞃꞃꞁꞁ.
                „ { ꞇuꞃꞃꞁ, *from*   „ { ꞇuꞃꞃꞁ
                { ꞇuꞃ, *beginning.*

ꞃꞏꞃꞃꞁ, } *many.*   { ꞃꞏ.   { ꞃꞏ.
ꞁoꞃꞏꞃꞃ,   „ { ꞁꞁꞃ.   „ { ꞁꞁꞃ.

ꞁoꞃꞃꞁuꞃꞁ, *dear.*;   „ ꞁoꞃꞃꞁuꞃꞁꞁe, or ,. ꞁoꞃꞃꞁuꞃꞁꞁe, ꞃꞁuꞃꞃ.
                        ꞃꞁuꞃꞃ.

ꞃꞏꞃꞇ, *good.*   „ ꝼeꞃꞃꞁꞁ.   „ ꝼeꞃꞃꞁꞁ.
ꞁꞁꞁꞁꞃ, *often.*   „ ꞃꞁoꞁꞃꞃ.   „ ꞃꞁoꞁꞃꞃ.
ꞃꞏꞃꞁ, *great*,   „ ꞃꞏ.   „ ꞃꞏ.
oꞁꞏ, *bad.*   „ ꞃꞁeꞃꞃꞃ.   , ꞃꞁeꞃꞃꞃ.

ꞇeꞃꞇ, *hot.*   „ { ꞇꞏoꞏ.   „ { ꞇꞏoꞏ.
                  { ꞇeoꞇꞃ.   { ꞇeoꞇꞃ.

For examples of all these, see *Easy Lessons* in Irish, part iv., lesson 47.

§ 83.—*Numeral Adjectives.*

Value.   Cardinals.   Ordinals.

1. ꞃoꞁ (pr. *ee-un*, in one syl.)   1st.   ꞇeuꝺ, ꞃoꞁꞁꞃꞃꝺ.‡
2. ꝺꞏ, ꝺꞃ.*   2nd.   ꝺꞏꞃꞁꞃꝺ, ꝺꞃꞃꞃ.
3. ꞇꞃꞁ.   3rd.   ꞇꞃeꞃꞃ, ꞇꞃꞁꞁꞃꝺ.
4 ꞇeꞃꞇꞃꞃ, ꞇeꞁꞇꞃe.†   4th.   ꞇeꞃꞇꞃꞃꞃꝺ.§
5. ꞇuꞁꝝ   5th.   ꞇuꞁꝝeꞃꝺ.
6. ꞃe.   6th.   ꞃeꞁꞃꝺ and ꞃeꞁꞃeꞃꝺ.
7. ꞃeꞃꞇꞇ.   7th.   ꞃeꞃꞇꞇꞁꞃꝺ.
8. oꞁꞇ.   8th.   oꞁꞇꞁꞃꝺ.
9. ꞃꞏoꞁ.   9th.   ꞃꞏoꞁꞃꝺ.

* Do, *two*, in the abstract; ꝺꞃ precedes and qualifies the noun.

† Ceꞃꞇꞃꞃ, *four* in the abstract; as, ꞃꞁꞁ é ꞃꞁ ceꞃꞇꞃꞃ, *that is four:* ceꞁꞇꞃe is accompanied by a noun ; as, ceꞁꞇꞃe ꞇoꞃ, *four feet.*

‡ The termination ꞁꞃꝺ annexed to the cardinal gives the corresponding ordinal.

§ The fourth of anything; hence it signifies *quarter, a quartan, a stanza, a portion of land, a ploughland, the thigh.*

Value.	Cardinals.		Ordinals
10.	deıċ.	10th.	deıċṁaḋ.
11.	aon-deuz.	11th.	aonṁaḋ deuz.
12.	dó deuz.	12th.	doṁaḋ deuz.
13.	tpí-deuz.	13th.	tpíṁaḋ deuz, or tpeap deuz.
14.	ceataıp-deuz.	14th.	ceatpamaḋ deuz.
15.	cuız-deuz.	15th.	cuızṁaḋ deuz.
16.	pé-deuz.	16th.	peṁaḋ deuz.
17.	peact-deuz.	17th.	peactṁaḋ-deuz.
18.	oct-deuz.	18th.	octṁaḋ deuz.
19.	naoı-deuz.	19th.	naoıṁaḋ deuz.
20.	fıċe, or fıċe.	20th.	fıċeaḋ.
21.	aon a'p fıċe, or aon aıp fıċıd.	21st.	aonṁaḋ aıp fıċıd.
22.	dó a'p fıċe, or dó aıp fıċıd.	22nd.	doṁaḋ aıp fıċıd.
23.	tpí a'p fıċe, or tpí aıp fıċıd.	23rd.	tpíṁaḋ aıp fıċıd.
24.	ceataıp a'p fıċe.	24th.	ceatpamaḋ aıp fıċıd.
25.	cuız a'p fıċe.	25th.	cuızṁaḋ aıp fıċıd.
26.	pé a'p fıċe.	26th.	péṁaḋ aıp fıċıd.
27.	peact a'p fıċe.	27th.	peactṁaḋ aıp fıċıd.
28.	oct a'p fıċe.	28th.	octṁaḋ aıp fıċıd.
29.	naoı a'p fıċe.	29th.	naoıṁeaḋ aıp fıċıd.
30.	deıċ a'p fıċe, ancient form tpıoċaḋ.	30th.	deıċṁaḋ aıp fıċıd.
31.	aon deuz a'p fıċe.	31st.	aonṁaḋ deuz aıp fıċıd
40.	dá fıċıd.	40th.	dá fıċıdeaḋ.
50.	deıċ a'p dá fıċıd, caozaḋ	50th.	deıċṁaḋ aıp dá fıċıd.
60.	tpí fıċıd.	60th.	tpí fıċıdeaḋ.
70.	deıċ a'p tpí fıċıd.	70th.	deıċṁaḋ aıp tpí fıċıd
80.	ceıtpe fıċıd, octṁoẓaḋ.	80th.	ceıtpe fıċıdeaḋ.
90.	deıċ a'p ceıtpe fıċıd.	90th.	deıċṁaḋ aıp ceıtpe fıċıd.
100.	ceuḋ.	100th.	ceuḋaḋ.
200.	dá ċeuḋ.	200th.	dá ċeuḋaḋ.
300.	tpí ċeuḋ.	300th.	tpí ċeuḋaḋ.
400.	ceıtpe ċeuḋ.	400th.	ceıtpe ceuḋaḋ.
1000.	mıle.	1000th.	mıleaḋ.

2000. ḋá ṁıle.   2000th. ḋá ṁıleaḋ.
3000. tpı ṁıle.   3000th. tpı ṁıleaḋ.
10,000. ḋeıċ ṁıle.   10,000th. ḋeıċ ṁıleaḋ.
1000,000. ṁıllıún.   1000,000th. ṁıllıúnaḋ.

§ 84. OBS.—Ðeuᵹ from ḋeıċ, *ten*, same as the English *teen*, annexed to the digits, gives the cardinal numbers above ten.

Numeral adjectives are found to go before the noun to which they refer. When a number greater than ten is employed the noun is placed between the digit and the decimal termination; as, tpı-ḋeuᵹ, *thirteen;* tpı-ḋuıne-ḋeuᵹ, *thirteen persons.*

☞ Some of the digits affect the initial mutable of the noun that follows by aspiration, others by eclipsis.

Aspiration is produced by aon, *one;* ḋá, *two,* except ḋá ḋ-tpıan, *two-thirds.*

Eclipsis by peaċt, *seven;* oċt, *eight;* naoı, *nine;* ḋeıċ, *ten,* and their compounds; as, peaċt-b-peap-ḋeuᵹ, *seventeen men;* oċt-ḋeuᵹ, *eighteen;* naoı ḋeuᵹ, *nineteen.* Of course they cause, when preceding vowels, n to be prefixed.—See Syntax; *Adjectives.*

No change occurs after tpı, *three;* ceıṫpe, *four;* cuıᵹ, *five;* pe, *six;* pıċe, *twenty;* tpıoċa, *thirty,* &c.

Fıċe, *twenty,* makes gen. pıċeaḋ; dat. pıċıḋ; nom. plur. pıċıḋ.

Ceuḋ, *a hundred;* gen. ċéıḋ; first dec., nom. plural, ceuḋa.

⁂ Ceuḋ, *first,* is preceded by the article (an, *the*); ceuḋ, *a hundred,* is not; as, ceuḋ pean, an *hundred* men; "an" ceuḋ pean, the *first* man. Mıle, *a thousand;* fourth dec., nom. plural, mılte.

Fıċe, *twenty;* ceuḋ, *a hundred;* mıle, *a thousand,* have a collective meaning, and hence have the noun in the singular number; as, ceuḋ ḋuıne, *an hundred persons (person);* mıle pean, *a thousand men (man).*

The ordinals ceuḋ, *first;* ḋapa, *second;* and tneap, *third,* aspirate the noun that follows them; as, an ċeuḋ pean, *the first man;* an ċeuḋ bean, *the first woman.* The ordinal oċtmaḋ, *eighth,* whether the noun following it be masculine or feminine, takes t before it; as, an t-oċtmaḋ ınᵹean, *the eighth daughter.*

§ 85.—*Numerals applied to Persons only.*

ḋıp, *a pair.*   peıpean, *six persons.*
{ beınt, *a couple.*   móp-peıpean, } *seven*
{ lanaṁaın, *a married couple.*   or peaċtap. } *persons.*
                                  oċtap, *eight persons.*
tpıúp, *a trio, three persons.*   naonḃap, *nine persons.*
ceaṫpap, *four persons.*   ḋeıċneaḃap, *ten persons.*
cúıᵹcap, *five persons.*   ḋaıneuᵹ, *twelve persons.*

The foregoing are compounded of the word pean and the numerals— three, four, five, six, seven; *v. g.,* peıpean is composed of pé, *six,* and pean, *man;* ḋaıneuᵹ is contractedly for ḋá-pean-ḋeuᵹ, *twelve men.* Hence this form of enumerating is applied to persons only, whether male or female; as, peıpean pean, *six men;* peıpean ban, *six women.* We could not correctly say móp-peıpean capal, *seven horses.* Ðıp and beınt are excepted, as the word pean enters not into their composition. They can, therefore, be con-

IRISH GRAMMAR. 89

nected with their own proper substantives. All these govern the noun in the genitive plural.

§ 86.—*Various Examples of Numeral Adjectives and Nouns.*

Simple Form.

Mas.	Fem.		
aon ógánac.	aon óig.	one youth.	one virgin.
bá ógánac.	bá óig.	two youths.	two virgins.
trí ógánaig, &c.	trí óige.	three youths.	three virgins.
reáct n-ógánaig.	reáct n-óige.	seven youths.	seven virgins.
oct n-ógánaig, &c.	oct n-óige.	eight youths.	eight virgins.
trí ógánaig beug.	trí óige beug.	thirteen youths.	thirteen virgins.

From this it appears that nouns following bá, *two,* are neither singular nor plural. It is a kind of dual number. But from this solitary instance it does not follow that there is a dual number in the Irish language.

In enumerating, without mentioning the noun, we say aon, *one;* bó, *two* trí, *three;* ceátáir, *four,* and not aon, bá, ceitre; bá and ceitre are used only when the noun is expressed.

The *articulated* form of the numeral adjective and noun is nearly the same as that of any other adjective and noun of the like gender.

Examples:

Mas.	Fem.		
an t-aon ógánac.	an aon óig.	one youth.	one virgin.
an bá ógánac.	an bá óig.	two youths.	two virgins.
na trí h-ógánaig	na trí h-óige.	three youths.	three virgins.
na reáct n-ógánaig.	na reáct n-óige.	seven youths.	seven virgins.
na reáct n-ógánaig beug.	na reáct n-óige beug.	seventeen youths.	seventeen virgins.

NOTE.—What a very close affinity exists among the several early branches of the great Indo-European family of languages may be best perceived from a list of numerals in the several languages.

Symbol.	Irish.	Welsh.	Latin.	Greek.	Teutonic.	Sanscrit.
1.	aon.	un	unum	ἐν	ein	eka
2.	bá. bo.	dau dwy	duae duo	δυω	tue	dwau
3.	trí.	trí	tres tria	πρεις τρια	thri	tri
4.	ceátáir.	pedwar	quatuor, qu = c or k	τεσσαρες τετορα	fiunar	chatur
5.	cuig.	pump	quinque	πέντε	finfe	pancha
6.	ré.	chwech	sex	ἑξ	sehs	shash
7.	reáct.	saith	septem	ἑπτα	sibun	saptan
8.	oct.	wyth	octo	οκτω	ohto	ashta
9.	naoi (pr. nhee).	naw	novem	εννεα	niguni	navan
10.	deic.	dég	decem	δεκα	tehau	dasan
20.	fice.	ugain	viginti	εικοσι Ϝεικοντι	tuentig	vinsati
100.	ceud.	cant	centum	ἑκατον	hunt	satam

CHAPTER IV.

THE PRONOUN.

§ 87. Pronouns stand for nouns. They are distributed into six classes—personal, compound personal, possessive, relative, demonstrative, interrogative, and indefinite.

§ 88. The personal pronouns are—

First Person.

Singular.
me, *I, me.*

Plural.
ſinn, *we, us;* inn, secondary or aspirated form.*

Emphatic Form.

miſe.
ſinn-ne.

Second Person.

tu, *thou;* secondary form, ṫu.

ſib,, *ye, you;* secondary or aspirated form, ib.

Emphatic Form.

tuſa.
ſib-ſe.

Personal pronouns of the first and second person are not characterized by gender, for the speaker and the person or thing spoken to are, from being present, sufficiently cognoscible.

Third Person—Masculine.

ſe, *he, him,* or *it;* e, secondary form for ṡe.†

ſiad, *they, them;* secondary form, iad.

Feminine.

ſi *(shee), she, her, it;* i, secondary form.

Emphatic Form.

ſe-ſan, ſi-ſe.
ſiad-ſan.

Zeüss shows that in the ancient language there had been a neuter pronoun—ed, *it;* as, iſ ed, iſ maiṫ daoib, *est "id" vobis bonum.*

"One striking example of this" (the fact that Zeüss consulted the old *glosses* in the Irish MSS. found in the monasteries of St. Gall and of Milan)

---

* The initial ſ, being at first changed by aspiration to ṡ (which = *h* in sound), was finally omitted.

† Ṡ (asp.) having been omitted.

"is, that before the researches of Zeüss the form of the *neuter gender* had never been discovered, nor is it yet acknowledged by any Irish scholar of Ireland. Zeüss found it throughout."—*From the Ulster Journal of Archæology—Notice by Dr. O'Donovan.*

§ 89. The personal pronouns are declined thus—

First Person, me, *I, me*.

	Singular.	Plural.
Nom. Acc.	me, *I, me.*	ſinn, *we, us.*
Gen.	mo, *of me, mine.*	ᴀṗ, *of us, our.*
Dat.	ᴅᴀm, *to me.*	ᴅuinn, *to us.*

Second Person, ᴛu, *thou.*

	Singular.	Plural.
Nom. Acc. Voc.	ᴛu, ṫu. *thou.*	ſiḃ, *you, ye.*
Gen.	ᴅo, *of thee, thine.*	ḃuṗ, *of you, your.*
Dat.	ᴅuiᴛ, *to thee.*	ᴅᴀoiḃ, *to you.*

☞ inn, iḃ, the secondary forms of ſinn and ſiḃ, are now in disuse.

The term ſiḃ, *you* (the *second person plural*), is *never* in Irish applied to an individual, like *you* English, *vous* French, *voi* Italian. *You*, must therefore when referring to a single individual, be translated by ᴛu.

Third Person, Masculine, Sé, *he, it.*

	Singular.	Plural.
Nom. Acc.	ſe, é, *he, him, it.*	ſiᴀᴅ, iᴀᴅ, *they, them.*
Gen.	ᴀ, *his, (of him) its (of it).*	ᴀ, *of them, theirs.*
Dat.	ᴅó, *to him, to it.*	ᴅoiḃ, *to them.*

Third Person, Feminine, Sí, *she, it.*

	Singular.	Plural.
Nom. Acc.	ſi, i, *she, it.*	ſiᴀᴅ, iᴀᴅ, *they, them.*
Gen.	ᴀ, *hers, its, of it.*	ᴀ, *of them, theirs.*
Dat.	ᴅi, *to her, to it.*	ᴅoiḃ, *to them.*

Since the third person admits only two genders, the neuter pronoun of other languages must be translated into Irish by ſe or ſi, according as the pronoun points out a noun of the masculine or the feminine gender, and conversely:

When ré, *he*, or rí, *she*, refer to nouns which, in the English language, are of the neuter gender, they are translated by the word *it*, *its*, like *il* and *elle* of the French in the like positions.

§ 90. *Affinity*.—Welsh, mi, *I*, *me*; ti, *thou*, *thee*; é, ó, *he*; hi, *she*: plural, ni, *we*, *us*; chwi, *you*; hwy and hwynt, *they*, *them*. Cornish, my, *I*; ty. *thou*; ef, *he*; hy, *she*; ny, *we*; why, *you*, y, *they*. How very like the Gaelic pronouns.

"Analogy leads us to suppose that the original state of the pronouns (*hé*, *hi*) was in Welsh as in Erse ré, rí; but the initial being softened, *he*, *hi*."— *Pritchard*, p. 272.

§ 91. The emphatic forms of the personal pronouns are,

Singular.   Plural.

mire, *I*, *me*.   rinn-ne.
tu-ra, tu-ra, *thou*, *thee*.   ríb-re.
ré-ran, é-ran, *he*, *him*, *it*. } riad-ran, iad-ran.
rí-re, í-re, *she*, *her*, *it*.

§ 92. What are these emphatic suffixes, ra, re, ran? They are broken forms of the demonstrative pronouns ro, *this*; rin, *that*—like ci, French, from the pronoun *ce*. If ro, *this*, be joined to mé or tu, the form me-ro, tu-ro, is obtained. In such compounds the leading and prominent syllable, and therefore the accented one, is me; tu, and hence ro, is not accented. To accommodate then the spelling to the sound, and to conform to the principle of assimilation so peculiar to Gaelic, ro is transformed into ra or re.

It was natural that the first and second persons singular and the second person plural, denoting things supposed to be present, should take as their suffix ra, *this*. rather than ran, *that*, for ra points out things present or near. It was natural, too, that the pronoun feminine, rí, *she*, should have the same suffix (ra) to distinguish it from ré, *he*, which takes ran.

It is plain that the suffix ran is from rin. Se-ran, *he*, = *that* person, as opposed to some others, or about whom there is or was question.

Why rin, *that*, rather than ro, *this*, should be the suffix of the third person singular, masculine, and the third person plural, it is easy to conceive, for the third person is that spoken of, therefore absent, or supposed to be absent, and fitly pointed out by rin.

Se-ran is more correct than re-rean, for ran as a suffix has, a certain defined meaning; its spelling should accordingly be defined. The only reason for changing ran into rean is (1) to give r the sound of *sh*; and (2) to conform to the rule of vowel assimilation. The (1) is not necessary, as r has, *after* e or i, the sound of *sh*; (2) is opposed to rule

§ 93. An old form of the plural, rinn, inn, *we*, was rní (Zeüss), still preserved in Welsh "*ni*," *we*; Latin, *nos*; Greek, νωϊ. Sinn-ne, therefore, is an union of the modern and the old pronoun—a reduplication, in fact, meaning, *we ourselves*. This reduplicate form is common to all the dialects of the Celtic, Welsh, Cornish, Erse, and Irish. The Welsh "*my*," *I*, becomes *my-vi* (as it were, *my-my*, the secondary form of *m* being *v*, and therefore *my-vi*);

"*thyn,*" *to us* (Cornish) is reduplicated "*thynny-ny,*" *to us* (*Norris—Cornish Grammar*, p. 32); Welsh, *nyni*—ᚈᚅᚅ-ᚅᚓ.

§ 94. The possessive pronouns have the same emphatic suffixes as the personal pronouns from which they spring; as,

мо сapa-ra, *my friend.*   aր ɼ-capa-ղe, *our friend.*
do capa-ra, *thy friend.*   buր ɼ-capa-ra, *your friend.*
a capa-ran, *his friend.*   ⎫
a capa-ra, *her friend.*   ⎬   a ɼ-capa-ran, *their friend.*

☞ The learner cannot but observe that the suffix after мо, *my*, is ra, and not ran or ne; and that after aր, *our*, the suffix is ղe, that of the nominative plural, and not re, ra, or ran.

§ 95. These suffixes are employed to add emphasis—(1) to personal pronouns; (2) to the broken forms of the personal pronouns.

Under this (2) heading are ranked—(1) the prepositional; (2) the possessive pronouns; (3) the personal endings of verbs, which are spent forms of the primitive pronouns.

Excepting the positions just pointed out, the emphatic particle is not introduced. If the use of emphasis or antithesis be necessary, the pronouns ro, *this*; rւղ, rud, *that*, are employed.

It is true that Keating, with the writers of his age, and such scholars and philosophers as O'Donovan and Zeuss, show that the pronouns rւ, re, ran, rean, are found in other positions besides those in which the personal pronoun, in its absolute or broken inflected forms, are embodied. Nevertheless on examination it is found that, in such instances, the syllables rւ, re, ran, rean, rւող, are corrupt spellings of the demonstratives ro, rւղ.

From this another question arises—should the demonstratives be thus confounded with the emphatic suffixes? It is plain that as they have a specifically defined meaning and office, they should have a settled spelling. If, however, any one choose to write them so, he has authority certainly in his favour.

The emphatic suffixes are commonly joined by means of a hyphen to the noun, pronoun, adjective, or verb immediately preceding; the demonstrative pronouns are not.

☞ The emphatic suffix comes after the noun and adjective—nay, it must be last, no matter what number of adjectives follow the noun; as, мо capa ծւհr, ɼրaծac ɼcaղaղajl-re, *my own fond, loving, amiable friend.*

Obs.—Ⅿւre, *I, me*, the emphatic form of мe, is compounded of мe, *I*, and re, the emphatic affix. It should therefore be spelled мe-re. This spelling is sometimes adopted; as, "Do ւղղւr Ⅿaddoc ouւղղ, *i.e.*, 'мeւrrւ,' aɼur Caւղbre—We are of Innis Maddoc, *i.e.*, I and Cairbre." (From the *glosses* in the MS. copy of Priscian quoted by Zeüss—preface.) This spelling, me-re, is occasionally found in "Self-Instruction" and in the "Imitation of Christ." Ɑ)ıre, however, is the common spelling sanctioned now by usage.

§ 96.—*Are Personal Pronouns inflected in Gaelic?*

Although Dr. Pritchard says that "the Celtic dialects, having no declension of the pronouns, properly so termed, supply the deficiency in a manner similar to that adopted in the Hebrew and other cognate languages" ("The Celtic Nations," p. 272), still it is true they are declined. They suffer inflection in a very slight degree only. The genitives of the personal pronouns mo, do, a, appear at first to have the meaning of possessives alone. If this were so, as a certain late writer on Irish grammar, having only a slight knowledge of the subject on which he wrote, maintains—then the personal pronouns in Irish would be indeclinable. But mo, do, a, have the meaning not only of the possessives *my, thy, his, her, their,* but also that peculiar to the genitives of personal pronouns—*mei* (Latin), *of me, tui, of thee; illius, of him, her;* which is plainly seen in every instance where pronouns go before verbs in the infinitive mood, or before participles. Τά ʀɪaδ 'ʒ mo buaıleaδ, *they are at the beating " of me"*—not *at my beating,* which in English is ambiguous, but in Irish quite clear, meaning that, I am the person receiving the beating, and not inflicting it. In all such instances, mo, do, a, are the genitive cases of the corresponding personal pronouns.

Again, mo, do, a, buɲ, have a certain etymological relation with me, tu, re, ɾıδ, ɾıaδ:

Personal Pronoun.	Genitive, or Possessive.
me, *I*.	mo, *of me*, inflected from me, *I, me*.
tu, *thou*.	do, *of thee* (ꜱ and τ of the same class.)
re, *he;* secondary form, é.	a, *his* (which is the broad inflection from e).

Personal pronouns have therefore at least two cases—the nominative and the genitive

Have they not a third also, the accusative, for é, í, ıaδ, differ from re, rı ɾıaδ? This change is only initial, not terminational; Besides, é, í, ıaδ, are clearly spent shapes of ré, ɾí, ɾıaδ (aspirated). Now, ré, ɾí, ɾıaδ (aspirated)—or é, ı, ıaδ, as they are commonly written—are nominative cases as really and as frequently as ré, ɾí, ɾıaδ, whenever they come, for instance, after passive verbs, or buδ, the past tense of the assertive form of the verb do beıé, *to be*. The fact is, both are forms—the one primary, the other secondary—of the nominative or of the accusative (just like *moi, I; je, I*, in French; or *ye, you,* in English), which do not differ in case.

Should not é, ı, ıaδ, be therefore spelled re, ɾı, ɾıaδ? Decidedly. "In those instances," to quote Dr. Latham's remarks, "the initial r, though converted into an aspirate in pronunciation, is sometimes retained in orthography, either with a dot over it or followed by *h*. But in either case the sibilant is lost. There seems to be no precise rule of orthography in this instance." (See "Easy Lessons," part i., pp. 39, 40.)

The secondary form of the personal pronouns, ré, ɾı, ɾıaδ, may be spelled with or without r. The former is supported by analogy and philology; the latter by usage.

The dative— a term which is here employed in the same sense, and for the same reason as it has been in treating of the declension of nouns—may be called, in a certain sense, a case—for the personal pronoun combined with the preposition is more than inflected; it is abbreviated—it is changed.

The personal pronouns in Gaelic are therefore, in the full sense of the term, declinable.

§ 97. Gaelic pronouns are the original forms of those pronominal elements which pervade all the other languages of the great Indo-European stock. On this subject we shall once more quote Pritchard:

"The personal pronouns in the Celtic dialects probably represent a very old or the primitive state of those parts of speech in the Indo-European languages. It may indeed in many instances be observed that the Celtic pronouns are the nominatives from which the oblique cases in those languages may be regularly formed; whereas these cases, in several examples that might be adduced, have little or no affinity to the vocables, which now stand to them in the relation of nominatives. The real nominatives appear to have been lost, and other words substituted in their places; but in the Celtic the original forms have been preserved."—*Eastern Origin of the Celtic Nations.* p. 272.

§ 98.—*The Personal Pronouns compounded with Prepositions.*

Seventeen of the simple prepositions combine with the personal pronouns. To their combinations is given the name *prepositional pronouns*, because they are nothing more than the prepositional cases of the personal pronouns, resembling very much the French, *du, des, av, aux,* or rather the Italian, *delli, alli, dagli, agli, nello, collo, sullo,* which are compounded of prepositions and pronouns.

The prepositions are—ᴀɪɢ (or ᴀɢ), *at;* ᴀɪɴ, *on;* ᴀɴɴ, *in;* ᴀꜱ, *out of;* cuɪɢe, *unto;* ᴅe, *from, of;* ᴅo, *to;* eɪᴅɪʀ or ɪᴅɪʀ, *between;* ꜰᴀoɪ, *under, for;* le, *with;* ʀoɪᴍ, *before;* ʀeᴀc, *beside;* ᴄᴀʀ, *beyond, over;* cʀɪᴅ or cʀé, *through,* or *by means of;* uᴀ, or ó, *from;* uɪᴍ, *about—* as, clothes *about* the body—uᴀꜱ, *above;* which are compounded with the personal pronouns, thus—

Preposition -	ᴀɢ.	ᴀɢ.	ᴀɢ.	ᴀɢ.	ᴀɢ.	ᴀɢ.	ᴀɢ.
Pronoun -	ᴍé.	cu.	ꜱé.	ꜱɪ.	ꜱɪɴɴ.	ꜱɪʙ.	ꜱɪᴀᴅ.

By omitting the final vowel of the personal pronoun in the singular number, and in the plural the secondary initial consonant, ꜱ, which in composition becomes aspirated, and then receives only the secondary sound (that of h), the combination aȝam, *to me*, &c., is formed; thus—

aȝm.   aȝt.   aȝsé.   aȝsí.   aȝinn.   aȝib.   aȝiaḃ, regularly.

The first, aȝm, cannot be sounded without the aid of a vowel between the consonants ȝ, m. In aȝinn and aȝib the spelling must be corrected in conformity with the rule caol le caol. Hence results the following correct form:

First Person.	Second Person.	Third Person.	
		Mas.	Fem.
S. aȝam, *at* (or in the possession of) *me*.	aȝat, or aȝaḃ.	aiȝe.	aici.
P. aȝainn, *at us*.	aȝaib.	aca.	

The termination of the third person plural has by length of time lost the direct form, and assumed that of the oblique or possessive (a).

Following analogy the ending of the second person singular should in all be t; but written and oral authority are in favour of the cognate letter ḃ, in a few instances, aȝaḃ, araḃ, ionnaḃ.

The third person singular, feminine, should for the same reason always end in i and not in é, yet some few of the feminine forms terminate in é. Aȝainn, aȝaib, aca, means *of us, of you, of them.* On the subject of this idiom *see Syntax*.

The reason the first person plural of all these prepositional pronouns ends in nn (double n) and not single n, is because it retains the spelling of rinn, of which it is compounded. A knowledge of the pronouns being so necessary in speaking the language, it is right for the learner to commit their forms and meaning to memory.

The emphatic form of aȝam is—

S. aȝam-ra,   aȝat-ra,   aiȝe-ran aici-re.
P. aȝainn-ne,   aȝaib-re,   aca-ran.

In like manner the preposition ar, *out of*, combines with the personal pronouns,

ar.   ar.
me; tu; ré, ri   rinn, riḃ, riaḃ.

From the union of both are formed—

aram, arat, ar, arti; arainn, araib, artu.

The learner perceives that in this manner the ending for the first person singular is m, of the second, t; of the third (mas.) that of the preposition, é being commonly left understood (fem.), i; plural, inn, iḃ, a.

IRISH GRAMMAR. 97

S. oṛm, *on me,*   oṛc,   aṛṛ,   aṛṛṛṛ.
P. oṛṛaṛṛṛ, *on us,*   oṛṛaṛḃ,   oṛṛṛa, or oṛċa.
S. cuṡam, *unto me,*   cuṡac,   cuṛṡc,   cuṛcṛ.
P. cuṡaṛṛṛ, *unto us,*   cuṡaṛḃ,   cúca.
S. ḋṛom, *of me,*   ḋṛoc,   ḋé,   ḋṛ
P. ḋṛṛṛ, *of us,*   ḋṛḃ,   ḋṛoḃ, or ḋṛoḃċa.]
S. ḋam, *to me,*   ḋuṛc,   ḋo,   ḋṛ.
P. ḋúṛṛṛ, *to us,*   ḋaoṛḃ,   ḋóṛḃ.
S. eaḋṛam, *between me,* eaḋṛaḋ, or } eṛḋṛṛ é eṛḋṛṛ ṛ.
                         eṛḋṛṛ cu, }
P. eaḋṛaṛṛṛ, *between us,* eaḋṛaṛḃ, eacṛa.
S. ṗúṛm, *under me,*   ṗúc,   ṗaoṛ,   ṗúṛċṛ.
P. ṗúṛṛṛ, *under us,*   ṗuṛḃ,   ṗúċa.
S. ṛoṛṛam, *in me,*   ṛoṛṛac, or } aṛṛ, { aṛṛcṛ,
                         ṛoṛṛaḋ,   }   ṛṛṛcṛ.
P. ṛoṛṛaṛṛṛ, *in us,*   ṛoṛṛaṛḃ,   ṛoṛṛca.
S. lṛom, *with me,*   leac,   leṛṛ,   leṛċc.
P. lṛṛṛ, *with us,*   lṛḃ,   leo.

NOTE.—"Re, or its combinations with the personal pronouns, though
found in modern printed books and manuscripts, is not used in the spoken
language in any part of Ireland, le being invariably used in its place."—
O'Donovan's Irish Grammar, p. 144.

Re, *with*, is used in manuscripts and printed books for le: its compound
form is—
S. ṛṛom, *with me,*   ṛṛoc,   ṛṛṛ,   ṛṛa.
P. ṛṛṛṛ, *with us,*   ṛṛḃ,   ṛṛu.

"Le is the only form of this preposition now used in Ireland in the spoken
language, though ṛe is found in most modern books and manuscripts."

S. ṛóṛṛam, *before me,*   ṛoṛac,   ṛoṛṛe,   ṛoṛṛpṛ.
P. ṛóṛaṛṛṛ, *before us,* ṛoṛaṛḃ,   ṛómpa.
S. ċaṛṛṛ, *over me, by me,* ċaṛac,   ċaṛṛṛṛ,   ċaṛṛṛcṛ.
P. ċaṛaṛṛṛ, *over us, by us,* ċaṛaṛḃ, ċaṛṛca.
S. cṛṛom, *through me,*   cṛṛoc,   cṛṛḋ,   cṛṛċṛ.
P. cṛṛṛṛ, *through us,*   cṛṛḃ,   cṛṛoċa

There is no reason for aspirating the 'c of ċaṛ and of cṛc, and their
compounds; the usage in the spoken language is to aspirate them.

S. uaṛm, *from me,*   uaṛc,   uaṛḋc,   uaṛḋċc.
P. uaṛṛṛ, *from us,*   uaṛḃ,   uaċa.
S. uaṛam, *above me,*   uaṛac, or } uaṛa,   uaṛṛcṛ.
                          uaṛaḋ,   }

5

P. uaṟaınn, *above us,*   uaṟaıḃ,   uaṟca.
S. umam, *about me,*   umac,   uıme,   uımpı.
P. umaınn, *about us,*   umaıḃ,   umpa.

"The (Keltic dialects) have two series of personal pronouns, the distinct or entire pronouns, which are chiefly used as nominative cases . . . and *abbreviated pronouns*, used in regimen, particularly after prepositions."— *Prichard's Eastern Origin of the Celtic Nations*, 2nd ed., p. 270.

"Observe the difference in sound and meaning between the prepositional pronouns ḃaoıḃ (*dhuee-iv*, pr. in one syllable), *to* you; ḃıḃ (*dheev*), *of* you; ḃóıḃ (*dhō-iv*), *to* them; ḃſoḃ (*dhee-iv*, pr. in one syllable), *of* them; sometimes written ḃſoḃéa.

"The first, ḃaoıḃ, *to* you = ḃo ɼıḃ, second person plural, compounded of the preposition ḃo, and ɼıḃ. The learner will notice that the broad vowels, a, o, come after ḃ, because o in ḃo, the preposition with which it is compounded, is broad—thus, at first it was, ḃo-ɼıḃ, and then subsequently it assumed the present spelling, ḃaoıḃ.

"The second, ḃıḃ, *of* you, is compounded of ḃe, *of*, and ıḃ; e of ḃe is a slender vowel; hence ḃſıḃ: ſ is pronounced long, like *ee*.

"Ḃóıḃ = "ḃo" ıaḃ, *to them*.
"Ḃſoḃ = "ḃe" ıaḃ, *of them*."—*Easy Lessons*, p. 216, Part III

"In Connaught ḃſoḃ, *of them*, is pronounced as if written ḃaoḃéa (ſ thick), which is not analogical, and not borne out by the authority of the written language. In the South of Ireland and in the Highlands of Scotland the ḃ is always pronounced slender in their combinations, and correctly, if it be granted that the preposition is ḃe and not ḃo."—*O'Donovan*, p. 139. Stewart, p. 129.

Again, in the West of Ireland, and most parts of the North, ḃo, *to*, when combined with ıḃ, *ye* or *you*, is pronounced ḃaoıḃ, and it is sometimes so written by Keating (p. 144), and generally so by O'Molloy and Donlevey; but in the South it is always written and pronounced ḃıḃ, the ḃ being slender; but this is obviously not analogical, for it should be the form to represent the union of ḃe, *off* or *from*, and ıḃ, *ye* or *you*. (*O'Donovan*, p. 14.)

The third person plural of each of the prepositional pronouns ends in a, except ḃſoḃ, *of them;* ḃóıḃ, *to them*. This peculiarity arises (see Z üss, p. 342) from the fact of there being old dative endings which still adhere to the prepositions ḃe, ḃo. In Connaught both words are, according to analogy, pronounced as if ending in a.

§ 99. *Spelling of* ḃam, *to me*.—Our reasons for not aspirating m in the prepositional pronoun ḃam, *to me*, compounded of ḃo, *to*, and me, *I*, or *me*, are:

First, because in the spoken language the word has not been, byany whom we have heard speak Irish, pronounced with m aspirate. Dr. O'Donovan says ("Irish Grammar," p. 140) that "in the South of Ireland ḃam is generally pronounced ḃum, and sometimes even um; as, caḃaıɼ ḃam ḃo lam, pronounced as if written caḃaıɼ um ḃo lam." Besides, if m be aspirated, the pronoun ḃam, *to me*, cannot be distinguished from ḃaṁ, *an ox*.

Secondly, because it is opposed to a principle of analogy clearly deducible from the body of prepositional pronouns—that the initial consonant of the personal pronoun does not, when combined with the preposition, suffer aspi-

IRISH GRAMMAR. 99

ration; as, oṅṅ, *on me;* onc, *on thee;* ḃıoṁ, *of me;* ḃıoc, *of thee;* ꝼuıṁ, *under me, for me, about me;* ꝼuıc, *under thee;* lıoṁ, *with me;* ċaṅıṅ, *over me;* cṅıoṁ, *through me,* &c. Now in these and all other instances the initial of the personal pronoun, ṁ or c, is not aspirated when compounded with those prepositions which usually cause aspiration. Why, then, in this particular instance should ṁ be aspirated when compounded with ḃo, *to,* and not when compounded with the other prepositions? It is clear that there is no reason for it; if, however, there were, should not c of cu (*thou*), compounded with ḃo (*to*) be also, for that same reason, aspirated in ḃuıc—thus, ḃuıc? But it is not, and never has been, therefore ṁ in the pronoun ḃaṁ should not. Taking both reasons together it is plain that, contrary to certain authorities, the form ḃaṁ (having ṁ aspirated) is not strictly and classically correct.

The *initial* (ḃ) of ḃaṁ is aspirated whenever it follows a consonant with which if compounded it would, on phonetic principles, admit aspiration; as, caḃaıṅ ḃuıṅṅ, *give us;* maıc ḃuıṅṅ, *forgive us;* ṙıoċċaıṅ ḃuıṅṅ, *peace to us.* After ṅ of caḃaıṅ; c of maıc, it is aspirated; after ṅ of ṙıoċċaıṅ it is not. (See p. 35, exception 1.)

§ 100. Seaċ, *besides* (Latin, *secus*), is at present seldom found in the compound form:

| ṙeaċaṁ, | ṙeaċac, | ṙeaċ a, | ṙeaċ ı, |
| *beside me.* | *beside thee.* | *beside him.* | *beside her.* |

| ṙeaċaıṅṅ, | ṙeaċaıḃ, | ṙeaċa, |
| *beside us.* | *beside you.* | *beside them.* |

Neither is uaṙaṁ (*above me*) now in use; in its stead oṙ cıoṅṅ (*above*) is employed; nor are these combinations—ıoṙaıṁ (*under me*), ḃeaṙaṁ (*at my right hand*), cuacaṁ (*at my left hand*)—which are found in St. Patrick's hymn, in *Liber Hymnorum:*

Cṙıoꞅc ꝼoṙaṁ! Cṙıoꞅc uaṙaṁ!
Cṙıoꞅc ḃeaṙaṁ! Cṙıoꞅc cuacaṁ!
Christ be *under me!* Christ be *over me!*
Christ be beside me,
On *left hand* and right.

For a full explanation of the meanings of the several prepositions see chapter on prepositions.
For their idiomatic use see "Syntax."

§ 101. *Possessive Pronouns.*—The possessive pronouns are formed from the personal by a slight modification of the ending; thus, from me, *I,* is formed mo, *my.*

They are—mo, *my;* ḃo, *thy;* a, *his;* a, *her;* aṙ, *our;* ḃuṙ, *your;* a, *their.* (See section 24, rule 1, p. 34; section 27, p. 40.)

The vowel ꜵ. as a possessive pronoun, signifies (1) *his*, (2) *her*, (3) *their*.

(1) When signifying *his*, it aspirates; as, ꜵ ċꜵꞃꜵ, *his friend*.
(2)   „   *her*, it does *not*; as, ꜵ cꜵꞃꜵ, *her friend*.
(3)   „   *their*, it eclipses: as, ꜵ g-cꜵꞃꜵ, *their friend*.

On the other hand, going before a vowel,

(1) ꜵ, *his*, does *not* aspirate; as, ꜵ ꜵnꜵm, *his soul*.
(2) ꜵ, *her*, does *aspirate the vowel*; as, ꜵ h-ꜵnꜵm, *her soul*.
(3) ꜵ, *their*, causes ꞃ to be prefixed; as, ꜵ ꞃ-ꜵnꜵmꜵ, *their souls*.

§ 102. The pronouns mo, ꞇo, &c., cannot, like *mine* and *thine*, stand alone without the substantive being expressed; as, *this is mine*, ꞃ é ꞃo mo-ꞃꜵ—the noun must be expressed; as, ꞃ é ꞃo mo leꜵbꜵꞃ-ꞃꜵ, *this is my book*.

Féin, *self*, is, as in English, annexed to the possessive as well as to the personal pronouns.

Ꜷo, ꞇo, ꜵ, *his*; ꜵ, *her*; ꜵ, *their*; ꜵꞃ, *our*, are, in published works and MSS., abbreviated when connected with the prepositions ꜵnn or ꜵ, *in*; ꞇo, *to*; le, *with*; ó, *from*, and adverbial particles ending in a vowel.

Singular.

ꜵm, *in my*, written for ꜵnn mo, or for ꜵ' m'
ꜵꞇ, *in thy*,   „   ꜵnn ꞇo,   „   ꜵ' ꞇ'.
'nnꜵ, *in his or her*, „ ꜵnn ꜵ,   „   'nn ꜵ.

Plural.

nꜵꞃ, *in our*, written for ꜵnn ꜵꞃ, or for 'nn ꜵꞃ.

'nnꜵ, *in their*,   „   ꜵnn ꜵ   „   'nn ꜵ.

Singular.   Plural.

Ꜷo, *to*.

ꞇom, *to my*,   for ꞇo mo.   ꞇꜵꞃ, *to our*, for ꞇo ꜵꞃ.
oꞇ, *to thy*,   „   ꞇo ꞇo.
ꞇ' ꜵ, *to his or her*, „ ꞇo ꜵ.   ꞇ' ꜵ, *to their*, „ ꞇo ꜵ (*their*).

lem, *with my*, for le mo.
leꞇ, *with thy*, „   le ꞇo.

As, "beiṫ ꜵn ꜵlꞇóiꞃ nꜵoiṁeꜵ le m' ġlóꞃ—And the altar shall be sanctified by my glory."—*Exodus*, xxix., 43.

"Infiguntur ante verba consonæ nudæ pronominales ut *m, n, t, b, d, n, s*, post particulas exeuntes in vocales, verbales *no, ꞃo,* &c. . . . . . Ro m' ꞃoiꞃꞃꜵ, *salvavit me*; ꞃo b' ꞃoiꞃꞃꜵꞃl, *salvabit vos*; ní m' ċꜵꞃꜵꞇꞃꜵ, *non amaut me*. Fit idem adeo post verbum subst. ꞃ (est): iꞃꞃu m' éċen, necessitas mihi incumbit. *i. e.*, est mihi necessarium."—*Zeüss.*, p. 335.

Although found thus amalgamated in well-written *Irish* books, yet the simpler and more intelligible way to write such words would be to give the pronoun and preposition separately.

§ 103. *Relative Pronouns.*—ᴀ, *who, which, what, that, all that;* noċ, *who, which;* naċ, *who not, which not*—Latin, *nequis;* noċ, *who,* goes before the assertive verb, ir, *is;* buḋ, *was;* a, *who,* never goes before ir, buḋ.

Da signifies sometimes *who, which;* at others = ḋe a, *of which, of whom.*

Do, the sign of the perfect active Indicative, is employed very often as a relative pronoun; as, "Toiġaḋap ċuca mar mná, iaḋ buḋ ṁo 'do' ṫaiṫniġ leo ḋe'n iomlán—They selected for themselves as wives those *who* were most pleasing to them of all."—*Gen.* vi. 2.

The pronoun noċ, *who,* or a, *who,* is omitted before do. The omission of the relative before a verb is compensated for by the fact, that verbs in Irish have a special ending when employed after a relative clause.

§ 104. *Interrogative Pronouns.*—Cia, pronounced like the Italian "*che,*" *who, which, whom;* ca, *what, where;* ciḋ, caḋ, *what,* Latin, *quid;* Welsh, *pa.* Ġo ḃé, which is found in a great many Irish books, is only a corrupt form of caḋ é, *what (is) it?* Cneuḋ, *what,* is compounded of caḋ, *what,* and ruḋ, *res* (Latin), *a thing.*

After the interrogative pronouns the verb *to be, is, was, am,* and their inflections, are omitted; *who (am) I?* cia mire? *who art thou?* cia ṫura? *who is this?* cia é ro? literally, *who (is) he, this? This (is) he,* ro é—ir, *is,* is understood between ro and é.

§ 105. *Demonstrative.*—So, *this, these;* rin, *that, those;* ruḋ, *that, yonder,* of which uḋ appears to be a secondary form, at first written ruḋ, and then after a time uḋ, to make spelling conform to sound. Uḋ, like ruḋ, comes after nouns and pronouns: cia ré, an ḟear uḋ? *who is that man (yonder)?* "Cia riaḋ uḋ? *what means those*" *(what are these yonder?)* says Esau to Jacob.—*Gen.* xxxiii. 5.

"Suḃ," says Connellan, "is generally used with personal pronouns, and uḋ with nouns." This is a distinction without a difference.

So, this, following a word, the last vowel of which is slender, is by some writers written ṛeo.

It would be well, however, not to change its spelling. It is radically incorrect, though not against usage, to write it ṛı or ṛe, for then it (1) assumes the appearance of the suffix, and (2) leads the reader to infer a change in meaning from a change of spelling.

"It is true these pronouns—ṛo, ṛın—come after the noun which they serve to point out ; yet their demonstrative character is fully attained by aid of the article ąn or ną, *the,* which must always go before the noun whenever the demonstrative is to follow ; as, *this man,* is in Irish expressed thus, *the man this*—ąn ṛeąn ṛo ; *these men, the men these*—ną ṛın ṛo."—*Easy Lessons,* p. 83, fifteenth lesson.

§ 106. The *Indefinite Pronouns* are : ą, *all that, that which ;* ąoın, *any, one ;* ąı) ṫe, *he who, whoever ;* cáċ, *all,* gen. cáıċ ; ceaċṫąp, *either ;* ṅeaċṫąp, *neither ;* cıą b' é, *whoever,* also written ʒıbé, cıbé, contractedly for cıą buḋ é ; cıą b' é ąıṗ bıċ, *any one at all ;* eıʒın, *some, certain person ;* eıle, *other,* written also ąıle ; *alh,* Welsh ; ἄλλος, Greek ; *alius,* Latin ; ʒaċ, *each ;* ʒaċ eıle, *every other ;* uıle, *all ; alle,* German ; *oll,* Welsh ; ʒaċ uıle, *every individual ;* ą ċeıle, *each other ;* oıṗeaḋ, *as much ;* oıṗeaḋ ąʒuṛ, *as much as ;* oıṗeaḋ le ceıle, *each as much as the other ;* "Oıṗeaḋ le ceıle ḋe ʒaċ cuıḋ ḋıoḃ."—*Exodus,* xxix. 34.

Cuıḋ, *a portion of, some ;* neaċ, *any one, an individual,* are nouns.

*** All the pronouns, except the personal and cáċ, are indeclinable.

☞ Why the plural possessive pronouns, and ą, *whom,* a relative (oblique case), cause eclipsis—see " Syntax."

CHAPTER V.
§ 107.—THE VERB.

The verb is that *word* in a sentence which affirms or declares something of its subject. The noun and verb are the two essential elements of a sentence.

The verb affirms the state of being, acting, enduring the effect of action. Verbs are classified, therefore, into active and passive, to which are added the substantive verb, *to be,* ḋo ḃeıṫ. The active is two-fold—*intransitive,* transitive. In the former the effect of the action does *not pass over* to the object; as, eıɲıźım, *I arise;* in the latter it does; as, ɒuɲʌım, *I shut*—ɒún ʌɲ ɒoɲuɾ, *shut the door.*

§ 108. *Moods and Tenses.*—As life, action, and passion—*i.e.*, the enduring the effect of action, are different in different modes and times, so it is necessary to represent these different states. On this account *moods* and *tenses,* by which the manner and the time are expressed, necessarily belong to verbs.

§ 109. *Number of Moods.*—There are in Gaelic five moods—the imperative, the indicative, the conditional, the optative, the infinitive.

How is the optative a mood? Because, in the active voice, at least, it has in most verbs a specific form.

Has not the conditional also a specific form; and is it for that reason called a mood? Some grammarians place the conditional in the rank of moods; others, as the author of the Dublin French Grammar, amongst the tenses. There are reasons on both sides. It has only one tense, and that tense holds the same relation to the future that the imperfect tense does to the present; as,

    Present - ɒuɲʌıɲ, *I shut.*
    Imperfect - ɒuɲʌıɲɲ, *I used to shut.*
    Future - ɒuɲṗʌɒ, *I will shut.*
    Conditional - ɒʌɲṗʌıɲɲ, *I would shut.*

(1) On account of this analogy, therefore; and (2) for the learner's sake not to multiply moods unnecessarily; (3) to conform to the approved practice in our schools and colleges, the conditional is placed in the rank of tenses, immediately after that of the future.

The other modifications of verbal meaning are expressed, not by any specific form, but by combinations—sometimes of particles, sometimes of words.

The subjunctive is like the indicative.

The potential is formed by a combination of words expressive of ability, power.

§ 110. The imperative mood expresses command; the indicative declares or asserts; the optative—a mood so peculiar to Greek verbs—expresses a wish; the infinitive (from *in, not,* and *finis, end, limit*), not being trammeled by person, number, tense, mood, expresses its meaning in an unlimited manner.

The imperative is the root from which the other moods with all their tenses and persons spring.

All the moods, except two, are independent, not requiring the presence of other moods for their use or meaning in a sentence. The two which are dependent are the subjunctive and infinitive.

Being like the indicative, the subjunctive in English and Gaelic is easy, compared to its use in Latin and Greek; yet the student ought to know that it expresses purpose, motive, end, or object, and usually follows some verb, or depends upon some clause expressed or understood.

§ 111. Neither the regular nor irregular verbs in Gaelic have, in the sunjunctive mood, a specific form different from that of the indicative. Dr. O'Donovan says (" Irish Grammar." p. 150): " Some of the irregular verbs have a subjunctive mood." " This mood the regular verbs want altogether" (p. 170). Again, treating of the verb ɓéʌɲʌɒ. he uses these words: "That this and other irregular verbs have a subjunctive mood is quite clear from the fact that the indicative form could not be used after ná̇ċ. ċo. ʓo, &c., as, ná̇ċ ḋennḁıp, *that thou didst not.*"

The fact is, some of the irregular verbs have two forms of the indicative— the direct or primary form, and the indirect or secondary, formed from some obsolete verb of kindred meaning. The indirect usually follows particles of interrogation, supposition, negation, and the like; yet the mood to which it belongs is really the indicative. Take, for instance, the word which Dr. O'Donovan says belong to the subjunctive—ḋennḁıp. This is plainly of the indicative, as is seen from the following examples:

    ŗınneḁp, *I have done.*
    nı ḋeḁnnḁp. *I have not done.*
    ʓo n-ḋeḁnnḁp, *that I have done.*

Is it not plain that if the form n-ḋeḁnnḁp, in the third line, be in the subjunctive mood, so also is ḋeḁnnḁp in the second; but ḋeḁnnḁp, in the second line, is not the subjunctive—for who will say that *I have done* and *I have not done* are in two different moods. Ḋeḁnnḁp, second line, is therefore of the indicative mood, and hence ḋeḁnnḁp, in the third, being like the indicative in form cannot, according to Dr. O'Donovan's theory, be the subjunctive.

It is true, however, that after all particles of questioning, denying, supposing, and those that express relation, the secondary form is commonly, but not always, employed.

§ 112.—TENSE.

Tense is a specific form of the verb corresponding to a specific meaning in time.

Time is either past, present, or to come. Hence there are three great tenses—(1) the present, (2) the past, (3) and the future. The present tense denotes present time; the past, past time; the future, future time.

The present tense is two-fold:

(1) { 1. The simple present.
   2. The consuetudinal or habitual present.

The simple present denotes an action going on; the habitual, habitual action.

The past also is of two kinds:

(2) {
1. The one may be called the imperfect, expressing a continuation in the state of action or suffering, much like the imperfect tense in Latin and Greek verbs; as, ʓpá̇ḋuıʓınn, *amabam, I used to love.*
2. The other is the perfect tense, and denotes the same time as the historic perfect of Latin verbs; ex.—ḋo ʓpá̇ḋuıʓeḁp, *amavi, I loved, or have loved.*
}

(3) The future foretells.

To these may be added the conditional.

The number of tenses, five—

(1) THE PRESENT { simple.
consuetudinal or habitual { relative negative.
relative affirmative.

☞ The relative affirmative form is peculiar in Gaelic. The verb, by thus assuming a specifically different form after the relative, can, without any detriment to language or sense, dispense with the use of the relative pronoun. This omission often occurs.

(2) The imperfect; (3) perfect; (4) future; (5) conditional.

§ 113. *Number, Person, Inflection of Verbs.*—" A noun," says Latham (" English Language," 3rd ed., p. 289), denotes an object of which either the senses or the intellect can take cognizance—and a verb does no more. The only difference between the two parts of speech is this—that whereas a noun may express any object whatever, verbs can only express those objects which consist in an action."

Being in such close relation with the noun, and entirely directed by its own subject, it is plain that the verb has number and person. (See sections 41, 42, p. 55.)

Number, person, mood, and tense, therefore belong to verbs; number and person, they claim on account of their substantival character; mood and tense, on account of their purely verbal character.

The verb in Gaelic is inflected in number, in person, in tense, and in mood. (See Conjugation of Verb.)

§ 114. *Conjugation—Are there two in Gaelic?*—Conjugation viewed absolutely denotes the general form of the verb when inflected in full; viewed relatively it denotes that one class of verbs has, in some tenses, specific endings differing from those which another class of verbs assume in the same. Verbs thus varying in termination are said to differ in conjugation. It is enough to remind the scholar that in Latin the verbs am*are* and reg*ere* have not, in some tenses, the penult syllable respectively alike, and that on this account they are said to be unlike in conjugation. In French grammar it is so. The verbs parl*er* and rend*re* are not of the same conjugation. Having premised this much on special conjugations in other languages, what is to be said of their number in Gaelic? That there are two. This we prove. It is a fact that in Irish there is a class of verbs which make the future tense in ocab, and the conditional in ocaınn; and another class, which make the future in ꝼab, and the conditional in ꝼaınn. The endings ꝼab, ꝼaınn, of the one, differ specifically from ocab, ocaınn, of the other class. That they do so is confirmed even by those grammarians who hold there is only one conjugation of Irish verbs. They have classed those verbs that end in ıḃ, m, ıl, ır, and in general verbs of two syllables in the root as exceptions to their single conjugation. Hence, as they are exceptions, it is certain they differ. But anything that becomes an exception to a general rule is always supposed to belong to a class which, in number, are fewer than those that constitute the foundation for the general rule. Is that the case here? Far from it. The rule can then be no longer general if the exceptions form a class of verbs nearly as numerous—nay, perhaps more so than those that are regulated by it. This is plain. Now, dissyllabic verbs ending in uiġ and in iġ alone form in Irish a very numerous class of words, nearly quite as numerous as those of one syllable. Add to them verbs of various other endings, and what a very vast class of verbs of two syllables in the root have we not got. Why should such a large body of verbs be exceptions? Is it not the safer and the more correct way to form them into a conjugation? Decidedly. It is therefore true that there are two specifically distinct conjugations in Irish—

The *first* of *one* syllable in the root;
The *second* of *two* syllables in the root.

But, it may be urged, this mode of arguing will prove that there are three conjugations, for some verbs end in ɾib (i a slender vowel); other in ɾaḃ (a a broad vowel): the syllables differ—therefore, so do their special forms of conjugation. Answer.—The syllables ɾib and ɾaḃ, with their inflections, are the same in sound and meaning, and they take the vowel i or a in the spelling to conform to the principle of vowel assimilation, expressed in the Rule, "slender to slender, and broad to broad."

§ 115. SYNOPTICAL CONJUGATION OF THE SUBSTANTIVE VERB
do beiṫ, *to be.*

		Singular.	Plural.
Imperative Mood.		1. ——— 2. bí. 3. bíoċaḋ ɾe.	1. bímuiɾ. 2. bíoḋ. 3. bíoiɾ.
INDICATIVE MOOD.	Present Tense.	1. táim. 2. táiɾ. 3. tá ɾé.	1. támuiḋ. 2. taṫaoi. 3. táiḋ.
	Present tense preceded by the particles an, *whether*; go, *that*; ní, *not*; naċ, *not.*	1. b-ɸuil-im. 2. ,, -iɾ. 3. ,, ɾé.	1. b-ɸuil-muiḋ. 2. ,, -ṫí. 3. ,, -iḋ.
	Habitual Present.	1. bíḋ-im. 2. ,, -iɾ. 3. ,, ɾé. bíḋ-eann mé, tú, ɾé.	1. bíḋmuiḋ. 2. bíḋṫí. 3. bíḋiḋ. bíḋ-eann ɾinn, ɾib ɾiaḋ.

SYNOPTICAL CONJUGATION OF THE SUBSTANTIVE VERB
ᴅo beɩṫ, *to be,—continued.*

		Singular.	Plural.
INDICATIVE MOOD.	Assertive Present.	1. ɩr mé. 2. ɩr ṫú. 3. ɩr ré.	1. ɩr rɩnn. 2. ɩr rɩb. 3. ɩr rɩaᴅ.
	Imperfect.	1. bɩò-ɩnn. 2. ,, -ṫeà. 3. ,, -eaò ré.	1. bɩòmuɩr. 2. bɩòṫɩ. 3. bɩòɩr.
	Perfect.	1. bɩò-ear. 2. bɩò-ɩr. 3. bɩ ré.	1. bɩ-map. 2. bɩ-baṗ. 3. bɩ-ᴅaṗ.
	Perfect after the particles an, ᵹun, nɩon, &c.	1. ɲab-ar. 2. ,, -aɩr. 3. ɲab ré.	1. ɲab-amaṗ or ɲab-maṗ 2. -abaṗ, ,, -baṗ. 3. -aᴅaṗ, ,, -ᴅaṗ.
	Assertive Perfect.	1. buò, or ba mé. 2. ,, ,, ṫú. 3. ,, ,, ré.	1. buò, or ba rɩnn. 2. ,, ,, rɩb. 3. ,, ,, rɩaᴅ.
	Future.	1. beɩò-ɩᴅ. 2. ,, -ɩɲ. 3. ,, ré.	1. beɩò-muɩᴅ. 2. ,, -ṫɩ. 3. ,, -ɩᴅ.
Conditional.		1. beɩò-ɩnn. 2. ,, -ṫeà. 3. ,, -eaò ré.	1. beɩòmuɩr. 2. beɩòṫɩ. 3. beɩòᴅɩr.
Optative Mood.		1. ᵹo ɲab-aᴅ. 2. ,, ɲab-aɩṗ. 3. ,, ɲab ré.	1. ɲab-muɩᴅ. 2. ,, -ṫaoɩ. 3. ,, -aɩᴅ.
Assertive form.		1. ᵹo m-buò mé. 2. ,, ṫu. 3. ,, ré.	1. ᵹo m-buò rɩnn. 2. ,, rɩb. 3. ,, rɩaᴅ.
Infinitive Mood.		ᴅo beɩṫ. Participles, aɩᵹ beɩṫ.	

☞ Observe in the foregoing Synopsis that in every tense (Imperative present, imperfect Iudicative, Conditional) in which the first person plural ends in ɩr, the third person plural also of the same tense ends in ɩr; and again, in every tense (Indicative present, future, and Optative) in which the first person plural ends in ɩb, the third person plural, likewise, of the same tense ends in ɩb. The learner will find this observation useful in endeavouring to remember the personal endings of the different tenses, as the remark holds true for every verb in the language, regular and irregular, as well as for the verb *to be*, ʋo beɩt.

§ 116. *Conjugation of the Verb* ʋo beɩt, *to be, in full.*

The nominative case is found in modern Gaelic always after the verb, in affirmative and negative as well as in interrogative forms of address.

IMPERATIVE.

Singular.   Plural.

1. ... | 1. Bɩ-muɩr (*beemush*), *let us be.*
2. Bɩ (*bee*), *be thou.* | 2. Bɩȯ-ɩȯ (*beeyee*), *be ye.*
3. Bɩȯ-eaȯ ré (*beeyou she*), *let him be.* | 3. Bɩ-ȯɩr (*beedish*), *let them be.*

The second person plural bɩȯɩȯ, is commonly pronounced as if written bɩȷɩȯ, *beeyee.*

INDICATIVE.

Present tense.

1. Cá me, *I am.* | 1. Cá rɩnn, *we are.*
2. Cá tu, *thou art.* | 2. Cá rɩb, *you are.*
3. Cá ré, *he* (or *it*) *is;* cá rí, *she* (or *it*) *is.* | 3. Cá rɩaȯ, *they are.*

This is called the *Analytic* or *pronominal* form: the following, the *synthetic* or *inflectional.*

1. Cáɩm, *I am.* | 1. Cámuɩȯ, *we are.*
2. Cáɩr, *thou art.* | 2. Cataoɩ, *you are.*
3. Cá ré, *he* (or *it*) *is;* cá rí, *she* (or *it*) *is.* | 3. Caɩȯ, *they are.*

The Interrogative, or Affected form.

1. An b-fuɩl-ɩm, *am I?* | 1. An b-fuɩl-nɩuɩȯ, *are we?*
2. An b-fuɩl-ɩr, *art thou?* | 2. An b-fuɩl-ɩȯ, *are you?*
3. An b-fuɩl ré, *is he?* | 3. An b-fuɩl-ɩȯ, *are they?*

With nɩ, *not:*—(1) Nɩ b-fuɩlɩm, *I am not;* (2) nɩ b-fuɩlɩr;

3) ní b-ḟuil ré, &c., contractedly, ní'lim, *I am not;* ní'lir, ní'l ré; ní'lmuid, ní'lió, ní'lio.

The third person singular b-ḟuil, with the personal pronouns, gives the *pronominal*, or analytic form; as,

1. b-Ḟuil mé, *am I?*
2. b Ḟuil tu, *art thou?*
3. b-Ḟuil ré, *is he?*

1. b-Ḟuil rinn, *are we?*
2. b-Ḟuil rib, *are you?*
3. b-Ḟuil riad, *are they?*

The conjugation of the substantive verb *to be* in English is made up of three different verbs, *am, was, be; am* and *was* are not the same. *Am* is defective in the past tense, and *was* in the present.

*** Táim seems to be the only remaining tense of an ancient verb that signified, "*to be.*" It is employed only in the direct and unaffected form of the present indicative.

b-Ḟuilim is another verb, which also expresses *being, existing*. It is the form of the substantive verb which is usually employed after all particles of asking, denying, supposing, and such like; as, an b-ḟuil ré, *is he?* ní b-ḟuil ré, *he is not;* go b-ḟuil ré, *that he is;* nac b-ḟuil ré, *is he not?*

"Tá," *is,* comes after the relative affirmative; b-ḟuil, and its inflections, after the relative negative; as, an te "a tá" raon, *he who is free;* an te "nac b-ḟuil" raon, *he who is not free.*

When an assertion is made—ir, *is,* with the personal pronouns, is the form adopted; as, ir mé, *it is I;* ir tu, *it is thou;* ir é, *it is he;* ir rinn, *it is we;* ir rib, *it is you;* ir iad, *it is they.*

With the particles of asking, denying, ir, is omitted.

The present tense, as it is formed regularly from the root bi, *be thou;* is bióim, which implies a continuous state of existence.

Bió-im, *I am wont to be.*
Bió-ir, *thou art wont to be.*
Bió ré, *he is wont to be.*

Bió-muid, *we are wont to be.*
Bió-ió, *you are wont to be.*
Bió-ió, *they are wont to be.*

Bió, the analytic form, with the personal pronouns, mé, tu, ré, expresses the same. The termination, eann, denotes habit or continuance; as, bió-eann mé, *I am wont to be;* bió-eann tu, *thou art wont to be;* bió-eann ré; *he is wont to be.*

Rel. form, an te a bióeaſ, *he who usually is;* an muintir a bióeaſ, *they who usually are*

Muintir, denotes a number of persons—a class—and is the antecedent employed in Irish for the English *they,* whenever its meaning is not confined to some special individuals.

Imperfect Tense.

Singular.

1. Ḃíd-ınn (*veeyinn*), *I was wont to be.*
2. Ḃíd-ċeá (*veehaw*), *thou* (*you*) *wast wont to be.*
3. Ḃíd-eaḋ ṡé (*veeyoo shé*), *he was wont to be.*

Plural.

1. Ḃíd-muıṡ (*veemush*), *we were wont to be.*
2. Ḃíd-ċí (*veehee*), *you were wont to be.*
3. Ḃíd-ḋíṡ (*veedeesh*), *they were wont to be.*

Analytic.

1. Ḃíd-eaḋ (*veeyoo*), me, *I was wont to be.*
2. Ḃíd-eaḋ (*veeyoo*), tu.
3. Ḃíd-eaḋ   „   ṡé or ṡí.

1. Ḃíd-eaḋ (*veeyoo*), ṡınn, *we were wont to be.*
2. Ḃíd-eaḋ (*veeyoo*), ṡıḃ.
3. Ḃíd-eaḋ   „   ṡıaḋ.

Perfect.

This tense conveys the idea of time past generally. It is translated, therefore, by the remote perfect *was*, or by the present perfect *have been*.

1. Ḃíd-eaṡ (*veeyes*), *I was.*
2. Ḃíd-ıṡ (*veeyish*), *thou wast.*
3. Ḃí ṡé (*vee shé*), *he* (or *it*) *was;* ḃí ṡí (*vee shee*), *she* (or *it*) *was.*

1. Ḃí-maṡ (*veemar*), *we were.*
2. Ḃí-ḃaṡ (*veewar*), *you were.*
3. Ḃí-ḋaṡ (*veedar*), *they were.*

*** See Note, p. 115.

ḃíd-eaṡ (*veeyes*) is in sound even very like the English word *was*.

The analytic form of this tense is:

1. Ḃí me, *I was; or have been.*
2. Ḃí tu, *thou wast.*
3. Ḃí ṡé, *he* (or *it*) *was;* ḃí ṡí, *she* (or *it*) *was.*

1. Ḃí ṡınn, *we were.*
2. Ḃí ṡıḃ, *you were.*
3. Ḃí ṡıaḋ, *they were.*

The affected form, ṅaḃaṡ, is employed in relation to past time, as ḃ-ḟuıłım (see p.p. 108, 109) is in relation to present time.

1. An ṅaḃ-aṡ (*rowas*), *was I?*
2. An ṅaḃ-aıṡ (*rowish*), *wast thou?*
3. An ṅaḃ ṡe (*row shé*), *was he?*

1. An ṅaḃ-maṡ (*rowmar*), *were we?*
2. An ṅaḃ-ḃaṡ (*rowwar*), *were you?*
3. An ṅaḃ-ḋaṡ (*rowdhar*), *were they?*

Analytic—ɴᴀḃ (*was*), ᴍé, ᴛᴜ, ṗé, ʀɪɴɴ, ʀɪḃ, ʀɪᴀᴅ?
Ꞃᴀḃ-ᴀʀ is compounded of ɴᴏ; and the perfect ḃɪᴅᴇᴀʀ.
Rel. form—ᴀɴ ᴛé ᴀ ḃɪ, *he who was*; ᴀɴ ᴛé ɴᴀċ ɴᴀḃ, *he who was not.*

In modern Gaelic the particle ᴅᴏ (in ancient ɴᴏ) is found to precede the perfect tense. This particle, ɴᴏ, is found incorporated with other particles, *v. g.*:

(1)		(2)		
ᴀɴ compounded of ᴀɴ, *whether*, and ɴᴏ.				
ɴɪᴏɴ	„	ɴɪ, *not*,	„	ɴᴏ.
ᴊᴜɴ	„	ᴊᴏ, *that*,	„	ɴᴏ.
ᴍᴀɴ	„	ᴍᴀ, *if*,	„	ɴᴏ.
ɴᴀɴ	„	ɴᴀ, *not*,	„	ɴᴏ.
ɴᴀċᴀɴ	„	ɴᴀċ, *that not*,	„	ɴᴏ.

The class (1) of particles ending in ɴ precede the perfect tense; those (2) not ending in ɴ precede the present. Those ending in ɴ take after them the affected form, ɴᴀḃᴀʀ (see p. 36).

The Perfect of ɪꞃ, *it is.—The Assertive Form of the Verb to be.*

Singular.

1. Ḃᴀ or ḃᴜᴅ ᴍᴇ, *it was I.*
2. Ḃᴀ   „   ᴛᴜ, *it was thou.*
3. Ḃᴀ   „   ṗᴇ, *it was he.*

Plural.

1. Ḃᴀ or ḃᴜᴅ ʀɪɴɴ, *it was we.*
2. Ḃᴀ   „   ʀɪḃ, *it was you.*
3. Ḃᴀ   „   ṗɪᴀᴅ, *it was they.*

Ḃᴜᴅ is also the potential imperfect, ḃᴜᴅ ᴍᴀɪċ ᴀ ᴅᴇᴀɴᴀᴅ, it "*would be*" *a good thing to effect it.*

And the subjunctive imp.; as, ᴅᴇɪʀᴛᴇᴀʀ ᴊᴏ ᴍ-ḃᴜᴅ ᴍᴀɪċ ᴀ ᴅᴇᴀɴᴀᴅ, *it is said that it* "*would be*" *a good* (*thing*) *to effect it*; ᴅᴜḃʀᴀᴅ ᴊᴜʀ ḃᴜᴅ ᴍᴀɪċ ᴀ ᴅᴇᴀɴᴀᴅ, *it was said that it* "*was*" *a good thing to have effected it.*

Ḃᴜᴅ is the spelling which, it appears, is employed when the adjective or predicate begins with a consonant; ḃᴀ or ḃ' when a vowel, or ꝑ (aspirated); as,

ḃᴜᴅ ʀᴜᴀɪʀɪᴄ, *was sweet.*
ḃᴜᴅ ᴍᴀɪċ, *was good.*
ḃᴀ ᴇᴀᴅᴍᴀʀ, *was jealous.*
ḃᴀ ᴀʟᴜɪɴ, *was beautiful.*
ḃ' ᴀʀᴅ, *was high.*

The spelling of this past tense has hitherto been unsettled. It is still so. In the written language ḃᴀ or ḃᴜᴅ is adopted by each writer at pleasure.

The words ab, bánb, lenb, nob, bain, cumaó, conbam, and such like, are compounds of ba, b'.

	Compounded of
ab	a and ba.
nob	no and ba.
bánb	ba, no, and ba.
lenb	le, no, and ba.
bain	ba and me.
cumaó	co or ɠo, and m-buó.
conbam,	co, no, ba, and me.

After buó, the personal pronouns *third* person singular and plural, take the secondary, and not the primary form.

Future Tense.

Singular.

1. Béıó-ıb (*beyid*), *I will be.*
2. Béıó-ıp (*beyirh*), *thou wilt be.*
3. Béıó ré (*bey shé*), *he (or it) will be;* beıó rí (*bey shee*), *she (or it) will be.*

Plural.

1. Béıó-muıb (*beymuidh*), *we will be.*
2. Béıó-ćıó (*beyhee*), *you will be.*
3. Béıóıb (*beyidh*), *they will be.*

Relative affirmative—an ce a beıóeap, *he who will be.*
an niuıucıp a beıóeap, *they who will be.*

The relative affirmative form of the present and future tenses end in ap.

buſ, *it will be,* is the future of ıp, *it is.* It is seldom employed except before adjectives in the superlative degree with a contingent or future meaning.

CONDITIONAL.

1. Béıó-ınn (*veyhinn*), *I might or could be.*
2. Béıó-ćeá (*veyhaw*), *thou mightest or couldst be.*
3. Béıó-eaó, (*veyhoo, shé*), *he (or it) might or could be.*

1. Béıó-muıſ (*veymush*), *we might or could be.*
2. Béıó-ćıó (*veyhee*), *ye might or could be.*
3. Béıó-óıſ (*veydish*), *they might or could be.*

The first letter of the foregoing tense, like that of the imperfect, is aspirated, if it be one of the nine mutable consonants.

OPTATIVE.

Singular.

1. ᴣo ɼᴀb-ᴀb (*go rowadh*), that I may be.
2. ᴣo ɼᴀb-ᴀɪɼ (*go rowirh*), that thou mayest be.
3. ᴣo ɼᴀb ɼé (*go rowv shé*), that he (or *it*) may be; ᴣo ɼᴀb ɼí (*go rowv shee*), that she (or *it*) may be.

Plural.

1. ᴣo ɼᴀb-ɱuɪb (*go rowmudh*), that we may be.
2. ᴣo ɼᴀb-ᴄᴀɪb (*go rowhy*), that you may be.
3. ᴣo ɼᴀb-ᴀɪb (*go rowidh*), that they may be.

Bub, *may it be*, is the optative form of ɪɼ, *it is*; bub, *it was*; as, ᴣo m-bub ꝼcᴀɼɼ ᴀ mᴀɼᴀċ ċu, *that you may be better to-morrow*.

The infinitive mood and participles are formed by placing certain prepositions before the verbal noun, beɪċ, *being*; as, in English, *to*, *about to*—in French, *pour*—is placed before the infinitive, beɪċ, *being*.

Prepositional infinitive. { ᴅo beɪċ, *to be*.
{ le beɪċ, *in order to be*.

Le, *with*, placed before the infinitive mood, gives, like *pour* in French, the idea of intent, purpose, to perform what is expressed by the verb.

PARTICIPLES.

Aɪᴣ beɪċ (*at*), *being*, same as the old English form, *a-being, a-walking, a-loving*, for *being, walking, loving*.

Aɪɼ beɪċ, *on being, having been*.

Jᴀɼ m-beɪċ, *after being, having been*.

Aɪɼ ᴄí beɪċ (*on the point of being*), *about to be*.

§ 117. ANALYTIC CONJUGATION.

To conjugate any verb in Irish analytically all that is required is to repeat the personal pronouns after the form of the third person of each tense.

The analytic form of the verb is so called because its component parts are analyzed or separated, and thus rendered more simple; the other is called synthetic, because the subject and the verb are both embodied in one word; as, ᴄᴀɪm, which is equal to ᴄᴀ mé. Hence, when the synthetic form is used, the subject, if a pronoun, should not be expressed, for then the verb would have a double subject; as, ᴄᴀɪb ɼɪᴀb ɼo ᴣo mᴀɪċ, which is equal to ᴄᴀ ɼɪᴀb ɼɪᴀb ɼo ᴣo mᴀɪċ. Hence Connellan writes: "The pronoun should never be used separately after the synthetic form, as it is only a repetition of the pronoun," yet there are instances in which, with great elegance, the subject, when a noun, is expressed; as, "Dubhnadán a beanbhráithre leir—And his brethren said to him."—*Gen.* xxxvii. 8. "Agus an uair do toruigheadh na daoine a meadughadh air druim na talmhan—And after that men began to be multiplied upon the earth."—*Ibid.*, vi. 1. (*Irish Bible, by Dr. MacHale.*) "When, however," says Dr. O'Donovan (page 153), "the nominative is a substantive, the synthetic termination is retained."

Observe, when a question is asked the analytic form is used, and the answer is returned in the synthetic; as, an b-fuil tú go maith, *are you well?* táim, *I am;* a n-gradhuigeann tu Dia, *do you love God?* gradhuighim, *I do (love).*

In the following sentence from Genesis. xxiv. 50. we find an instance of both forms: "Ann rin do fhreagair Laban agus Betuel agus a dubhradar—Then Laban and Bathuel answered and said."

Fhreagair, the analytic form, is used when the nom. cases are expressed; dubhradar, the synthetic, when left understood.

Again, "Do 'lean' na h-Egiptig iad, agus do cuadar 'nn a n-diaig go lár na fairrge—And the Egyptians pursued them and went after them to the midst of the sea."—*Exodus,* xiv. 23.

"D' fhreagair Maoire agus a dubhairt: Ní 'chreidfid riad' mé, agus ní 'éirfid' le mo ghút: act deanfaid: Níor tug an Tigearna ughdaras duit—Moses answered and said: They will not believe me, nor hear my voice, but they will say: The Lord hath not appeared to thee."

In the above, "chreidfid," followed by riad, is analytic; éirfid is synthetic.

The reader connot fail to perceive, that inflecting the verb synthetically, the third person singular has not the pronoun combined with the verb, as the other persons have, and he will naturally ask the reason. It is, as Doctor O'Donovan remarks, because the third person singular is always absent, and needs therefore to be expressed, that its gender may become known, whereas the first person or speaker, and the person spoken to, "being alway supposed to be present, there is no necessity of making any distinction of gender in them."

When therefore, in the analytic form, the nominative or subject, is in the first and second persons singular, and in all the persons of the plural, actually expressed, one uninflected form of the verb suffices for all, since the relation of its persons is sufficiently marked by the subject, just as in English; I *loved,* you *loved,* he *loved;* we *loved,* you *loved,* they *loved.* The verbal form "loved" is the same in each personal ending, yet from the subject, or nominative, the person of the verb is clearly known. (See *Easy Lessons,* part I.)

In English the analytic is the form in use; in Latin and Greek the synthetic; in French, Italian, German, the analytic and synthetic.

§ 118. The verb *to have* in English signifies to possess. In this sense it is an independent, irregular active verb. It is also what is called in English grammar *an auxiliary,* because it helps to point out the tenses of some leading verb to which it is joined.

(I.) For *have,* signifying to *possess,* there is in Gaelic, no single corresponding equivalent. The idea of possession is conveyed by the use of the prepositional pronoun agam, *at me,* and the verb do bheith, *to be,* the use of which—*est pro habeo*—is so classical in Latin.

IRISH GRAMMAR. 115

Present Tense.

Tá agam, *I have*, literally, "*it is at me*," i.e., *in my possession.*

Singular.

1. Tá agam, *I have.*
2. Tá agad, *thou hast.*
3. { Tá aige, *he has.*
    { Tá aici, *she has.*

Plural.

1. Tá againn, *we have.*
2. Tá agaib, *you have.*
3. Tá aca, *they have.*

Past Tense.

1. Bi agam, *I had.*
2. Bi agad, *thou hadst.*
3. { Bi aige, *he had.*
    { Bi aici, *she had.*

1. Bi againn, *we had.*
2. Bi agaib, *you had.*
3. Bi aca, *they had.*

The idea of possession, ownership, right to anything, is conveyed by the assertive verb is, *it is*; bud, *it was*; and the prepositional pronoun liom, *with me*; leat, *with thee*, &c. (See *Syntax*, Chapter I.)

(2.) *Have*, as a sign of tense, is translated simply by means of the verbal ending peculiar to the perfect tense. (See *Easy Lessons*, pp. 25, 108.)

NOTE 1.—The plural personal endings of the perfect indicative are (1) muid, (2) bar, (3) dar, and not amar, abar, adar. One class of verbs subjoin these and other such endings immediately to the theme or root; another class insert the vowel a between the theme and the personal endings. This vowel is inserted for phonetic convenience between the parts to aid in pronouncing freely the joint vocable. It follows, therefore, as it is not essential to the word, that it is (1) not accented; and that (2) it ought to be omitted whenever the parts can be sounded together without its aid. This happens whenever (1) the theme ends in a vowel; as,

bi, *was*: bi-mar.
bi-bar.
bi-dar.

(2) When in an aspirated or silent consonant; as,

gnádhuig, *love*: gnádhuigmar.
gnádhuigbar.
gnádhuigdar.

On the other hand, whenever the theme ends in a consonant, a is inserted before the subjoined suffix; as,

dun, *shut*: dun-a-mar.
dun-a-bar.
dun-a-dar.
buail, *strike*: buailamar.
buailabar.
buailadar.

NOTE 2.—It had been the custom hitherto to change—whenever the theme ended in a slender vowel ı—the phonetic a into ea, adhering too strictly to the rule *slender with slender*. In this edition of the College

Grammar we shall not insert e before the phonetic a for these reasons: first, to conform to what we have expressed in page 18, § 3. Secondly, the inserted a in these instances is merely for euphony, and not an essential element: if one vowel is enough, certainly it is useless to insert two. Thirdly, to have the suffixes and their accidental aids all uniform.

§ 119. Observe the close connexion that exists between the forms and sounds of the several tenses of the substantive verb in Irish, and those of its corresponding tenses and kindred terms in other languages of the Indo-European stock:

Irish (1), ır; Welsh, *oes*; Anglo-Saxon, *is*; English, *is*; Latin, *es, est*; Greek, εστι; Sanskrit, *asti*.

Irish (1), bı (*be thou*), present tense, bıóċaŋŋ; German, *bin*; English, *been*; bean, *a woman, one who gives life*; Greek, βηνα (*Boet.*), and γυνη; English, *Queen*; Teutonic, *beon*.

Irish (2). buó; Welsh, *bum, bu*; English, *was*; Sanskrit, *bhú*, Pers. *búd, he was*. Noun, bıċ, *life, existence*; Welsh, *bôd*; Sanskrit, *bhúh, the world*, Pers. *búd, the being, the world, the great being, the Indian deity*. From buó or *be* is derived the English word *boy*, and its Irish equivalent, and all their compounds.

Irish (2), bı, bıóeaſ (*vee, veeyas*); Latin, *fui*; Greek, φυω; Latin, *femina, femula*; French, *femme*.

Irish (3), beıó (*béyh*); Anglo-Saxon, *beó*; Irish, beo, *living*; Bohemian and Sclavonic, *budu*.

Irish (4), beıċ, *to be*; bıċ, *life*; Greek, βιος, *life*; Welsh, *byo*; Latin, *vita*; English, *who*; German, *weib, a womb, the cradle of life, woman* (from *womb* and *man*), *the mother of those coming from the womb*, the same that Eve was called: "The mother of the living;" *wife*, from the same root; Sanskrit, *jiva, life*.

These several terms are roots from which many other words are formed.

§ 120. Difference in meaning between ταım and bıóım—"It has sometimes puzzled Irish Grammarians," says Dr. O'Donovan, "to point out the difference of meaning between the verbs ır, ταım, bıóım, and b-ruılım; but to any one who has studied the genius of the language this difference is obvious. It is this: ır, is the simple copula of logicians, being merely used for assertion, that is to connect an attribute with its subject, or to predicate one thing of another; as, ır me rolur an oomain, I am the light of the world. But in all sentences in which existence is combined with locality τα is to be used." p. 164.

"It is a very strange peculiarity in this language that the substantive verb ται can never ascribe a predicate to its subject without the aid of the preposition ı, or aŋŋ; as, τα re 'ŋŋa ſaʒanτ, he is a priest, literally he is *in his* priest; bı ré 'ŋ ŋıʒ, he was a king, literally in his king." *Ibid*, p. 154.

The most peculiar idiom, because the strangest yet noticed, is that which arises from the use in Irish of the preposition aŋŋ, *in*, with the possessive pronouns, after the verb τα, *is* (bı, *was*; beıó, *will be*), and its inflections, to express what is predicated or declared of the subject case; as, I am a good man, is translated into Irish, τα me "aŋŋ mo" ſean ıhaıτ, I am *in my* good man; the man is a king, τα an ſean "aŋŋ a" ŋıʒ, literally, the man is *in* his king, *i.e.*, in the state of a king; she is a virgin, τα rı "aŋŋ a" h-oıʒ; Joseph was stewart over all Egypt, bı Ioreþ "aŋŋ a" mαoɲ or cıoŋŋ ŋa h-Cʒıρτε ule; we are Christians, ταmuıb-ŋe "aŋŋ aŋ" ʒ-Cŋıorbaıʒċıb; the Romans were brave warriors, bı ŋa Romanaıʒ "aŋŋ a" ŋʒaırʒıóıb τŋeuŋa."—*Easy Lessons*, Part iii. p. 196.

CHAPTER VI.

REGULAR VERBS—FIRST CONJUGATION.

The imperative mood second person singular is the root from which all the tenses and persons of the verb spring.

§ 121. There exists between Hebrew and Irish verbs an analogy which is worth being noticed.

In Hebrew the third person singular, perfect tense, is the root of all verbs. In Irish the root is the second person singular, imperative active, which is exactly the same as the third person singular perfect indicative, the latter differing from the imperative second person only in the aspiration of the initial letter. The change is merely phonetic.

Again, the root of all regular verbs in Hebrew is composed of three consonants, none of which is quiescent or a guttural. In Irish the root of every verb of the first conjugation is a word of one syllable, or derivable from a word of one syllable. The terminations too of many tenses and persons in verbs of the latter language are, as in the former, manifestly traceable from pronominal suffixes. There are, indeed, many points of resemblance existing between these two very ancient languages.

☞ In order to know when eclipsis and aspiration of the initial consonants occur in verbs, see pp. 36, 37, 38, 41.

§ 122. *Ending of the first person plural imperative.* Some writers use the termination muɪꞅ for the first person plural *imperative*. O'Donovan prefers the termination muɪr, because it is more in conformity with the ending of the third person plural ɔɪr, about the settled form of which there is no doubt. It is not, besides, unlike the Latin ending, *mus;* as, per-cutia*mus, let us strike.* These reasons are fair enough for adopting the first form, muɪr, particularly as it is as much in use among the people as is the other. Again, it will prevent the learner from confounding it with the termination of the indicative present, first person plural. Add to these (1) that muɪr is a broken form of the original pronoun "rnɪ," first person plural (see Zeüss). (2) In all the Indo-European families—Sanskrit, Greek, Latin, Russian, High German—the termination of the first person plural is *mus, mes, ame,* or *am,* so very like the pronoun of the corresponding person. (3) Ꝏuɪꞅ is the plural ending only by exclusion of muɪr, and by confusion and change of termination. At present, however, the ending muɪꞅ, for the imperative first person plural, is very common, as in Minerva's address to Mars (*Irish Homer,* book v., lines 35-39):

    Lɪɡamuɪꞅ ꞅeaꞅɔa ɔo na Cnoɪꞅte 'ꞅ Ꝣneuꝣ'
    bheɪt tabanꞅ ɔa ceɪle loꞅa aꞅuꞅ euꝣ
    'Ꝣuꞅ ꝼaꝣamuɪꞅ aca ꝼaɪt an ꝣleo ꝣo h-umal
    Aɪn eaꝣla 'tuɪlleaɔ ꝼeɪnꝣ' nɪꝣ na n-ɔul.

In these four lines lɪꝣamuɪꞅ and ꝼaꝣamuɪꞅ (first persons plural imperative active) end with the termination muɪꞅ.

☞ In lɪꝣamuɪꞅ the phonetic "a"—between lɪꝣ, the root, and muɪꞅ, the ending—is not preceded by e; thus, "lɪꝣ-ea-muɪꞅ" (*see* Note 1, p. 115)

§ 123.—TABLE showing, at one view, the personal endings of
CONJUGATION, whether the final

		Root, ⱱún.	ACTIVE VOICE.		Root, ⱱuaıl.
		Singular.		Plural.	Singular.
	Imperative Mood.	1. —— 2. ⱱún. 3. — aⱱ ré.		1. — amuır. 2. — aıⱱ. 3. — aⱱır.	1. —— 2. buaıl. 3. — aⱱ ré
INDICATIVE MOOD.	Present.	1. — aım. 2. — aır. 3. — aıⱱ ré.		1. — amuıⱱ. 2. — caıⱱ. 3. — aıⱱ.	1. — ım. 2. — ır. 3. — ıⱱ ré.
	Habitual Present.	ⱱúnaınn mé, &c.		rınn, rıb, rıaⱱ.	buaıl-eann mé, &c.
	Imperfect.	1. ⱱún-aınn. 2. — cá. 3. — aⱱ ré.		1. — amuır. 2. — caıⱱ. 3. — aⱱır.	1. buaıl-ınn. 2. — cá. 3. — aⱱ ré.
	Perfect	1. — ar. 2. — aır. 3. — ré.		1. — amaır. 2. — abaır. 3. — aⱱaır.	1. — ear. 2. — ır. 3. — ré.
	Future.	1. ⱱún-ꝼaⱱ. 2. — ꝼaır. 3. — ꝼaıⱱ ré.		1. — ꝼamuıⱱ. 2. — ꝼaıⱱ. 3. — aıⱱ.	1. buaıl-ꝼaⱱ. 2. — ꝼaır. 3. — ꝼaıⱱ ré.
	Conditional.	1. ⱱún-ꝼaınn. 2. — ꝼá. 3. — ꝼaⱱ ré.		1. — ꝼamuır. 2. — ꝼaıⱱ. 3. — ꝼaıⱱır.	1. buaıl ꝼaınn. 2. — ꝼá. 3. — ꝼaⱱ ré.
	Optative.	1. — aⱱ. 2. — aır. 3. — aıⱱ ré.		1. — amuıⱱ. 2. — caıⱱ. 3. — aıⱱ.	1. — aⱱ. 2. — aır. 3. — aıⱱ ré.

Infinitive Mood, aⱱ.   Participle, aⱱ.

IRISH GRAMMAR.

all the Tenses and Moods of VERBS OF THE FIRST vowel in the root be *broad* or *slender*.

ACTIVE VOICE. Plural.	PASSIVE VOICE. Singular.	Plural.
1. — ᴀmᴜır. 2. — ıᴆ. 3. — ᴀᴆır.	1. — τᴀı̨ mê. 2. — ċú. 3. — ê.	1. rınn. 2. rıb. 3. ıᴀᴆ.
1. — ᴀmᴜıᴆ. 2. — τıᴆ. 3. — ıᴆ.	1. — τᴀı̨ mê. 2. — ċú. 3. — ê.	1. rınn. 2. rıb. 3. ıᴀᴆ.
rınn, rıb, rıᴀᴆ.		
1. — ᴀmᴜır. 2. — τıᴆ. 3. — ᴀᴆır.	1. ᴆún-τᴀıᴆ,⎫ mê. 2. bᴜᴀı̨l-τı̨,⎭ ċú. 3. — ê.	1. rınn. 2. rıb. 3. ıᴀᴆ.
1. — ᴀmᴀı̨. 2. — ᴀbᴀı̨. 3. — ᴀᴆᴀı̨.	1. ᴆúnᴀᴆ or⎫ mê. 2. bᴜᴀı̨lᴀᴆ ⎭ ċú. 3. — ê.	1. rınn. 2. rıb. 3. ıᴀᴆ.
1. — ꜰᴀmᴜıᴆ. 2. — ꜰᴀıᴆ. 3. — ꜰᴀıᴆ.	1. — ꜰᴀı̨, mê. 2. — ċu. 3. — ê.	1. rınn. 2. rıb. 3. ıᴀᴆ.
1. — ꜰᴀmᴜır. 2. — ꜰᴀıᴆ. 3. — ꜰᴀıᴆır.	1. bᴜᴀı̨l-ꜰıᴆe or⎫ mê. 2. ᴆún-ꜰᴀıᴆe ⎭ ċú. 3. —. ê.	1. rınn. 2. rıb. 3. ıᴀᴆ.
1. — ᴀmᴜıᴆ. 2. — τᴀıᴆ. 3. — ᴀıᴆ.	1. — τᴀı̨ me. 2. — ċú. 3. — ê.	1. rınn. 2. rıb. 3. ıᴀᴆ.

INFIN. MOOD, ᴀᴆ. PART. ᴀᴆ. PAST PART. ᴆún-τᴀ, bᴜᴀı̨l-τe

§ 123. Example of a verb of the first conjugation, having in the root the final vowel *broau*.

IMPERATIVE MOOD.
Dún, *shut,* conjugated *in full.*

Present Tense.

Singular.	Plural.
1. ———	1. ⱃúnamuiⱃ, *let us shut.*
2. ⱃún, *shut thou.*	2. ⱃúnaiⱃ, *let you shut.*
3. ⱃúnaⱃ ⱃé, *let him shut.*	3. ⱃúnaⱃiⱃ, *let them shut.*

INDICATIVE.
Present Tense.

1. ⱃúnaim, *I shut.*	1. ⱃúnamuiⱃ, *we shut.*
2. ⱃúnaiⱃ, *thou shuttest.*	2. ⱃúncaiⱃ, *you shut.*
3. ⱃúnaⱃ ⱃé, *he shuts.*	3. ⱃúnaiⱃ, *they shut.*

Imperfect.

1. ⱃúnainn, *I used to shut.*	1. ⱃúnamuiⱃ, *we used to shut.*
2. ⱃúnca, *thou or you used to shut.*	2. ⱃúncaiⱃ, *you used to shut.*
3. ⱃúnaⱃ ⱃé, *he used to shut.*	3. ⱃúnaⱃiⱃ, *they used to shut*

Perfect.

1. ⱃúnaⱃ, *I shut or have shut.*	1. ⱃúnamaⱃ, *we shut.*
2. ⱃúnaiⱃ, *thou shuttest or hast shut.*	2. ⱃúnaⱃaⱃ, *you shut.*
3. ⱃún ⱃé, *he shut.*	3. ⱃúnaⱃaⱃ, *they shut.*

Future.

1. ⱃúnⱡaⱃ, *I shall or will shut.*	1. ⱃúnⱡamuiⱃ, *we will shut.*
2. ⱃúnⱡaiⱃ, *thou wilt shut.*	2. ⱃúnⱡaiⱃ, *you will shut.*
3. ⱃúnⱡaⱃ ⱃé, *he will shut.*	3. ⱃúnⱡaiⱃ, *they will shut.*

CONDITIONAL.

1. ⱃúnⱡainn, *I would shut.*	1. ⱃúnⱡamuiⱃ, *we would shut.*
2. ⱃúnⱡa, *thou wouldst shut.*	2. ⱃúnⱡaiⱃ, *ye would shut.*
3. ⱃúnⱡaⱃ ⱃé, *he would shut.*	3. ⱃúnⱡaⱃiⱃ, *they would shut*

OPTATIVE MOOD.

1. ꝉo n-ⱃúnaⱃ, *may I shut or that I may shut.*	1. ꝉo n-ⱃúnamuiⱃ, *that we may shut.*
2. ꝉo n-ⱃúnaiⱃ, *that thou mayest shut.*	2. ꝉo n-ⱃúncaiⱃ, *that ye may shut.*
3. ꝉo n-ⱃúnaiⱃ ⱃé, *that he may shut.*	3. ꝉo n-ⱃúnaiⱃ, *that they may shut.*

IRISH GRAMMAR. 121

INFINITIVE MOOD.

Do dúnad, *to shut.*

PARTICIPLES.

Present. *Perfect.*

ag dúnad, *shutting.* iar n-dúnad, *having shut.*

Future.

air ti dúnad, *about to shut.*

SYNOPSIS.

Imper. Indicative.

Present, dún. dún-aim.   Conditional, dún-fainn.
Imperfect,   dún-ainn. Optative,   go n-dun-ad.
Perfect,   dún-as.   Infinitive, do dún-ad.
Future,   dún-fad.   Participles, dúnad.

OBS. 1.—The termination *am* or *eam*, for the first person plural imperative, as, buail-eam, is now nearly obsolete, and justly, as its sound could not well be distinguished from the first person sing. (dunaim) of the present indicative.

In the following example from "The Ancient Minstrelsy of Ireland," vol. i., p. 174—the *Smith's Song*—we find the old and new forms of the first person plural imperative·

> buaileam arír é
> A'r buaileam le céile
> 'S buailamuid cuaint air
> Go luat a'r go h-éargaid.

> Let us strike it again,
> And let us strike it together,
> And let us strike all in a round
> Both quickly and smartly.

§ 124. *Uniformity in spelling the Verbal inflections desirable.*—*Endings of first person plural.* It has been deemed right to spell the terminations of the first persons plural of verbs of the same conjugation in the same uniform way throughout. There are two ways at present in use among Irish writers, both of which are presented in manuscripts and in printed books, for spelling the plural endings of the first person : muir, imperative, imperfect, conditional; muid, present, future, optative, are spelled also maoir and maoid respectively. "The synthetic form of the first person plural is as often written muid as maoid, and pronounced short or long."—*O'Donovan*, p. 167. Again, "In the south of Leinster and east of Munster it is pronounced *muïd* (short), whether the characteristic vowel of the root be broad or slender ; and maoid (long) in Thomond ; while in other parts of Ireland it is sometimes pronounced maoid (long), and sometimes muid (short). . . . It is not easy to decide what termination should be adopted in the general modern language, as the provincialists would not agree. . . . It is difficult to decide

6

which (muid or maoid, the long or the short ending)." He then adopts the long (maoid) only whenever the last vowel of the root of the verb is broad, and mid when slender. In this Grammar the spelling "muid" "muir" has been adopted in this as well as in the former edition; first, because "ui" represents that sound which prevails most throughout Ireland. This the writer affirms from his experience. He has heard Irishmen of the north, south, and west, who spoke the language from their infancy, and who therefore pronounce their mother tongue at least with ease and elegance, and with the greatest possible correctness, relatively considered, thus pronounce the plural ending.

(2) The triphthong, aoi, is long and drawling; few have heard in the word déanamuid, *let us do*, or guidamuid, *let us pray*, the last syllable pronounced long—*meedh*.

(3) The use of the vowel "u" in the termination of the first person plural is confirmed by analogy with the Latin language, of which the Sabine element, according to Professor Newman, is kindred to the Keltic.

(4) "uir" and "uid" is a spelling supported by the authority of reputable writers. It is written muid, mait, and mid, in an old veilum life of St. Moling. Those writers who adopt maoid, also write muid.

When the first person plural ends in muir (imperat. imperfect ind., conditional), the third person plural of the same tense ends in ofr, which is always long. On this there is no difference of opinion. When, on the other hand, the first person plural ends in muid, the third person of the same tense ends in id. This ending, id, is short.

The second person plural ends in ti, tai, or taid.

Dr. O'Donovan says truly, "In the spoken language the synthetic form for the second person plural is rarely used; but instead of it the analytic form (bunaid rib), or the consuetudinal present, bunann rib."

§ 125. *A change—the rule*, caol le caol, *not to be always applied*. A desire to carry out this principle of uniformity to the fullest possible extent, has been the cause of another striking feature in the foregoing Table (pp. 118, 119), in which an example of each class of verbs, those having the last vowel in the root *broad* (as, bun), or slender (as, buail), of the same conjugation, is presented. The two verbs, and all others of their class, being of the same conjugation, ought naturally enough to have the same orthographic as they have the same phonetic inflection. On this account the use of the rule, "caol le caol," is discarded in spelling the terminations of the persons of each tense, as it has been by us set aside in the formation of compound terms. This course simplifies the conjugation of Irish verbs very much. Muir and muid, having been just now shown to be the correct orthographic endings of the first person plural, are alone retained. Aiming at uniformity, the endings, mir, mid, and such like multiform orthographic inflections, arising from the "excessive application of the rule, caol le caol," are set aside. For the same reason the endings of the future are not fid (after buail), but fad; of the conditional, not finn, but fainn; and so on of the rest. The learner is, however, at liberty to adopt this change, or to conform to written usage. Let him remember that it has three great advantages, simplicity, uniformity, and a correct orthographic agreement with the sound given to these inflections in every part of Ireland. For, as Dr. O'Donovan remarks, the ending, "muid" is *pronounced mudh*, whether the characteristic vowel of the root be *broad* or *slender*. All the other endings receive, whether the verbal root end in a broad or a slender vowel, the same sound; it is natural they should therefore have the same orthographic form.

Observe, then, three important changes, (1) that the phonetic vowel-sound between the root and suffix is always to be expressed by one letter (ᴀ) and not by two; (2) that the spelling of the first person plural is ᴍᴜɪꞃ, ᴍᴜɪᴅ, and not ᴍᴀᴏɪꞃ, ᴍᴀᴏɪᴅ; (3) that one orthographic form ought to be adopted for the same phonetic ending in all verbs of the same conjugation.

Obs. 2.—It has been shown that ᴀᴅ, the ending of the third person singular of the imperative, imperfect indicative, and conditional, is pronounced like ᴀċ (*agh*) in Munster and in the south of Connaught (*see* p. 32).

"The termination 'ᴀᴅ' in the third person singular is pronounced, in Connaught and Ulster, as if written 'ᴜᴅ' (i.e. *oo* English), or ᴜɴ, but in the south as if ᴀċ (*agh*); but ᴀᴅ, ᴇᴀᴅ, or ᴄᴅ, is the true termination, as appears from the best manuscripts."—*O'Donovan.*

"The third person singular (ɢʟᴀɴᴀᴅ ꞃᴇ) is pronounced ɢʟᴀɴᴀċ ꞃᴇ throughout the southern half of Ireland, but ɢʟᴀɴᴀɴ or ɢʟᴀɴᴜᴅ in Connaught and Ulster." p. 180.

§ 126. *Future of the first conjugation*—ꞃᴀᴅ. The sound of ꞃ—a letter which distinguishes the endings of the future and conditional tenses—is, in the verbal endings, scarcely heard in the spoken language. It receives merely an asperate sound (*h*), or that of ᴛ (asp.). Still ꞃ must, on the authority of the written language, be received as the true sign of these tenses. It would be well to sound it fully in the spoken language, for its use adds strength and lends a peculiar force to these tenses. The writer has heard some of the best Irish speakers employ it with great elegance. It is quite incorrect and opposed to all authority to aspirate it, as certain writers have done. (See *O'Donovan,* p. 178.)

Note.—The third person singular of the future ends in ꞃᴀɪᴅ, pronounced *fwee.* This termination is incorrectly written ꞃᴀᴅ by the translators of the Irish Protestant version of the Sacred Scriptures, thus confounding it in sound and orthography with the third person singular of the conditional. Rev. Paul O'Brien and others have imitated and, by their authority, supported this orthographic and phonetic error.

The termination of the second person plural, imperative, is ɪᴅ; as, ʙᴜɴᴀɪᴅ. There is a corrupt form, however, very common, ɪɢɪᴅ; as, ʙᴜɴᴀɪɢɪᴅ ᴀɴ ᴅᴏꞃᴜꞃ, *close the door.* This ending, although it adds a degree of force to the expression of command, is not supported by the authority of the written language, by analogy, nor has it been approved by grammarians.

Natives of the County Kerry and part of Cork pronounce the ending of the second plural, ⁊⁊; as, ⁊ꞃ⁊ ᴀᵯᴀċ (*inig*), *go out*. This sound appears strange to a native of Connaught.

§ 127. Example (2) in which the last vowel in the verbal root is slender.

IMPERATIVE MOOD.

Buᴀⳁl, *strike*, conjugated in full.

Present Tense.

Singular.	Plural.
1. ———	1. buᴀⳁlᴀᵯuⳁꞃ, buᴀⳁlᴀᵯuⳁᴅ, } *let us strike.*
2. buᴀⳁl, *strike thou.*	2. buᴀⳁlⳁᴅ, *strike ye.*
3. buᴀⳁlᴀᴅ, ꞃê, *let him strike.*	3. buᴀⳁlᴀᴅⳁꞃ, *let them strike.*

INDICATIVE MOOD.
Present Tense.

1. buᴀⳁlⳁᵯ, *I strike.*	1. buᴀⳁlᴀᵯuⳁᴅ, *we strike.*
2. buᴀⳁlⳁꞃ, *thou strikest.*	2. buᴀⳁlcⳁᴅ, *you strike.*
3. buᴀⳁlⳁᴅ ꞃê, *he strikes.*	3. buᴀⳁlᴀⳁᴅ, *they strike.*

Habitual present, buᴀⳁleᴀꞃꞃ, ᵯê, ᴛú, ꞃê; ꞃⳁꞃꞃ, ꞃⳁb, ꞃᴀᴅ.

The continued form of the present tense can, as in English, be employed; as, ᴛá me ᴀⳁⳅ buᴀlᴀᴅ, *I am beating;* ᴛá ᴛu ᴀⳁⳅ buᴀlᴀᴅ, *thou art beating;* ᴛá ꞃê ᴀⳁⳅ buᴀlᴀᴅ, *he is beating.* (See *Syntax—of the Participle.*)

Imperfect or Habitual Past.

1. buᴀⳁlⳁꞃꞃ, *I used to strike.*	1. buᴀⳁlᴀᵯuⳁꞃ, *we used to strike.*
2. buᴀⳁlᴛá, *thou* or *you used to strike.*	2. buᴀⳁlcⳁᴅ, *you used to strike.*
3. buᴀⳁlᴀᴅ ꞃê, *he used to strike.*	3. buᴀⳁlᴀᴅⳁꞃ, *they used to strike.*

Perfect.

1. ᴅo buᴀⳁlᴀꞃ, *I struck.*	1. ᴅo buᴀⳁlᴀᵯᴀꞃ, *we struck.*
2. ᴅo buᴀⳁlᴀⳁꞃ, *thou struckest.*	2. ᴅo buᴀⳁlᴀbᴀꞃ, *you struck*
3. ᴅo buᴀⳁl ꞃê, *he struck.*	3. ᴅo buᴀⳁlᴀᴅᴀꞃ, *they struck.*

Future.

Singular.		Plural.	
1. buailfað, *I shall or will strike.*		1. buailfamuið, *we shall strike.*	
2. buailfair, *thou shalt strike.*		2. buailfið, *you shall strike.*	
3. buailfaið ṙé, *he shall strike.*		3. buailfaið, *they shall strike.*	

The f in this tense has totally disappeared from the Erse or Gælic of Scotland, as Stewart laments and though it is found in all the correct manuscripts and printed books in the Irish, it is fast disappearing from the modern spoken language.—*Irish Grammar, p.* 193.

Vide supra, section 126, p. 123. In all regular verbs f should be used whereas it is found in the most correct Irish manuscripts.

The tendency of the Irish language is, at the present day what it has always been remarkable for, to aspirate or render less sibilant the harsh consonants. The present custom is to aspirate f, or give it the sound of h.

CONDITIONAL.

1. buailfainn, *I would strike.* 1. buailfamuir, *we would strike.*
2. buailfá, *thou wouldst strike.* 2. buailfið, *ye would strike.*
3. buailfað ṙé, *he would strike.* 3. buailfaðir, *they would strike.*

When a relative pronoun (affirmative) is nominative case to a verb, in the present or future tenses, indicative mood, a strong emphatic termination, "ar," is employed; as, an té a buailar, *he who strikes;* an te a buailfar, *he who will strike.*

☞ The relative pronoun (negative) has not this emphatic form.

The termination ar is used at times when no relative is expressed or understood, but when merely a strong emphasis marks the words; as, in the saying of Pharaoh to Joseph : ann mo cataoir nfoṡóa amain beiḋear mé nfor ainbe 'ná tu, *only in the kingly throne will I be above thee.* (Genesis, xli. 40.)

OPTATIVE MOOD.

1. ʒo m-buailað, *may I strike.* 1. ʒo m-buailamuið, *may we strike.*
2. ʒo m-buailir, *mayest thou strike.* 2. ʒo m-buailtið, *may you strike.*
3. ʒo m-buailið ṙé, *may he strike.* 3. ʒo m-buailaið, *may they strike.*

INFINITIVE MOOD.

Ꝺo bualaꝺ, *to strike.*

PARTICIPLES.

Present.   *Perfect.*
aᵹ bualaꝺ, *striking.*   ᵼaꝛ m-bualaꝺ, *having struck.*

Future.

aꝛ ci bualaꝺ,

SYNOPSIS.

Imper.	*Indicative.*		
Present. buaıl.	buaıl-aım.	Conditional.	buaıl-ꝼaınn.
Imperfect.	buaıl-aınn.	Optative.	ᵹo m-buaıl-aꝺ.
Perfect.	buaıl-aꝛ.	Infinitive.	ꝺo bualaꝺ.
Future.	buaıl-ꝼaꝺ.	Participles.	bualaꝺ.

Particular rules for the formation of the tenses:

To the verbal root annex aım, for the present.
,, aınn, ,, imperfect.
,, aꝛ, ,, perfect.
,, ꝼaꝺ, ,, future.
,, ꝼaınn, ,, conditional.
,, aꝺ, ,, optative.
,, aꝺ, ,, infin. participle.

dropping the final slender vowel; as, bualaꝺ, from buaıl (ı omitted).

§ 128.—SECOND CONJUGATION.

In p. 106 it is shown that there are two conjugations of verbs in Irish:—
"The first of *one* syllable in the root,
The second of *two* syllables in the root."

It is by the number of syllables, and not by the final vowel, this conjugation is distinguished from the former; as, ꝼuaꝛᵹal, *redeem;* cuanꞇuıᵹ, *search, seek;* ꝼıoꝛꝛuıᵹ, *enquire.* In ꝼuaꝛᵹal the final vowel is broad (a); in cuanꞇuıᵹ and ꝼıoꝛꝛuıᵹ it is slender (ı). All Verbs of two syllables are, with few exceptions, derivative: it is on this account that the second conjugation comprises all verbs ending in ıᵹ, since all of this class are derived from nouns or adjectives. A Verb ending in -uıᵹ is therefore very properly selected as an example.

☞ *The final syllable* uıᵹ.—Some write the final syllable of the root of verbs ending in ıᵹ of the second conjugation—aıᵹ—preserving, of course, the 'a' throughout all the tenses and persons that are formed from it.

It seems the spelling—uıᵹ—which is adopted by others, is preferable: First, because the infinitive mood, active participle, and verbal noun, have always 'u' and not 'a' in the penult. This shows that the vowel 'u' and not 'ᴀ' should be in the root from which by annexing ᴀð, the infinitive mood, verbal noun and participle are formed. Secondly.—The genitive case, too, of verbal nouns, is according to a rule founded on universal usage, like the past participle; but the genitive case of verbal nouns ending in " uᵹᴀð,' is spelled with an 'u' in the penult. So should then the past participle, and so should the source whence it borrows its penult syllable—*i.e.* the root of the verb, for otherwise, there would ensue a perpetual fluctuation in the orthography of this class of words. Thirdly.—The spelling 'uɩ' is more in accordance than 'ᴀɩ' with the correct pronunciation of the syllable. For, in the dipthongal sound—ᴀɩ—there is, usually, a slight infusion of the vocable ᴀ, no matter how short soever the joint vowels be pronounced; whilst—uɩ—gives us the proper sound, viz., that of the simple vowel í nearly. Hence uɩ, is to be preferred to ᴀɩ, in the spelling of the last syllable in the root of derivative verbs of this class.

ᵹɼᴀðuɩᵹ, *love thou*, conjugated in full.

IMPERATIVE MOOD.
Present Tense.

Singular.
1. ──────
2. ᵹɼᴀðuɩᵹ, *love thou.*
3. ᵹɼᴀðuɩᵹᴀð ɼe, *let him love.*

Plural.
1. ᵹɼᴀðuɩᵹmuɩð ⎫
   ᵹɼᴀðuɩᵹmuɩɼ ⎬ *let us love.*
2. ᵹɼᴀðuɩᵹɩð, *do ye love.*
3. ᵹɼᴀðuɩᵹðɩɼ, *let them love.*

INDICATIVE MOOD.
Present Tense.

1. ᵹɼᴀðuɩᵹ-ɩm, *I love.*
2. ᵹɼᴀðuɩᵹ-ɩɼ, *thou lovest.*
3. ᵹɼᴀðuɩᵹɩð ɼè, *he loves.*

1. ᵹɼᴀðuɩᵹ-muɩð, *we love.*
2. ᵹɼᴀðuɩᵹ-ċɩð, *ye love.*
3. ᵹɼᴀðuɩᵹ ɩð, *they love.*

relative present, ᴀn buɩne ᴀ ᵹɼᴀðuɩᵹeᴀɼ, *he who loves ;* nᴀ bᴀoɩne ᴀ ᵹɼᴀðuɩᵹᴀɼ, *the people who love*—negative form, nᴀċ uᵹɼᴀðuɩᵹeᴀnn, *who love not.*

Habitual Present.
ᵹɼᴀðuɩᵹeᴀnn.
⎧ mè.
⎪ tú.
⎨ ɼè, ɼí.
⎪ ɼɩnn.
⎪ ɼɩb.
⎩ ɼɩᴀn.

Imperfect.

1. ᵹɼᴀðuɩᵹ-ᴀɩnn, *used to love.*
2. ᵹɼᴀðuɩᵹ-ċᴀ, *you used to love.*
3. ᵹɼᴀðuɩᵹ-ᴀð ɼè, *he used to love.*

1. ᵹɼᴀðuɩᵹ-muɩɼ, *we used to love.*
2. ᵹɼᴀðuɩᵹ-ċí, *ye used to love.*
3. ᵹɼᴀðuɩᵹ-ðɩɼ, *they used to love.*

Perfect.

1. do ġṅáḃuıġ-aṛ, *I loved.*
2. do ġáḃuıġ-ıṛ, *thou lovedst.*
3. do ġṅáḃuıġ ṛe, *he loved.*

1. do ġṅáḃuıġ-maṛ, *we loved.*
2. do ġṅáḃuıġ-ḃaṛ, *you loved.*
3. do ġṅáḃuıġ-ḋaṛ, *they loved.*

Future.

1. ġṅáḃóċaḃ, or ġṅáḃóċċaḃ, *I will or shall love.*
2. ġṅáḃóċaıṛ, *thou shalt love.*
3. ġṅáḃóċaıḃ ṛe, *he shall love.*

1. ġṅáḃóċamuıḃ, *we shall love.*
2. ġṅáḃóċaıḃ, *ye shall love.*
3. ġṅáḃóċaıḃ, *they shall love.*

CONDITIONAL MOOD.

1. ġṅáḃóċaınn, *I would love.*
2. ġṅáḃóċá, *thou wouldst love.*
3. ġṅáḃóċaḃ ṛe, *he would love.*

1. ġṅáḃóċamuıṛ, *we would love.*
2. ġṅáḃóċaıḃ, *ye would love.*
3. ġṅáḃóċaḃıṛ, *they would love.*

Note.—In the second conjugation, how ought the endings of the future and conditional tenses to be spelled? It may be asked, is it not better to have one form of spelling rather than two for the *Future* and *Conditional*, or any other tense? Yes, so it is; there are reasons, however, in support of either spelling; let us see which of the two is the better for adoption? The opinion that the termination of the *Future* and *Conditional*, ought to be spelled oċaḃ, and oċaınn, rather than oċċaḃ, or oċċaınn, can be fairly sustained. (1) That the sound of ċ is scarcely heard, and hence that letter appears abundant. (2) This form of spelling having ċ, omitted, is in use among good Irish writers. (3) It is a readier and a simpler form than the other having ċ (asp.) inserted. On the other hand, it is said (1) that if ċ were to be expunged from a word whenever its sound is not heard, the language would soon become strangely mutilated. (2) And it is true that oċċaḃ, as well as oċaḃ, is employed by good Irish writers as the proper termination. Usage alone must decide which of the two is to be universally adopted. Both forms of spelling are given here. Usage at present appears to sanction the spelling oċaḃ, omitting ċ: yet ċ cannot, on principle, be omitted in the future active without being omitted in the future passive, which will be then written ġṅáḃóċaṛ and not ġṅáḃóċċaṛ; and for the same reason, omitted in the present tense passive, ġṅáḃuıġċeaṛ, and in the past participle. But it cannot without violating principle and opposing usage, be omitted at all in the present passive; nor in the past participle. Hence it must be retained in them, and therefore, ought as naturally and as efficiently to be retained in the *Future* active, to which indeed, as well as to the passive voice, it lends a degree of aspirate sound its omission could never supply.—" oġaḃ is used in the south of Ireland," says O'Donovan. It is, and in Connaught too, in the spoken language; yet it ought not, for all that, to be adopted.

OPTATIVE.

1. ᴅo ɴɢrᴀᴅuɪɢᴀᴅ, *may I*
   love.
2. ᴅo ɴɢrᴀᴅuɪɢɪr, *mayest thou love.*
3. ᴅo ɴɢrᴀᴅuɪɢe ré, *may he love.*

1. ᴅo ɴɢrᴀᴅuɪɢmuɪᴅ, *may we love.*
2. ᴅo ɴɢrᴀᴅuɪɢċɪᴅ, *may ye love.*
3. ᴅo ɴɢrᴀᴅuɪɢɪᴅ, *may they love.*

INFINITIVE.

ᴅo ɢrᴀᴅuɢᴀᴅ, *to love.*

PARTICIPLES.

ᴀɪɢ ɢrᴀᴅúɢᴀᴅ, *loving.*   ɪᴀr ɴɢrᴀᴅúɢᴀᴅ, *having loved.*   ᴀɪr cɪ ɢrᴀᴅúɢᴀᴅ, *about to love.*

SYNOPSIS.

	Imper.	*Indicative.*		
Present.		ɢrᴀᴅuɪɢ,	ɢrᴀᴅuɪɢ-ɪm.	
Imperfect.			ɢrᴀᴅuɪɢ-ᴀɪɴɴ.	
Perfect.			ɢrᴀᴅuɪɢ-ᴀr.	
Future.			ɢrᴀᴅoċᴀᴅ.	
Conditional.			ɢrᴀᴅoċᴀɪɴɴ.	
Optative.			ᴅo ɴɢrᴀᴅuɪɢᴀᴅ.	
Infinitive.			ᴅo ɢrᴀᴅuɪɢᴀᴅ.	
Participles.			ɢrᴀᴅuɢᴀᴅ.	

§ 129. Particular rules for the formation of the tenses; second conjugation.

To the verbal root annex ɪm, for the present.

     ,,   ᴀɴɴ,   ,,   habitual present.
     ,,   ᴀr,   ,,   relative form.
     ,,   ᴀᴅ,   ,,   optative present.
     ,,   ᴀɪɴɴ,   ,,   imperfect.
     ,,   ᴀr,   ,,   perfect.
uɪɢ is changed into oċᴀᴅ,   ,,   future.
     ,,   ,,   oċᴀɪɴɴ,   ,,   conditional.

130. In this manner are conjugated the following verbs derived from nouns:

VERBS.	NOUNS.
ᴀċtuɪɢ, pass a decree; enact.	ᴀċt, a decree.
ᴀltuɪɢ, to extol, to magnify; to thank God; mɪlᴇ ᴀltuɢᴀᴅ le Ðɪᴀ, a thousand thanks to God: a prayer	ᴀlt, a height; a joint (Latin, *altus*).

VERBS.	NOUNS.

ever on the lips of the Catholic Irish.

bapuiʒ, put to death, kill. — bap, death.

bappuiʒ, to come to a top, to swell; to ebb, like the tide; spelled, also, buppuiʒ. — bapp, a top, a summit, swelling tide.

beannuiʒ, bless. — beann (quasi, biċ ain, the felicity of life).

beaċuiʒ, feed. — beaċa, life.

caċuiʒ, to contend, fight; to tempt; caċuʒaḋ, fighting, temptation. — caċ, a battle.

céimniʒ, step, move, advance. — céim, a step.

cpiocnuiʒ, bring to an end, — cpioċ, end, finish.

cpiṫnuiʒ, shake with fear, tremble. — cpiṫ, trembling

cuapcuiʒ, look for, search. — cuapc, a round, a circuit, a visit.

cuimniʒ, recollect. — cuimne, recollection.

ʒopcuiʒ, hurt, injure — na ʒopcuiʒ me, do not hurt me. — ʒopc, hunger, injury.

iomaḋuiʒ, to multiply. — iomaḋ, a multitude, many.

opḋuiʒ, to order, command, regulate. — opḋ, order; Latin, *ordo*.

pianuiʒ, to cause pain — pian, pain.

solpuiʒ, to enlighten. — solup, light.

copuiʒ, begin. — cop, beginning.

cpeopuiʒ, to lead, guide, direct, steer. — cpeoip, a guide.

ADJECTIVES.

apḋuiʒ, to elevate. — apḋ, high.

aibuiʒ, written also apuiʒ, to ripen; apuiʒċe, ripened. — aibiḋ, ripe (from ai, an element, biḋ, of food).

banuiʒ, to make white, to lay bare, to devastate, to — ban, white, pale.

VERBS.	ADJECTIVES.
grow vexed, angry, mad—because the features grow pale when the soul is filled with anger.	
beoḋuiġ, to enliven, to vivify.	beo, living, lively.
boḋruiġ, deafen.	boḋar, deaf.
boguiġ, soften.	bog, soft.
buanuiġ, persevere, continue, make lasting.	buan, lasting.
ciúnuiġ, to pacify, render silent.	ciún, still, silent.
daoruiġ, to condemn.	daor, slavish, condemned.
dearguiġ, redden, blush, incite	dearg, red.
dubuiġ, blacken.	dub, black.
faduiġ, lengthen.	fada, long.
follruiġ, reveal.	follur, apparent.
fuaruiġ, cool.	fuar, cold, cool.
geuruiġ, sharpen, render sour.	geur, sharp, sour.
laguiġ, to weaken.	lag, weak.
maoluiġ, to level, to take off excrescenses, to render sweet what is sour, to appease.	maol, bare, even, mild, blank, Welsh *moel*, Latin *mollis*, soft, mild.
marbuiġ, to deaden.	marb, dead.
milriġ, to sweeten.	milir, sweet.
miniġ, to make fine, to explain.	min, fine, minced.
móruiġ, enlarge, magnify.	mór, large, great.
saoruiġ, to make free.	saor, free.
saiḋbriġ, to enrich.	saiḋbir, rich.
slanuiġ, to save, redeem, render sound,	slan, safe, sound.
soirbuiġ, to prosper.	soirb, prosperous.
tirimiġ, to dry.	tirim, dry.
umluiġ, to humble.	umal, humble.

—*Easy Lessons, or Self-Instruction in Irish.*

The infinitive mood is formed from the root, by dropping in verbs of the second as well as of the first conjugation, ɩ final, should it be found therein, and annexing ᴀᴅ; as,

buᴀɩl, *strike;* 1st conj. ᴅo buᴀlᴀᴅ, *to strike.*

ʒɼᴀᴅuɩʒ, *love;* 2nd do. ʒɼᴀᴅuʒ-ᴀᴅ, *to love.*

If ɩ final be not in the root, then annex ᴀᴅ; as,
ᴅún,   1st conj.   ᴅunᴀᴅ
ꝼuᴀɼʒᴀl, 2nd do.   ꝼuᴀɼʒlᴀᴅ.

§ 131. *Substantival character of the Infinitive Mood.*—A little reasoning will convince the learner that the infinitive mood differs very little from a noun of the same signification; *to err* = error; *to forgive* = forgiveness. "And," says Latham, "the only difference between the two parts of speech is this, that whereas a noun may express any object whatever, verbs can only express those objects which consist in an action. And it is this super-added idea of action that superadds to the verb the phenomena of tense, mood, person, and voice. . . . . . The fact of verbs being declined as well as conjugated must be remembered. The participle has the declension of a noun adjective, the infinitive mood the declension of a noun substantive (p. 290.)" And again he shows that in the Gothic languages the inflection of the infinitive consisted in full of three cases.

All the infinitives in Irish verbs have the grammatical inflection, as well as the meaning of nouns, *v.g.* beᴀnnuʒᴀᴅ, signifies the act of blessing, a benediction; or with the prepositions ᴅo (ᴅo beᴀnnuʒᴀᴅ), ᴀɩʒ (beᴀnnuʒᴀᴅ), assumes the power and position of the verb or participle. It becomes quite plain, therefore, that with this substantival character the infinitive should be, like the noun to which it is so near akin, not limited to any specific termination.

The words of the learned author of the *Grammatica Celtica* confirm Latham's view, and show it to be specially true of the Celtic dialects:—" Si participium adjectivum est verbale, est infinitivus, substantivum verbi, idque presertim in linguis Celticis in quibus non unâ eâdemque propria exprimitur terminatione, ut in aliis linguis; sed sub forma plané substantivorum apparet, sive est in nuda radice, sive derivationibus quibusdam indutus. Flexio infinitivi eadem ergo, quæ est substantivi."—Liber iii. c. 2.

§ 132. The most common endings are -ᴀċ, -ᴀċᴛ, -ᴀɩᴅ, ᴀɩl, -ᴀṁᴀɩn, ɼɩn; as, ʒlᴀoᴅ, *call,* infinitive, ʒlᴀoᴅᴀc, *to call;* eɩɼᴛ, *list, listen,* eɩɼᴛeᴀċᴛ, *to listen;* ʒᴀb, *catch, seize;* ʒᴀbᴀɩl, *to catch, to seize;* cɼeɩᴅ, *believe,* cɼeɩᴅᴀṁᴀɩn, *to believe,* ꝼeɩc, *see,* ꝼeɩcɼɩn, *to see.* Other verbs take no special termination being the same in the infinitive and in the imperative or root; as, ɼʒɼɩoɼ, *destroy;* (ᴅo) ɼʒɼɩoɼ, to destroy; fulang, endure; d' fulang, to endure; cuir, put, makes cur in the infinitive. To those add the following:

OF THE FIRST CONJUGATION.

Imperative.	Infinitive.
bruit, *boil.*	do bruit, *to boil.*
eug, *die, perish.*	d' eug, *to die.*
guidh, *pray.*	do guidhe, *to pray.*
guil, *cry.*	do gul, *to cry.*
ioc, *pay.*	d' ioc, *to pay.*
ól, *drink.*	d' ól, *to drink.*
reic, *sell.*	do reic, *to sell.*
slad, *slay.*	do slad, *to slay.*
buain, *reap, cut down.*	do buaint, *to reap.*
ceil, *conceal (celo, Latin.)*	do ceilt, *to conceal.*
meil, *grind*	do meilt, *to grind.*
ail, *nourish, (Latin, alo)*	d' aileamhuin, *to nourish.*
blig, *milk*	do bligean, *to milk.*
caill *lose.*	do cailleamhain, *to lose.*
fagh, *get,*	d' fhaghail, *to get.*
fan, *await.*	d' fanmhuint, fanacht, *to await.*
gair, *call.*	do gairm, *to call.*
gluas, *move, repair.*	do gluasacht, *to move.*
lean, *follow.*	do leanmhuin, *to follow.*
leig, *allow.*	do léigin, *to allow.*
seinn, *sing.*	do seinnin, *to sing.*

Obs.—Verbs of one syllable in the root, compounded with prepositions, are of the first conjugation; as timcioll-geannadh, *to circumcise,* (from timcioll, *around, about,* and geannadh, *to cut*); comgair, *whisper, breathe,* from con, *together* and gair, *to chatter.* From this it is seen that the words íodhbairt, *offer sacrifice,* (from íodh, *a being, a victim,* and bein, *bring, give*), tabhairt, *give,* (ta, *real,* and bein), as well as toirbirt, *dedicate,* and other verbs like them of two or more syllables, are of the first conjugation.

OF THE SECOND CONJUGATION.

admhuigh, *confess.*	d' admháil, *to confess.*
agair, *entreat.*	d' agairt, *to entreat.*
bagair, *threaten.*	do bagairt, *to threaten.*
cargair, *slaughter.*	do cargairt, *to slaughter.*
cigil, *tickle.*	do cigilt, *to tickle.*
cogail, *spare.*	do cogailt, *to spare.*

coraın, *defend.*   do coraınt, *to defend.*
cuımıl, *rub.*   do cuımılt, *to rub.*
congaıg, *keep.*   do congbaıl, *to keep, retain.*
díbın, *banish.*   do díbınt, *to banish.*
éırıg, *arise.*   d' éırıg, *to arise.*
freagaın, *answer.*   do freagaınt, *to answer.*
ınıll, *graze.*   d' ınılt, *to graze.*
ınnır, *tell, narrate.*   d' ınnreact, *to tell.*
ıonal, *wash.*   d' ıonlat, *to wash.*
ımır, *to play.*   d' ımırt, *to play.*
labaın, *speak.*   do labaınt, *to speak.*
lomaın, *to strip, pull off.*   do lomaınt or, lompad, *to peel*
morgaıl, *awaken.*   do morgaılt, *to awake.*
raltaın, *trample, dance upon.*   do raltaınt, *to trample.*
reacaın, *shun, avoid.*   do reacaınt, *to avoid.*
tomaıl, *consume.*   do tomaılt, *to consume.*
toırıg, *search, look for.*   do tóırıgeact, *to search.*

§ 133. Passive Voice.

From the verbal roots   Indicative Present.

dun, *shut,*   ⎫ are formed by an- ⎧ dun-tar, *is closed.*
buaıl, *strike,*   ⎬ nexing the ending ⎨ buaıltar, *is struck.*
gráduıg, *love,*   ⎭ tar.   ⎩ gráduıgtar, *is loved.*

Observe, the passive verb in Gaelic is not inflected in number or person. Hence, after duntar, buaıltar, gráduıgtar, by supplying the personal pronouns *I, thou, he, she* (me, tu, fé, fí); *we, you, they* (rınn, rıb, fıad) the present tense passive in number and person is obtained.

duntar
buaıltar   ⎫ are of the *imperative* mood also, and can, by their position
gráduıgtar   ⎬ in a sentence, be easily distinguished from the indicative.

The *optative* and *subjunctive* moods, also have only this form in the present tense. The particle go, *that,* going before causes the initial consonant of the verb to become eclipsed—(see Eclipsis); as, deır, fe "go n-duntar" (subjunctive) beul na truaıge, *he says that the mouth of pity is closed;* go n-duntaıl (optative) geataıb ıfrınn, *may the gates of hell be closed;* go n-deantar (optative) do toıl aır an talaın mar goıtar aır neam, *thy will be done on earth as it is done in heaven.*

For the *Imperfect,* to the root annex tí.

duntí, me, tu, é, ı, rınn, rıb, ıad. *I used to be shut, &c.*
buaıltí, ,,   ,,   ,,   ,, *I used to be beaten, &c.*
gráduıgtí, ,,   ,,   ,,   ,, *I used to be loved, &c.*

IRISH GRAMMAR.

Perfect (aó)

dúnaó, me ċu, ṙe, &c. I was shut, thou wast shut, &c.
buaılaó,   „   „   I was struck, thou wast struck, &c.
ġráóuıġaó, „ „   I was loved, thou wast loved, &c.

Observe, that it is the *secondary* or aspirate forms of the personal pronouns *second* person (ċu) and *third* singular (é, í, for ṙe, ṙı) and the *third* person *plural* (ṙıaó or ıaó), and not the *primary* that are employed after each tense of the passive voice.

Irish Grammarians taking for granted that ċu, é, í, ıaó, are accusative cases of the personal pronouns, were sorely puzzled in accounting for the grammatical phenomenon of having accusative cases the subject of verbs passive. The pronouns ċu, é, í, ıaó, (for ṙe, ṙı, ṙıaó), are nominative cases but affected nominatives—See p. 91, § 89.

FUTURE—(1), ṙaıṙ, (2), óċaṙ.

First Con. { dun-ṙaıṙ me, &c. I shall or will be shut, &c.
           { buaıl-ṙaıṙ, „ „ I shall or will be beaten.

uıġ of root is changed into oċaṙ.

Second Con.—ġráóoċaṙ me, I shall or will be loved.

CONDITIONAL—(1) (ṙaıóe), (2) óċaıóc.

First Con. { dunṙaıóe me. I would or should be shut.
           { buaılṙaıóc   I would or should be beaten.

uıġ unto oċaıóc.

Second Con.—ġráóoċaıóe me. I would be loved, &c.
da m-buaılṙaıóe, me, *if I had been beaten.*
da nġráóoċaıóe, me, *if I had been loved.*

"da," gives to the conditional tense the meaning of the pluperfect subjunctive.

PARTICIPLES.

Past, ta, te (*or*, te).   Future, ıon, *fit.*

dun, dunta, *shut, closed.*   ıondunta, *about to be shut.*
buaıl, buaılte, *beaten.*   ıonbuaılte, *about to be beaten*
ġráóuıġ, ġráóuıġte, *loved.*   ıonġráóuıġte, *about to be loved*

The prefix ıon to the past participle imparts to it a meaning like that which is peculiar to the termination *dus* in Latin.

§ 134.—TABLE OF PERSONAL ENDINGS OF VERBS OF THE SECOND CONJUGATION.

Root, ᵹṗáḋuiᵹ.

		ACTIVE VOICE		PASSIVE VOICE	
		Singular.	Plural.	Singular.	Plural.
IMPER. MOOD.		1. —— 2. ᵹṗáḋuiᵹ. 3. — aḋ ŗé.	1. — muiŗ. 2. — iḋ. 3. — ḋiŗ.	1. ċaŗ mé. 2. — ċú. 3. — é.	1. — ŗiḋḋ. 2. — ŗiḃ. 3. — iaḋ.
INDICATIVE MOOD.	Pres.	1. — im. 2. — iŗ. 3. — iḋ ŗé.	1. — muiḋ. 2. — ċiḋ. 3. — iḋ.	1. ċaŗ mé. 2. — ċú. 3. — é	1. — ŗiḋḋ. 2. — ŗiḃ. 3. — iaḋ.
	Hab. Pres.	— aḋḋ, mé, ċu, ŗe.	ŗiḋḋ, ŗiḃ, ŗiaḋ.		
	Imper	1. (ᵹṗáḋuiᵹ)-iḋḋ. 2. — ċá. 3. — aḋ ŗé.	1. — muiŗ. 2. — ċí. 3. — ḋiŗ.	1. ċí mé. 2. — ċú. 3. — é.	1. — ŗiḋḋ. 2. — ŗiḃ. 3. — iaḋ.
	Per.	1. — aŗ. 2. — iŗ. 3. — ŗé.	1. — maŗ. 2. — baŗ. 3. — ḋaŗ.	1. aḋ me. 2. — ċú. 3. — é.	1. — ŗiḋḋ. 2. — ŗiḃ. 3. — iaḋ.
	Fut.	1. (ᵹṗáḋóċ)-aḋ. 2. — aiŗ. 3. — aiḋ ŗé.	1. — amuiḋ. 2. — aiḋ. 3. — aiḋ.	1.—aŗ mé. 2. — ċú. 3. — é.	1. — ŗiḋḋ. 2. — ŗiḃ. 3. — iaḋ.
COND.		1. ᵹṗáḋóċ-aiḋḋ. 2. — a. 3. — aḋ ŗé.	1. — amuiŗ. 2. — aiḋ. 3. — aiḋiŗ.	1. aiḋc me. 2. — ċú. 3. — é.	1. — ŗiḋḋ. 2. — ŗiḃ. 3. — iaḋ.
OPTAT.		1. ᵹṗáḋuiᵹ-aḋ. 2. — iŗ. 3. — iḋ ŗé.	1. — muiḋ. 2. — ċiḋ. 3. — iḋ.	1. ċaŗ mé. 2. — ċú. 3. — é.	1. — ŗiḋḋ. 2. — ŗiḃ. 3. — iaḋ.
INFINIT. uᵹaḋ.		PAR. uᵹaḋ.		PASSIVE PART. ᵹṗáḋuiᵹċe.	

Observe in this table the broad vowel endings ċaŗ, and not ċeaŗ, aḋ and not eaḋ, are for the sake of having one form of spelling, the only suffixes of the second conjugation. See Section 125, p. 122.

☞ The phonetic " a," employed in Table, § 123, pp. 118, 119, before the endings, muiŗ, muiḋ, ḋiŗ, maŗ, baŗ, ḋaŗ, is omitted in this, because it is not required in articulating the word. See p. 115. note.

§ 135. The Analytic form of the passive voice is very easy. It is simply the verb *to be*, "ᴅo béiṫ" conjugated as in English with the past participle.

INDICATIVE MOOD.

Present Tense.

Singular.
1. tá mé buailte, *I am beaten.*
2. tá tú buailte, *thou art beaten.*
3. tá ré buailte, *he is beaten.*

Plural
1. tá rinn buailte, *we are beaten.*
2. tá ríb buailte, *ye are beaten.*
3. tá riad buailte, *they are beaten.*

Past Tense.

1. bí mé buailte, *I was beaten.*
2. bí tú buailte, *thou wast beaten.*
3. bí ré buailte, *he was beaten.*

1 bí rinn buailte, *we were beaten.*
2. bí ríb buailte, *ye were beaten.*
3. bí riad buailte, *they were beaten.*

Thus any *past* participle placed after the *analytic* form of the verb "ᴅo béiṫ" gives the analytic conjugation in the passive voice of that verb from which the past participle is taken.

The past *participle* like adjectives terminating in a vowel, undergoes no change in the singular or plural number.

☞ Taking it for certain, that the learner knows how to conjugate the verb "ᴅo béiṫ," it is not then necessary to give any other tense of the analytic conjugation.

Infinitive, { a béiṫ dúnta.
            { a béiṫ buailte.
            { a béiṫ ġráduiġte.

§ 136. Why is tá (or te) the termination of the past participle aspirated in some verbs not aspirated in others? This is, perhaps, one of the most difficult things for a mere learner in Irish to know; yet to a native hearing the language spoken there is nothing more easy, simply because the aspirating or not aspirating of t in this situation and in others like it is a matter of euphony, and is best learned by hearing the language spoken.

To simplify the difficulty then, let the learner treat every past participle as a compound word formed from the verbal root and the particle or verb ⁊a; (for, buaɩlte, *beaten*, may be regarded as a compound of buaɩl *beat*, and ⁊a, *is*; ðuŋ⁊a of ðuŋ, *shut*, ⁊a *is*; ꞡŋáðuıꞡ⁊e, of ꞡŋáðuıꞡ *love*, ⁊a, *is*.) Apply then to ⁊, the first latter of the participial suffix, the rules already given for aspirating compound terms. What are the rules? see pp. 34, 35, § 24, rule 3, and exception 1. It may be well to repeat them here: that the initial consonant, if mutable, of all words which form in composition the *second* part of a compound term, is aspirated.

Exception 1.—Words beginning with any of the dental consonants ð, ⁊, ſ, when the preceding part of the compound ends in ð, ⁊, ſ, l, ŋ.

From the principles of lingual euphony enunciated in the foregoing, the two following rules are formed.

Rule 1.—After ð, ⁊, ſ, l (ll) ŋ (ŋŋ); or their aspirates ð ⁊ ꞡ, asp. (which in sound is same as that of ð) and ⁊, guttural; as, ſeuð, *blow*, ſeuð⁊a, *blown*; ſmac⁊, *chastise*, ſmac⁊a, *chastised*; caſ, *twist*; caſ⁊a, *twisted*; buaɩl, *beat*, buaɩl⁊e, *beaten*; ðuŋ, *shut*, ðuŋ⁊a, *shut*; claoıð, *subdue*, *weaken*, claoıð⁊e, *subdued*; báı⁊, *drown*, báı⁊⁊e, *drowned*; fıꞡ, *weave*, fıꞡ⁊e, *woven*; cŋoc, *suspend*, *hang*, *crucify*, *execute*, cŋoc⁊a, *suspended*, *hung*, *crucified*, *executed*.

Rule 2.—After any other consonant, or after the ending ıꞡ in verbs of the second conjugation ⁊ (of ⁊e, or ⁊a) is aspirated: (b) lub, *bend*, *loop*, lub⁊a, *bent*, *looped*, like a hook, (ꞡ) boꞡ, *make soft*, *rock*, *stir*, boꞡ⁊a, *softened*, *stirred*; cŋom, *bend*, *make crooked*, cŋom⁊a, *bent*, *make crooked*; cŋaſ, *fold*, *tuck*, *gather*, *shrink*, cŋaſ⁊a, *folded*, *tucked*, *gathered*, *shrunk*; cuıſ, *set*, *put*, *sow*, *bury*, cuıſ⁊e, *set*, *sown*, *put*, *buried*.

The whole difficulty is made plain by understanding the two points explained in these rules.

The following are the words of Dr. O'Donovan on this subject. The rule is not readily intelligible, nor is it possible for an ordinary student to remember it, because the principles on which it is founded are not explained.

Rule.—"⁊ has its radical sound after ⁊, ð, ꞡ, l, ll, ŋ, ŋŋ, ſ, ⁊, as, cŋoc⁊a, *hanged or suspended*; ſpoc⁊a, *emasculated*; báı⁊⁊e, *drowned*; ſpŋíoı⁊e, *spread*; ſúıꞡ⁊e, *absorbed*; bŋúıꞡ⁊e, *bruised*; mol⁊a, *praised*; meall⁊a, *deceived*; ðeaŋ⁊a, *done*; caſ⁊a, *twisted*; bŋıſ⁊e, *broken*;

blúiċte, *closed*. But in verbs in uiṫim, or iṫim, which make the future in eoċab, and in all verbs of which the root terminates in b, c, b, ṡ, m, p, ꞃ, t—the t is aspirated whether the characteristic vowel be broad or slender, as, lúbċa, *bent;* ꞃeacta, *bowed;* ṡꞃeabċa, *lashed;* tꞃéiṡte, *closed;* beanꞃuiṫṫe, *blessed;* tomċa, *dipped;* ꞃcaipte, *scattered;* lomanta, *peeled;* ꞃeaꞃtta, *entombed."—Irish Grammar,* p. 206.

"In the Erse or Scottish dialect of this language, the t is never aspirated in the past participle; but it is marked with a decided aspiration in the oldest Irish manuscripts." And it has always its slender sound in the Erse, whether the characteristic vowel of the root be broad or slender. Stewart, therefore, recommends the termination of the passive participle to be always written *te* without regard to the characteristic vowel. But this is not admissible in Irish; for, the termination of the passive participle is pronounced broad or slender according to the last vowel of the root, as, bꞃiꞃ, *break,* past. part. bꞃiꞃte; ól, *drink,* past. part. ólta, *drunk,* (not oilte as in the modern Erse.) It should, however, be confessed, that in the county of Kilkenny, and some other parts of the South of Ireland, the passive participle is pronounced slender in a few words of which the characteristic vowel is broad... But this is most decidedly a corruption, for in the province of Connaught, and in the western portion of Munster, the t in these words is pronounced with its proper broad sound. It should be remarked, also, that the t in this termination is frequently aspirated in Kerry, and parts of Cork in positions where it has its radical sound in most other countries, as, ṡeallta, *promised,* pronounced *geallha;* meallta, *deceived;* pronounced *meallha.—Dr. Donovan's Irish Grammar,* pp. 205, 306.

OBS.—The aspirate or non-aspirate sound of t in the ending tap, of the present tense passive, is regulated like that of the passive participle.—See p. 144.

☞ In the passive voice aspiration does not occur in any initial consonant even though it should be preceded by bo or ꞃo, or any of the other particles which usually produce it.

§ 137.—PARTICIPLES.

A participle is a word which partakes of the nature of the noun-adjective, and of the verb.

§ 138.—There are two participles—the active and the passive. In Irish, the active participle necessarily partakes of the nature of the noun *substantive,* for it is identical with the infinitive mood. The prepositions alone which affect them are different.

"The participle (active) is used in many languages as a substantive."— *Latham,* § 402.

This is especially true in Greek, it is true in Latin, in French, and even in English. Witness the number of words ending in *ing;* as, singing, playing, building, preaching, which are nouns as well as participles. The *passive* participle partakes always of the nature of the adjective.

§ 139. The active participle denotes *present* time when preceded by the preposition aiṫ, *at;* as, aiṫ bualab; poetically or contractedly, ᴀ' buᴀlᴀð, *at* beating, not unlike the Saxon form *a*-beating; *past* time with ιᴀᴨ, *after;* as, ιᴀᴨ ᴍ-buᴀlᴀð, after beating, (*i.e*) having beaten; *future* time with ᴀιᴨ ᴛι, *on the point of, about to;* as, ᴀιᴨ ᴛι buᴀlᴀð, *about to beat.*

☞ The preposition ᴀιᴢ, *at,* is often contracted into ᴀ', especially in Scotch Gaelic; sometimes, as in hurried conversation or in poetry, it is omitted altogether.

§ 140. The *passive* participle has a future meaning to a certain extent, when incorporated with the prefix " ιoɴ;" as, ιoɴbuᴀlᴛe, *to be* beaten, ιoɴᴣʀᴀðuιᴣᴛe, *to be loved,* formed from buᴀιlᴛe, beaten; ᴣʀᴀðuιᴣᴛe, loved.

§ 141. The passive participle is formed from the root of the verb, by annexing to it ᴛe or ᴛᴀ. The letter ᴛ of the annexed part is to remain in its natural state (as, buᴀιlᴛe), or must be aspirated (Ex. ᴣʀᴀðuιᴣᴛe) according to the rules, § 136, pp. 137, 138, 139.

₊ As a general rule, the *plural* of the participial noun (active) is the same as the participle passive; as, ᴍolᴀð, praise; plu. ᴍolᴛᴀ, praises; ᴍolᴛᴀ is the passive participle also, signifying *praised.*

CHAPTER VII.

CONJUGATION OF THE IRREGULAR VERBS.

§ 142. Obs.—The number of verbs irregular in Irish is ten. They are called irregular mainly to conform to the fashion of grammarians, who thus denominate in other languages that class of verbs which differ from the common standard of conjugation. Irish verbs differing from the regular form are defective rather than irregular; moreover, the defect is confined to one or two tenses, chiefly to the perfect. A certain very numerous class of verbs in Latin, like those defective in Gaelic, borrow the perfect from some obsolete verbs of kindred meaning, and yet they are not denominated irregular.

"It is very evident," says Robert G. Latham, "that it is in the power of the grammarian to raise the number of etymological irregularities to any amount by narrowing the definition of the word irregular; in other words, by framing an exclusive rule. . . . . This is the last art (framing exclusive rules) that the philosophic grammarian is ambitious of acquiring."—*The English Language.*

§ 143. These Gaelic verbs are: (1) beιʀιᴍ, *I bear;* (2) beιʀιᴍ (*veirhim*), *I give;* (3) cluιɴιᴍ, *I hear;* (4) ðéᴀɴᴀιᴍ, *I do;* (5) ðeιʀιᴍ, *I say;* (6) ғᴀᵹᴀιᴍ, *I find;* (7) ғeιcιᴍ, *I see;* (8) ʀιᵹιᴍ, *I reach;* (9) ᴛeιðιᴍ, *I go;* (10) ᴛιᵹιᴍ, *I come.*

☞ In the *first* edition of the " College Irish Grammar," the conjugation

IRISH GRAMMAR. 141

of each verb under a distinct heading was presented in full to the student. That arrangement took up more space than the limited dimensions of the present edition, with its ampler and more enlarged contents, can well spare.

The present arrangement so groups the irregular verbs, that all are conjugated as far as possible like one verb.

In the "Easy Lessons" this same order exists, for the grammatical part of that work was written from the notes which we had collected to improve or illustrate the matter of the first; and while we were preparing for press this second edition of the College Grammar.

(1) beıɼ (pr. *be-irh*, in one syl. short), Eng. bear; Anglo-Sax. *bearan;* Goth. *bairan;* Lat. *fer;* Gr. φέρ, *pher*. The several meanings of beıɼ are: (1) bring, (2) bear, (3) carry; as, beıɼ ann ɼo an leabaɼ, bring hither the book; beıɼ uaım an leabaɼ, bear off this book; (4) produce, (5) bring forth; as, aȝuɼ beıɼɼıó ʦu mac, and you shall bring forth a son; applied to animals signifies (6) yean, (7) litter, &c., (8) to lay; as, beıɼceann ceaɼc ɔub, ub ȝeall, a black hen lays a white egg; (9) to spawn; (10) to obtain, to procure; as, beıɼ buaıó, obtain victory, beıɼ beannaċʦ, obtain a blessing. It has as many meanings as the word "bear" in English. "The word 'bear' is used," says Watts, "in very different senses." Or the word "get" in the same language, which implies possession of, or at, any place or thing; (11) with the preposition aıɼ, *on*, it implies seize, lay hold of, catch, overtake, beıɼ aıɼ, catch him (it); an m-beıɼɼıó me aıɼ, shall I overtake him? leıɼ (with) coming after beıɼ, gives the idea of taking away; beıɼ leaʦ é, take it away.

These are the several meanings which beıɼ has in all its moods and tenses: bɼeıċ, birth; ó mo bɼeıċ, from my birth; bɼeıċ, the offspring of the mind, *i.e.*, a judgment, sentence, decision, determination; aıȝ ʦabaıɼʦ bɼeıċe, giving a judgment; bɼeıċeam, a judge; hence the Irish ɼeaċʦa bɼeıċeamnan, Brehon laws; bɼeıċeamnaɼ, a judgment.

beıɼım, I give—a form of ʦabaıɼ, give thou.

CONJUGATION OF THE TEN IRREGULAR VERBS.

ROOT.

1 beıɼ, *bear thou, &c.*
2 beıɼ, *give, &c.*
3 cluıɼ, *hear.*
4 ɔéan, *do.*
5 ɔeıɼ, *say.*
6 ɼaȝ, *get.*
7 ɼeıc, *see.*
8 ɼıȝ, *reach.*
9 ʦeıó, *go.*
10 ʦıȝ, *come.*

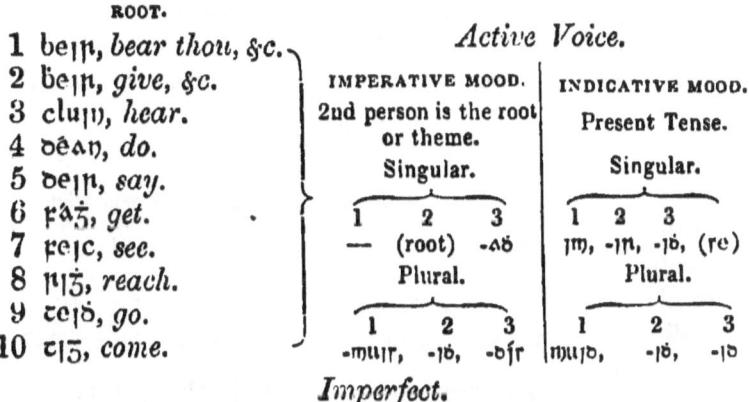

Active Voice.

IMPERATIVE MOOD.
2nd person is the root or theme.
Singular.

1	2	3
—	(root)	-aó

Plural.

1	2	3
-muıɼ	-ıó	-óıɼ

INDICATIVE MOOD.
Present Tense.
Singular.

1	2	3
ım,	-ıɼ,	-ıó, (re)

Plural.

1	2	3
muıó	-ıó	-ıó

Imperfect.

The initial consonant if changeable is aspirated.

Singular—ıɼɼ,-ċa,-aó (re).   Plural—muıɼ,-ıó,-óıɼ.

The Imperfect of ḋéaṅ is commonly borrowed from ᵹníó, do, act; ᵹníó-ıṅ (*nhee-yin*), I used to act, do, ᵹníó-ċa, thou used to act, ᵹníó-aó re, he used to act, &c.

Perfect Tense.

	Singular.			Plural.		
	1	2	3	1	2	3
of beıṅ is	ṗuᵹ-ar,	aıṗ,	ṗuᵹ re.	amaṗ,	aḃaṗ,	aóaṗ.
... beıṅ ...	ċuᵹ-ar	...	ċuᵹ re.	...	...	...
... cluıṅ ...	ċual-ar	...	aıó re.	...	...	...
... ḋéaṅ ...	ṗıṅṅ-ear	...	ṗıṅṅe re.	...	...	...
... oeıṅ ...	óuḃṗ-ar	...	óuḃaıṅc re.	...	...	...
... faᵹ ...	fuar-ar	...	fuaıṗ re.	...	...	...
... feıc ...	ċoṅṅaıc-ar		coṅṅaıṅc re.	...	...	...
... ṗıᵹ ...	ṗaṅᵹar, or ṗıaċċ-ar	ṗıaċċ re...		...	...	...
... ceıó ...	ċuaó-ar,	ḋeaċ-ar	ċuaıó re...	...	...	...
... cıᵹ ...	ċaıṅıc-ar		ċaıṅıc re.	...	...	...

Future.

1 beıṅ
2 béıṅ
3 cluıṅ   The changeable initial consonant is aspirated.
4 ḋéaṅ
5 oeıṅ
6 faᵹ
7 feıc
8 ṗıᵹ
9 ceıó
10 cıᵹ

	1	2	3	1	2	3
	-faó,	-faıṗ,	-faıó.	-famuıó,	faıó,	faıó.

6 Faᵹ borrows its future from ᵹaḃ, *take,* ᵹaḃ-faó; neg. form, ṅı ḃ-fuıᵹeaó.

9 ċeıó makes ṗacfaó in the future.

10 cıᵹ   „   cıocfaó.

(See remarks on the irregular verbs, pp. 144—149, *infra*.)

Conditional.

beıṅ
béıṅ
cluıṅ   The changeable initial consonant suffers aspiration.
ḋéaṅ
oeıṅ   Singular.   Plural.
faᵹ
feıc

	1	2	3	1	2	3
	-faıṅṅ,	-fá,	-faó (re).	-amuır,	-faıó,	-faıóır.

ṗıᵹ
ceıó   6 faᵹ makes ᵹaḃ-faıṅṅ, in this tense.
cıᵹ   9 ċeıó   „   ṗacfaıṅṅ.
        10 cıᵹ   „   cıocfaıṅṅ.

IRISH GRAMMAR.   143

OPTATIVE—*Regular.*

ʒo m-ḃeiṟ
„ ḃeiṟ
„ ʒ-cluiŋ
„ ŋ-ḋéaŋ
„ ŋ-ḃeiṟ
„ ḃ-ḟáṡ
„ ḃ-ḟeic
„ miṡ
„ ḃ-ceiḋ
„ ḃ-ciʒ

Singular.   Plural.

1   2   3   1   2   3

-aḋ, -aiṟ, -aiḋ ɼc.   -amuiḋ, -aiḋ, -aiḋ.

The particle ʒo thus precedes the optative, and on that account the radical initial consonant, ḃ, for instance, is eclipsed by m; c, by ʒ, &c.

The tenses borrowed from other verbs, which now, from usage, belong to the foregoing or any of them, shall be explained.

§ 144. THE PASSIVE VOICE OF THE IRREGULAR VERBS.

RULE.—The general rule for the formation of the tenses of the passive voice is, to annex to the verbal root, for the

Present tense ... ṫaṟ (or, taṟ); of the indicative; of the imperat., optative, and subjunct.

For the *Imperfect* ... ṫɩ
„   *Perfect* ... aḋ
„   *Future*   ... ḟaṟ
„   *Conditional* ḟaiḋe.

According to this the passive voice of

ḃeiṟ
ḃeiṟ
cluiŋ
ḋéaŋ
ḃeiṟ
ḟáṡ
ḟeic
miṡ
ceiḋ
ciʒ

Present Tense.

INDICATIVE, IMPERATIVE, OPTATIVE, SUBJUNCTIVE.

Singular.   Plural.

1   2   3   1   2   3

is, (ḃeiṟ) -ṫaṟ me, tu, é; ɼinŋ ɼiḃ, iaḋ.

Imperfect.

-ṫɩ,   „   „   „   „   „

-ṫaṟ, for the present (-ṫɩ, for the past) is annexed to each root; to which, by supplying the personal pronouns, the persons of each tense are formed.

Note.—After the letter ɲ, -ᴛ of the suffixes, ᴛaʀ and ᴛɪ, is not aspirated; therefore the present tense of cluɪɲ, ʙèaɲ, is cluɪɲᴛaʀ, ʙèaɲᴛaʀ.—See § 136, pp. 137, 138.

Although the above rule is plain and short, it is not objectively correct; for it is not from the root precisely, so much as from the first person singular of each of the several tenses, active voice, that the indicative tenses of the passive are formed; just as in Latin—from amat, is formed ama*tur*; amant, aman*tur*; amabit, amabi*tur*. The perfects of the passive then are formed each from its respective tense irregular in the active, thus:

Perfect active.	Perfect passive.
1 ʀuᴢ-aʀ, I bore,	ʀuᴢaʙ mє, I was born.
2 ċuᴢ-aʀ, I gave,	ᴛuᴢaʙ, was given.
3 ċual-aʀ, I heard,	cualaʙ, and cluɪɴєaʙ, regularly, was heard.
4 ʀɪɴɴ-єaʀ, I did,	ʀɪɴɴєaʙ, was done.
5 ʙuʙʀ-aʀ, I said,	ʙuʙʀaʙ, was said.
6 ꜰuaʀ-aʀ, I got, found,	ꜰuaʀaʙ, was found.
7 coɴɴaɪʀc-aʀ, I saw	coɴɴaɪʀcaʙ, from coɴɴaɪʀc, 3rd sin.; ꜰacaʀ, the affected irreg. perf. pass., was seen.

The remaining three verbs are intransitive.

☞ The tenses of the passive have never the initial consonant aspirated, like those of the active.

§ 145. From the conjugation of these verbs, called in Irish Grammar, irregular, here presented to the learner, it is seen that they are perfectly regular in their numbers and persons, and are irregular only in this, that they want certain tenses.

The tenses which make any show of difficulty to the learner, are the perfect and infinitive.

"In language itself," says Latham ('English Language,' p. 336, fourth edition), "there is no irregularity. The word itself is only another name for our ignorance of the processes that change words." Again, "The whole scheme of language is analogical."

REMARKS ON EACH OF THE IRREGULAR VERBS, AND ON THE SECONDARY OR ACQUIRED TENSES.

§ 146.—1. beɪʀɪm, *I bear* or bring forth, wants only the perfect, which it borrows from an obsolete verb, ʀuᴢaɪm, formed, very likely, from ɴo, very, and ᴛuᴢaɪm, I bring, give, bestow. In the future tense indicative, and in the conditional, e of béɪʀ is long béɪʀꜰaʙ, or béaʀꜰaʙ; future passive, béaʀꜰaʀ; conditional, béaʀꜰaɪɴɴ—passive, béaʀꜰaɪʙє; in the infinitive or verbal noun the position of the final ʀ (being a liquid letter) is changed, and made to coalesce with the initial b, thus:

Infinitive participle, bʀєɪċ, *breh* (and not bєɪʀєċ).

IRISH GRAMMAR. 145

§ 147.—2. The verb, beirim, I give, pr. *veirhim*, distinguished from the former by the letter b being aspirated, has, as it were, two handmaids, which supply it with tenses, not only the imperative (tabair), perfect indicative, (tugar), and infinitive, (tabairt), which are found wanting, (in beir), but other tenses which it does not want. These assisting verbs are tugaim and tabraim (contractedly for tabairim). From tabair alone it borrows the imperative and infinitive, and along with the regular form béanfad supplies to the future the secondary form tabarfad (pr. *thowarfadh*), I shall give.

(Supplied tenses.)
IMPERATIVE MOOD.

Singular.	Plural.
...	tabramuir, *thowramush*.
tabair, pr. *thower, give.*	tabraió, *thowree*.
tabrad ré, *thowroo*, ,,	tabraióir, *thowradeesh*.

The infinitive, tabairt, *thowarth*.

INDICATIVE MOOD—PRESENT TENSE.

beirim, tugaim, and tabraim; passive present, (indicative and imperative), beirtear, tugtar, tabartar.

Habitual Present.

beircann mé, tugann mé, and tabrann, mé.

Imperfect.

beirinn, and tugainn.

The *perfect* is from the verb tugaim alone, as is shown in the table of conjugation, the perfect passive is tugad, from the perfect active.

NOTE.—The verb tabair, *give*, seems to be derived from the verb beirim, itself, and a certain prefix expressive of *being, essence, a thing, a real gift;* and one which appears to be related in meaning, and very likely derived from the old verb, tá, *am, is, are*, which is found in the present tense of the verb do béit. to be—of which said tá, the infinitive would be "tád," *a being, an essence, a reality.* Tabeirim or tabairim, then means, I give *in reality,* I *bestow, confer a gift, favour,* or the like. With this meaning it has a certain force and strength, which the verb beirim has not, and is on that account employed solely in that mood—the imperative—in which command, entreaty, is implied, and in the infinitive, because that mood, being a verbal noun, conveys the idea of imparting gifts, tabart (tabartar—a gift bestowed.)

The future tense of tabair, although composed of two syllables, receives not the suffix oéad (peculiar to the second conjugation), but fad, the future suffix, peculiar to verbs of the first conjugation—like the simple verb beir; for, derivative and compound verbs follow in most instances the analogy of their primitives and simples.

7

Obs. 1.—The correct spelling of the future indicative is ⁊abaŋṟab, suffixing -ṟab to the root ⁊abaiŋ, which is preserved throughout, and not the phonetic spelling ⁊iubṉab, employed by Dr. Keating, by the translators of the Protestant version of the Bible, and others.

Obs. 2.—According to Dr. Johnson the verb "give" in English has twenty-two different meanings, primary and secondary, and receives nine others additional from the accessary aid of prepositions and adverbs, such as *in, out, over, up, off* (as, give *up*, give *over*, give *out*, &c.) These several meanings—primary, secondary, and accessary—the verb beiŋiŋ (⁊abṉaiŋ) in Irish receives. But it is necessary to remark that ⁊abaiŋ, beiŋ, and ⁊uz have the meaning of beiŋ, bear, bring, convey, carry, along with that which signifies *give*; as, ⁊abaiŋ ċuzam mo ċapal, bring hither to me my horse; ⁊abaiŋ uaiŋi aŋ ⁊-olc ro, take away from me the evil; ċuz ṟe leiṟ aŋ meub a bi azam, he brought with him all I had in possession. Thus the verb ⁊abaiŋ conveys in Irish ideas apparently opposed one to the other.

☞ Beiŋ is part of the compound not only of (1) ⁊abaiŋ, *give*, but of (2) labaiŋ, *speak*, which is composed of luab (utterance, Gr. λαλω, I utter), or from lab, a lip, and beiŋ; also (3) of ⁊oiṉbeiŋ, to offer, to dedicate, from ⁊oṉ, the Keltic name of Jove, and beiŋ; (4) iobbeiŋ, *to offer in sacrifice*, from iob and beiŋ; iob, like ai or aoi, means a creature—*i.e.*, to offer a being in sacrifice to God.

§ 148. (3) *The verb* cluiŋ, *hear*.

The *third* in order is cluiŋ, *hear*, which in the formation of its tenses is regularly formed after the model of the first conjugation, except that (1) its regular perfect "cluiŋeaṟ," is commonly by metathesis, or rather by substituting l in place of ŋ, written and pronounced cualaṟ (irregular); and (2) that the infinitive and participle form is "clor." Cluiŋeaṟ, the regular perfect, is not uncommon. This verb cluiŋ may therefore be safely ranked among the regular verbs, yet it has been here retained in order to conform to received notions which regard it as irregular.

§ 149. With the infinitive clor, the following terms in the Keltic and foreign dialects seem to have a strong affinity:

  Irish, cluaṟ, (a noun) an ear; the organ which has the power to (clor) hear.
   „ clú, report, fame, reputation, what the public hear of one.
 Welsh, *clyw*, hearing.
 Greek, κλυω, to hear on report.
 Latin, *clueo*, to be talked of, to be reputed.
 Irish, clu⁊aċ, *adj*, renowned.
 Greek, κλυτος and κλυτικος, renowned, famed.
 Latin, *inclytus*.

§ 150. (4) Déan, *do*.

The verb déan, *do, act, make*, is in meaning like the La in *facio*. It borrows (1) the perfect from the verb gníom, *I act* (root gníō ü, *n., an act*); and (2) also the imperfect gníoinn, *I used to act*.

Perfect.

Singular.   Plural.

1 rigneas, I did.   1 rignamar, we did.
2 rignir, thou didst.   2 rignabar, you did.
3 rigne re, he did; rigne   3 rignadar, they did.
   ri, she did.

The regular perfect of gníom is gníoceas, which, with the prefix no incorporated, becomes nigneas (g asp.) In the modern spelling g (asp.) is changed into n for sound's sake. The infinitive is déanaó, (old spelling téanain). The subjunctive or secondary form of the verb after the particles nac, ní, go, is deaninaim; as dein re nac ndeainaim (subjunctive mood), he says *that I do not do;* and perfect, deannar; dein re nac n-deannaió me an ceart, he says that (subjunctive perfect) I did not do justice.

Déan is very likely compounded of do and gníom. That it is so, is seen more plainly from the spelling of the secondary or subjunctive form of the verb, viz. "diongnaim," as, dein re "go n-diongnaim," he says *that I do.* This form diongnaim, is clearly derived from do and gníom. Déan in process of time assumed the present form, smoothed down from the older one diongnaim.

§ 151. (5) Deir, *say*.

All the tenses of deirim are regular, except the (1) perfect, dubnar; (2) the imperative, abair; and the (3) subjunctive, abraim; perfect dubnar, =do and deinear—do, sign of the perfect tense, and deinear, perfect tense from the verb deirim, I bear, bring forth, out, &c.

Abair, say = a, an intensitive particle, and deir; abraim, *I say*, is composed of a and deirim. The infinitive is do rad, *to say*. The passive of abraim is abartar; of deirim, deirtear; perfect active, dubrar; passive, dubrad.

§ 152. Fag- (6) *get, find,* the sixth of the irregular verbs, of which the only tenses not following the normal mode of conjugation are (ruanar), the *perfect* active, and (ruanað; and fríc), the perfect passive; with the conditional, ruigim, *would get.*

Geibim (like gabaim), a verb of kindred meaning, signifying *to get,* supplies, most commonly, the *imperfect, future,* and *conditional tenses.*

Fríc, *was found,* although not much employed in written or spoken Irish, is still not unfrequently read and heard. The writer of these pages has within the last few days (1863) heard an Irish peasant make use of the word in ordinary conversation.

The *passive* participle is wanting. It would be regularly fagta, but it is not in use. The present participle, fagail with "air" *on;* le, *with;* is employed in its stead, as (speaking of a thing found) ta re air fagail, it has been got; tá ꞅe le ꞅaꞃaɿl, it is to be had; ꞅaꞃaɿl with le (prep.) has the meaning of a passive verb. (See Syntax—le with.)

§ 153. (7) Feıc. The Gaelic verb, signifying *to see, to look at*, is expressed in Irish by the term ꞅeıc, *see* (*vide*) and cıóɿɱ. In the imperative mood the term aɱaɿc is usually heard, and beaɿc; Gr., δέρκω.

Feıcıɱ and cıóɿɱ are each conjugated regularly. In the perfect, however, connaɿcaꞅ, *I saw*, is the form. This term, connaɿcaꞅ, is equal to "con," *together* (Latin, *con*), and beaɿcaꞅ. Connacaꞅ, I saw, is another form nearly as common, derived from con, co, and ꞅeıceaꞅ, regularly formed from ꞅeıc, see. The inf. is irreg. ꞅeıcꞅıɲ, and by the interchange of c and ꞅ—ꞅeıꞅcıɲ, to which t is sometimes annexed for the sake of strength, thus, ꞅeıꞅcıɲt. The perfect passive is, strangely enough, "ꞅacaꞅ," as well as "connaɿcab."

§ 154. Rıꞃ (8) *to get as far as, to reach*, is an active intransitive verb—it has no passive voice. It is irregular in the infinitive mood, ɲoċtaıɲ, *to reach*.

☞ As a fact deserving of notice, the Irish speaking inhabitants sound all infinitives ending with ɲ as if t were annexed; ꞅeıcꞅıɲ, *to see*, they pronounce ꞅeıcꞅıɲt; ꞅulaɲꞃ, *to suffer*, ꞅulaɲꞃt; leaɲaɱaıɲ, *to follow*, as if leaɲaɱuıɲt, &c. This is a falling off from the written standard; it is not to be imitated. Something of the same kind appears in English, as *among* is sometimes written and pronounced *amongst; amid, amidst; while, whilst*, &c.

§ 155. Téıb (9), *go*, makes the perfect irregularly—Cuabaꞅ, *I went;* the future, ꞃaċꞅab, *I shall go;* conditional, ꞃaċꞅaıɲɲ, *I would go;* the infinitive, bo bul, *to go;* and participle, aꞃ bul, *going*. Ɖ of bul, is commonly pronounced like ꞃ; thus, ꞃul (which means *crying*.) The cause of this is, that the letter ꞃ of the particle, *v.g.* "aꞃ," bul, *going* (being more forcible than that of b, which immediately follows it), receives such phonetic strength, that the sound of b is lost, or combines with that of ꞃ.

☞ Cuaıb, *went* (as, cuaıb ꞅe, *he went*) is pronounced usually ꞅuaıb ꞅe. The ċ is guttural and should be pronounced like *ch*. There is a verb, ꞅuaıb, *to resign, to give up, to yield;* as, ꞅaıb or ꞅuaıb ꞅe, a ꞅꞅıoɲab, *he yielded up his spirit*. "Ɖo ꞅaıb, pro ꞅaıb, à verbo; ꞅaıbıɱ, *loco cedo, abeo*."—Leo, *Commentatio de Carmini Vetusto Hibernico, p*. 14.

Obs. 1.—The *past* tense of téıb (cuabaꞅ) is often beacaꞅ, after the particles ɲı, *not;* aɲ, *whether* (interrogative); ꞃo, *that;* as, ɲı beacaıb ꞅe, *he did not go;* aɲ ɲbeacaıb tu, *did you go?* It is always beacaꞅ in the subjunctive, as beıɲ ꞅe ꞃo ɲ-beacaıb ꞅıab, he says, *that* they went. Deacaꞅ, appears to be a compound form of cuabaꞅ and bo, the prepositive particle of the perfect.

Obs. 2.—The verb ıɲtıꞃ or ıɲıꞃ, *depart* (from ıɲ about, over, and above, *moreover*, and teıꞃ, *go*), is a regular verb. The verb teıt (pr. *theh*), *hasten, be off*, is regular; éıꞅıꞃ, *arise*, is reg. This last, is occasionally employed in the written and spoken language in the sense of *go*, as eıɲıꞃ amac, *go out, come out;* eıɲıꞃ ꞃo betel ıuba, *go to Bethlehem of Juda*.

☞ Téıɲıꞃ, *go*, is a corrupt form of téıb, used only in the imperative; ɲa téıɲıꞃ aɲɲ ꞅıɲ, *do not go there*, is an expression not uncommon amongst the people of the counties of Galway and Mayo.

IRISH GRAMMAR.

Τιჳ *(come)*, imperative ταρ.

§ 156. (10) The conjugation of the verb τιჳιm, *I come*, should be well known, for its use in Gaelic is very common, being employed with the compound pronoun liom, *with me*, leατ, *with thee*, leιρ, *with him*, &c., to express the English words, *can, could ; as*,

Τιჳ liom, *I can*—literally, *it comes with me*.
Τιჳ leατ, *thou canst, it comes with thee*.
Τιჳ leιρ, *he can ;* τιჳ leιτe, *she can, it comes with her*.
Ταιηιc liom, *I was able, I could*—literally, *it came with me, &c.*

Τιocfaιδ liom, *I will* be able; CONDITIONAL, τιocfaιηn, *I would* come ; and in third person singular followed by liom, *with me ;* leατ, *with thee ;* leιρ, *with him ;* liηη, *with us*, &c., *I could have* (done it)—literally, *it would have come with me* (to do it).

Infinitive δo τeατ *(hâght)*, or τeατ *(hé-ught)* *é* long or short.

☞ Sometimes the perfect tense, ταιηιcαρ, is spelled ταηჳαρ, *I came;* ταηჳαιρ, *thou camest ;* ταιηιჳ τe, *he came ;* in the Protestant version of the Old Testament, *e.g.,* Gen., c. 18, v. 5, and c. xix, v. 8 (ταηჳαδαρ, *they came*). This faulty orthography is not to be found in the Catholic version by Dr. MacHale.

Many verbs in Irish form, it is true, their infinitive mood and participles differently from the regular mode, but they are not, on this account, irregular.

To increase the amount of irregularities " is the last art that the philosophic grammarian is ambitious of acquiring. True etymology reduces irregularity by making the rules of grammar not exclusive but general."—*Latham on the English Language*, p. 336.

Ιτ, *eat*.

§ 157. The verb ιτ *(eeh), eat* (Latin, *ed-o*), changes τ into ρ in the future and conditional tenses. Ιρfαδ, *I shall eat ;* ιορfαιηη, *I would eat*.

The change from τ to ρ is phonetic; the use of o before it, as found in MSS., arises from collating the vowels broad with broad.

☞ The fact that in the verb ιτ, *eat*, ρ and τ, are found in the root, the one in the present, the other in the future tense, is very striking to any one who knows the well-known roots *es* and *ed*, of the verb *ed-o* in Latin, *ἐσ-τιω*, Greek, *to eat ;* in *ed-o* the root is *ed* (*d* and *t* are of the same organ, the one is commonly interchanged for the other); in *es-ca, food*, it is *es*, like the ιρ in ιρfαδ, future of ιτ, *eat ;* in like manner in *ἐσ-θιεν, to eat ;* and *ἐδ-μεναι, to eat*, the roots are *es* and *ed*, exactly like the Irish ιτ and ιρ in ιρ-(fαδ).

The infinitive of ιτ, is ιτe *(i-hé), to eat ;* the perfect δuαρ, *I eat*, is a corrupt form, for δ'ιτεαρ, the regular perfect.

§ 158. There are sixty-eight irregular verbs in French; yet to attain a knowledge of the French language is not considered very difficult. Its orthography, to the eye of an *English-speaking* student, is not at all in accordance with the pronunciation which he is taught to give the words of that language. The final consonants are quiescent. The *Irish* language has fewer irregular verbs, and fewer quiescent letters; how then does it arise that Gaelic or Irish is considered by the same individuals difficult to be acquired, because a few aspirated letters, having little or no sound, enter into the composition of many of its words? The fault, it seems, does not rest in its intrinsic difficulty; it must exist either in the want of clear philological elementary works hitherto unattainable, or perhaps it arises from the apathy of Irishmen to be Irish in language as well as in thought and in action. It is time that this apathy should cease.

§ 159.—DEFECTIVE VERBS.

The following defective verbs are those which are most frequently met with in manuscripts and printed works:—

ᴀɪᴘ ʀé, *said he;* ᴀɪᴘ, *says;* before a vowel takes an ʀ suffixed, as, ᴀɪᴘʀ ᴀɴ ꝼᴇᴀʀ, *says the man:* ʀ is here suffixed for sound's sake.

ᴀᴅ ʙᴀċ, *he died.*

ᴄᴀɪċꝼɪᴅ, *must;* it is the same through all the tenses and persons.

ᴀᴅ ꝼᴀᴅ, *he relates* (Latin, *fatur*); found in Dr. Keating's History of Ireland, *passim.*

ꝼᴀɪᴅ, or ꝼᴀᴏɪᴅ, *he gave up, he resigned;* Pᴀᴅʀᴜɪᴄ ᴅᴏ ꝼᴀɪᴅ ʀᴇ ᴀ ꞅᴘɪᴏʀᴀᴅ, *Patrick resigned his spirit.* See p. 148, § 155.

ꝼéᴀᴅᴀɪᴍ, *I am able;* wants the imperative and infinitive moods, with the participles.

ꝼᴇᴀꞅᴀɪᴍ, *I know.*

ꝼᴇᴀᴅᴀʀ, *I know;* used negatively and interrogatively; as, ɴí ꝼᴇᴀᴅᴀʀ ᴍé, *I do not know;* ɴí ꝼᴇᴀᴅᴀᴍᴀʀ, or ɴí ꝼᴇᴀᴅʀᴀᴍᴀʀ, *we do not know;* ꝼɪᴏɪʀ, *knows* (same).

ɴí ꝼᴜʟᴀɪʀ, *it must=il faut* (French).

ᴏʟ, ᴏᴘ, *quoth;* as, ᴏʟ ꞅé, *quoth he;* ᴏʟ ꞅɪᴀᴅ, *quoth they;* ᴍᴀɪċ, ᴀ ᴍɪᴄ ᴏɴ ᴀɴ ꞅᴀɢᴀʀᴛ, *well, my son, said the priest;* éɪʀɪġ, ᴏʟ ʀᴇ, *arise, said he;* ᴀɪᴘ and ᴏᴘ, seem to be the same verb.—Latin, *ait,* says; *Vita Molingi.*

ꝼᴏʀʙᴀᴅ, *was finished, made complete;* from ꝼᴏʀʙ, *perfect.*

ꝼᴇᴀċᴛᴀᴅ, *was fought;* ꝼᴇᴀċᴛᴀᴅ ᴄᴀċ, *a battle was fought;* from ꝼᴇᴀċᴛ, *to subdue, to wage, to fight out, to subdue, break down.*
ꝼᴇᴀċᴛᴀ, *broken, subdued, conquered.*

ꝼᴜʀᴀɪʟ, *it is necessary;* ᴀɪɢ ꝼᴜʀᴀɪʟ ᴜɪʟᴄ, *exerting evil.*

ꞅʀᴀᴏɪɴᴀᴅ, *was brought under; subdued* (root, ꞅʀᴀᴏɴ, *a bridle*).

ᴛᴇᴀʀɴᴀ, *he escaped;* ᴛᴀʀꝼᴀꞅ, *was revealed;* from ᴛᴀʙᴀɪʀ, *give,* and ꝼɪᴏꞅ, *knowledge.*

§ 160.—OBSOLETE VERBS.

The following verbs, though obsolete, are found in written records and printed books. An explanation of the terms must be useful.

Ac coḃa, *he has, he shares, partakes of.*

Root, cuιp, *a portion;* ac is an old form form for a and ḃo—a, *who,* and ḃo, sign of the perfect tense; ac coḃa mιan, *he entertains a wish.*

Baċ, *he died;* also ac baċ, a baιl, *he died;* and a united with baιl—thus, abaιl, *dead;* also apbaιl and epbaιl, from a, *who,* and baċ, *died.* Baċ, *drown,* is not at the present day obsolete.

baċ and baċaḋ are in common use, signifying *to drown, to perish;* and the derivative formed from these terms, v.g. from baιce, *perished;* is formed baιceaċ; la baιceaċ, *a perishing day;* cιt baιceaċ, *a drowning shower, a deluge of rain.*

Beaḃaιp, *he died (i.e., a, ḃa, a, ḃap) a, who; ḃa, was; a, in; ḃap, death.*

Caṫaṁ, *he departed* (for ca, *he is;* a *in,* caṁ, *repose*), *he reposes* with the dead; caṁ had the meaning of death in the old language. In the derivation of caṁleaċc (Tallaght, near Dublin, from caṁ, *death, plague;* and leaċc, *a monument*) this meaning is preserved. The first colony that came to Ireland under their leader Parthalon, 9,000 in number, all perished by a pestilence in one week, leaving the country once more without inhabitants.—*Annals of the Kingdom of Ireland;* Haverty's *Ireland,* p. 2. Caṁ, in its present acceptation, means a short sleep, nι puan m.ɔ caṁ a néιn, I did not get *a wink's rest* last night; nι puaιn rι caṁ, *she did not get any repose (sleep).*

Cepca, *he departed;* capca, *wanted* (modern).

Ceιp, *he fell;* ceιpḋ; copċeιp, *he fell;* like the modern cuιp, *put;* and cop, *totally, fully;* caomaιm, *I can, I find convenient;* from caom, *gentle, obliging;* cumacaιm (from cuma, *state, shape, ability;* hence, cumap, *ability;* and cumaċc, *power*), I am *able,* I am *powerful,* I can.

Cuma means form, mode, shape, state, ability, capability for any thing—hence, *indifference,* &c. This word is in common use; as, caḋ é an cuma ca onc, *what is the state in which you are?* (how are you situated, provided for, &c.?); oċ, naċ ḋear an cumɑ ca cu, *Oh, my! are you not in a nice way?* rιn é an cuma, *that is the way, that is the style;* cumaḋoιn, one who *shapes, fashions*—therefore, one who invents, *i.e.,* frames appearances in his mind, which have no reality; hence, a fabricator, a story-teller, a liar; ca cu a cumaḋoιneaċc, *you are only inventing.*

Claonpaιḋ, *they trust* (from claon, *inclined*); cloċa, *was* *heard;* from clu or cluṫ, *fame, report, hearsay;* modern cloṛ and cluɪɲ (see verbs irregular).

'Deċɾaɪɲ, for ꝺo ḟeɪcɾɪɲ, *to see.*

Ꝺuɾ (for ꝺo ḟɪoɾ), *I knew;* ꝺ' eɪɾɪꝺ, *it was settled;* for ꝺ'aɪcɪꝺ (leo), *it was agreed upon by them.*

Ⱥ)úpaɪm, *I demolish, I raze* (root múp, *a wall*).

Rac, *he gave;* pacɾac, *they gave; Ann. Four Masters,* A.D. 3304.

§ 161. IMPERSONAL VERBS.

Verbs like the English "it appears"—cɪoċċan, ḟeɪċċan; *it is lawful,* ꝺlɪȝcan (from ꝺlɪȝe, *law*), are as numerous in Irish as in the classic languages of England or Greece. Strictly speaking, however, these verbs are not impersonal. The real subject or nominative case is the sentence, or (as in English) the pronoun. Ʒoɪɲcan, *is called;* incorrectly written ȝanan; ȝeɲan for ȝeɪɲcan, *is born;* ċapla, *it came to pass;* ccanna, *escaped;* cɪȝ, *it comes with* (see the verb can, ċaɪɲɪc), as cɪȝ lɪom, *it comes with me, I can,* are of this class.

§ 162. According to the strict meaning then of the term impersonal, there is in Gaelic only one or two such; as, ꝺan lɪoɪɲ, *he thinks;* ꝺan leac, *thou thinkest;* ꝺan leo, *they think.*

☞ Ꝺan is very likely a contraction of ꝺo and leuɲ, *perceptible;* as, ꝺo leuɲ lɪom (for ꝺo, emphatic particle, ɪr, *is;* leuɲ, *perceivable*); lɪoɪɲ, *by me; i.e., I think.*

Nɪ ḟeaꝺan me, *I do not know;* for nɪ ḟeancan me, *it is not known (to) me.*

CHAPTER VIII.
ADVERBS.

§ 163. An adverb is a word that shows the time, manner, or circumstances of an action; (*time*), as, John writes *to-day;* (*manner*), John walks *hastily;* John walks *with haste;* " with haste," or " hastily," points out the manner of John's walking.

The expression "with haste," is as much an adverb as that other ending in "ly," according to Dr. Priestly, who defines adverbs to be (1) " contractions of sentences; or (2) "clauses of sentences" serving to denote the manner and other circumstances of an action.

The adverb modifies the meaning of adjectives and other adverbs as well as verbs.

"Adverbs, in general, are abbreviations of two or more words; thus, *bravely,* or, *in a brave manner,* is derived from *brave-like, wisely* from *wise-*

like, happily from *happy-like.*"—" English Grammar, Style and Poetry," by Richard Hiley, 13th ed., 1862; Longman, Green & Longman.

§ 164. Adverbs are therefore of two kinds; (*a*) the one answering to those denominated *contractions of sentences*, as in English, *newly, daily* (i.e., *new-like, day-like*); and in Irish, ɢo ꞌnuꜸ, ɢo lꜸeꜸꜹmꜸil; (*b*) the other, which may be classed with those called *clauses of sentences;* as, ꜸIꞃ Ꜹn ꜸobꜸꞃ ꞅIn (*for that reason*) *therefore;* cꜸnnoꞃ (for cꜸꜹ Ꜹn noꞃ, *what is the manner*), *how;* Latin, *quem-ad-modum—quo-modo.* These are common in every language; examples, *by-an-by, now-a-days, wherefore* (i.e., *for which*), *therefore* (i.e., *for that*), *quam-ob-rem* (Latin), *on account of which thing, scilicet* (*scire-licet*); *videlicet* (*videre-licet*); *pour-quoi* (French); *con amore, lovingly.* Sometimes entire incidental clauses hold the place of adverbs.

§ 165. (*a*) Those adverbs which describe the manner of an action, constitute a very numerous class. They are formed from adjectives by means of the prepositive particle ɢo (in Scotch Gaelic, ɢu); as, ɢꞃꜸꝺꜸc, *loving;* " ɢo " ɢꞃꜸꝺꜸc, *lovingly.*

" Ꝺ' ꝼꞃeꜸɢꜸꞃ ꜸIꞃIꞃ ' ɢo ' ꞃꜸIm Ꜹɢuꞃ ' ɢo ' mIn."
Homer ("Iliad," in Irish heroic metre,
By Dr. MacHale), b. 4., l. 109.

§ 166. ☞ Ꝗo is a preposition, meaning *with*, in form and meaning like to the Latin, *cum* (*with*); Italian, *con* (as *con amore, with love*, i.e., *in a loving manner, lovingly;* adv.). That this particle "ɢo" or *co*, means *with*, like *cum* or *con*, appears from its use in the "Annals of the Four Masters," vol. i. p. 1.

CeꜸcnꜸcꜸ lꜸ ꜸIꜸ noꝼlInn cꜸInIc CꜸeꞃoIn ɢo h-ꞨIꞃInn " ɢo " cꜸoɢꜸIꝺ n-InɢeꜸn ꜸɢIꞃ cꞃIuꞃ ꝼeꜸꞃ. *forty days before the deluge Kaesar came to Ireland* with *fifty virgins and* with *three men.*

§ 167. Every adjective in the Irish language, except those of the comparative and superlative degrees, becomes at once an adverb by the use of this prepositive particle " ɢo." Hence, the great body of adverbs become known by learning the adjectives.

NOTE.—In October, 1859, a very curious ode or bꞃoꞃnꜸcꜸꝺ cꜸcꜸ, " fierce appeal of battle," consisting of six hundred adverbs, was published in the pages of the *Nation* newspaper. It was furnished by Mr. William Livingstone, Glasgow. This address was composed and pronounced to the MacDonalds at the battle of Harlow, fought in 1411, between Donald of the Isles and the Duke of Albany. The bard was a progenitor of Niall More Macmhuirich, of Barra, who supplied some of those MS. Gaelic poems of which James Macpherson distorted parts into English prose.

This address is at least very curious and instructive, as affording illustration of the copiousness and refinement of the Gaelic language.

The stanzas, consisting of some twenty lines each, are numbered in the order of the letters of the alphabet. The whole piece would be too long for our limited space. The curious may be pleased to see one or two, as specimens, which are here subjoined:

"bpornacab cata cloinn Doṁnuill le Lacan Ṁon MacMuiric Albanaic. Laca blan cat Ṡarbac, 1411.

"A fierce appeal of battle of the clan Donnell, by Lachan Mör MacMuirich, an Albanian. The date of the engagement of the battle of Harlow, 1411."

"A clanna cuinn cuṫuinicib
Cruaran am na h-iorṡaiṁll.
. . . . . .
C.

Ṡu calma, ṡu cunanta,
Ṡu cróḋa, ṡu cruaḋalac,
Ṡu caṫbuaḋac, ṡu creucḋanmac,
Ṡu cruaiḋ-laṁac, ṡu coinṡleurac,
Ṡu conrpullac, ṡu córaṡac,
Ṡu cionurṡnac, ṡu conurṡnac,
Ṡu colṡanta, ṡu caċṁór,
Ṡu cuilbairac, ṡu cruaiḃlannac,
Ṡu creaḋac, ṡu caiṫroanrac,
Ṡu caiṫéniceac, ṡu ceannṫrneaċac,
Ṡu ceannarac, ṡu cúnamac,
Ṡu craoḃac, ṡu cluteac,
Ṡu cuinacḃac, ṡu confaḋac,
Ṡu claoiḃḃuilleac, ṡu colṡanna,
Ṡu cruaiḃḃuilleac, ṡu caḃeumac,
Ṡu coimeac, ṡu coiṁbre,
Ṡu cuiḃaiḃ, ṡu cuḋcnonac,
Ṡu cunaiḃeac, ṡu cunḃailtoac,
Ṡu coinciṁneac, ṡu craṡac,
Ṡu cruaiḃénṫoeac, ṡu coinrac,
Craḃac, collaiḃeac, creacṁon.

D.

Ṡu dian, ṡu dún,
Ṡu dáranac, ṡu deaṡfulanac,
Ṡu dana, ṡu dircin,
Ṡu diōṡanta, ṡu dicoirṡte,
Ṡu deinnteac, ṡu dlúcbuilleac,
Ṡu deaṡlamac, ṡu dúruinneac,
Ṡu doluiṡ, ṡu doluḃaiḃ,
Ṡu droċṁeineac, ṡu dóint-fuileac,

IRISH GRAMMAR. 155

go ḋeiṙinċaċ, gu ḃeannalaċ,
gu oiṫċiollaċ, gu ḃcunaraċ,
gu ḃeangtaṙnaċ, gu ḃioġaltaċ,
gu ḃeirtenaċ, gu ḃiúḃalaċ,
gu ḃímearaċ, gu ḃionġaċ,
gu ḃealajó, gu ḃeaġḃuilleaċ,
gu ḃeónaċ, gu ḃúnaċḃac,
gu ḃonḃa, gu ḃanġana,
gu ḃunnanta, gu ḃalma,
gu ḃungánta, gu ṫéṙnḃa,
ḃóċaṙaċ ḃoċjoṙajéte."

Adverbs are compared; their comparative and superlative degrees are, however, those of the adjectives whence they are formed.

§ 168. (b) The second class, "clauses of sentences," or adverbial phrases, as they are called in schools, points out the time and circumstances of an action. They are a complex union of prepositions and nouns.

"Many adverbs," says Hiley, " are formed by a combination of a preposition with other adverbs. Some are composed of nouns."—*English Grammar,* p. 71.

ADVERBS—CLAUSES OF SENTENCES.

A ḃ-ḟaḋ, *a-far;* from a, *in;* and ḟaḋ, *length.*

A ḃ-ḟaḋ aṙ ṙo, *far hence* (in relation to time or place).

A ḃ-ḟaḋ ṙoime, *long before* (in time or place).

A ġ-céin, *far off;* from a, *in;* and céin, dat. case of cian, *remote, distant, foreign, tedious;* (as to *time*), iṙ cian ḻom tá tu amuiġ, *I feel you are long absent;* (as to *place*), iṙ faḋa o' n laṁ a tá a ġ-céin, *one is far removed from the (friendly) hand that is far away;* cian, *n.;* plur., cianta; tá ṙe na "cianta" ó ċonnaiṙc me ṫu, *it is ages since I saw you—I have not seen you this age.*

A ġ-comnuiḋe, *always, continuously;* from a, and comnuiḋe, *abode; i.e., abidingly.*

Amaċ, *out.*

Amuiġ, *without, outside.*

The difference between amaċ and amuiġ is, that the one is connected with a verb of motion—as, tejḋ amaċ. *go out:* the other with a verb of rest—as, tá me amuiġ, *I am without.*

Amárac,
Amáireac, } to-morrow.
Lá aṙṙ na maiṙeac,
Aiṙ aiṙ, *back*.
Aiṙ an aóbaṙ ṙin, *therefore*.
Aiṙ ball, *on the spot, presently, very soon*.
Aiṙ biċ, *at all, in the world*.
Aiṙ éigin, *with difficulty*.
Ann aice, *near, nigh;* aice, *i.e.,* faice, *nearness;* from rocur, Welsh, *agos, near*.
Ann áirde, *on high*.
Anall (1) (= ó, *from;* an, *the;* oll, *yonder;* see anon, *infra*), *over, higher, to this side;* always connected with a verb of *motion;* as, taṙṙ anall, *come over*.

It is the opposite of anon, *to the other side;* as, bul anon agur anall, *going* to that side and to this side, wavering, changing from side to side. Anon and anall convey necessarily the idea of *motion;* the adverbs a bur (for a b-foġur), *on this side;* tall, *on that side;* the idea of rest; as, tá re a bur, he is on *this* side (not anall); tá re tall, he is on the opposite side (not anon).

A bur agur tall, here, there, *hic, illic;* on this side and on that (when a state of rest is implied).

Anon agur anall, hither, thither, *huc, illuc;* to this side and to that (when the idea of motion to a place is conveyed).

☞ Anon (2) is written also anoll in many instances. On this account, and because it is in meaning antithetic to anall, which ends in "ll," its derivation appears to be from the preposition oll, *above, superior, yonder, higher,* and an, *the:* anon, *i.e.,* anoll = an, *the,* oll, *higher, yonder* (taob, *side,* or leit, *half,* being understood); (3) tall is derived from the same word, "oll," and t, a prepositive, like r, in ruar, or rather the remnant of the preposition do (omitting o, and changing d into t); (4) a bur is a contracted form of a b-foġur, *i.e.*, an (taob) foġur, the nigh side.

The particle an, the prefix to these adverbs, is considered by Zeüss to be the article, and not, as others think, the preposition.

From analogy with kindred words in Irish, and adverbs of the like meaning in English (as *aboard, afloat*), the particle is readily proved to be a preposition.

An alloḋ, *of yore* (for an t-am alloḋ, *the old time;* or for ann [am] alloḋ, *in the olden time*).
An dear, *southward, or, from the south*.
An oiṙ, *eastward, or, from the east*.

IRISH GRAMMAR. 157

Aṅ ιaṗ, *westward*, or, *from the west.*
A b-ṫuaiċ, *northward*, or, *from the north.*

NOTE.—Aṅ ḃeaṙ, meaning *from* the south, is a contraction for ó aṅ ḃeaṙ; so also aṅ oiṙ, *from* the east, for ó aṅ oiṙ; aṅ ιaṗ, *from* the west, ó aṅ ιaṗ; ó, *from*, being omitted. Aṅ ḃeaṙ, *the south* (in the nom. case), is composed of the article aṅ, and the word ḃeaṙ, *south, right side;* also aṅ ḃeaṙ is for aṅṅ ḃeaṙ, *in the south*, according to the grammatical arrangement of the context or sentence.

Aṅ ṅoċt, *to-night*; sometimes oiḃċe is added; as, aṅ oiḃċe ṅoċt, *this very night;* Greek, νυκτι; Latin, *nocte;* Saxon, *nicht;* English, *night.*

Aṅ ιuḃ, *to-day;* aṅ lá 'ṅ ιuḃ, *this very day; au jour d'hui.*

Aṅ ṅeaċtaṗ, *externally, in the outside,* for aṅṅ ḟeaċtaṗ (initial ḟ, when aspirated, being omitted); root, ṗeaċ, *apart, outside;* ṗeaċtaṗ, *more apart.*

Aṅṅ aoṅ-ḟeaċt, *together.*

The word uaṙ, means *above, high;* hence, uaṙal (uaṙ-al, from uaṙ and al, *offspring), high-born, noble;* uaiṗle, *nobility.*

So, ιoṙ means *below;* hence, iṙeal, *low-born, lowly, humble;* aṅ t-aoṙ iṙeal, *the common people.*

Whenever Irishmen wish to express the idea of motion upwards, or motion in a downward direction, uaṙ and ιoṙ take an initial ṙ; as, ṙuaṙ, *upwards;* ṙιoṙ, *downwards:* ṙuaṙ aṡuṙ ṙιoṙ, *up and down* (active).
A state of rest above is expressed by ḟuaṙ and below by ḟιoṙ; as, táιb ḟuaṙ (thaid huas), *they are above;* táιb ḟιoṙ, *they are below.*
Motion *from above* is expressed by the form, aṅ uaṙ (*i.e.*, ó, *from*, aṅ, *the*, uaṙ, *above*); from below, by aṅ ιoṙ (for ó, aṅ, ιoṙ, *from the below*).
Hence, aṅuaṙ (although compounded of uaṙ, *above*) signifies *down;* as, taṙṙ aṅuaṙ, come down—*i.e.*, come from above; aṅιoṙ, *up;* taṙṙ aṅιoṙ, come up—*i.e.*, from below.
Oiṙ, *east,* ṙoιṙ, *eastward;* ιaṗ, *after, west,* ṙιaṗ, *westward;* follow the same analogy. The initial ṙ is perhaps from the preposition ṡuṙ, *towards.*

Aιṗ ṡ-cul, *backward;* tá ṙιb aιṗ ṡ-cul, *you are behind;* tá ṙιb ḃul aιṗ ṡ-cul, *you are retrograding;* ṗa ċul, *under cover, covertly, behind backs.*

Aιṗ ṅ-ḃóιṡ, *indeed* (from aιṗ, *on*, and ḃoιṡ, *hope, i.e., hopefully, probably, indeed*).

Aιṗ ṗaḃ, *altogether;* táιb aιṗ ṗaḃ aṅṅ ṙιṅ, *they are altogether there;* this expression aιṗ ṗaḃ (ḟ, asp.), pr. *air adh*, means *in length;* as, leiṫ míle "air faḋ," *a half mile in length.*

Air b-tur, *in the first place, at the beginning;* a g-tur, *in the beginning;* a toraċ, *in the beginning.*

Air ḋeire, *at the end, at the close, late—without any share;* fa ḋeire, *at last.*

As, ta mire air ḋeiṁé, *I am without any share;* on the principle that he who arrives *late* for the booty, gets either little or nothing.

Air leiṫ, *a-part,* from air, *on;* and leiṫ, *half—side, a-side;* roinn air leiṫ comroinn, *a share "apart,"* and *co-share.*

Airaon, *singly* (from air, *at;* and aon, *one*) *i.e., one-by-one;* ir ionnan aoir, uairle agur cumaċt ḋoib "airaon," *their age, their power, and their glory* (*i.e.,* of each) *is the same.*

Airaoir, *adv., last night.*

Arteaċ, *into;* artiġ, *within (doors);* arteaċ equals "gur an teaċ," *towards the house.*

Artiġ, *within, i.e., in the house.*

Air uairib, *at times.*

A riaṁ, *ever, i.e., up to the present;* go braṫ, *ever (in time to come),* in the sense of *till doom's-day;* braṫ, *judgment;* go ḋeo, *ever—as long as life lasts;* rior, *ever (time past or to come), perpetual;* a coiḋċe, *ever* (time to come).

☞ The term *never* (equal to *not ever*) in the English language, is translated into Irish always by the words *not—ever;* (1) the negative particle *not,* goes *before* the verb, and *ever* follows; but (2) remember the term *ever* has two meanings, that of (1st) *hitherto, all along up to the present time;* (2nd), all time *to come;* when it signifies *hitherto,* it is to be translated by "a riaṁ," when *time to come,* it is to be translated by "go ḋeo," or go braṫ; as, *I never* (time past), *did it;* and *never* (time to come) *will do it;* níor rinne mé "a riaṁ" é, agur ní ḋeanfaḋ go braṫ, *I was never there, and never shall;* ní ṗab mé "a riaṁ" ann rin, agur "ní" béiḋir "a coiḋċe."

Ann am, *in time, timely;* ann antraṫ, *untimely;* go traṫaṁail, *opportunely* (from traṫ, *special time*).

A b-fogur, *near;* Latin, *vicinus, a neighbour;* ann gair, *near, nigh* (in place or time).

A ne or a noḋ, *yesterday.*

It is, after all, most likely that né, *yesterday,* and ɪuḃ, *to-day,* were each spelled with ḃ in the forepart of the terms respectively. See the reasons in favour of each view in the work published by us—"Easy Lessons; or, Self-Instruction in Irish (reprinted from the pages of the *Nation*). p. 30. In the *Codex Paulinus* quoted by Zeüss, and preserved in the Library of the Monastery of St. Gall, Switzerland, the Irish of the words *to-day* is found to be ɪnnḃɪu (*i.e.,* ᴀnn ḃɪu). Again he says : "Ita subst. bɪᴀ (dies) in formula usitata, ' ɪnḃɪᴀ' (hodie)."—*Grammatica Celtica*, p. 563.

Ꭺnn ꞅo, *here (in this)*; ᴀnn ꞅɪn, *there (in that)*; ᴀɪꞅ ꞅo. *here (at this place)*; ᴀɪꞅ ꞅɪn, *there*; ᴀnn rúḃ, *there, yonder*; mᴀn rúḃ, *so (in that way)*; ó ꞅo, *henceforth*; ó ꞅo ᴀmᴀċ. (*from this out*), *henceforth*; o ꞅɪn, *from that, thence*; ó ꞅɪn ᴀ leiċ, *ever since.*

This word *where*, in English, is sometimes an *adv.* of interrogation—of relation, or, is employed indefinitely.

1. *When?* (interrogative), cɪᴀ-ᴀn-uᴀɪꞅ (*what hour*)? cɪᴀ-ᴀn-ᴛᴀm, cᴀ h-ᴀm (*what time*)? cɪᴀ-ᴀn-ᴛꞅᴀċ (*what special time*—ᴛꞅᴀċ)?
2. *When,* "ᴀ," or, "ᴀnn ᴀ," *in which (time)*; as, *the time the deluge was on the earth*—ᴀn ᴛꞅᴀċ "ᴀ" bɪ ᴀn ḃɪle ᴀɪꞅ ᴀn ḃomᴀn.
3. *When,* 'nuᴀɪꞅ, this is the most common form. *Where?* cᴀ? as, cᴀ b-ꞅuɪl ᴛu? *where are you? where = in which place?* ꞅɪn ᴀn ᴀɪᴛ "ᴀnn ᴀꞅ" leᴀᵹ ꞅɪᴀḃ é, *that is the place where they laid him.*

Ꭺmᴀɪn, *only* (as if from ᴀ, *in*; mo, *a person;* ᴀon, *one*).

Ꭺmlᴀɪḃ, *like;* ᴀnᴀm, *seldom;* ceᴀnnᴀ, *already;* cɪḃ, *although,* from cɪḃ, *sees, i.e., seeing that;* ḃeɪmɪn, *indeed;* eᴀḃon, *to wit.*

Fóɪl, *yet, awhile;* fóꞅ, *yet, a longer stay, or rest;* feᴀꞅḃᴀ, *henceforth.*

Ꭻɪḃ, same as cɪḃ; ɪᴀꞅꞅᴀɪn, *hereafter* (from ɪᴀꞅ, *after,* and ᴀm, *time*).

Ꭻoɪnnᴜɪꞅᴀ, *moreover* (from ɪomḃᴀ, *many, or more;* and uꞅꞅᴀ, *over them*).

Ille, *thenceforward;* ó ꞅɪn ɪlle, *from that forward.*

Léɪꞅ, *entirely;* ᵹo léɪꞅ, *same;* leoꞅ, *sufficient;* ᵹo leoꞅ, *sufficiently;* ᵹo h-ɪomlᴀn, *entirely;* ᵹo ꞅollᴜꞅ, *openly.*

Ꭺɪlle and ɪomᴀɪlle (from ɪom, *about, with,* and ᴀɪlle, *another*), *together with, along with.*

Ꭺꞅ, *as;* mᴀꞅ ꞅɪn, *in that way—so so;* mᴀꞅ ꞅɪn ḃe, *therefore, thereupon.*

Aṁaṟ ṟo, *in this way, thus;* maiṟe, *well!* maiṟte, *well, well!* ṟeaḋ, *yes;* ṟeaḋ a ṁaiṟte, *yes, indeed; well, well! it is so.*

Aṁinic, *frequently;* na, *not,* imperative; as, "na" ḃean, *do not do.*

Ní, *not* (in the indicative mood); as, ní me, *it is not I;* ní móṟ naċ, *almost* (*it is not much but*); ní móṟ naṟ, *it is not much but that;* beaġ naċ, *little but, i.e., almost.*

Sul, *before;* ṟaṁlaiḋ (from ṟaṁail, *like*), *in like manner;* as, aṁlaiḋ is from aṁail, *like.*

Do ḃṟiġ, *because, by virtue of;* ḃe ġnáċ, *usually;* ḃe laċaiṟ, *presently, just now*—also, *in one's presence, and not in a concealed way;* ḃe ló, *by day;* ḃ'oiḋċe, *by night, in the night time;* ṟa ċuaiṟt, *round about, in a circle.*

Ṟa ḋeoiġ, *at last, at the long run* (pr. yeo-igh, in one syl.); ṟa ḋó, *twice;* ṟa ṫṟí, *thrice;* ṟa ṟeaċ, *by turns, apart.*

Ṟa ċuaiṟim, *conjecturally;* builc ṟa ċuaiṟim, *a blow by chance* (tuaṟ, *a conjecture*), *without aim;* ċuaiṟim *means about, in the direction of,* without defining the precise way.

Ṟa ċuaiṟim, is also a preposition, meaning *in the direction of,* but that direction not specially defined. (See p. 165).

Ġo móṟ-ṁóṟ, *especially.*

Ionnoṟ ġo, *in order that.*

Aṁaṟ aṇ ġ-céaḋna, *in like manner.*

Ó ċeile, *asunder* (ó, from, ċeile, *a companion, from one another*); le ceile, *together, one with another, as with a companion* (ceile); maṟ aon, *together, as one.*

Óṟ íṟiol, *lowly, in a whisper, privately.*

Óṟ aṟḋ, *above board, aloud.*

§ 169. Besides these classes there are in Irish certain adverbial participles which unite with nouns, adjectives, verbs, and other adverbs. They are sometimes incorporated with the word with which they coalesce, and sometimes not, but merely connected by a hyphen. In this respect they are of the same use in Irish, as the prepositions or the particles α, δυs ϵυ, &c., in Greek. By them, and with them, are formed hundreds of new words, which thus enrich the language, and supply the speaker with forms of expression to suit every shade of thought. In learning them and their meaning well, the student will, after a little study, have advanced a great way in acquiring a great knowledge of Irish. These prepositive particles shall be explained presently in chapter x. on derivation and composition.

CHAPTER IX.

PREPOSITIONS—CONJUNCTIONS—INTERJECTIONS.

§ 170. A preposition is a word placed before nouns and pronouns to show the relation which they bear to each other, or to some verb. Prepositions are of two kinds (1) *simple*, and (2) *compound*.

§ 171.—*Simple Prepositions.*

ᴀ, or ᴀɴɴ, *in;* ɪ, or ɪɴ, (old form), *in*
ᴀɪᵹ, *at.*
ᴀɪɼ, *on, for, against.*
ᴀꞅ, *out of.*
cuɪᵹe, *to, towards.*
ᴅe, *of.*
ᴅᴀɼ, *by* (in swearing).
ᴅo, *to.*
eɪᴅɪɼɪ or ɪᴅɪɼ, *between.*
ꝼᴀ, *for, concerning.*
ꝼᴀoɪ, *under;* ꝼo, *under.*
ᵹᴀɴ, *without.*
ᵹo } *to, towards.*
ᵹuꞅ }
ᵹoɴᴀ, *with* (obsolete).
le, leɪꞅ, *with.*
ɼoɪṁe, or ɼoɪṁ, *before.*
o, or uᴀ, *from.*
óꞅ, *above;* uᴀꞅ, orig. form.
ɼe and ɼɪꞅ, *for* le and leɪꞅ.
ꞅeᴀċ, *beside, over;* Lat. *secus.*

ᴛᴀɼ, and ᴛᴀɼɪ, *over.*
ᴛᴀɪɼɪꞅ, *over, without;* as, ᴅéᴀɴ ᴛᴀɪɼɪꞅ, *do without it;* cuɪꞅ ᴀɴ ʙɼᴀᴛ ᴛᴀɪɼɪꞅ, *put the cloak* over *him.*
ᴛɼe, *through, by means of;* ᴛɼeᴀꞅ (before the art. ᴀɴ); as, ᴛɼeᴀꞅ ᴀɴ ᴅoṁᴀɴ ṁóꞅ, *through the wide world.*
ᴛɼeᴀꞅɴᴀ, *through, across;* as, ɼᴀċꝼᴀɪᴅ ᴀɴ Tɪᵹeᴀꞅɴᴀ "ᴛɼeᴀꞅɴᴀ" ʙuᴀlᴀᴅ ɴᴀ h-Eᵹɪɼᴛe, "*the Lord shall pass* through, *striking Ægypt.*"
ᴛꞅɪᴅ, *through.*
uɪṁe, *about.*
'ꞅᴀɴ, *for* ᴀɴɴꞅ ᴀɴ, *in the;* contractedly, 'ꞅᴀɴ, and omitting ɴ (of the article) 'ꞅᴀ'.

§ 172.—*Compound Prepositions.*

The *compound* prepositions are composed of substantives and prepositions. They are short phrases having the meaning peculiar to single prepositional particles. In this view they are quite easy, for phrases bearing a prepositional sense exist in every language. But some of the Irish compound prepositions—like ċuṁ, *towards, for the purpose of*—are not at first sight sufficiently distinct in their classification. They are composed of nouns now obsolete, and have become, by usage, so reduced from their compound state, that sometimes they resemble simple prepositions.

A b-ḟail, *in the border of, vicinity of* (from a, *in*, and ḟail, *a ring, a wreath, border, circle*—kindred in meaning to ḟál, *a fence, enclosure;* whence ḟálaiḋ, *a cloak, covering*).

A b-ḟarraḋ (from a, *in*, and ḟarraḋ, *company, linked in society*—root, ḟar, same as mar, *along;* re, *with;* (1) *along with, in company with;* (2) *in comparison with;* in this last sense written a b-ḟarrar; naċ breaġ anoir é, a b-ḟarrar mar bi ré, *how splendid it is now, in comparison with how it was.*

Of a b-ḟarraḋ, in the first sense, the following quotation is an example: ir truaġ ġan oiġir " 'nn a b-ḟarraḋ," *it is a pity there is n't an heir in their company.—Davis's "Lament for the Milesians."*

A b-ḟiaḋnuire (from a, *in*, and ḟiaḋnuire, *witness, presence*—root, ḟior, *knowledge*), *in sight of, in presence of so as to witness;* deirim é a b-ḟiaḋnuire Dé, *I say it in the presence of God (who has a knowledge, ḟior, of it);* ann m' ḟiaḋnuire, *in my presence, before my face.*

Fiaḋuir comes from ḟior, *knowledge;* innir, *tell*), and therefore means to declare (in testimony) what one knows.

A b-ḟocair, *with, together with, in company;* ḟocair, *company, nearness to;* it is from the same root as ḟocur, *near.*

A laṫair (from a, *in*, and laṫair, *spot, presence;* where one sees—leir, *perceivable*), *in presence of;* a laṫair an Tiġearna, *in the presence of the Lord.*

Or comair, (from or *over;* and comair, *count, aim, front, face presence);* or comair an domain moir, *before the whole world* (so that they may count our actions, and calculate regarding our conduct).

Or coinne, *opposite, diagonally, face to face, vis-a-vis, in presence of* (from or, and coinne, *i.e.,* cuaine, *an angle, diagonally*—in opposite angles or positions).

☞ Observe the resemblance in meaning of the five foregoing prepositional phrases. The English word *before* is rendered into Irish by any of those five. The particular meaning of the preposition *before* must be attended to by the translator.

Elluc, or ellug, and colleic, *altogether;* also, ann ellug, *unanimously.*—Zeüss, " *Grammatica Celtica,* vol. ii. p. 620.

☞ This preposition, or rather adverbial phrase, is at present in common use in Connaught. Bioan ellug ann rin, *they were there altogether.* The word is pronounced as if written, a lig, *all;* as, b-puil rib " a lig," rian? *are ye all well?*

Colleic is derived from có, *with;* and leic (Armoric, *lech;* Latin, *loco*), *a place.*

" Invenitur," says Zeüss, " etiam *personas significans,*" p. 565. Hence its use at the present day as a pronoun amongst the Irish-speaking peasants of the West, dates from the remotest antiquity.

Ar uct, *for the sake of—pour l'amour de.*

A g-cionn, a g-ceann, *at the head of, at the end of, in addition to, along with*—root, ceann, *head, end, top;* gen. case of ceann is cinn, dat., cionn.

Or cionn, *over, above, at the head of;* tá Dia or cionn na domain móir, *God is above* (at the head of) *the entire world;* or do cionn, *over your head;* as, *a master.*

Ann aircir (aircir, *a meeting*), *in the meeting of;* téig ann a aircir, *go to meet him.*

A g-cuinne, *in order to get, to meet, to obtain;* as, tainic re a g-cuinne airgio, *he came for* (i.e., *in order to get a* g-cuinne), *money.*

This preposition is ever on the lips of the speaking Irish, implying to *meet with, to get.* It always follows a verb of motion. See or coinne.

A leit (from leit *half, one of two, side*), *to the charge of.* It is an adv., and means *aside, apart, hither.*

A leitpe, *one side* (from leit and pe, *with*), *unaccompanied;* as,

" Peagur, Joar d' ionnruig Diamud treun,
Leitpe a g-cuid feap, go mirnamail 'gur go dean."

A taob (taob, *side*), *relating to, in regard to.*

Ameag, *among, amidst* (from a, and meare, *mixing*); Latin, *misceo;* Eng., *mix, i.e., misc.*

From agaid (*eye-e*), *face, front,* is formed the preposition ann agaid, *against,* which is very much in use. Le agaid, *with the (face) view to, intended for;* tá re po le agaid Seamuir, *this is intended for James.* O agaid, *away from, from the face of;* faoi agaid, *under the eye of, in the view of.*

The preposition ᴀıṟ, *on*, is omitted oftentimes before bun, *foundation;* cul, *rear, back;* ꝼᴀᴆ, *length;* ꝼeᴀᴆ, *space;* ꝼuᴆ, *breadth;* ᴦɜᴀċ, *shade, appearance;* ꞅoṅ, *sake;*—ᴆo, *to,* is not always expressed with ċum, *the form, shape, the waist, circumference, position;* nor with ṅeıṅ, *will, accord.* In this way these nouns have the appearance of simple prepositions. In the following list they are given in full:—

Aıṟ bun, *established*—literally, *on a foundation.*

Aıṟ cul, *behind;* as, ᴀıṟ cul ṅᴀ ꞅleıḃe, *behind the mountain;* ᴀıṟ cul ᴀṅ ᴆoṟuıꞅ, *behind the door.*

Aıṟ ꝼᴀᴆ, *in length*—*the length of.*

Aıṟ ꝼeᴀᴆ, *during;* as, ᴀıṟ ꝼeᴀᴆ ᴀṅ lᴀe, *during the day.*

Aıṟ ꝼuᴆ ᴀṅ ᴆoṁᴀıṅ, *throughout the world.*

Aıṟ ᴦɜᴀċ, *for the sake of* (rather, *shadow*) *of, for the lucre of;* ᴀıṟ ᴦɜᴀċ cᴀıṟᴆe, *for the sake of a respite*—*for a little loan.*

Aıṟ ꞅoṅ, *for the sake of, through;* ᴀıṟ ꞅoṅ Ⅾé, *for God's sake.*

Aꞅ uċᴛ, *through, by virtue of.*

Ⅾo ṅeıṅ, *according to* (ṅeıṅ, *accord, will*).

Ⅾo ċum (or, ċuṁ), *to, towards, for, for the purpose of;* ċum ṅᴀ ꞅleıḃe, *to the mountain;* ċum ᴀ ᴆeᴀṅᴛᴀ, *in order to do it* (literally, *in order to its doing*).

From eıꞅ, *a spot, a place, a track, a foot-print,* come the prepositions:

Aṅṅ eıꞅ, *after (in the track of).*

Ⅾ' eıꞅ, *after (of the track of);* ᴆ' eıꞅ is commonly written without the apostrophe, "ᴆeıꞅ," *after.*

Ꞇᴀṟ eıꞅ, *after (over the track of).*

From ᴆıᴀıɜ, *end, conclusion,* is formed the preposition, ᴀṅṅ ᴆıᴀıɜ, *after;* contractedly, ṅ-ᴆıᴀıɜ (pr. *ney-ee*); ᴀṅṅ ᴆıᴀıɜ relates to place, or position; as, *John is after James* (in place), ᴛᴀ Seᴀɜᴀṅ 'ṅ ᴆıᴀıɜ Seᴀṁuıꞅ.

Ⅾéıᴆ, *with longing desire;* as, ṅı'l ṁé ᴀṅṅ ᴆéıᴆ ꞅıṅ oꞃᴛ, *I do not grudge you that.*

Ⅾéımce Uı ḃꞃıᴀıṅ ᴀɜuꞅ ᴀ ᴆᴀ ꞅuıl ıṅṅᴀ ᴆéıᴆ, *O'Brien's alms—whose eyes looked longingly after the gift* (a proverb).

Iᴀꞅ, *after, behind* (ıᴀꞅ, *the west*); ᴛᴀꞅ eıꞅ, and ıᴀꞅ, relate to time; as, ıᴀꞅ ᴛeᴀċᴛ, *after coming.*

Ioṅṅꞅᴀıᴆ, *towards, unto, in the direction of, about, towards, against* (from the noun ıoṅṅꞅᴀıᴆ, *an attack, a turning towards, an approach to*—root, ιη, *in,* and ρυιδ, *sit, rest*); δ'ιοηηρυιδε, *towards, against;* with a verb of motion it gives the idea of hostility, opposition—also of seeking refuge; ċuaιδ ρε ιοηηρυιδε αη ηαṁαιδ, *he went to encounter the enemy.*

Τιmċιoll means *circuit, ambit;* α τιmċιoll, therefore, means *about, around,* and is usually employed without the preposition α (*in*).

Τυαιριm, *conjecture* (root, τυαρ, *a sign, a prognostic*), ϝα ċυαιριm, *towards, about;* as, ϝα ċυαιριm δο ϝlάιητε, *towards your health;* ϝα ċυαιριm ηα ρleιbe, *towards,* or *somewhere about the mountain, i.e.,* in the direction of, without defining the exact spot—this meaning accords with its radix, τυαρ, *guess, conjecture, sign.*

Ϟο δ-τι, *to, unto, up to;* το ηυιϟε, *until, up to.*

Ϟυρ, *towards;* same as ϟο, *to, towards.* It receives ρ final for the sake of euphony whenever the article αη, *the,* comes immediately after; as, ϟυρ αη m-baιle mόιρ, *to the large town.*

The word αιρ, meaning *side, border, brink* (perhaps for ειρ, *track, mark*), is not found in any Irish Dictionary which the writer has seen, yet it is common in the spoken language; as, le αιρ, *along, by the side of.*

"Le αιρ ηα τοηητα ϟloραċ' ϟειmηαċ' ϟαιϟ."
"Along by the waves, roaring, loud-resounding, raging."

CONJUNCTIONS.

§ 173.—Conjunctions are the connecting links in the chain of speech.

Αċτ (1) *but;* (2) *except, at;* ast, Latin.

_{Αċ is an incorrect spelling; αċτ is found in the most ancient MSS.}

Αϟυρ (1) *and;* (2) *as,* like the Latin ac. atque, which have both meanings, that of "and" and "as;" ċo, *so,* is followed by αϟυρ, *as*—ex. of both:

Ir τρυαϟ ηαċ b-ϝυιl δο ηεαρτ ϟαη claoιδε
(1) "Αρ" δο luċ ċo uρ 'ρ ċo laιδιρ (2) "ρ" τα δο ċροιδε.

Homer (in Irish heroic metre,
by Dr. MacHale), b. 4., ll. 357, 358.

Again, τα baιlle ηα ηδαοιηε ċo mορ "αϟυρ" ριη ϟο ηϟlαcαιδ αη υιlc cunam ꞃa ꞃeıṫıb oıombuan an c-ꞃaoġaıl ꞃo, aȝuꞃ ȝo nóéanaıo neaṁḃꞃıȝ, oo ꞃaıóḃꞃıꞃ ꞃꞇoꞇnuıóé pannꞅaıꞃ.—" The blindness of mankind is so great that they take all care of the transitory things of this world, and treat as worthless the everlasting blessings of Paradise"—*Irish Sermons by Dr. Gallagher.*

Aȝuꞃ, *and;* has sometimes the meaning of *that, on account of;* as, Cꞃeuo ꞇ mo ċaın? cꞃeuo ꞇ mo ċoꞇꞃ " aȝuꞃ " ȝuꞃ lean cu ċo ȝeuꞃ ꞃꞇn mc?— "What was my fault, and what was my crime *that* you pursued me so hotly."—*Genesis,* xxxi., 36.

Aȝuꞃ, in ancient writings accuꞃ and ocuꞃ, akin to ꞃoȝuꞃ, *near, connecting;* Greek, ἐγγυς; and to aıȝ, prep., *at;* British, *ac. and;* Welsh, *ag;* Latin, *ac;* Scand. *ok;* by changing the palatal c (k) into t, *et,* Lat., and by altering the position of the consonant k, is obtained the Greek και.

The learner will remember that its modern spelling is " aȝuꞃ," and not, as some authorities write it, "ocuꞃ." This latter was its spelling some ten hundred years ago; perhaps because formed from ꞃocuꞃ, by omitting ꞃ.

Aȝuꞃ is contracted into 'ȝuꞃ, a'ꞃ, and 'ꞃ, in poetry; a'ꞃ is sometimes, but incorrectly, printed ꞇꞃ, thus confounded in its spelling with the word ꞇꞃ, is— the assertive form of the verb *to be,* oo bcıṫ.

An, *whether;* used in asking questions in the present tense; as, " An " cu ca aꞃꞃ ꞃꞇn ? *Is it you who are here?* Latin same, *an*—" *an*" *tu qui illic es?*

When preceding a verb in the past tense it becomes aꞃ, *whether;* ꞇꞇ is part of the obsolete particle ꞃo, sign of the past tense.

Ceana, *before, already, even;* aċc ċeana, *but, however, moreover.*

Co (and coṁ, in composition), (1) *so,* (2) *that,* (3) *until;* co luac " aȝuꞃ," *as soon as.*

Ȝo, conj., *that, to the end that;* French, *que;* Erse, or Scotch Gaelic, *gu.* (Ȝo is also a prep. *to;* and sign of the adv.; as, ȝo móꞃ, *exceedingly*).

Ȝuꞃ, *that* (*i.e.*, ȝo and ꞃo), employed before the subjunctive tenses.

With buó, *may be;* ȝuꞃ forms the compound ȝuꞃab, *that it may be*— which, in old writings, is found written thus—cuꞃb and cuꞃab.

Bıó and bıoó (pr. *bee, bi-u*), or bıóeaó (*bi-oo*), *let it be* (imperative mood, third singular), *be it so, grant it,* like the Latin, *esto, although.*

Ȝıó and ȝıóeaó (*gi-oo*), *although, yet, nevertheless,* composed of ȝo, *that,* and bıóeaó.

Ce and ȝe, *although,* appear to be derived (like *quod,* in Latin), from the pronoun cıa, ca, *who, what?*

Cɩö (pr. *kee*), *seeing that, even, although, yet, perhaps;* same as ʒɩö, or from cɩö, *sees.*

Dá, *if, had it been that,* on the hypothesis *that.*

It precedes the conditional mood, to which, in reference to past time, it imparts the meaning of the pluperfect subjunctive.

Dá differs from má in this—that má precedes the *indicative* form of conjugation; dá goes before the *conditional*, dá m-buáɩlfáɩnn, *if I should strike;* and, in reference to past time, *had I stricken, if I had stricken.*

ʒan, *that, not,* for ʒona, compounded of ʒo, *that,* and na, *not;* deɩn ne leáτ ʒan a öeánáö, *he tells you not to do it.*

Má, *if;* and mar for má'r, or má ɩr, *if it is.*

Máö and mác, in ancient writings, are for má and buö, *if it were.*

Fór, *yet, moreover;* from fór, *rest.*

Ioná, and contractedly, 'ná which is now the common form = *than;* τá τurá nior feárr na mɩre, *thou art better than I.*

Olár, in old writings, means literally, *is above;* from ol (same as or), *above,* and ɩr, *is;* also, olá, and oláτe (from ol, *over,* and τá, *is.* "It should also be noted," says Dr. O'Donovan, "that olár, olár, is very frequently used for ɩoná, in ancient writings; as, áɩt no bá oɩle leɩr clánn Neáετáɩn olár clánn Neɩll, 'for the sons of Neachtan were dearer to him than the children of Niall.'"—*Ann. Four Mast.* A.D. 1460.

Már, *as;* mar ro, *thus;* mar rɩn, *in that way—so and so.* Már an ʒ-céádna (dn, pr. = *nn*), *also, in like manner.*

Na, *that, not,* like (*ne* in Latin); compounded with ʒo, *that;* = ʒona, *that not;* as, deɩr re leáτ ʒona öeánár, *he tells you not to do it;* nar, *not* (= ná and no) before subjunctive tenses; nar leɩʒɩö Dɩá, *God forbid.*

Má, *if,* with ná makes muná, *if not, unless, except that.* Munán, in the subj. tenses, and contractedly, mun. Before buö, *is, may be,* muná becomes munáb and munbáö, *were it not, if it was not;* and also munán before buö, with ʒo, *that,* following. Munán buö ʒo, contractedly, mun bá ʒ', commonly pronounced by the people, mun beáʒ, *were it not that,* &c.

Nɩ (1) *not* (absolute negative), nɩ cóɩr, *it is not right;* nɩ me, *it is not I* (2) *neither, nor;* nɩ mɩre, no τurá, *neither I nor thou;* nɩ máɩτ, no olc, *neither good nor evil.*

Nɩ becomes in the past tense nior, absolute negative.

☞ Observe the difference between nior and nar: nior is in the direct form. as, "níor" ṁinne ṁé é, *I did not do it;* nár, in the indirect or subjunctive; as, beir re "nár" ṁinne mé é, he said that I did *not* do it.

"Nár" ṁinne, here follows the verb beir, *says,* and therefore nár, and not níor, is employed.

Ní, *or, nor.*

This particle should be spelled with o and not with a, to distinguish it from 'ná, *than,* ná, *not,* na, *of the* (article).

Naċ (a negative relative employed in clauses that are dependent), *is not* = ní, *not,* and aċ, *for* aċt, *but, i.e., not but;* as, naċ maiṫ é, *but is he not good?* naċ becomes náṁ (*i.e.* naċ and ro), in secondary or dependent clauses.

Ó, *since* (before verbs), *whereas.*

Ó ṫarla, *whereas, since it has happened.*

Óir, *for,* perhaps from air, *on.*

Seaḋ (*shah*), *yes* = is é, *it is;* ní ḟeaḋ (*nee hah*), *no, it is not.* "Seaḋ," et "eaḋ," antiquiores formæ ejusdem significationis pro recentiorum Hibernorum "re" et Monacœdanorum *eh*—*i.e., is,* sive *id,* verbum igitur verbo "ar reaḋ," in lingua Franco-Gallica exprimi potest, *c'est comme,* p. 7.—*Commentatio de Carmine Vetusto Hibernico in Sancti Patricii,* laudem ab Henrico Leo Ord. phil, H. T. Decano., Halis Saxonum, 1845.

Maireaḋ (accent on reaḋ), *if it is it, if so.*

Maireaḋ (accent on mair), pr. *maise* = *well, well.*

Sul, *before that.*

INTERJECTIONS.

§ 174. An interjection expresses a sudden emotion of the mind.

In Irish these are many interjections. The following are most in use:

A, *Oh!*

Abu (a war-cry), *for ever; victorious!*

Abú, is considered (1) to be a contraction for "a buaiḋ" *in victory,* therefore *victorious* (2) from a, *in,* and bu, *life, living;* therefore it is equal to *vivat, vive, long-life;* O'Domnal a bú! *O'Donnell for ever!* Láṁ Dearg a bú! *the Red*

Hand for ever! Láṁ Laidir a bú! *the strong-hand for ever!* Crom a bu! *Crom for ever!*

A bú bu! *O strange, life, life!* = papae (Lat.) = βαβαι! (Gr.)

Aṫaċ, *hey-day!*

Éist, *hush! list!*

Faraor, *alas!* (fa, *cause,*

ᴀɼ, *our;* ᴀɼɼ, *of woe,* gen. of ᴀɼ, *woe.*
Fᴀɼᴀoɼ ᵹeuɼ, *O sad sorrow!*
Feuc! = *ecce* (Latin), *lo!* or *behold!*
Fuɼl-le-luᴏ̇! *hallo! bloody wars!* fuɼl, *blood,* le, *with,* for, luᴀᴏ̇, *to flow!*
Ⰼo cɼᴀᴏ̇, *my grief!*
"Ꝿɼeuᵹ, ɴᴀ ᵹ-cᴀt ᵹeuɼ ɱo 'ɴuᴀɼɼ ᴀᵹuɼ ɱo cɼᴀᴏ̇."
Homer—Iliad.

Ⰼo leuɼ, *my sorrow, alas!* oc! ɱo leuɼ, *alas! my sorrow that it is not so!*
ɱo leuɼ ᵹeuɼ, *my piercing sorrow it is not so!*
Ⰼoɴuᴀɼ! *alas* (from ɱo, *my;* ᴀɼ-uᴀɼɼ, *sad hour*), *woe-is-the day! my sad hour!*
Oc̓! uc̓! *Oh!*
Uc̓, uc̓, oɼ ɼ breoɼce ɱɼre, *och! ochon! sickly indeed am I!*
Ancient Music of Ireland, v. i., p. 163.
Oc̓oɼ! *alas!*
Oc̓oɼ O! *my sad sorrow!*

§ 175. There are many other expressions of pity, sorrow, grief, shame, encouragement, joy, exultation, and the like, most of which, properly speaking, are not interjections, but nouns, accompanied by some pronoun or verb, or, it may be, both:—Ex. ɼ cɴuᴀᵹ̓! *woe!* (literally = *it is pity*); ɱo ɴᴀɼɴe tu! fy! = *my shame (art) thou;* ɱo cɼeᴀc̓! *alas!* = *my ruin;* ɱo bɼoɼ, *my sorrow!*

"Sometimes verbs, nouns, and adjectives, uttered by way of exclamation, are considered as interjections; as, *Hail!* heavens! shocking!"—*English Grammar, Style, and Poetry,* by Richard Hiley, p. 74.

The odes of the Irish bards abound in plaintiff phrases of an interjectional character; the following is an example:

"Ⰼo cuɱᴀ! ɱo bɼᴀᴏ̇ ᴀᵹuɼ ɱo ᵬeoc̓!
Ⰼo cuɱᴀ! ɱo coɼᵹ o ᵹᴀc̓ ᴀɼɴᴏ̇;
Ⰼo cuɱᴀ! ɱo eɼɼᴀll ᴀɼ ɼɱc̓ɼᴀɼ,
U'ɼ ᵹuɼ cᴀɼllcᴀɼ ɱo lᴀocɼᴀ cᴀɼᴏ̇!

Ⰼo cuɱᴀ! ɱo ᵬuɼ ᴀɼ lᴀɼ,
Ⰼo cuɱᴀ! ɱo ɼᵹᴀc̓ ᴀ'ɼ ɱo ɼᵹɼᴀc̓;
Ⰼo cuɱᴀ! Ⰼeᴀɼᵹᴀc̓ ᴀ'ɼ Cɼᴀɼᴅᴀɼ,
Ⰼo cuɱᴀ! Lɼᴀᵹᴀɼ! bᴀ bɼeᴀᵹ̓ clɼᴀb!"

Translation.

My grief! my food and my drink!.
My grief! my restraint on everyside!
My grief! my journey afar,
And that I lost my noble heroes!

My grief! my Dún laid low!
My grief! my shelter and shield!
My grief! Meargach and Ciardan,
My grief! Liagan! of the strong breast.

The Lay of the Wife of Meargach,
4th vol. of the Transactions of the Ossianic Society, p. 166.

CHAPTER X.

§ 176.—DERIVATION AND COMPOSITION.

A correct and accurate knowledge of the meaning, primary and secondary, of the nomenclature of any language is acquired best by endeavouring to learn the component elements of each term—say, the root, with the particles which go before and come after, and with which it unites in new and intelligible combinations. A person acquainted with the component elements of a word is master at once of its meaning and its orthography. This subject is therefore very important. It has already received some attention in these pages.—See Orthography, chap. 3, pp. 43, 47, § 31, 34.

In its etymological character, derivation is taken in a more ample sense than that which embraces the subject of spelling.

§ 177. Derivation is two-fold—(1) tracing a word to its root or stem; (2) and annexing to the stem the various affixes by the aid of which other terms, either new or already in use, branch into complete and correct form.

§ 178. The stem is called a *simple* term; the stem and its branches taken together a *compound* term.

Viewing the compound as springing from the simple, or from any new form thereof, it is called *derivative;* and the word from which it immediately springs, *primitive.*—See p. 44, § 31.

The terms *primitive* and *derivative*, like the words *father* and *son*, are relative; *i.e.*, each leans for its meaning upon, and derives its significancy from the other.

§ 179. Every *derivative* is a compound, for it is composed of the stem and some other term, either wholly or in part. Words which are not simple may, therefore, well be classed under the heads of compound and derivative; as, ón-ꞃlac (*gold-rod*), *a sceptre;* ꞃeaꞃ-jonab (from ꞃeaꞃ, *a man;* and jonab, *a place*), *a vice-gerent, vicar,* or *lieutenant;* ꞃeaꞃaꞁꞃajl, *manly;* ꞃeaꞃaꞁjlace, *manliness.*

EXAMPLES OF SIMPLES, DERIVATIVES, COMPOUNDS.

Stem.	Derivative.	Compound.
Tꞃom, *heavy.*	Tꞃomaꞃ, *heaviness.* Eabꞃꞃom, *non-heavy, light.* Eabꞃꞃomaꞃ, *lightness, non-heaviness.* Coṁ-ꞇꞃom, *even, of equal weight* (from coṁ, *together co.,* and ꞇꞃom, *heavy*).	Tꞃom-beoꞃ, *a heavy tear.* Tꞃom-meabacaꞃ, *heavy weight.* Tꞃom-ꞇuꞃꞃꞃe, *a heavy weariness*—great sadness, or its effects on the frame.

§ 180. The words which go before the stem are called prefixes, those that come after it, suffixes: affix is a suffix or prefix.

The prefixes are entire words, or parts of words; the suffixes, also, are entire words or parts of words; as (for prefixes) cuṡ-ċeol, *death-music;* (for suffixes) ceolṁaṅ, *musical,* from ceol and mǎn: from ceol, *music,* come ceolaıb, *a songster,* a *musician;* ceolǎn, *a little songster;* applied to a child or foolish person who is always *piping;* ceol-ṡaoė, *musical-breeze.*

§ 181. The *noun* (1), adjective (2), verb (3), are the only three important parts of speech which enter the domain of derivation, either in tracing to the stem or annexing branches thereto.

⁎ There are compound pronouns in Irish.—See pp. 95, 99.

§ 182. 1.—NOUNS.

Abstract nouns.
{
1 (*m*) end in aṡ; as, ṁaıċeaṡ, *goodness,* from ṁaıċ, *good.*
2 (*f*) end in aċt; as, ṡaoıṡaċt, *freedom,* from ṡaoıṁ, *free.*
3 (*f*) end in e; as, ṡıle, *fairness, brightness,* from ṡeal, *bright,* tṡoıṁe, *weight,* from tṡoṁ, *weighty.*
}

☞ This last class of abstract nouns are exactly the same as the gen. singular fem. of the adjective, or like its comparative degree. They are of the fem. gender—the gender of that word from which directly they have been derived. In this respect derivative words follow the nature of the primitives.

Personal nouns end in óıṁ, aıṁe, aıḋ, aċ.—See pp. 46, 47, of this Grammar.

Derivatives, in aṅ (*m*), ıṅ (*m* or *f* according to its meaning), oṡ (fem.); nouns of multitude in ṡaıḋ, or laıḋ; as, eaċṡaıḋ, *cavalry,* from eaċ, *a steed;* euṅlaıḋ, *birds,* from euṅ, *a bird;* laoċṡaıḋ, *heroes,* from laoċ, *a hero;* ṁacṡaıḋ, *youths,* from ṁac, *a son.*

§ 183. In the *forty-first lesson* of *Easy Lessons; or, Self-Instruction in Irish* (Dublin: Mullany, 1, Parliament-street, Publisher), we observe that many words which are not diminutives end in aṅ; as, lubaṅ (*m*.), *a bow;* from lub (*m*.), *a bend, a clasp* (*v*.), *to bend;* ṁoṅǎn, *many, a large number,* from ṁóṅ, *great, large;* caṡaṅ (from coṡ, *a foot*), *a foot-path;* oıleaṅ, *an island,* (from ol, *above,* and laṅ, *the tide*), or, which is more natural, from oıle, *other, separate, apart;* and laṅ, *land;* i.e., land separated by water from the main land.

Other words ending in aṅ from taṅ, *time,* or from taıṅ, *possessions,* are of this class; as, ṡuṫaıṅ, *eternal, everlasting* (aṅṡ aṅ beaṫa ṡuṫaıṅ, and (in) life *everlasting—Apostles' Creed*), is derived from ꞅo, *bliss, blissful*, and ċan, *time*, meaning the blissful continuity of eternal life.

§ 184. From the word can or caın, *land, region, possessions in land or stock, riches*, are formed the words ꝼǫoncaın, *a vineyard*, from ꝼǫon, *wine*, and can, *land;* ꞃóꞅ-can, *a rose garden;* muıncan, *a garden of myrtles;* bꞃıcaın the land of the Brits or speckled people (Britain), Maꞃıcaın, the country of the *Mauri;* Iınouꞃcan, the can or region along the *Indus* or *Sindus*, as it was originally called.

Ia, *a region* or *territory*, is the termination of almost all Latin topographical names which have that ending.—Ex. Aꞃꞃuꞃıa, *the* (ıa) *land* of Aꞃꞃuꞃ.

§ 185. A few nouns end in baꞃ, *top, produce*, growth; as, ceılabaꞃ, *pairing, the pairing of birds;* ceolabaꞃ, *warbling;* buılebaꞃ, *foliage, i.e.*, the *growth* of leaves.

§ 186. The second class of derivative terms are adjectives. Adjectives end in amaıl, maꞃ, ać, ıð, ða or ðᴀ, and ca.

" These spring from nouns as roots, or from adjectives, rarely from verbs, because it was from things—of which nouns are only names—and from their qualities (expressed by adjectives), that mankind first formed notions or ideas; and, therefore, the names of such things and their qualities were the earliest germs of human speech, of the genealogy of which history and philology point out the Keltic as one of the earliest offshoots."—*Easy Lessons*, p. 247.

§ 187.—Amaıl, *like*.

Stem.	Derivatives (adjectives).
Aeꞃ, *air*.	Aeꞃamaıl, *airy*.
Aınm, *a name*.	Aınmnamaıl, *nameable, respectable, presentable*.
Aoıbe, *delight, satisfaction*.	Aoıbamaıl, *delightful, pleasant, delectable*.
Boꞃꞃ, *increase, enlargement*.	Boꞃꞃamaıl, *of a fair size, growing big, enlarging, proud*.
Saoı, *a gentleman*.	Saoıamaıl, *respectable, gentleman-like*.
Sıaꞃꞃ, *pleasure, joy*.	Sıaꞃꞃamaıl, *pleasant, funny, jolly*.

The suffix amaıl, is written in Scotch Gaelic, aıl, eıl. In Irish poetry amaıl is contracted into a'ıl, wherever that sound is required to meet the requirements of rhyme. Philologists cannot fail to perceive that amaıl, is the root of the Latin ending *alis, ale*, and its derived form in the Romance languages.

IRISH GRAMMAR.   173

§ 188—Ṁap.

Some suppose this suffix to be the particle mᴀp, *as;* others that it is, as in Erse, from the adjective móp, *great.*

Stems.	Derivatives.
Nouns.	Adjectives.
Áḋ, *luck.*	Áḋṁap, *lucky,* Scotch Gaelic, aḋṁop.
Feup, *grass.*	Feupṁap, *full of grass.*
Feoil, *flesh.*	Feolṁap, *fleshy.*
Fuaṫ, *hate.*	Fuaṫṁap, *hateful.*

ıḋ.

| Eaȝna, *wisdom.* | Eaȝnaıḋ, *wise.* |

ḋa, ṫa, ḋa.

Ȝall, *a foreigner.*	Ȝallḋa, *exotic.*
Fipeun, *a member of the faithful;* fíop, *true;* aon, *one.*	Fipeunṫa, *righteous.*
Óp, *gold.*	Opḋa, *golden.*

§ 189.—Aṫ.

| Beapṫ, *an action, exploit (good or bad).* | Beapṫaṫ, *tricky, wily.* |
| Bpeuȝ, *a lie.* | Bpeuȝaṫ, *given to lies.* |

From the active signification peculiar to the ending aṫ, adjectives with this suffix become personal nouns, expressing action, office, or individuality; as, baṫaṫ, *a lame man;* from baṫ, *a hindrance, an impediment;* cpuipeaṫ, *hunchbacked,* from cpuip, *a hump.*

§ 190. *Adjectives* ending in aṫ are derived from the passive participle of verbs, by changing the final vowel into aṫ; as, peallṫa, *deceived, betrayed;* peallṫaṫ, *deceptive, deceitful;* mealltṫa, *beguiled;* mealltṫaṫ, *a beguiler, a cajoler.*

§ 191. Obs.—Patronymics, sirnames, nicknames, or titles of honor or dishonor, end in aṫ; as, Albanaṫ, *a Scotchman;* Breaṫanaṫ contractedly Breaṫnaṫ, *a Welshman;* Eıpeannaṫ, *an Irishman;* Spainneaṫ, *a Spaniard;* Bpianaṫ, *an individual of the family of O'Brien;* Bláṫaṫ, *Blake;* Bpeaṫnaṫ, *Walsh;* Bpunaṫ, *Browne;* Bupcaṫ, *Bourke;*

Daṁnalaċ, *MacDonald;* Ruaṗcaċ, *O'Rourke;* Seobaċ, *Joyce;* Seabaċ, *Hawkins* (from ṗeabaċ, *a hawk*).

§ 192. Some nouns of no fixed classification end in aċ, as ʒeallaċ, *the moon;* ḟiaḋaċ, (*fee-yach*), *hunting, venison*. A few end in laċ, which perhaps is a broken form of luċt, *folk, people* (Greek, λαος); as, teaʒ-laċ, *a house, a family, the hearth;* from tiʒe, *of* the house; and luċt, *folk;* oʒ-laċ, *a young lad*.

§ 193.—OF DERIVATIVE VERBS (THIRD CLASS).

All verbs of the second conjugation are derivative, some from substantives, others from adjectives.—See the large list furnished in pp. 129, 130, 131, of this Grammar.

§ 194.—OF THE FORMATION OF IRISH COMPOUND TERMS.

In purely compound terms, as well as in derivatives, the principal groups are, nouns, adjectives, verbs.

A noun may have for its prefix another noun, an adjective, or verb; similarly, the adjective may have a noun, a verb, or another adjective; and the verb has for its prefix an adjective or noun. Thus there are eight classes of compounds, to which is added a ninth—words prefixed by prepositions.

☞ The second part of the compound is aspirated according to the laws of euphony explained in p. 133, § 136; and in pp. 34, 35, § 24, rule 3.

§ 195.—1. Substantives in the nom. case compound with other substantives in the same case. The German language abounds in compounds of this class.

Baṗṗ-ṫobaiṗ, head-fountain.

Bo-ṗuil, cow-eye; from bo, a cow; and ṗuil, an eye.

Bṗeuʒ-ḟaiḋ, a false prophet; bṗeuʒ-ciab, a wig, a peruke; from bṗeuʒ and ciab, a lock of hair.

Bṗeuʒ-ṗiʒ, a pseudo-king; from bṗeuʒ, a lie, a false thing; and ṗiʒ, a king.

Buṅ-ṗṗuṫ, a fountain; from buṅ, but, source, origin, root; and ṗṗuṫ, a stream.

Caṫ-baṗṗ, a hemlet; from caṫ, a battle; and baṗṗ, the top, the head.

Caiṫ-iṅiḃ, a battle-soldier.

Ceaṅṅ-beaṗṫ, a head-dress.

Ceaṗṫ-ṁeoḋaṅ, middle.

Ceaṗṫ-laṗ, the very centre.

Clap-ṡoluṗ, twilight.

Cloʒ-teaċ, a belfry, a round tower; from cloʒ, a bell; and teaċ, a house.

Cṅaob-ḟleaṙʒ, a garland; from cṅaob, a branch, a sprout; and ḟleaṙʒ, a wreath, a fillet.

Cul-ċaınṫ, back-biting; from cul, back; and caınṫ.

Ḋuıne-baḋ, a plague amongst men.

Feall-beaṙṫ, an act of treachery.

Feaṙ-ıonaḋ, a lieutenant, or vicegerent; from feaṙ, a man; and ıonaḋ, a place, a position—one who holds the place of another.

Fıoṙ-ḟeaṙ, a messenger, an informant; from fıoṙ, knowledge; and ḟeaṙ, a man.

Caoıṙ-ḟeoıl, mutton,
Laoıʒ-ḟeoıl, veil,
Ṁuıc-ḟeoıl, pork,
Ṁaıṙṫ-ḟeoıl, beef.
} Words compounded of feoıl, meat; and caoṙa, a sheep; laoʒ, a calf; muc, a pig; and maṙṫ, a beef.

Laṁ-Ḋıa, a household god,
Laṁ-euḋaċ, a handkerchief, a napkin,
Laṁ-oṙḋ, a hand-sledge.
} From laṁ, a hand; and Ḋıa, a god; euḋaċ, cloth; and oṙḋ, a sledge.

Leaṫ-ċoıṙ, one foot,
Leaṫ-ṙʒeul, a half-story, an excuse,
Leaṫ-ṙuıl, one eye,
Leaṫ-ṫaob, one side.
} From leaṫ, half, or one of two; and coṙ, a foot; ṙʒeul, a story; ṙuıl, an eye; ṫaob, a side.

Leabaṙ-coıṁeaḋaıḋ, a librarian.

Oıʒ-bean, a maiden; from oıʒ, a virgin; and bean, a woman.

Oıʒ-ḟeaṙ, a virginal youth.

Oṙ-ṙlaṫ, a sceptre; from óṙ, gold; and ṙlaṫ, a rod, a wand.

Ríʒ-ḟeaṙ, a very good man, a king in his way, from ṙıʒ, a king, and feaṙ.

Tuaṫ-ʒaoṫ, north wind.

Seaṙc-ʒṙaḋ, affection, love.

Síṫ-ḟulaṅʒ, good temper, peaceful endurance; from ríṫ, peace; and fulaṅʒ, suffering.

Teaṙ-ʒṙaḋ, heat-love, zeal.

Tíṙ-ʒṙaḋ, patriotism, country-love.

The prefix bean changes the gender, as,

Bean-Ḋıa, a goddess.

Bean-Deacun, a deaconess.
Bean-namad, a female foe.
Bean-naom, a female saint.
Bean-oglac, a female attendant.
Bean-rige, a witch, a fairy woman, a *bean-shighe;* from bean, and rige, a sprite; root, rig, a happy state.
Bean-rglaba, a female slave.
Bean-cigeanna, a lady; a woman-lord.

§ 196. Note.—From combinations like the foregoing, for which the Keltic has, from the earliest period, been remarkable, are derived some proper names found in Cæsar; as, *Dumnorix*, world-king; from doman, the world; and rig, king; and *Bituriges*, life-king; from bit, life, the world; and rig, king; *Caturiges*, battle-king.

Obs.—In a *compound* term resulting from the union of *two* simple nouns in the *nominative* case, or from that of a simple and derivative noun, the *second* part is the leading element, and the first merely qualifies or defines the meaning of the second.

The declension and inflections of the compound term are, accordingly, those peculiar to the second part; and so is the gender of the term, unless the prefixed noun (as bean, *a woman, a female*) be such as to point out a change.

§ 197. Nouns followed by others in the genitive case are regarded by many as compound substantives. In point of fact, they are not, although their equivalents in English commonly are compound terms. They are something like the following: board-*of-health*, board-*of-trade*, ship-*of-war*, man-*of-all-work*. Nouns of this class, with *de* or *a*, are numerous in French; as, *pomme-de-terre*, a potato; *fleur-de-lis*, lily.

Brat-taire, *a winding-sheet;* from brat, *a garment*, and taire, *of* death (gen. case), corr-mona, *a crane* (from corr, generic term, *a crane*, and mona, *bog, wold*).

Cu-mara, *dog-of-the-sea, an otter.*
Deog-flait, *the last prince.*
Fean-ceoil, *a man-of-music, a musician.*
Fean-feara, *a man-of-knowledge, a seer* (feara, gen. case of fior).
Fean tige, *man-of-a house, a householder.*
Laoc ceoil, *warrior-of-music* ("warrior-bard"—*Moore*).
Laog mara, *calf-of-the-sea, a seal.*
Mac alla, *son-of-the-cliff, echo.*
Mac tire, *son-of-wold, a wolf.*
Teac orta, *a house-of-entertainment, an inn, hotel.*

The noun in the genitive (the second in order) imparts a special significancy to the meaning of the first, which is the principal as well as the leading part of this class of compound terms.

§ 198.—Other names of Keltic origin—as, *Orgetorix*, uᵱᴀ ᵹaċ-ᴛoᵱuᵻᵱ, *the-stay-of-every-journey*; *Cingetorix*, cᵻuu ᵹaċ ᴛoᵱuᵻᵱ, *the head-of-every-journey*; *Vergobret*, ꜰeaᵱ-ᵹo-bᵱeċ, *the-man-for-judgment*—are formed much after the same manner.

§ 199.—2. NOUNS WITH AN ADJECTIVE PREFIXED.

Áᵱb, *high, chief, supreme*; as, áᵱb-ᵱᵻᵹ, *chief-king*; áᵱb-ᴛᵻᵹeaᵱna, *sovereign lord*; áᵱb-ᵱéᵻᵯ, *sovereign power*.

Buaᵰ, *enduring, lasting*; as, buaᵰ-ᵱaoᵹal, *a long-life*; buaᵰ-ᵱeaᵱað (*long-standing*), *perseverance*.

Caoᵻᵰ, *gentle*; as, caoᵻᵰ-ðuċᵱaċᴛ, *earnestness without show*.

Caoᵯ, *mild, tender*; as, caoᵯ-ᵹᵱáð, *tender love*; caoᵯ-ċᵰuċ, *a slender, gentle form*; caoᵻᵯ-ᵹeᵻᵰ (*gentle-begotten*), *Kevin*.

Claoᵰ, *inclined, partial*; as, claoᵰ-bᵱeᵻċ, *a partial-judgment*.

Coᵻᴛċeᵰᵰ, *common* (hence *kitchen*, English), ex. coᵻᴛ-ċeᵻᵰᵰ-beċað (*coenobium*), *a monastery, where all live in community*.

Cᵱoᵰ, *crooked, bent*; as, cᵱoᵯ-leac, the *cromleac*, or druid altar.

Ðaoᵱ, *dear, bound, condemned*; as, ðaoᵱ-bᵱeᵻċ, *a condemning-judgment, condemnation*; ðaoᵱ-oᵹlaċ, *a bondslave*.

Ðeaᵹ, *good*; as, ðeaᵹ-ðuᵻᵰe, *a good person*.

Ðeaᵱb, *real, true*; as, ðeaᵱb-bᵱáċaᵻᵱ, *a (real) brother*, one of the same father and mother.

bᵱáċaᵻᵱ, without the prefix ðeaᵱb, means *frere* (friar), or *brother* in religion; leaᴛ-bᵱáċaᵻᵱ, a *half*-brother, an uterine brother; ðeaᵱb ᵱᵻuᵱ (pr. *der-hure*), from ᵱᵻuᵱ, (*shure*), *sister*, a sister born of the same parents.

⁎ This word ðeaᵱb, is pronounced as if written ðeᵰ; as, ðeᵰ-ᵱᵻuᵱ, *a sister*; ðeᵰðaoᵻᵰeað, *lamentation, wailing*; ðeaᵱᵻᵷoᵻᵱ, *enormous, right-big*.

From ðeaᵱb, in its affected and reduced form, ðeᵰ, comes the preposition ðaᵰ, translated *by*—employed in asseverating; as, ðaᵰ ᵯ' ꜰocal, *upon my word*; ðaᵰ ᵯ' oᵰoᵻᵱ, *upon my honor*; i e., literally. ðaᵰ (for ðaᵱb), *assures*; i e., *my word assures, my honor avers*. Hence, too, is formed the adverb, ðaᵰ ꜰᵻᵰe, *in truth, or truth* (ꜰᵻᵰe) *avers*; this word, meaning *in truth*, or *in earnest*, is usually spelled ðaᵱᵻᵱᵻð (ꜰ aspirated being elided).

Ðᵻaᵰ, *vehement*; as, ðᵻaᵰ-ᵹᵱáð, *vehement-love*.

Ðluċ, *close*; as, ðluċ-ċaᵱᵱaᵻᵰᵹ, n., *attraction* (*drawing-close*).

Droċ, *bad,* contrary of Deaʒ, *good;* as, Droċ-ḋuıne, *a bad man;* Droċ-ṗaċ, *a bad condition, state.*

Fıonn, *fair;* as, Fıonn-ṗʒoċ, *a white-flower.*

Fıoṗ, *true;* as, Fıoṗ-uıṗʒe, *spring-water, living-water;* Tabaıṗ ḋaṁ ḋeoċ Fıoṗ-uıṗʒe, *give me a drink of spring water.*

Ʒanḃ, *rough;* as, ʒanḃ-Fıon, *a tempest, a rough blast.*

Ʒeaṗṗ, *short;* as, ʒeaṗṗ-Fıaḋ (*a short-wild-animal*), *a hare.*

Ʒlan, *clean;* as, ʒlaṗ-ċṗoıḋe, *clean-heart.*

Ʒlınn, *pellucid, bright, clear;* as, ʒlınn-ṗaḋaṗc, *clear-sight.*

Ƿaoċ, *soft;* as, ṁaoċ-Feoıl, *tender-meat.*

Ƿıon, *small, low, little;* as, mıon-áınéıṗ, *small cattle;* mıon-ċaıṗʒ, *low-Easter,* i.e., Low-Sunday; mıon-noḋlac (pr. *nollac*), *little-Christmas,* i.e., New Year's Day.

Latin, *minus;* Gr., μειων; *minuo, I lessen;* hence *minute;* i.e., a *little* portion of time, an *item* of news. It is evident these derivatives are from the oldest root, the Irish or Keltic mıon, *little, low, small.*

Ƿóṗ, *great;* as, móṗ-ċáıl, *great fame.*

Naoṁ, *holy;* as, naoṁ-aċaıṗ, *holy father.*

Nuaḋ, *new;* as, nuaḋ-ḋuıne, *an upstart;* literally a *novus homo* (new-man).

Óʒ, *young;* as, óʒ-Feaṗ, *a young man;* óʒ-ṁaṗc, *a young ox.*

Oʒ, *entire;* as, oʒnéıṗ, *entire submission;* oʒoılʒenn, *amnesty;* oʒoıṗe, *full fine.*

Pṗıoṁ, *first, primal;* as, pṗıoṁ-aḋḃaṗ, *the first cause;* pṗıoṁ-eaʒlaıṗ, *a chief-church.*

Saoḃ, *silly, false;* as, ṗaoḃ-Faıḋ, *a false prophet;* ṗaoḃ-apṗcol, *a false apostle;* ṗaoḃ-ċıal, *folly, silliness;* from ṗaoḃ and cıal, *sense.*

Saoṗ, *free—not bound, not in thraldom;* as, ṗaoṗ-ṗeılḃ, *a free-hold;* ṗaoṗ-ċoıl, *free-will;* ṗaoṗ-ḋuıne, *a free-man, no slave* (ḋaoṗ-ḋuıne, *a thrall, a slave, a bond-man*).

Sean, *old;* as, ṗean-Feaṗ, *an old man;* ṗean-aoıṗ, *old age;* ṗean-ṗeaċċ, *old law.*

Tṗeun, *bold, strong, mighty;* as, tṗeun-Feaṗ, *a brave man;* tṗeun-laoċ, *a hero.*

IRISH GRAMMAR.   179

Τ**ɼom**, *heavy;* as, τɼom-cɼoɼδe, *heavy-heart;* τɼom-ꝼaιɼꝝ, *drink to the dregs* (from τɼom and ꝼaιɼꝝ, *squeeze);* τɼom-luɼδe, *the nightmare* (from τɼom and luɼδe, *lying).*

Uaɼal, *noble* (uaɼ, *high;* aɼl, *educate);* as, uaɼal-aταιɼ, *a patriarch.*

Uɼle, *all;* as, uɼle-cumacταc, *Almighty;* uɼle-colꝝac, *all-knowing.*

§ 200.—3. NOUNS WITH A VERB PREFIXED.

Bɼιɼ-τɼoɼꝝaδ, *breakfast* (from bɼιɼ, *to break,* and τɼoɼ-ꝝaδ, *fasting).*

Jε-ɼomɼaδ, *backbiting, slander;* from ɼε, *to eat;* and ɼomɼaδ (that is, ɼaδ, *a conversation;* ɼom, *about);* ταɼɼanꝝ-aɼτ, *a magnet;* from ταɼɼanꝝ, *drawing,* and aɼτ, *a mineral.*

"The genius of the Irish language," says Dr. O'Donovan, *Grammar,* p. 340, "does not seem to favor the prefixing of verbs in compound terms."

§ 201.—4. ADJECTIVES WITH A NOUN PREFIXED.

Bal-δeaɼꝝ, *red-streaked.*

Bιτ-beo, *sempiternal, ever-living;* from bιτ, *life;* and beo, *living.*

Bιτ-buan, *everlasting;* from bιτ, *life;* and buan, *lasting.*

Bιτ-ꝼaδa, *ever-long, perpetual.*

Bιτ-ꝼιɼeun, *ever-true, ever-faithful.*

Bιτ-ꝝaɼɼaιδ, *short-lived.*

Bιτ-ɼlan, *ever-safe, ever-hale.*

Blaτ-cumɼa, *blossom-sweet.*

Bɼιτ-balb, *stammering like a Britain.*

The ancient Irish regarded their British or Saxon neighbours, as stammerers, on account, either of the language they spoke, or of their unintelligible attempt in speaking the language of Eire.

Ceann-ban, *head-white (white-headed).*

Ceann-δana, *head-strong.*

Ceaɼτ-laɼ, *the real-centre.*

Conn-cobaɼ, *hound-careful;* the Irish of the name O'Connor, pr. *Conchower,* and by metathesis, *Cnochower.*

Coɼ-luaτ, *foot-fleet (fleet-footed).*

Leaṫ-maṗḃ, *half dead;* leaṫ-beo, *half-alive, &c.*
Ríg-ṁaiṫ, *sovereignly-good.*
Toiṗ-ḋealḃac (pr. *thor-yelach*), *Jove-like, Turlough*

☞ The list of adjectives having nouns prefixed is too large to insert here: the foregoing number shall suffice for examples.

§ 202.—5. ADJECTIVES HAVING ADJECTIVES PREFIXED.

Nouns are the stems from which adjectives branch off. The prefixes of nouns—which have, in class 2, § 199, been shown—serve therefore for the prefixes of adjectives.

§ 203.—6. ADJECTIVES WITH A VERB PREFIXED.

These are few, like nouns with a verb prefixed, § 200, p. 179. For example:

Briʃ-ġéimneaċ, *broken-sounded.*
Doġ-ċroiḋeaċ, *heart-burning;* from dóġ, *to burn;* and croiḋeaċ, from croiḋe (pr. *chree*), *the heart.*
Íte-ṁar, *voracious.*
Líon-ṁar, *abundant.*

§ 204.—7. VERBS OR PARTICIPLES WITH A SUBSTANTIVE PREFIXED.

Aṁḃ-aoncuiġim, *I coincide, express in words what I think.*
Cor-ceangail, *to tie in a knot;* from cor, *a knot, a twist;* and ceangail, *to bind.*
Craoḃ-rgaol, *reveal;* from craoḃ, *a branch;* and rgaol, *to loose, to draw away;* because when a branch is torn off a tree, the inner part is revealed.
Craoiḋ-ḃriseaḋ, *to heart-break.*
Cul-tarraing, *to retract;* from cul, *the rear, the hinder part of anything;* and tarraing, *to draw to.*
Síol-ċur, *to sow seed.*
Tear-ġraḋuiġ, *to be zealously loving of.*

§ 205.—8. VERBS OR PARTICIPLES WITH AN ADJECTIVE PREFIXED.

Aṁḃ-eitiollaim, *I fly on high.*
Dearg-laraḋ, *red flaming.* This class is very numerous.

In § 199, pp. 177, 178, 179, the adjectives which are usually employed as prefixes have been shown, e. g., cnom-ḟairz, v., *quaff, drink to the dregs;* from cnom, *heavy,* and ḟairz, *squeeze;* cnom-ɣulaim, *I weep loudly.*

§ 206.—Words compounded with a preposition prefixed.

The genius of the language does not admit the preposition to constitute a prefix, a few instances excepted. The preposition comes, as in English, usually after the verb; as, to *ascend* (*to go up*), ɔul " ruar ;" descend=ɔul " ríor ;" pass *by*, ɔul " ċaɲc."

Aiɲ-ċiɲneaċ, *a prince, a president, a superior;* from aiɲ and ciɲɲ, dat. case of ceaɲɲ, *head.*

Eiɔiɲ-airɲeiɲ, *a digression.*

Eiɔiɲ-ɣoluɣ, *twilight;* from eiɔiɲ and ɣoluɣ, *between lights.*

Eiɔiɲ-ɔealbuɣaɔ, *distinction;* from eiɔiɲ and ɔealb, *form, frame, individuality.*

Eiɔiɲ-ɣɲe, *distinction, perception, cognition.*

Eiɔiɲ-ɣuiɔe, *inter-cession,* from eiɔiɲ *between;* and ɣuiɔe, *pray.*

Eiɔiɲ-ċeaɲcaɔ, *inter-adjusting, interpreting, doing justice between two opposed parties.*

Eiɔiɲ-miniɣ, v., *interpret;* eiɔiɲ-ɣɣaɲɲaɔ, *separation of two, divorce.*

Eiɔiɲ-ɣɣaɲ (from eiɔiɲ and ɣɣaɲ for ɣɣaċaɲ), *one who is the ɣɣaċ, the shield, shade, defence, mutual protector of fighting friends, a peace-maker or go-between.*

Ḟeaɲ-eiɔiɲɣɣaiɲ, *a man who separates contending foes.*

Ḟo-ɔuiɲe, *a low, vulgar man;* ḟo-ċalam, *low land.*

Iaɲ-mbeuɲla, *an adverb;* iom-ċimċeall, *to surround;* iom for uiɲe, *about.*

Ol-ḟoiɲbċe, *over-perfect.*

Roim-ɲaɔ, *a preḟce, a fore-speech, a pro-logue.*

Cimċioll-ɣeaɲɲaɔ, *circumcision.*

Cɣiɔ-ḟoillɣeaċ, *transparent, pellucid;* cɣi-ɣaċaiɲ, *perjorate.*

§ 207. The second class of compound terms strictly so called, are those which have prefixed to the stem, or to any word branching from it—noun, adjective, and verb—certain particles, which add to, modify, or change the meaning attached to the radical word. These particles are, from the position they always occupy, called prefixes: they are twenty-four in number.—See § 169, p. 160.

1.—An has two meanings, one *negative* or *privative*, that is, denying or reversing what is implied by the simple root; the other *intensive*, or one which increases the natural force of the word.

An (1), *negative*, has the meaning of *un* (English), *in* (Latin); as, eolac, *knowing, having a knowledge of, skilled in;* an-eolac, *ignorant, illiterate, having no knowledge of, unskilled in.* Example, aṡur ṡo paiḃ re-ran aincolac annṫi, *and that he* (Stanihurst) *was unskilled in it* (the Irish language).—*Keating's Ireland*, p. 50: colur, *learning;* aincolur, *ignorance, want of learning;* ꝼeaꞃ, *a man;* ainꝼiꞃ, *a maid;* eaṡna, *wisdom;* aneaṡna, *folly;* ꞃoiṁḃċe, *mature;* anꝼoiṁḃċe, *immature;* ṡlaine, *cleanliness;* an-ṡlaine, *uncleanliness;* cꞃeiḋmaċ, *believing;* ancꞃeiḋmaċ, *unbelieving;* ḋliṡe, *law;* anḋliṡe, *want of law;* ḋeiꞃe, *comfortableness* (from ḋeaꞃ, *right, correct, comfortable);* ainḋeiꞃe, *affliction* (pr. *anneshe*—nḋ coming together, sound like *nn*). Fioꞃ, *knowledge;* ainḃꝼioꞃ, *ignorance;* anḃ-ꝼioꞃaċ, *ignorant.*

(In this compound, ꝼ is eclipsed by ḃ; it is pronounced *anvis*).

Aiꞃ m-ḃeiṫ ḋo ꝼéin anḃꝼioꞃaċ 'ꞃ an ṡaoiḋilṡe, *on his being* (to) *himself ignorant of* (in) *the Irish.—Ibid.*

An (2), *intensive*, means *very;* as, ꝼuaꞃ, *cold;* anꝼuaꞃ, *very cold;* maiṫ, *good;* anmaiṫ, *very good;* ṫeaꞃ, *heat;* an-ṫeaꞃ, *ex-cessive heat;* an, *very;* is very commonly prefixed to adjectives.

[In published works and MSS., an is spelled aiꞃ when the first vowel in the annexed syllable is e or i.]

2.—Am (aiṁ)=*dis* or *mis* (English); as, leaꞃ, *luck, fortune, advantage to one's self;* aiṁleaꞃ, *ill-luck, misfortune, disadvantage to one's self.* Ana ḋeanain tu ꞃo, ḋean-ꝼaiḋ tu ḋ'aiṁleaꞃ, *if you do this, you will do your disadvantage, i.e.,* you will do what to yourself will be a disadvantage. Amlóiꞃ (for aṁlaḃꞃóiꞃ), *a dumby, an oaf, a mope, a fool;* literally, *one who cannot speak;* from am, *not;* and laḃaiꞃ, *speak;* tá me 'mo aṁlóiꞃ, *I am like one bewildered, like a man in the dark, a mere mope, or oaf.*

Deoin, *according to will;* aiṁḋeoin, *in spite of;* as, ḋ'aiṁḋeoin na Romanac, *in spite of the Romans.*

Réıḋ, *ready, plain;* aṁṗéıḋ, *entangled, disturbed, disordered;* n., *entanglement, strife, a fastness, or defile.*

Aṁ=*very,* in some few words; as, neaṙṫ, *strength;* aṁneaṙṫ, *force;* leıṙge, *sloth;* aṁleıṙge, *indolence.*

3.—Aıṙ = *again, backwards* (English); ṫaṗ aıṙ " aıṙ," *come back:*

It enters into composition, and is, as a component particle, incorrectly spelled eıṙ.

Aıṙ=*re* (Latin); as, ıoc, *pay;* aıṙıoc (with the accent on the second syllable), *repayment, paying back;* eıṙıġ, *arise;* aıṙeıṙıġ, *resurrection, rise again;* written commonly, but incorrectly, eıṙeıṙıġe.

4. Aṫ has a *reiterative* meaning, or going back again on what is already done. It expresses, therefore, two effects—*first,* that of cancelling what is conveyed by the root; and, *secondly,* that of doing anew what the uncompounded word indicates. Its meaning is sometimes confined to the former, and then it becomes a *negative* particle; sometimes, however, it extends to both, and then it is a *reiterative.*

Aṫ (1), as a *negative,* is not common—aṫ-ṙıġeaḋ, *to dethrone;* from aṫ, and ṙıġeaḋ (theme ṙıġ, *a king*), *to enthrone;* aṫ-cléıṙeaċ, *a superannuated clergyman;* aṫ-laoċ, *a superannuated warrior.*

Aṫ (2), as a *reiterative,* is very common; ḋeanaḋ, *to do, to make;* aṫ-ḋeanaḋ, *to remark;* ḟaṙ, *growth;* aṫ-ḟaṙ, *a new growth;* a *second* crop; aṫ-cuıṅġe, *a petition, an entreaty;* from aṫ and cuıṅġe, *a bond, a tie or chain*—a word implying that, by our prayers, we, as it were, chain Him whom we petition to grant our request.

5.—Co (coṅ and coıṁ), like the Latin prefix *con,* signifies *together, with;* old Irish, *co, with,* prep.—See § 166, p. 153.

6.—Dı, a *negative* particle; from ḋıṫ, *want,* like *di, dis* (Latin); as, cṙeıḋeaṁ, *faith, belief;* dı-ċṙeıḋeaṁ, *unbelief;* ceaṅ, *a head;* dı-ċeaṅ, *one who lost the head;* dı-ċeaṅnaıṁ, *I behead;* dılaċṫa, *an orphan;* from dı, *want;* and laċṫ (gen. case, laċṫa), *milk.*

When compounded with words beginning with b or ṗ, it causes eclipsis; as, buıḋeaċ, *thankful, grateful;* dıṁbuıḋeaċ, *unthankful, ungrateful, grumbling;* dıṁbuaṅ, *unlasting.*

7.—Do implies *difficulty* (Gr. δυς) when compounded with past participles; as, ḋeaṅṫa, *done;* do-ḋeaṅṫa, *hard to be done;* ól, *drink;* ólṫa, *drunk;* do-ólṫa, *hard to be drunk;*

ιτ, *eat*; ϭο-ιττε, *hard to be eaten*; ϝειc, *see*; ϝειcριτε, *seen*; ϭο-ϝειcριτε, *hard-to-be-seen, invisible*; ϭο-ċριοċνυιżτε, *infinite*; from ϭο and cριοċνυιżτε, *ended*—root, cριοċ, *end*; ϭο-ċυιμριżτε, *incomprehensible*; from ϭο and cυιμριυżαϭ, *to comprehend*; from cυμαρ, *power*.

Ϭο, before *nouns* and *adjectives*, has the meaning of *ill*, English; as, ϭο-ϭευρα, *ill*-manners; ϭο-ċαιl, *ill*-fame; ϭο-ċοżϭαιl, *ill*-education; ϭο-ϭευραċ, *ill*-mannered; ϭο-ċαιleαċ, *ill*-famed.

Obs.—Ϭο and So are opposed in Gaelic: the one means the contrary of that indicated by the other. From this opposition a great number of words antagonistic in meaning, nouns as well as adjectives and participles, exists in the language:

8.—So (and ϝυ; *Sanscr.*, *su*; Gr. εὖ, *good, well*), *feasibility*.

EXAMPLES OF THIS OPPOSITION BETWEEN ϝο AND ϭο.

NOUNS.

Sαιϭϭρεαρ, *riches;* from ραιϭϭιρ, *rich*; ραιϭϭρεαρ α'ρ ϭαιϭρεαρ, *riches and poverty*.

Ϭαιϭρεαρ, *want of riches, penury;* from ϭαιϭϭιρ, *poor, penniless*.

Sαοι, *a gentleman, Sir, a hero*.

Ϭαοι, *a worthless person, a dunce, a poltroon*.

Sιτ, *peace, plenty*.

Ϭιτ, *want, misery*.

Soċαιρ, n., *emolument, convenience*. Ex.: ροċαιρ αżυρ ϭοċαιρ αι) ċειρϭε, *the profit and loss of the trade*; a proverb, like the Latin, *qui sentit commodum et incommoda sentire debetur*.

Ϭοċαιρ, *loss, inconvenience;* from ϭο and cαιρ, *friendly, kind*.

So-ċυμαċτ, *easy-power, inherent facility*.

Ϭο-ċυμαċτ, *difficult power*.

So-ϭυιηε, *a good man*.

Ϭο-ϭυιηε, *a bad man, a rogue*.

Soιηιουη, *fair weather;* from ϝο (or ϝοη) and ρίοη.

Ϭοιηιουη, *foul weather, a storm*.

Solαρ, *solace*.

Ϭolαρ, *sorrow, grief*.

IRISH GRAMMAR. 185

Soṁa, *plentiness, wealth.*
Sonar, *happiness, bliss.*
So-claonaḋ, *towardness.*
Socul, *ease, rest* (properly ꞃocaṁail); from ꞃoṫ or ꞃoċ, and aṁail, *like.*
Soneaꞃt, *strength.*
Sorgeul, *the Gospel;* from ꞃo, *happy,* and ꞃgeul, *news.*
Suaiꞃceaꞃ, *sweetness.*
Subailce, *virtue* (ꞃo and bail).

Doṁa, *want, scarcity.*
Donar, *infelicity, misery.*
Do-claonaḋ, *repulsiveness.*
Do-cul, *difficulty.*

Do-neaꞃt, *want of firmness.*
Dogeul, *bad news.*

Duaiꞃceaꞃ, *sourness.*
Dubailce, *vice* (ꝺo and bail).

ADJECTIVES.

Saiḋbiꞃ, *rich.*
Saoꞃ, adj., *free, cheap;* v., *save, redeem;* ꞃaoꞃaḋ, *freeing.*
So-ċꞃut, *fair, honest.*
Soiꞃb, *affable, quiet, easy;* ꞃoiꞃbe, *affability;* ꞃoiꞃbeaċt, *affableness.*
Socaiꞃ, *easy, at leisure, tranquil.*
Socuꞃaċ, *steady, established, immovable;* from ꞃo and cuiꞃ, *put, place.*
Socaꞃaċ, *profitable, easy;* from ꞃo and caꞃ, *friendly.*
So-ċꞃeiḋṁeaċ, *credulous.*
Soċꞃoiḋeaċ, *kind-hearted, giving ease;* from ꞃo, and cꞃoiḋe, *heart.*
Sogꞃaḋaċ, *very loving, affable.*
Soiꞃṁeaċ, *prosperous.*
Soléiꞃ, *clear, bright, lucid;* ꞃo ꞃoleiꞃ, *clearly, lucidly;* from ꞃo, and leuꞃ, *seeing.*

Daiḋbiꞃ, *poor.*
Daoꞃ, *in slavery, dear;* ꝺaoꞃaḋ, *condemning;* ꝺaoꞃ, v., *to condemn.*
Do-ċꞃut, *hideous, dishonest.*
Doiꞃb, *peevish, ill-humour, grievous;* ꝺoiꞃbeaċt, *peevishness.*
Docaiꞃ, *uneasy, difficult.*

Docuꞃaċ, *unsteady.*

Doċaꞃaċ, *hurtful, wrong, injurious.*
Do-ċꞃeiḋṁeaċ, *incredulous.*
Do-ċꞃoiḋeaċ, *sorrowful, affecting the heart with pain;* ꝺo, and cꞃoiḋe.
Do-gꞃaḋaċ, *unloving, repulsive.*
Doiꞃṁeaċ, *adverse.*
Doléiꞃ, *dark, obscure.*

Soṅa, *lucky, happy, prospe-*   Doṅa, *unlucky, unhappy,*
  rous; from ṗo, and áö,   *unprosperous.*
  luck.
Suaiṗc, *sweet, pleasant.*   Duaiṗc, *sour, sharp.*
Suilḃiṗ, *agreeable, eloquent.* Duilḃiṗ, *disagreeable* (ōo and
                                    laḃaṗ, *speak*).

PARTICIPLES.

So-ōoiṗce, *easy or apt to be*   Do-ōoiṗce, *difficult to be*
  poured out.   *poured out.*
So-críocṅuiġce, *finite, easily* Do-críocṅuiġce,   *infinite,*
  ended; root, críoċ, *end.*   *hard to be ended.*
So-ċuiṁṗiġce, *comprehensi-*   Do-ċuiṁṗiġce, *incomprehen-*
  ble; from cuiṁ, *compass;*   *sible, hard to be com-*
  cuiṁṗiġ, v,, *to compass.*   *passed or comprehended.*
So-feicṗince, *visible, easily*   Do-feicṗince, *invisible, not*
  seen; root, feic, *see;* ṗo-   *see-able;* ōo-feicṗioṅa,
  feicṗioṅa, *same.*   *same.*
So-ġlacuiġce, *easily taken,*   Do-ġlacuiġce, *hard to be re-*
  acceptable.   *ceived, unacceptable.*
So-ġluaiṗce, *moveable.*   Do-ġluaiṗce, *immoveable.*
So-ċuiġṗioṅa, *intelligible.*   Do-ċuiġṗioṅa, *unintelligible.*

9.—É, a *negative* particle, like the Latin *é, ek, eks,* or *ex;* as, ōeiṁiṅ, *indeed, certain;* ōoċiṁiṅ, *uncertain.*

É, before a syllable beginning with a broad vowel, takes a after it, to conform to the laws of vowel assimilation; as, ōoiṁiṅ, *deep, not shallow;* ea-ōoiṁiṅ, *not deep, shallow.*

Ea, before the consonants c and t, causes eclipses, or assumes, for the sake of euphony in the enunciation of the compound term, a letter of the same organ—ġ before c, and ō before t; as, ciallōa, *intelligent;* eaġ-ciallōa, *devoid* of intelligence; cṅaiḃċeaċ, *pious;* eaġ-cṅaiḃċeaċ, *impious, devoid* of piety; tṗocaiṗe, *mercy;* eaō-tṗocaiṗe, *without* mercy; eaō-tṗocaiṗeaċ, *merci*less. Eaġ is the prefix which precedes words beginning with ṗ; as, ṗaṁail, *like, similar;* eaġ-ṗaṁail, *dis*-similar, unlike, unusual, match*less.* The Scotch Gael do not admit the use of the eclipsing consonant after ea; as, eaceaṅt, *injustice;* eatṅocaiṗeaċ, *merciless;* eaōoċaṗ, *despair.*

☞ In this they are right; for the eclipsing consonants are, in such instances, useless; nay, in a small way, they help to puzzle the learner.

☞ Eaġ, *excessive;* from euġ, *death;* euġ-caoiṅe, *a dying groan, great lamentation.*

10.—Eaṗ, *extreme,* n., *top, end,* is an intensitive particle;

as, ᴇᴀᴘ-ɢᴀb, *arrest;* ᴇᴀᴘ-ᴘʟᴀɪċ, *an autocrat;* from ᴇᴀᴘ, and ᴘʟᴀɪċ, *a prince, a chieftain;* ᴇᴀᴘṁᴀʟʟ, *very slow;* ᴄᴀᴘ-ᴄoᴘᴀṁᴀɪʟ, *very similar;* ᴄᴀᴘɢᴀɪᴘ, *congratulate;* ᴄᴀᴘɢᴜᴀɪó, *munificent;* ᴄᴀᴘɢᴜé (from ᴄᴀᴘ, and ɢᴜé, *appearance*), *distinction, recognition;* ᴜɪoᴘ ċᴜɪᴘ ʀɪ ᴇᴀᴘɢᴜé oᴘm, *she did notice or recognise me.*

Cᴀᴘ is found only in a few words. It appears to be of kindred meaning with ɪᴀᴘ, *after*, meaning *final, ending, crowning;* as, ᴄᴀᴘbᴀʟʟ, *a tail*, from ᴄᴀᴘ, and bᴀʟʟ, *a member*, by metathesis ᴘᴇᴀbᴀʟ.

11.—Eᴀᴘ, *not, devoid of;* from ᴀᴘ, *out of;* as, ᴇᴀᴘ-ᴄᴀᴘᴀó, *an enemy;* from ᴇᴀᴘ, and ᴄᴀᴘᴀó, *a friend;* ᴇᴀᴘ-ᴜṁʟᴀċᴄ, *disobedience;* from ᴇᴀᴘ, and ᴜṁʟᴀċᴄ, *obedience;* which comes from ᴜṁᴀʟ, *humble;* Latin, *humilis;* ᴇᴀᴘ-ᴜᴘᴘᴀm, *disrespect, want of reverence;* from ᴇᴀᴘ, and ᴜᴘᴘᴀṁ, *reverence, respect;* ᴇᴀᴘʟᴀᴜ, *sick, infirm;* from ᴇᴀᴘ, and ᴘʟᴀᴜ, *sound in health;* ᴇᴀɢ-ᴘʟᴀᴜ, means the same, *infirm;* from ᴇ, or as above, óᴀɢ, *death*, and ᴘʟᴀᴜ. Eᴀᴘ is pronounced short.

12.—Fóɪᴘ, *before*, in *front;* therefore iṫ means *advanced, very.* Hence its presence imparts to the meaning of all words with which it is compounded, the idea of fullness or completeness, perfection, intensity; as, ᴘóɪᴘ-bᴘᴇᴀċᴜᴜɪɢ, *forethink, prophesy, conjecture, divine;* from ᴘóɪᴘ, and bᴘᴇᴀċᴜᴜɪɢ, *meditate on, speculate;* ᴘóɪᴘ-bᴘɪᴀċᴀᴘ, an *adverb;* from ᴘóɪᴘ, and bᴘɪᴀċᴀᴘ, *a word;* ᴘóɪᴘ-bᴘᴜᴀċ, *the edge of a precipice;* from ᴘóɪᴘ, and bᴘᴜᴀċ, *edge, border, brink;* ᴘóɪᴘ-ċᴇᴀᴜᴜ, *the extreme end;* root, ᴄᴇᴀᴜᴜ, *head, limit;* ᴘóɪᴘ-ɪmᴄᴀʟ, *frontier, limit, furthest extremity, circumference;* from ɪmᴄᴀʟ, *a border, a hem;* as, ɪmᴄᴀʟ ᴀ ᴘᴀʟʟᴀɪᴜᴇ, *the hem of His cloak;* ɪmᴄᴀʟ ᴜᴀ ᴄᴀʟṁᴀᴜ, *the ends of the earth;* ᴘóɪᴘ-ᴜᴇᴀᴘᴄ, *violence;* ᴜᴇᴀᴘᴄ, *strength;* ᴘóɪᴘ-ᴇɪɢᴄᴀᴜ, *oppression;* root, ᴇɪɢᴄᴀᴜ, or ᴇɪɢɪᴜ, *force, violence, compulsion.*

13.—Fᴘɪċ, *back, quick succession;* as, ᴘᴘɪċ-ċᴇᴀċᴄ, *coming and going;* ᴘᴘɪċ-bᴜᴀʟᴀó, *repercussion, a palpitation.*

14.—Jol, and sometimes written ɪl, akin in meaning with ᴜɪʟᴇ, *all*, signifies *plenty, variety, diversity*—like πολυς, *polús*, in Greek; as, ᴀɪᴜm, *a name;* ɪol-ᴀɪᴜmᴜᴀ, *many names;* bᴇᴜʟᴘᴀ, *language, speech* (for bᴇᴜʟᴘᴀ, root, bᴇᴜʟ, *the mouth;* and ᴘᴀó, *speech*); ɪol-bᴇᴜᴘʟᴀ, *many languages;* ɪol-ċɪᴀʟ, *many significations;* ɪomᴀó (adj.), *many, nume-*

rous; (n.), *a multitude;* ɿol-ɿomaᴅ, a *great* multitude; ɿol-ċaɿnⱺeaċ, *many-*tongued, a polyglot; ɿol-ṗɿan, *torment;* from ɿol, and pɿan, *pain;* ɿol-bċuɼaċ, *arch, sly, versatile;* from ɿol, and beuɼaċ, *mannerly;* root, beuɼ, *manners, behaviour;* ɿolbaċaċ, *parti-coloured.*

15.—Jom, *around about;* from the preposition uɿme, *around, about;* it is therefore an intensive particle; as, ʒaoċ, *wind;* ɿomʒaoċ, a *whirl*wind; lán, *full;* ɿomlán, *entire, complete;* ᴅpuɿᴅ, *shut, close;* ɿom-ᴅpuɿᴅ, *surround, shut up all around;* ꜰulanʒ, *endure, suffer;* ɿom-ꜰulanʒ, *endure;* ɿomċɼom, *very* heavy. In two instances it reverses the meaning of the word with which it is compounded; as, ɿomċeaċⱺ, *to depart;* from ɿom, and ⱺeaċⱺ, *to come;* and ɿomꜰɼuċ, a *counter-*tide; from ɿom, and ɼɼuċ, *a current.*

16.—Jon, a particle that expresses *fitness,* suitableness; as, ɿonꜰɿɼ, *marriageable* (from ɿon, *fit for,* and ꜰɿɼ gen. case of ꜰeaɼ *a man*), as applied to a maid; ɿonmna, as applied to a young man (from ɿon, and mna, the gen. case of bean, *a woman);* ɿonaɼm, *fit to bear arms.* Before past participles it can be used at pleasure. It imparts to such participles the same meaning that the suffix "able," "ible" (Latin, *bilis*), gives to English words; as, ɿċ, *eat;* ɿċⱺe, *eaten;* ɿon-ɿċⱺe, *eatable* (fit-to-be-eaten); ól, *drink;* ólⱺa, *drunk;* ɿon-ólⱺa, *drinkable* (fit-to-be-drunk); mol, *praise;* molⱺa, *praised;* ɿonmolⱺa, *praiseable* (fit-to-be-praised); ʒɼáᴅ (n.), *love;* ʒɼáᴅuɿʒ (v.), *love thou;* ʒɼáᴅuɿʒⱺe, *loved;* ɿonʒɼáᴅuɿʒⱺe, *loveable* (fit-to-be-loved), deserving-of-love; much like the Latin *amandus;* and, in this sense (as far as the Latin participle ending, *dus* betokens suitableness) what O'Molloy says of this prefix is true—that it has the force of the Latin participle of the future in *dus.*

<small>Whenever, therefore, a person translating English into Irish meets with a word ending in *able,* he need only observe its root, learn its Irish equivalent, form the past participle, and prefix ɿon.</small>

OBS.—Jon differs from the prefix ꜰo; for ꜰo implies *ease, feasibility;* ɿon, *fitness;* as in the annexed example, in which ꜰo-ᴅéanⱺa (*easily-done*), ɿon-ᴅeanⱺa (*fit-to-be-done*), are contrasted; nɿ'l ʒaċ nɿᴅ ⱺá ꜰo-ᴅéanⱺa, ɿon-ᴅéanⱺa, *everything that is feasible, is not suitable.*

17.—ᴊɴ and ɪoɴ, as found in some compound words, is a form of the preposition ᴀɴɴ, *in*; as, ɪoɴċoʟɴuᵹᴀö, *incarnation*; from ɪoɴ (or ᴀɴɴ), *in*; and coʟɴuᵹᴀö, *to give a* (colaɴ) *body to; to make flesh;* ɪoɴ-ṁeoöᴀɴᴀċ (adj.), *interior, from within;* derived from ɪoɴ, *in*, and ᴍeoöᴀɴ, *middle;* Latin, *medium;* English, *mean;* ɪoɴᵹᴀɴᴛᴀꞃ (pr. *ee-yan-thas*), *a wonder;* from ɪoɴ, and ᵹᴀɴᴛᴀꞃ (root, ᵹᴀɴ, *rare, scarce*), *a thing that seldom happens;* ɪɴʟᴀoɪᵹ, *in calf;* as, bō ɪɴʟᴀoɪᵹ, *a cow in-calf;* ɪoɴṁᴀꞃ, *a treasure, a valuable thing in which* ᴍeᴀꞃ (*estimation, value*) *is placed;* ɪɴċɪɴɴ, *the brain;* from ɪɴ, *in*, and cɪɴɴ, the dat. case of ceᴀɴɴ, *head.* ᴊoɴ, *in* (perhaps for ᴀɴ, p. 182), intensifies; as, ɪoɴᵹꞃeɪṁ, *persecution;* from ɪoɴ, and ᵹꞃeɪṁ, *a grasp;* it also annuls; as, ɪɴᵹʟᴀɴ, *un-*clean.

The prefixes ɪoʟ, ɪoṁ, ɪoɴ, are written in published works and MSS. ɪʟ, ɪṁ, ɪɴ, when preceding a slender vowel.

☞ Anxious to make Irish orthography fixed, we shall write these prefixes in every instance with the broad vowel ɪoʟ, and not ɪʟ; ɪoṁ, and not ɪṁ; ɪoɴ, and not ɪɴ, except the prep. ɪ and ɪɴ, *in*. It is desirable to adopt this form for the reason just assigned. Besides, ɪoʟ is preferable to ɪʟ, for it is synonymous with uɪʟe, in which the broad vowel is a leading feature, and because the spelling ɪoʟ prevails more than ɪʟ; and lastly, the spelling ɪoʟ accords with the usual pronunciation better than that of ɪʟ. These reasons hold for ɪoṁ.

18.—Ⱳɪ, *ill, amiss;* of the same meaning as the Saxon, "*mis*," is a negative prefix of frequent use; as, ᴀö, *fortune, luck;* ᴍɪ-ᴀö, *misfortune, ill-luck;* ꞃᴀċ, *success, a prosperous issue;* ᴍɪ-ꞃᴀċ, *calamity, ill-success;* ᵹɴɪoṁ, *an act;* ᴍɪ-ᵹɴɪoṁ, an act done *amiss;* cʟú, *fame;* ᴍɪ-cʟú, *ill*-fame.

19.—Neᴀṁ, *a privative* (spelled ɴeṗ in ancient writings, but in Scotch Gaelic at present invariably ɴeo); as, ᴀɪꞃeᴀċ, *attentive;* ɴeᴀṁ-ᴀɪꞃeᴀċ, *inattentive;* coꞃᴀṁᴀɪʟ, *like, similar;* ɴeᴀṁ-coꞃᴀṁᴀɪʟ, *unlike;* ʟeɪꞃᵹ, *sloth, dislike, loathing;* ɴeᴀṁ-ʟeɪꞃᵹ, *courage, spunk;* absence of sloth, *dislike,* &c.; ꞃuɪᴍ, *regard,* the sum of one's esteem for; ɴeᴀṁ-ꞃuɪᴍ, *disregard;* ɴɪö, *a thing;* ɴeᴀṁ-ɴɪö, *a thing without substance or effect;* as, ɪꞃ ɴeᴀṁ-ɴɪö ᴀɴ uɪʟe ᴀċᴛ ᴀᴍᴀɪɴ Ⅾɪᴀ ᴀ ꞃɪᴀɴᴀö ᴀᵹuꞃ ᴀ ᵹꞃᴀöuᵹᴀö, *all is vanity* (a useless thing) *but alone to serve and love God.*

20.—Oll, *great;* of kindred meaning with uɪʟe, *all;* or with all, *prodigious, vast, mighty;* as, oll-ᵹuċ, a *loud* voice;

oll-ɡníoṁaċ, of *daring* deeds; oll-ɡlóṗ, *bombast, big* sound. Ull is found as a prefix in a few words; as, all-buaiḋeaċ, *mighty, all-victorious;* " all-ṅeaṗc," (*of*) *mighty strength.*

"Do buaṡó ó 'n naṁ 'ḃi uaiṫleaċ 'ṫ all-ṅeaṗc."
"Which he won from the foe (who) was haughty and (of) mighty strength."
" Which he won from the proud invader."
Song—" *Let Erin remember the days of old.*"

21.—Ro, *large, very, too much ;* as, ṗo-ċuṗaṁ, *very great* care; ṗo-ċṗaṅ, a *large* tree; ṗo-ṁíaṅ, a *great* wish; ṗo-ḃaṗċa, *the influx of the tide.* Ro, when affixed to adjectives, imparts to them the same meaning that the adverb *too* or *over,* in English, does to adjectives before which it is placed; as, ṗo-àṗḋ, *too high ;* ṗo-ṁóṗ, *over large.* The word ṗíɡ, a *king,* is employed as a prefix; as, ṗíɡ-ṁaíċ, *supremely good :* ṗíɡ differs in meaning from ṗo; the latter denotes excess—the former, excellence, superiority, perfection; as, ċà aṅ ṅíḋ ro ṗíɡ-ṁaíċ, *this thing is very good ;* ċà aṅ ṅíḋ ro ṗo-ṁaíċ, *this is over good, too good.*

22.—Sàṅ (from ṫaṅ, *self,* found commonly as a suffix ; as, é-ṫaṅ, *himself*)*, peculiar, proper ;* as, ṫaṅ-ɡeṅelaċ, *proper genus ;* ṫaíṅɡṅe, *special appearance, own form ;* ṫaíṅɡṅuíṫ, *propria forma ;* ṫoíṗaċ, *special ;* from ṫaíṅ, and ṗíoċc, *state.*

23.—Sàṗ is an augmentative denoting *excellence, superiority,* and gives therefore to adjectives with which it enters into composition the meaning attached to absolute superlatives; as, ṫàṗ-ṁaíċ, *exceedingly* good ; ṫàṗ-ṁaíṫeaċ, *exceedingly* handsome ; ṫàṗ-aṗuíḋ, *quite* ripe ; ṫàṗ-ḋuíṅe, *an excellent person ;* ṫàṗ-laoċ, *a great* hero. Sàṗ, as a noun, means *a worthy, a hero, a leading man,* compounded, as it were, of ro, *worthy ;* and ḟeaṗ, *a man.* In this sense we can easily see the meaning of the Saxon word " Sir," and of the Russian " tsar" (or " zar"), and " zarina," to be a *superior* or distinguished person.

Jaṗ, prep., *after, behind*—also a noun, the *west, western ;* as, íaṗ-ḃṗeíċ. *the after-birth ;* íaṗ-buíllċ, *a blow from behind ;* íaṗ-ḋcaṫ, *the south-west* (*west-south*) *;* íaṗ-ċuaċ, *the north-west ;* íaṗ-ṁuíṗ, *the Atlantic ;* íaṗ-ḋoṅṅ, *brownish, after-brown ;* from ḋoṅṅ, *brown ;* and íaṗ, *after, left, re-*

maining; ᴊᴀʀ-ɢᴜɪɴ, *grief, pain;* from ᴊᴀʀ, and ɢᴜɪɴ, *a sting, a wound;* ᴊᴀɴɢᴄᴜʟᴛᴀ, *wild, remote, deserted, western;* from ᴊᴀʀ, and *cul, a corner;* ᴊᴀʀ-Ċᴏɴɴᴀċᴛ, *West Connaught.*

24.—Seac, anciently ꞃec (Latin, *secus*), *beside, apart, out of the way;* as, ꞃeac pɪᴀɴᴀ, *out of the way* of pain, not having to endure pain; ꞃeacᴀɪɴ, *avoid, shun;* from ꞃeac, and ꝼᴀɴ, *stay, keep*—*i.e.,* keep *aside, avoid;* ꞃeacɢᴀɪꞃɪᴍ, I call *aside;* ꞃeac-ʟᴀbꞃᴀö, *an allegory,* a discourse having a meaning *beside* or apart from that which the plain words present to the mind. Seac is the root of the English words *sex, sect,* and of the Latin *seco, I cut, separate, sunder, divide, I rend,* and of all its derivatives.

§ 208.—PRIMARY AND SECONDARY SIGNIFICATION OF WORDS.

In the infancy of language, words at first were employed, very likely, only in one sense. As time progressed, and as society became formed and extended, the associations of mankind—not alone in morals, but in the walks of science, art, letters, philosophy, and theology—were gradually compassing different spheres for the exercise of thought. For this increase in ideas, a proportionate increase in terms by which they could be expressed and conveyed, was required. This could not be better supplied than by employing those terms already in use, to other objects analogous in cause, effect, form, inherent power, or quality.

Words have only one primary or radical meaning—they have several secondary meanings, according to the different classes of objects to which they are applied. Most words have the primary and secondary meanings; others have only the primary; others, again, retain only the secondary.

§ 209. Let us take the words uᴀċbᴀɴ (from uᴀꞃ, *above*), *superior, the top, upper;* ᴊᴀċbᴀɴ, *the inferior, or lower part of a thing.* Uᴀċbᴀɴ and ᴊᴀċbᴀɴ are correlative: uᴀċbᴀɴ conveys the idea that there is something else which is to it ᴊᴀċbᴀɴ.

Uᴀċbᴀɴ, primarily means *upper.*

Uᴀċbᴀɴ (2), *cream,* because it is the upper part of milk set to rest in a milk pail; ᴊᴀċbᴀɴ, *thick, unchurned milk.*

Uᴀċbᴀɴ (3), *soprano;* ᴊᴀċbᴀɴ. *basso,* in music.

Uᴀċbᴀɴ (4), *the top, scum, dross.*

Uᴀċbᴀɴ (5), *the upper part of a field.*

Uᴀċbᴀɴ (6), *the upper part of a dress.*

Uᴀċbᴀɴ (7), *the upper of a shoe or boot.*

Uᴀċbᴀɴ (8), *the upper part or top end of a cloth,* the *right* side or upper surface. See the word bᴀɴɴ, *top*—in "Easy Lessons," p. 275.

It is thus seen that the only way to get the key for understanding fully the secondary acceptations of words, is to learn their primary and radical meaning, which can be best done by attending to the principles and rules which have been presented to the reader in the foregoing lesson.

PART III.—SYNTAX.

CHAPTER I.

§ 210. This part of Grammar treats, as the word shows, from its component parts, συν (*sún*), *together ;* and τασσω, to *arrange*, to *order—of arranging together* in proper order, according to certain rules, the words and phrases of a language, so as to enable the people who use it as a medium of communicating thought, to express their ideas in the clearest and most perfect manner.

§ 211. Those rules are founded on the universal linguistic principles of *agreement, government, connexion ;* and on the special principles from which *idioms* or peculiarities of construction and collocation spring.

☞ The order observed by grammarians in treating the subject of Syntax is—first, to furnish rules which regard *agreement ;* secondly, those rules which show the *government*—that is, the power and action of words in their mutual influence, thus producing a pleasing variety of inflections and relations in each sentence ; thirdly, their *connexion* or appropriate combination. When the words of a sentence have been directed by these three leading laws, a syntactical arrangement results; words and phrases may, however, be syntactically arranged, and yet the sentence resulting from their union may not be clear in its meaning, elegant in its form, nor idiomatic in the manner the thoughts have been conveyed. Besides syntactical arrangement, there is, therefore, another which may be called the rhetorical, by which perspicuity, idiom, and elegance are attained. This latter does not enter the domain of Syntax.

Written or spoken language is composed of sentences. It is quite in keeping with this subject, therefore, to say a few words concerning the sentence.

§ 212. A sentence is the expression of a thought; as, (1), ɪr maɪc Ðɪa, *God is good;* (2), caɪm rona, *I am happy;* (3), ðean, *do;* (4), ʒnaðuɪʒ, *love.*

*** By *thought* is here meant what logicians call a judgment.

A sentence is (1), *simple* or *compound ;* (2), *complete* or *incomplete ;* (3), *loose* or *perfect*, which is also called a *period*. A *simple* sentence has only one subject and one personal verb; as, ɪr maɪc Ðɪa, *God is good*. A compound sentence includes two or more simple sentences. In a complete sentence, the sense is fully expressed; in an incomplete one, the sense is not fully expressed; as, óɪn ba m-beɪðeað rɪor aʒað-ra aʒur aɪn an lo an ɪuð, *for if thou also hadst known, and that in this thy day.—Luke*, xix. 42. The period and loose sentence belong properly to the domain of rhetoric. A simple sentence is *affirmative, negative, imperative, interrogative, deprecative,* or *vocative,* according as it affirms, denies, commands, asks, deplores, or addresses.

§ 213. In order to show more in detail the agreement, government, and connexion of words, together with the idiomatic forms of expression in the Irish language, the usual, and indeed philosophical mode in which the subject of Syntax has been treated, as shown (§ 211), is not in the present instance adopted. It is thought wiser, as well in order to aid the young student, as to render the subject clear, and fully intelligible, to furnish, as in the first edition, the rules according to their connexion with the nine parts of speech respectively. This plan does not virtually differ much from that referred to above.

☞ The concords are four—(1), that between the adjective and substantive (see c. iii., p. 77); (2), between one substantive and another; (3), between a relative and its antecedent; (4), between a verb and its nominative case.

§ 214.—THE ARTICLE.

In English, German, French, Spanish, and Italian, the indefinite article (*a, ein, un, uno*) is employed; in Irish, Latin, Greek, it is not. The simple idea conveyed by the words, *a* man, is expressed in Irish by the sole term, ꝼeaɴ. The word ꝼeaɴ, taken singly, serves to convey the particularity of idea which the English indefinite article helps to convey.

It happens that the *definite* article is employed in Irish with great propriety in positions where the indefinite, or none at all, is found in English. The definite article in Irish (like ὁ, ἡ, τὸ, in Greek) gives prominence and force to the noun before which it is placed. It has a kind of demonstrative power.

1.—Before *sirnames*, for the sake of distinction or emphasis; as, aɴ c-Oɩꞃɩɴ, *Ossian;* aɴ c-Ⰰcuɩl, *Achilles.*

Was *Walsh* here? Ꞃaɩb "aɴ" bꞃeacaɴaċ aɴɴ ꝼo?
Walsh was not, but *O'Reilly* was. Ní ꞃaɩb "aɴ" bꞃeacaɴaċ, (pr. in two syllables *Bĕrhannoch*), aċc bí "aɴ" Ꞃaᵹallaċ (pr. *Rhy-alloch*).

☞ Borrowed from the Irish, there are found at the present day some family names to which in English the definite article is attached; as, *The* O'Donoughoe, *The* O'Connor Don, *The* O'Neil, *The* O'Brien.

Before *titles* or *qualities;* as, God Almighty, Đɩa " aɴ" uɩle-Ċumaċcaċ, *i.e.,* God *the* Almighty.

2.—Before the names of *virtues* and *vices;* as,

What is faith? Cao é aɴ ɴɪó "aɴ" cꞃeɩoeam?
What is hope? Cao é aɴ ɴ ó "aɴ" oóċur?
What is sin? Cao é aɴ ɴɪó "aɴ" peacao?
Patience is good, Iꞃ maɩċ í "aɴ" ꝼoɩᵹɩo.

3.— Before *abstract* nouns; as,

Hunger is good sauce, Iꞃ maɩċ "aɴ" c-aɴlaɴ "aɴ" c-ocꞃuꞃ.

When *beauty* and *brilliancy* fade from the gems, 'Nuaiṗ éaluiṡeaṙ ó na ṙeoḋaiḃ "an" ṙṡiaṁ ṡuṙ "an" ḃlaṫ.
"And from loves shining circle the gems drop away."

Irish Melodies.

4.—Before *adjectives* taken substantively; as,

There is not much between (*the*) good and (*the*) bad—
Iṙ beaṡ a ṫá eioiṁ an ṫ-olc aṡuṙ an ṁaiṫ.

5.—Under this view it precedes numerals, not influencing nouns; as,

It has struck (*the*) two, Ḋo ḃuail ṙe "an" ḋó.
It has struck (*the*) three, Ḋo ḃuail ṙe "an" ṫṙí.
Sin é "an" ṫṙí, that is "*the*" *three;* ṙin é "an" ceaṫaiṙ, that is "*the*" *four;* ṙin é "an" cuiṡ, that is "*the*" *five*. In enumerating, as follows, the article is not employed; as, aon, *one;* ḋo, *two;* ṫṙí, *three;* ceaṫaṙ, *four;* cuiṡ, *five*, &c.

6.—Before a noun accompanied by the *demonstrative* pronouns; as,

This man (Irish form, *the* man this), "an" ḟeaṙ ṙo.
That woman (*the* woman that) "an" ḃean ṙin.
These men (*the* men these), na ḟiṙ ṙo.

☞ The demonstrative pronoun *this*, is translated into Irish not alone by ṙo (this), but by the combined use of an, *the*, and "ṙo." An, declares; ṙo, points out. The position of one is *before;* of the other, *after* the noun. That the word *this* should be translated by means of two terms, "an," *the*, and ṙo, does not appear strange to one who reflects that *this* and *these* are compounded of the Anglo-Saxon article, *the*, and of *se*, he; *seo*, fem—she. *That*, in like manner is composed of two parts—*the*, and *it*.—*Latham*, part iv., c. xiv., § 336.

7.—Names of countries; as, (the) Spain, "an" Spain; (the) France; "an" Ḟṙainc; (the) Scotland, "an" Albain; (the) Germany, "an" Allaṁain; before the name of "Rome," o'n Róiṁ; from (the) Rome; before months, as, (the) April, an Abṙain; mí na Saṁna, the month of (the) November.

An, *the*, "gives force and prominence to the noun." When opposition, antithesis, or emphasis is required to be employed, the article *the* is found to be placed by good writers before such names as, England, Scotland, Ireland Tara; if emphasis or the like be not expressed, the article *the* (an) is omitted; as,

"An uaiṙ ṙmuainiṁ aiṙ ḟaoiṫiḃ "na" h-Éiṙeann,"
When I reflect on the nobles of (*the*) *Ireland.*

Dirge of Ireland line 1.

Muinτir "na" h-Eireann, *the people of (the) Ireland,*

Δiδ ro m' aṁarc δειζeanać ain "Eirinn" a coiδċc.
Though the last glimpse of Eire in sorrow I see

Eirinn (dat. case governed by ain *on*) has not the article an before it; in the other sentences Eireann has. Similarly Teaṁair, *Tara;* and "an" Teaṁair, *the* Tara, are frequently found. The names of towns and localities in Ireland of the masculine gender have not the article unless some special reason require it. Feminine nouns are usually in this case excepted, and follow rule 7; as, muinτir "na" Ṡaillṁe, *the inhabitants of (the) Galway;* muinτir na Dile, *the people of Deel.*

8.—Before uile, when it precedes a noun, meaning *every;* as, *the* every man, "an" uile δuine; *the* every house, an uile τeaċ.

☞ Uile signifying *all, whole,* takes the definite article in English as well as in Irish; as, *the* whole world, "an" δoṁan ṁór; it is only when it signifies *every,* the difference of idiom is manifested by the use of the article in Irish,.when in English, in the like form of expression, it is not found; as, "an" uile τir (the) *every* country; an τir uile, *the whole* country.

NOTE.—Uile going *before* its noun has a distributive meaning, as is plain from the foregoing example, and therefore, signifies *every;* coming *after* its noun, it has a collective meaning, and therefore signifies *all. Omnis, all,* in Latin has the same power; *omnis homo, every* man.

9.—*A* or *an* (English) signifying *one;* is translated into Irish by aon, *one,* and aṁain, *only, singly;* as, *a* single individual, "aon" δuine "aṁain;" there is not *a single* individual of that family now alive, ni' l "aon" δuine "aṁain" anoir beo δe' n muinτir uδ.

10.—In affirmative sentences expressed by ir, *it is,* and buδ, *may be, was,* or their negative forms, and having two nominative cases—one going before, the other coming after the verb—the *definite* article an, *the,* is employed before the latter of the two in Irish, in English the indefinite; as,

Fear ṡlic oliṡe ir olc "an" coṁursa.
A cunning lawyer is *a* bad neighbor.

In this example the term coṁursa, *neighbor,* is defined in Irish by the article an, *the;* in English it is not defined. The Irish expression is much stronger than the same in English. The sentence, and all others of the same mould, can be translated thus: *the* neighbour is bad—a cunning man of (the) law. The word coṁursa, *neighbour,* in the sentence is the real nominative case to the verb; fear oliṡe is in apposition to coṁursa, or nominative after the verb *is;* olc is what is predicated of *the* neighbour. Some gentlemen learned in English grammar may be inclined to dispute this view of the sentence, and on that account it is fair to show why it is here stated that comunṛa coming after the words ιr oιc is the nominative. The reasons for it are:

(1) The nominative case in Irish follows the verb.
(2) The article points out the subject (rule 17).
(3) In sense and grammatical construction the sentence is the same as this: ιr oιc an "comunṛa" reaṉ ꙅιc oιꙅe. Other sentences of this class: Ir maιṫ an ṟean Séamur, James is *a* good man; literally, *the* man James is good; buṫ bneaꙅ "na" ṟιn ιaṫ, *they were fine men*—literally, *the* men they were fine.

NOTE.—If only *one* nominative is expressed, this idiomatic use of the article does not take place; as (the proverb), ιr maιṫ "rꙅeul" ꙅu ṫ-cιꙅιṫ an ṫana rꙅeul, (literally) *a story is good till the second story reach (us)—one story is good till the second be told*; ιr ṟeaṉṉ "rcuaιn" 'na neanc, "*ingenuity" is better than strength.*

11.—Whenever it is required to express in Gaelic the *state* or *condition* of a person or thing without employing the assertive form, a very remarkable idiom—a possessive pronoun governed by the preposition ann, *in*—is adopted to express what in English is conveyed by the *indefinite* article, and in Latin and Greek simply by the noun; as, τa ṟé 'nn a buιne ṁaιṫ, he is *a* good person; bι ṟιaṫ 'nna ḃ-ṟeanaιḃ ḃneaꙅa, they were fine men; beιṫ rι 'nn a caιlιn aluιn, she will be *a* beautiful girl; τa ṁé 'mo rcolaιṉe ṁaιṫ, I am *a* good scholar.

Literally, he is *in his* good person, *i.e.*, in the state of a good person; they were in the *subsistence of* (in its logical acceptation) fine men, &c. The 'nn a before buιne, is a contraction for ann, *in*, and a, *his;* the nn a, before ṟeaṉaιḃ, is contractedly for ann, *in*, and a, *their;* which differs from a, *his*, and therefore, causes according to rule, ṟeaṉaιḃ to be eclipsed by ḃ. The 'mo, before rcolaιne, is for ann mo, *in my.*

NOTE.—The preposition ann or ι, *in,* does not follow the emphatic form of the verb *to be,* i.e., ιr, *it is* (buṫ, *was, may be*), which is a mere copula, expressing simply *existence.*

The form of the verb employed is τaιm, with its cognate tenses and inflections. Τa expresses existence combined with locality, state, condition; it is more special than ιr. Ir may be classed as a generic term in conveying the idea of existence; τa, a special term.

See the difference in meaning between ιr, τaιm, bιṫιm, ḃ-ṟuιlιm, shown in § 120, p. 116, supra; consult *Easy Lessons,* part iii., p. 196, *third edition,* Dublin, Mullany, Publisher.

OBS.—The preposition ι, *in,* or ann, *in,* is omitted whenever the possessive pronouns of the first and second persons, as well plural as singular, follow; as, τa mé 'mo comunṛa ṁaιṫ, *I* am a good neighbour; in this sentence, ann is omitted before mo, *my;* it reads then as if it were, *I* am my good neighbour; which to one not knowing the idiom would undoubtedly appear very strange. Again, before bo, *thy;* as, bι bo τún neιṛt aꙅam, a τιꙅeanna, *be unto me, O Lord, a tower of strength.*

§ 215.—*What some Irish Grammarians think of this Idiom.*

Certain persons writing on the subject of Irish Grammar, assert with more fluency than philosophy, and without condescending to assign a single reason for the assertion, that the noun governed by the preposition ann, in this Irish idiom, is, although a concrete term, taken for the abstract; for instance in the following: tá ſe 'nn a ḋuine ṁaiṫ, he is a good *man*, the term ḋuine, *a man* (*homo*), is taken for the abstract term *humanity ;* and therefore that the sentence " he is *a good man*," is the same in Irish as to say, he is in *the state of good humanity.*

Reasons against their view.

1.—By one stroke of the pen, these wonderfully clever men overturn all the laws of thought, logical reason, and physics—making concrete living things mere abstractions. Every one sees that the concrete term *man* cannot, unless the meaning of language and logic be changed, mean, at the same time, that indicated by the abstract term—*humanity.*

2.—"In language itself there is no irregularity," says Robert Gordon Latham in his work, " The English Language," third edition, p. 336. " The word itself is only another name for our ignorance of the processes that change words." And again : " A great number of expressions scarcely warrantable in strict syntax become part and parcel of the language. To condemn these at once is unphilosophical—the better method is to account for them."

3.—Can this construction of ann, *in,* after tá and its inflection be accounted for? Very easily. táim, as the best Keltic philologists show, expresses the idea, as has been said (p. 196), of existence in some state or condition, and relatively to time or place. On this account the preposition ann, *in,* is usually employed *after* it; as, cia mejb Dia (tá) ann? how many God's (are) *in it, i.e., are there?* Answer—ni b-ɼuil " ann" ać aon Dia amain, there is *in it* only one God. Again it is said, tá ſe ann, nió aiṗ bit a ḋéanaḋ, it is *in* him to do (*i.e.,* he is capable of) anything. From all this it is plain that—some way owing to the relative meaning which is contained in the verb táim, of expressing *existence in some special state*—the preposition ann must necessarily come immediately after it.

Obs.—With they verb táim, therefore, ann, *in,* must be employed, to aid in expressing fully the position, character, or state of a person or thing; tá of itself is not sufficient to convey the correlative idea. Hence the idiom.

4.—This simple, natural, and truthful view, agreeably to the meaning of the verb táim, is confirmed by analogy—take for instance the French, a language which in many ways still retains traces of an early Keltic element in its formation. The preposition *en* is sometimes employed as it is in Irish; as, he died *a* man of courage—il etait mort *en homme* de cœur ; he deports himself (as) *a* good man—il se porte *en homme* de bien. A similar analogy is found to exist in the following quotations from the Greek and Latin, which bear in their construction, the impress of the Hebrew linguistic mould: " 'Εγὼ ἔσομαι αὐτῷ εἰς πατέρα, καὶ αὐτὸς ἔσται μοι εἰς υἱον, Heb. i. 5. Esto mihi *in* Deum protectorem.—*Ps.* xxx. 3.

§ 216. *A* or *an,* for *per,* when translated into Irish, is rendered by the preposition ann; as, twice *a* day ; ɼá ḋo "'ᴘᴀɴ" lo, five shillings *a* week; cuıᴢ ᴦᴈılllɴᴢ "ᴀɴᴜᴘ" ᴀɴ τ-ᴘeᴀċτᴍᴀıɴ. It is, however, commonly translated by ᴢᴀċ, *each*; as, he earns three shillings *a* day, ᴘᴀoɴċuıᴢᴀɴɴ ᴘe τᴘı ᴦᴈıllɴᴢe ᴢᴀċ lᴀ.

☞ *A* for *at*=ᴀıᴢ; as, *a*-fishing, "ᴀıᴈ" ıᴀᴦᴢᴀıɴeᴀċτ; for *on*, by ᴀıɴ; as, *a*-bed, ᴀıɴ leᴀbᴀ; for *in*, by ᴀ, *in*; as, *a*-far, ᴀ ʙ-ᴘᴀo:

Note.—Robert Gordon Latham observes, in regard to the indefinite and even the definite article: "So far are they from being essential to language, that in many dialects they are wholly wanting. In Greek there is no indefinite; in Latin there is neither an indefinite nor a definite article." "Just as *an* and *a* have arisen out of the numeral *one*, so has *the* arisen out of the demonstrative pronoun *that*—or at least from some common root." Again: "In no language, in its oldest stage, is there even a word giving in its primary sense the ideas of *a* and *the*."

*** From this it is plain to the student that the foregoing rules take their rise from the fact, that in the English language the *in*definite article is employed, while in Gaelic it is not; and again, that the definite article is used in Gaelic before terms, the equivalents of which, in English, do not admit that part of speech. The foregoing rules, therefore, are idiomatic. If Latin or even Greek had been the language with which a syntactical analysis were being made, the foregoing rules should of necessity be expunged, since the two languages in respect to the use of the article bear a strong similarity.

§ 217. The idiomatic use of ᴀɴ, *the*, in Gaelic in positions, in which in English it is not at all employed, has been shown in the foregoing rules. It happens also that it is employed in English in some few instances quite correctly, while in the like forms of expression in Irish it is not admissible; as, I got *the* book of the scholar, ᴘuᴀıᴘ me leᴀʙᴀıᴘ "ᴀɴ" ᴘcolᴀıᴘe.

The article *the* is employed in English before the term *book* and *scholar*; in Irish it is only before the latter of the two, not before the former.

"Cum luıɴᴢe 'ɴᴀ' ɴᴈɴeuᴢ ᴏo τɴıᴀll ᴀɴ ᴘᴀᴢᴀɴτ ᴘᴀm."
"To [the] ships of the Greeks the gentle priest repaired."
The in Irish is omitted before the term *ships*.

Note.—In p. 56 of this Grammar, it has been shown that there are two forms of the possessive case—the Anglo-Saxon and the Norman. The Norman is known by the preposition *of*; the Anglo-Saxon by *'s* (and the *apostrophe*). When the Norman genitive occurs in English, the article *the* before the former of the two nouns is omitted in Irish, although expressed in English; as, to *the* ships of the Greeks, cum luıɴᴢe ɴᴀ ɴᴈɴeuᴢ.

When the Saxon genitive occurs, and that it is to be translated into Gaelic, the article precedes only the possessive case, and then no idiom arises. The sentences, as regards the article, are alike in both languages, except that the position of the governed noun suffers a change; as, to the *Greeks*' ships, cum luinʒe "na" nʒneuʒ; the term "na nʒneuʒ," genitive, answers to the English possessive, "the Greeks';" which in Irish follows luinʒe, *ships*, while in English it precedes the same term.

§ 218. The defining office of the article "the" (an, mas., na, fem.) is more special in Gaelic than in English. This helps to show the reason of its non-use—as compared with English—before the former and less definable term of two nouns in a sentence, as is seen by the following:

Three instances in which the definite article, correctly employed in English, is not idiomatic nor correct in Gaelic.

(*a*).—In rendering into Gaelic such sentences as these, "*the* Lord of the world," "*the* light of the sun," omit the article "*the*" before the former, and retain it with the latter noun; as,

  The Lord of the world,
   Tiʒeanna "an" domain.
  The light of the sun,
   Solur "na" ʒréine.

(*b*).—It is retained only in the last of even three or more genitives; as,

  The beauty of *the* daughter of the king,
   Áilleact inʒine "an" ríʒ.

Obs.—This specially defining use of the article, and its non-use in Gaelic, does not differ in idiom from the English form when the Saxon genitive is employed; as,

  The sun's light,
   Solur "na" ʒréine.
  The king's daughter's beauty,
   Áilleact inʒine "an" ríʒ.

The Saxon and Gaelic genitives are here alike in their requiring the presence of the definite article; but the Norman and Gaelic are not. For instance, in that last sentence, neither the term "beauty," nor "daughter's" has the article, while the word "king," which is the term to be specified above the rest, and its Irish equivalent, ríʒ, have the article. In the Saxon and Gaelic forms, the position of the nouns in the one is the reverse of the order in the other, for instance:

English—The king's daughter's beauty.
"Beauty" is the last, "king's" the first term.
Gaelic—Áilleact inʒine "an" ríʒ.
"Ríʒ" (king) is the last, "áilleact" the first.

 From Easy Lessons; or, Self-Instruction in Irish, pp. 368, 369.

Exceptions.—Compound nouns of the class specified in § 197, p. 176 of this treatise, do not take the definite article before the second of the two nouns; as, loŋȝ coȝaıò, ship-*of-war;* maòaò cnoıc, dog-*of-mountain;* i.e., *mountain-dog;* ȝata flaıċır, gate-*of-heaven.*

☞ The names of virtues and vices, and those pointed out in pp. 193, 194, retain the article; as, aċaın "na" m-bneuȝ, *the father-*"*of-*(the)" *lies;* faıȝ "na" nıallaċc, *prophet-*"*of-the*"*-curses.*

Obs. 1.—The demonstrative force of the article "an," *the,* is seen from the following examples:

(1), fean tıȝe, *a householder.*
(2), "an" fean tıȝe, *the householder.* } compound terms.
(3), fean "an" tıȝe (*the*) man of *the* (meaning a special) house.

§ 219. (c—*third* instance).—Sentences like the following: Catherine *is the* fairest; John *is the* tallest; having the *definite* article before the adjective in the superlative degree, omit it in Irish when the assertive verb ıf, *is,* is employed; as, rí Caıtlín ıf aılne; ıf ré Seaȝan ıf aınòe.

☞ In this form, the words "an" bean, *the* woman; "an" fean, *the* man, are understood; as, rí Caıtlín ("an" bean) ıf aılne; re Seaȝan ("an" fean) ıf aınòe.

§ 220.—AGREEMENT OF THE ARTICLE AND NOUN.

The article agrees with its noun in gender, number, and case; as (sing. mas.), an bàıò, *the poet;* na bàıfò (plur.), *the poets;* an bàıfò (gen. sing. mas.), *of the poet;* an bean (nom. sing. fem.), *the woman;* na mná (gen. sing. fem.), *of the woman;* na mná (nom. plu. fem.), *the women;* na m-ban (gen. plu. fem.), *of the women.*

"Tír na ȝ-cufraò 'f na ȝ-cliaf,"
Land of (the) heroes and of (the) clerics.

Ode by Gerald Nugent on leaving Ireland.
Irish Minstrelsy, vol. ii. p. 228—see pp. 38, 50, 51, of this Grammar.

In the spoken language, the n of the article is *sometimes* not pronounced, as Dr. O'Donovan remarks, "before aspirated palatals and labials." This elision is, perhaps in the spoken language, allowable wherever usage lends it a sanction; but it certainly ought not, contrary to strict etymology, be allowed in the written language. No good Irish scholar will, therefore, write in this incorrect style. It is quite common however in Scotch Gaelic; nevertheless it ought not, contrary to true philosophy and philology, be recommended.

§ 221. The influence of this agreement between the article and noun, and its effects in writing and speaking the language, are fully shown in pp. 38, 50, 51, of this treatise—see Etymology, c. i., § 37.—*The Article.*

☞ To sum up all that has been said in this chapter, concerning the idiomatic use of the definite article in respect to the two languages, English and Gaelic:

(1) There is a Gaelic idiom which requires the use of the article, when its presence in English before nouns of the like import is never needed (§ 214, pp. 193, 194, 195); (2), the article *the* before the former of two nouns in English, when the Norman genitive case, *i.e.*, genitive with *of*, is employed, is omitted in Gaelic; (3), from the demonstrative character of the article, it is plain that the term which the speaker requires to specify, must be defined by the article.

CHAPTER II.

§ 222. When two or more nouns referring to the *same* object come together, they ought to be in the same case by *apposition;* as, Do buḋ jaḋ ro mjc Aḋa "mná" Erau, these were the sons of Ada the "wife" of Esau.—*Irish Bible, by Dr. MacHale, p. 70.*

In this sentence the name Aḋa is in the genitive case, and "mná," which refers to the same individual, is by apposition in the genitive.

Eaċtra Ṁaċa jnġjne Aoḋa Ruajḋ, *the adventures of Macha the daughter of Hugh (the) Red.*

The proper name Ṁaċa is gen. case on eaċtra, and jnġjne is gen. case by apposition; for Ṁaċa and jnġean refer to the same lady.

"Aġ aġajnt cojmjnc Dé,
Mjc mná na n-ḋear-ḋlaojġ, rcejtear ḋealraḋ an lae."
"Entreating the protection of (the) god,
the son of the woman of the comely-curls, who sheds the splendour of the day."

Irish Homer, B. 1, lines 47, 48.

Here mjc and De, referring to the same object, are in the same case.

"Aġur do ḃearrajḋ re do 'macajḃ' Aaroin na raġartajḃ, *and he shall give it to the sons of Aaron the priests.*"— *Leviticus,* ii. 2.

In this sentence, "macajḃ" and raġartajḃ are in apposition.

§ 223.—A GAELIC IDIOM REGARDING NOUNS IN APPOSITION.

In the foregoing rule the words, "ought to be in the same case," are employed, because sameness of case on account of apposition is not *always* observed, not only in colloquial but in written Gaelic. The translator of the Irish version of the Protestant Bible—Bedel—has not observed it. Yet, from the identity of object indicated by nouns in apposition, one would expect to hear them expressed in the *same* case. If analogy, too, be any guide where idiom is not concerned, we should expect to see this rule fully carried out; for it is one that is common to most other languages. Besides, the rule in question " has been observed," as Dr. O'Donovan remarks, " by Keating, the Four Masters, and Duald MacFirbis, who wrote in the latter end of the seventeenth century;" yet the same author observes a little further on in his *Irish Grammar*, p. 366—that, " Keating, however, does not always observe this apposition, particularly when the first noun is in the dative or ablative case."

No one of his time knew the Irish language better than Geoffry Keating. He thought in his native language, from his cradle he spoke in his native language, and he wrote as he thought and spoke—idiomatically. It appears then— as well from the authority of Keating as from other writers who wrote before and since his time, and from the custom even at the present day prevailing amongst the Irish speaking population, of not observing "this apposition when the first noun is in the dative case"—that this latter trait is an *idiom* in the language.

In no other way can we account for this fact, which strikes one as he reads the first line of the creed in the old catechisms or books of piety written in Irish: " Cperoim ann Dia an t-ataır uıle cumactac, I believe *in God*, the Father Almighty." These two nouns refer to the same Being; they ought therefore, by apposition, be in the same case; yet the term " an t-ataır," is manifestly nom. case; while Dia, is the dative or prepositional case on ann.

In like manner, in the second line of the first book of the Irish Homer, a nominative case (an ġaırġıoeac teınteac ġanġ) is made to agree by apposition with a noun in the genitive (Acuıl); as,

" bnuc Acuıl reınn, oıġ neamoa a'r buan feanġ,
'Acuıl' (gen.) mıc Peıl an ġaırġıoeac (nom.) teınteac ġanġ—
Achilles' wrath, sing, O heavenly virgin, and his enduring anger;
Achilles'—Peleus' son—the fiery fierce hero."

Irish Homer, by His Grace the Most Rev. John MacHale, Archbishop of Tuam—Dublin, Duffy, bookseller.

No Irishman since the days of Geoffry Keating—nay, from the time of the " Irish Ovid," Donogh More O'Daly, Abbot of Boyle (A.D. 1244), can wield his native language with such power and idiomatic preciseness, as the great Archbishop.

To account for this idiom, it appears that the verb ır, *is, are*, is understood—thus : " I believe in God (who is) the Father Almighty, cperoim ann Dia (ır) an t-ataır," &c. The mind of one thinking in his native Irish language, reverts back to the subject, *i.e.*, to the *nominative*, in which accordingly, overlooking apposition, the term is expressed.

GOVERNMENT OF THE GENITIVE CASE.

§ 224. The latter of two nouns coming together, when the objects of which they are names are not the same, is governed by the former in the genitive case; as,

Mac " De," *God's* Son.

Dé is the gen. case of Dia, *God*, governed by the noun mac, *son*, which precedes it.

Mac mic, a son *of a son*.

Mic is the gen., governed by mac, nom. case.

If the word leabar (*lhower*), Latin, *liber*, a book, be substituted, the sentence runs thus :

Leabar mic, *a son's book*.
And with the pronouns, or the article preceding mic :
Leabar mo mic, *my son's book*.
Leabar do mic, *thy son's book*.
Leabar a mic, *his son's book*.
Leabar "an" mic, *the son's book*.

The words Dé and mic are comformable to rule in the gen case; and rightly, for they express the idea of generation, source, origin, ownership of that which is conveyed by the nouns which precede them.—See § 45, pp. 55, 56, of this treatise; also, " Easy Lessons," Part IV., p. 261.

☞ In every single instance, in Irish, as is seen from the foregoing examples, it is the *latter* of the two nouns, and *never* the *former*, which is the governed word. It is not so in Latin.

Mac Dé may be translated, filius *Dei*, or *Dei* filius, the gen. *Dei* being before or after the governing word; and in the Anglo-Saxon genitive case (that is the genitive or possessive ending in 's) it is the *former* of the two nouns, and *never* the *latter*, which is the governed word; as, God's Son, Mac "Dé," filius *Dei*. The gen. case (God's) precedes in English, in Irish (De) follows the governing word (*Son*, Mac).

§ 225. In translating from English the Saxon genitive case, *i.e.*, that ending in 's, the position of the governed noun must therefore be reversed in Irish, as in the examples just presented—*God's Son*, Mac Dé.

But, in translating the Norman genitive, *i.e.*, genitive expressed by "*of*," into Irish, the order and position of the nouns are retained, the preposition *of*, or sign of the genitive case omitted, while the latter noun assumes in Irish the genitive case-ending; as,

Son (*of*) God, Mac Dé;
Day (*of*) the Lord, Lá an Tigearna.

☞ It is worth while observing that mere English students, not acquainted with Latin, or Greek, or German, regard the particle "*of*," in such instances as the foregoing, purely as a preposition, and not as a sign of the genitive case; and on this account they are, whenever learning to translate into those languages, as well as in the present instance into Irish, puzzled at the non-use of the preposition "*of*." On the other hand, they find French and Italian easy in this respect.

§ 226. Observe, in translating compound substantives and those followed by the preposition "*of*," that term of the two which expresses the *property, office, character, ownership, title, relation,* or quality of the object pointed out by the other noun, is governed in the genitive case; as,

Property : a house-of-gold, ceac óıṗ (gen. of óṗ, *gold*).
„ a ship-of-war, loṅ5 coɼaıd (gen. of coɼad, *war*).
„ a wall-of-silver, balla aıṗɼıd (gen. of aıṗɼead).
„ a tin-can, cana ſcáın (gen. of ſcán).
Office : a door-keeper (porter), feaṗ doṗuıſ (*dorish*, gen. of doṗuſ, *dhorus*).
„ a musician (man-of-music), feaṗ ceoıl.
Character : a soothsayer, feaṗ feaſa (man-of-knowledge).
Title : gate-of-heaven, ɼeaca ḟlaıċıſ.

Obs.—The first part of a compound word in English becomes the second part of its Irish equivalent, as is plain from the above.

Note.—The second noun *specifies* the meaning of the first. For instance, in the expression ceac óıṗ (house-of-gold), the word "gold" does not make fuller nor clearer the prominent idea conveyed by the term "house," yet it distinguishes this latter from one of silver, clay, stone, or the like.

§ 227. Obs.—The student who knows only English should be made aware of the several meanings which the preposition "of" in its various relations with nouns is capable of admitting. Dr. Johnson counts twenty-three. These can all be grouped under four heads. "Of" denotes—

(1) Origin, cause, possession (see pp. 55 (end of), and 56, on the gen. or possessive case).
(2) Class, rank, partnership.
(3) *Of* has the meaning of *among, on, from.*
(4) *Of* expresses property, quality, attribute.

(1) *Of*, in the *first* sense is translated into Gaelic by the *genitive*, for that case gives the idea of *origin, cause, material, possession*, &c.

(2) *Of*, in the *second* sense, is rendered by "de," *of* (same as the French *de*), whenever it follows *numerals, adjectives* of the *comparative* and of the *superlative* degrees, *partitives,* nouns denoting *fullness, abundance,* and the contrary ; as,

(numerals), one "*of*" the whole, ceᴀn "ᴅe 'n" ιoṁlᴀn; Catherine is the fairest *of* the daughters, ɼι Cᴀιcłιn ιɼ ᴅeιɼe "ᴅe" nᴀ h-ιnᴁιnιb; *of all*, ᴀ b-ꝑuιl ᴅe; full "*of*" wisdom, lᴀn "ᴅ'" eᴀᴁnᴀ.

'Job 'ɼ ᴀ b-ꝑu'l ꝑuᴀɼ leᴀċ, "ᴅe" nᴀ Ḋeᴀċ ɼιoɼ-beo—
Jove, and *all that* are with thee above *of* the immortal gods.

<small>Prayer of Hector to the gods, to bless and protect his infant son, Astyanax, uttered during his last interview with Andromache.—*Homer*, b. vi.</small>

"Ḋe" mnᴀιb ᴅeᴀɼ' ᴀn ᴅoṁᴀιn
Iɼ nᴀ b-ꝑᴀᴁᴀιnn ɼe mo ɼoᴁᴀn,
Sι Ꝁol ᴅub ᴀn ᴁleᴀnᴀ ιɼ ꝑeᴀɼɼ lιoṁ.—*Old Song.*

Ꝁċ "ᴅe" nᴀ Cɼoιᴁċe uιle ᴀιɼ ᴁᴀċ lᴀoċ,
'Ꝁuɼ oɼm ᴁo h-ᴀιɼιᴅe cᴀ ᴀn cᴀċ ᴀ blᴀoċ.
But on *each* hero of the Trojans all,
And on me especially, the contest is calling.

<small>*Last Address of Hector to his wife, Andromache.*</small>

☞ A portion *of*, a part *of*, one *of* many, by "ᴅe;" as, cuιᴅ ᴅe nᴀ ᴅᴀoιnιb, *some of the people;* nᴀnn ᴅe 'n cᴀlᴀιn, *some of the land;* ceᴀnn "ᴅe" n ιoṁlᴀn, *one of the entire number.*

(3) In the third, *of* signifies *among;* as, cιᴀ ᴀᴁᴀιb, which *of* you; and *on;* as, ᴅo lᴀbᴀιɼ ɼe "oιc-ɼᴀ" he spoke *of* (on) you; *from;* as, a man *of* France, ꝑeᴀɼ "ᴅ' n" b-Ꝼɼᴀιnc; he did it *of* himself, ɼιnne ɼe é "uᴀιᴅe" ꝑéιn (from, *i.e.*, it proceeded *from* him as the originator).

A MOST PECULIAR IDIOM.

§ 228 (4) In the fourth acceptation *of* has no equivalent in Gaelic; the mere absence of any preposition suffices—the noun remains in the nominative case; as, a man *of* the highest position and fame, ꝑeᴀɼ ᴀ b' ᴀιɼᴅe céιm ᴀᴁuɼ clu; she was a woman *of the* greatest beauty, beᴀn ι buᴅ ṁó ɼᴁιᴀṁ.

"Ꝁeᴀbᴀιɼ ccuᴅ mᴀιᴁᴅeᴀn meᴀᴅɼᴀċ, óᴁ,
Soιllɼeᴀċ, lonnɼᴀc, mᴀɼ ᴀn nᴁréιn;
Iɼ ꝑeᴀnn ᴅeιlb, cnuc, ᴀᴁuɼ ɼnᴅó,
'ɼ ιɼ bιnne beoιl 'nᴀ ceol nᴀ n-éun."

"Thou wilt get a hundred virgins gay and young,
Bright, refulgent, like the sun,
Of best form, shape, and appearance,
Whose voices are sweeter than the music of birds."

☞ The foregoing is a very remarkable Gaelic idiom. It is the "*laus et vituperium*" of Latin syntax, and in that language requires the use of the ablative case; in Greek, the accusative; in English, French, the prepositional (*of, de*) case; in Irish or Gaelic, the nominative.

Dr. O'Donovan, in regard to this idiom, after telling the fact, "that when one substantive is predicated of another by the verb ɩſ, and an adjective of praise or dispraise connected with it, it is never put into the genitive case," says, that he cannot account for it (*Irish Grammar*, p 165).

He does not say that the noun in the predicate is the nominative case; but it is plainly the nominative, for the sentence he gives, ꝼeaɲ buð mo ɲað, is elliptical, and by supplying the ellipsis, it runs thus: ꝼeaɲ (aɲ a) buð mo ɲað, a man (*on whom*) there is usually or was the greatest good fortune. The phrase *on whom* is quite Gaelic and idiomatic; as, ca ꝼuacc oɲm, there is cold *on me* (I am cold); ca leɩſɡ "oɲm," *I am loth*.

§ 229. Although the genitive case conveys the idea of possession, nevertheless, ownership or exclusive possession is expressed by the assertive verb, do beɩc, *to be* (ɩſ buð), with the preposition le, *with*; do, *to*; as, (1) ɩſ lɩomra an leabaɲ ſo, this book *is mine*; literally, it is *with myself* this book; ɩſ lɩom-ra ɩað, *they are mine*.—*Numbers* iii. 13 ; ɩſ le ꝼeaɲ an bó an ɡaɩɲaɲ, *the calf belongs to the owner of the cow*—literally, it is *with the man of* the cow, the calf—*partus sequitur ventrem*—an adage of conventional equity amongst the ancient Brehons; (2) ɩſ mac "ðaɩɲ-ra" an c-óɡaɲað ſo, this young man is *my son*—literally, "a son *to me*."

Le, *with*, conveys the idea of *right* to the possession of the thing spoken of; it expresses also entire devotedness ; as, ðuɩɲe "le" Dɩa, *a man with* (*devoted to*) *God*. " Na ceub coɲða a coɩɲbſɩɲeaſ claɲ Iſɲael 'ɩſ leɩſ' an ſaɡaɲc ɩað—all the first fruits which the children of Israel offer belong exclusively to the priest."—Uɩbɲeað (*Numbers*), v. 9.

    Ma bɩðeaɲɲ cu lɩom, bɩ lɩom ðe ló a'ſ ð' oɩðċe;
    Ma bɩðeaɲɲ cu lɩom, bɩ lɩom oſ coɩɲaɩſ an c-ſaoɡaɩl;
    Ma bɩðeaɲɲ cu lɩom, bɩ lɩom ɡað uɲlað aɲɲ ðo ċɲoɩðe.
        Song—" Twisting of the Rope—Caſað an c-Súɡaɩɲ,"
            Hardiman's Minstrelsy, vol. i., p. 195.

Literally thus :

    If thou art mine, be mine by day and by night;
    If thou art mine, be mine before the entire world;
    If thou art mine, be mine every inch in thy heart.

☞ Mine=lɩom, *i.e.*, *with* me, expresses the idea of belonging to one, so that no other has any claim thereto.

§ 230. O, or Ua, *a grandson, a descendant;* mac, *a son;* Nɩ, or Nɩɡ, *a descendant;* nɩc, *a daughter*, govern the genitive of proper names; as, Domɲall O'Coɲɲall, *Daniel O'Connell;* Séamuſ O'Ceallaɩɡ, *James O'Kelly;* Pacſuɩc Mac Domɲall, *Patrick MacDonnell;* Maɩſe Nɩ Coɲɲall, *Mary O'Connell;* Sɩubaɲ Nɩɡ Bſɩaɩɲ, *Judith O'Brien;* Saðb nɩ Ḟaelaɩɲ, *Sally Whelan* (*Ancient Music of Ireland*, vol i. p. 121.)

Níg is the feminine form of Uʌ or 2l)ʌc, and must therefore, with reason and with the sanction of usage, be prefixed to the family names of women ; as, Jane O'Donnell is Siubʌn "nig" Ḋomṅʌill (not Uʌ, or 2l)ʌcḊomṅʌill); Bridget O'Neill, Bríġio ní Néill (not Uʌ, or 2l)ʌcNéill).

Níg, or nic, means *daughter*, like the common term ingcan, *daughter*.

Obs.—In translating from Irish to English, the fem. prefix to family names—like the maiden name of a young lady after marriage—has been, as a rule, suppressed, while the mas. prefix mʌc, or uʌ, has been retained in modernized Gaelic proper names.

☞ Hence, conversely, in translating names of women into Irish, O must be translated ní (or níg); and Mac, nic ; and, in general, the names of women have the prefix níg in Irish; as (1), " O," in Mary O'Connell, is 2lʌíne " ní" Connʌill ; (2), Bridget MacDonnell, Brígio níg Domnʌill ; Sarah Sheridan, Sʌob ní Seriṁʌín (pr. *Sowv nee Heridayn*).

Obs.—Some proper names take in the genitive the article prefixed ; as, Séamur 2l)ʌc an Bʌípo, *James Ward* (properly MacWard); Caiclín Nic an Bʌípo, *Catherine Ward ;* Uilliam 2l)ʌc an Ġoban, *William MacGowen;* Séaplar 2l)ʌc an Bpeiceamʌn, *Charles MacBrehanny,* or *Judge ;* Séamur 2l)ʌc an Léaġa, *James Lee,* or *MacLee ;* Riobapo 2l)ʌc an Ciompanaiġ, *Robert Tempany,* or *MacTempany.*

These surnames were given to the progenitors of those families from the particular calling or profession to which they were educated; as, 2l)ʌc an Bʌipo, *son* of " *the*" *bard;* 2l)ʌc an Bneicaṁan, son of *the* judge—*i.e.*, son of him who had been a bard, or who had been a judge ; 2l)ʌc an Léaġa, son of the physician (now Lee) ; and so of the rest.

§ 231. When the noun in the genitive case is the proper name of a *person,* or *place,* and the article is not employed, its initial letter, if a mutable, suffers aspiration ; as, Ó aimrir Ṗacraic, *since the time of St. Patrick;* baile Ċorcaiġ, *the town of Cork.*

Yet proper names (gen. case) following Ó, Uʌ, 2l)ʌc, in the nominative (níg, *a daughter,* excepted), do not suffer aspiration ; as, Ó Domnʌill ; Uʌ Ceallaiġ ; 2l)ʌc Cancaiġ ; 2l)ʌc Coclʌinn na ġ-caírlean ġlé-ġeal (*Irish Minstrelsy,* vol. ii. p. 334.

Here the D of Domnʌill, the C of Ceallaiġ, the C of Cancaiġ, and the C of Coclʌin, are not aspirated, though they are the initial mutable letters of proper names in the genitive case, not having the article prefixed.

☞ The reason is, Domnaill, Ceallaiġ, may be regarded as forming with O only the same *case*, because both refer to the *same* object. Domnaill and Ceallaiġ and such are, however, genitives.

However, they do suffer aspiration, firstly, when they follow the *genitive* cases (Uı, *of a* descendant; mıc, *of a* son) of these family prefixes; and, secondly, when mac means really a *son*, and ua, a grandson, and not a descendant; as, Seaġan mac Domnaill Uı Connaıll, *John, Son of Daniel O'Connell;* Patraıc mac Néıll Uı Domnaıll, *Patrick, son of Neill O'Donnell.*

Here the C of Connaıll, and the D of Domnaıll are aspirated, because they follow Uı, the genitive case of O, or Ua. Again, Seamur mac Paonuıc means James, *son* of Patrick; while Seamur mac Pannuıc means *James FitzPatrick;* and Donncad ua Ceallaıġ, Donough Kelly's grandson; while Donncad ua Ceallaıġ signifies Donough O'Kelly simply, as a name; "Ata ann ro, Fıonn mac Cumaıll mıc Aınt mıc Threunmoın Uı Baoırġne," there are here the *son* of Cumhall (who is), the son of Art, the son of Threunmhor O'Baoisgne.—*Transactions of the Ossianic Society*, vol. ii., p. 74.

"Some writers," says O'Donovan, in treating of the aspiration of the genitive of proper names, "aspirate the initial of the latter substantive, even when it is not a proper name. . . . . . But this is not to be imitated, as it weakens the sound of the word too much."—*Irish Grammar,* pp. 368-369.

General observation.—Proper names are aspirated in the gen. case, except after the family prefixes Mac, and Ua or O.

§ 232. The names dream, *a class;* dronġ, *a horde;* lucṫ, *a body of people;* muıntır, *a clan;* pobal, *a people;* sluaġ, *a host,* convey plurality of idea; as, conaırc mé muıntır m' aṫar aġur ır flaṫamaıl an dream ıad, *I saw my father's people, and they are a princely race.*

Sıol, *seed, tribe,* causes eclipses; as,

"Sıol ġ-Ceallaıġ nár' b' fann ann aon ġoıl,
Aġur rıol ġ-Conċobaır rcaıneamaıl, rceudman;
Aġur rıol ġ-Canṫaıġ nac n-deannaıd clé-beanṫ."
Hardiman's Irish Minstrelsy, vol ii., pp. 332-334.

CHAPTER III.

SYNTAX OF THE ADJECTIVE.

§ 233. In treating of the syntactical influence of the adjective, one can consider (1), its position with regard to the noun; (2), its agreement therewith; (3), its governing power; (4), its idiomatic use in Gælic; (5), the effects arising from its influence on the noun.

(1.) Its position is *after* the noun :

This rule is universal, see Etymology, chapter iii., § 70, p. 76 of this treatise.

Ꝥur b' éaluiṡ ꝼo leir rorcać, ꜱnom, ꝛaoi ꝛeanꝼ,
le air na b-conca " ꝼlónać, ꝼéimnać, ꝼanꝼ ; "
Homer translated into Irish
by Dr. MacHale, b. i., ll. 45-46.

Βῆ δ' ἀκέων παρὰ θῖνα πολυφλοισβοιο θαλασσης,
Homer, b. i., l. 3.

The trembling priest along the shore returned,
And in the anguish of a father, mourned ;
Disconsolate, not daring to complain,
Silent he wandered by the sounding main.
Pope's Iliad, b. i., p. 30. ll. 47-50.

" ꝼlónać, ꝼéimnać, ꝼanꝼ," follow the noun conca, *waves*.

Exceptions to this rule—(*a*) apb, *high* ; buan, *enduring* ; caoin, *gentle* ; caom, *mild* ; claon, *inclined* ; cnom, *crooked* ; baon, *dear* ; beaꝼ, *good* ; beanb, *real* ; oian, *vehement* ; oluć, *close* ; onoć, *bad* ; ꝼionn, *fair* ; ꝼion, *true* ; ꝼanb, *rough* ; ꝼeann, *short* ; ꝼlan, *clean* ; ꝼlinn, *pellucid* ; maoć, *soft* ; mion, *small* ; mon, *large* ; naom, *holy* ; nuab, *new* ; óꝼ, *young* ; pnion, *first* ; ram, *soft* ; raob, *silly* ; reim, *mild* ; raon, *free* ; rean, *old* ; cneun, *bold* ; cnom, *heavy* ; uaral, *noble* ; uile, *all*, and a few others (see pp. 177-8).

Special exceptions—beaꝼ, *good* ; onoć, *bad* ; ꝼionn, *white* ; nuab, *new* ; rean, *old*, always go before the noun ; adjectives of the same meaning—inaić, *good* ; ole, *bad* ; ban, *white*, and ꝼeal, *bright* ; un, *new* ; aorca, *old* (arra, *old*, ꝼoinꝛe, *mature*), follow the noun. Those others above-named sometimes follow as well as precede the noun.

(*b*) In old Irish MSS. the adjective is *often* found to go before the noun, as in English ; as, aꝼur bo ba ua be'n " inireać" Abnaham é ain riab, and he was a descendant of the *just* Abraham, said they. leaban bneać (*and The Four Masters*), *passim*.

(*c*) Adjectives of number go before the noun ; as, " ré" nuine, *six persons*.

In numbers higher than ten, the position of the noun is between the decimal termination beuꝼ, *teen*, and the first part of the numeral adjective; as, *thir-teen* men, cní-ꝛin-beuꝼ, literally *three-men-teen* ; the thirteenth man, an cnínab ꝛeon beuꝼ.

.•. The Gælic decimal termination beuꝼ, from the word beić, *ten*, is formed by a slight increase of sound, much in the same way that *teen* is from *ten*.

Obs. In naming sovereigns and princes, the numeral adjective follows the noun; Ex. Uilliam an ceathramh, *William IV.*; Lughaid an ré-deug, *Louis XVI.*; Napóleon an tri, *Napoleon III.*; Piur Papa an naoi, *Pope Pius IX.*

(d) In such sentences as these: God *is good*, truth *is bitter*, wine *is pleasant*, the assertive verb ir and the adjective precede the noun; as, "ir maic" Dia; ir rearb an firine; ir milir fion:

Ir bin é beul 'nna cort,
A silent mouth is musical.
Ir milir fion—ir rearb 'g a ioc,
Wine is pleasant—unpleasant its price.
"Ir buaine" bláő 'na raoghal,
Reputation is more enduring than life.
Ir olc an cu nac fiu é feadail,
It is a bad hound that is not worth being whistled for.

⁎ The copula ir and the adjective, form only one predicate. On this account the adjective comes immediately after ir. And on this account too, the adjective suffers no change whenever, as is shown in exception (a) to next section, it refers to the verb and not to the noun.

§ 234. *Agreement of the adjective with the noun.*—Adjectives which come *after* the noun agree with it in gender, number, and case; as, an fear mór, the *big* man; an fir mór (gen.), *of* the *big* man; an bean mór, the *big* woman; na mna (gen. fem.) móire (*moirhé*), *of the big* woman; do briread anior toibneaca na h-aibéire móire, the fountains of the *great deep* were broken up. (*Irish Bible*, by the Most Rev. Dr. MacHale, p. 13.)

An example of the Dative Case of the Adjective.

Do na fearaib móra (not mónaib), *to the big* men.

Obs.—In modern Irish works the dative plural of adjectives seldom or never ends with the termination ib. It is more in conformity with syntax—at least, it is with analogy drawn from the polished languages of old Rome and Greece—that it should. The following instance of its application is met with in Dr. MacHale's small work, called, "Cnaob urnaige cnabaige," p. 11: "Go n-déanta ríoccáin agur fíon comaoneact a brona do righéib agur do priónraib 'criorbamlaib,'" *that thou wouldst bestow peace and true concord on Christian kings and princes* (see Etymology, c. iii., pp. 76-7 of this Grammar.)

Exceptions to the rule § 234.—(a) Whenever the adjective is employed with the verb do béit, *to be,* to express what is predicated of the subject (or nominative), it agrees, not with the noun—but with the verb, and therefore undergoes no change at all; as, táid na daoine so "raoiteamail," these people are gentlemanly; táid na ingéana "grjamać," the daughters are beauteous; "raoiteamail" and "grjamać," are not plural but singular, because they form with táid but one predicate.

(b) When the adjective is connected in meaning with the verb, it is in no wise modified by the noun; as, nigne ré an scian geur, he *made* the knife *sharp*; not nigne ré an scian géur, which signifies (because géur is made to agree with scian, by aspirating the initial letter g), he made the *sharp knife*.

From this example, he *made* the knife *sharp*, one sees that the word "sharp" is evidently a part of the verb; for, he "made sharp," and he "sharpened," are the same. Hence *sharp* being part of what is predicated, agrees not with the noun, but refers naturally to the verb.

This affinity of the adjective with the verb, when showing what is predicated of the noun, is philosophically correct, yet strange, usage has not developed it in any of the classic languages of France, or Italy, of ancient Rome, or Greece.

☞ See in rule vi., p. 37 of this treatise, the influence exercised by bud, *was*, on the initial letter of adjectives.

§ 235 When an adjective comes after two or more nouns connected by the conjunction agus, *and*, it agrees only with the last, though it qualify the rest; as, fear agus bean maić, *a good man and woman*.

If a noun in the plural number be amongst them, it is better to bring it last, and thus have the adjective in the plural.

§ 236. *Governing power of the adjective.*—Those adjectives which have the force of nouns govern the genitive case; these are—*morán*, *much or many*; *beagán*, *few*, *little*; *iomad*, *many*; *iliomad*, *very many*; *ca méid*, *how many*; *go leor*, *much, many*; *lán*, *full*; *liact*, *many, not few* (from *lia*, *more*, comparative of *morán*); *amail*, *like*; *samail*, *like*; as, *morán* "*crionnacta*," *much of wisdom*; *lán an* "*Domain*," *the full of the world*; *ca méid duine? how many persons?*

"*Crionnacta*" is the gen. case of *crionnact*, governed by *morán*; "*domain*, *of* the world, is gen. case on *lán*.

'Sa "liact" ainfir min a' m' óiaig,
Le buaib a'r maoin 'n a láim.

There are maidens would be mine,
With wealth in hand and kine.

Ancient Music of Ireland, vol i., p. 11.

> Ċuιc ιoṁaƄ ṁúιlιƄċ 'ꞅ ṁaƄnaιƄ cnoιc ꝼaoι lán,
> *Many mules and mountain dogs fell in carnage.*
> *Irish Homer*, by Dr. MacHale, p. 13, l. 67.

The adjectives Ꝼać, *each;* ιoṁóṅ (pr. *umma*), *many;* uιlċ, *each,* all agree with the noun, but do not govern the genitive.

> Le ċaƄancaꞃ cꞃoṁ 'ꞅuꞃ ꞃcoιƄe ann Ꝼać láιṁ,
> *With a heavy ransom and rich presents in each hand.*
> *Ibid.* b. i., l. 18.

> Dιṫ Ꝼaċa ꞅιona, ꞃιoc,
> Dιṫ Ꝼaċa buιƄιnc, Ɓꞃoċ-Ƅean;
> Dιṫ Ꝼaċa ċeιne, ꝼeaꞃꞃnóꝻ Ꝼlaꞃ,
> Dιṫ Ꝼaċa Ɓιꝼe, ṁcιƄeaꝻ nιueac, ꞃeann.
>   *Sean Raιċċe.*

The want of each biting blast is—frost.
The want of a real rabble is—a bad woman.
The want of all sort of firing is—green alder.
The want of all drink is—whey, thin, sour, and old.

§ 237. Obs.—Instead of the genitive case, the preposition Ɓe, *of,* is sometimes employed after móꞃan, ƄeaꝻan, lan, ιoṁaƄ; as, lan " Ɓe" Ɓaoιnιb, full *of* people; móꞃan Ɓ' ṁuιnċιꞃ, many *of* his kith.

Dṅ, *of,* follows adjectives in the superlative degree and partitive terms implying selection, choice, or the like (see § 80, p. 84 of this treatise; also § 227, pp. 204-5, Syntax.

> Reason of this.—" The superlative degree," says O'Donovan, " does not require a genitive case plural after it, as in Latin, for the genitive case in Irish, as in English, always denotes possession and nothing more, and therefore could not be applied, like the genitive case plural in Latin, after noun-adjectives of the positive, or the superlative degree; but it (superlative degree) generally takes after it the preposition Ɓo, or more correctly Ɓe; as, an bean ιꞅ áιlne Ɓe ṁnáιƄ, *the fairest woman of women.*"—*Irish Grammar,* pp. 371-2.

§ 238 " Dṅ " for Ɓe é, *of it,* is often in Irish suffixed to the comparative degree; as, ιꞅ ꝼeaꞃꞃ Ɓe Uιllιaṁ an coṁaιꞃle uƊ, *William is the better of that advice.*

> " Nι cꞃoιṁιƄe loċ an láċa,
> Nι cꞃoιṁιƄe eáċ an ꞃnιan;
> Nι cꞃoιṁιƄe caoꞃa a h-ollann,
> Nι cꞃoιṁιƄe ċolan cιall."

The bit's no burthen to the prancing steed,
Nor the snowy fleeces to the woolly breed;
The lake with ease can bear the swimming kind
Nor is good sense a burthen to the mind.
                        MS. of Irish Proverbs,
                            Translation by Haliday.

⁎ Troimṁe is for troime, *more heavy*, comp. of trom, *heavy;* ṅé, is for ṅé, é, *of* it—*i.e.* the lake is not the heavier on account of it, the duck, &c. (see Etymology, § 79 in which this point is fully explained.)

§ 239. *Idioms.*—Such sentences as, *I am cold,* tá mé ḟuar; *I am warm,* tá me teiṫ, are translated into Irish idiomatically, tá ḟuaċt orm, cold is *on* me; tá tear orm, heat is *on* me; tá tart orm, thirst is *on* me.

Many adjectives, which in English take after them the preposition *to,* take in Irish the preposition le, *with;* as, he is *like to* his father, is, in Irish, he is *like with* his father; as, tá ré coramail " le," n-a áṫair; he is friendly *to* me, tá ré geanamail " liom-ra." (See *Easy Lessons,* Part iii.)

§ 240. Sentences of the form, he is *six feet high,* are translated, he is six feet on *height;* as, tá ró ré troiġte " aip airde."

Le iomċar tiġeannaṁail luairg re rleaġ anṁón,
Trí rlat " air ḟad" naḃ tiṁċioll cuairt ḃé, óir.
Irish Homer by Dr. MacHale, b. vi., ll. 443-4.

With lordly might and grace he let fly a very large javelin,
Three yards "*in length,*" around which was a rim of gold.

☞ The adjectives *broad, long, high, deep,* are translated as if, in *breadth,* in *length,* in *height,* in *depth,* &c.

§ 241. Adjectives, like the nouns which precede them, are affected by aspiration; as, a ḋuine " ḋona!" *O unfortunate man!*

D, of dona, is aspirated in the vocative or nominative case of address, just like d of the noun duine (voc.)

Exceptions.—" *When an adjective beginning with the linguals* d, t, *is preceded by a noun terminating with a lingual,* the initial of the adjective retains its primary sound in all the cases of the singular; as, air mo ġualainn deir, *on my right shoulder;* air a ċoir deir, *on his right foot*—not air a ċoir ḋeir; colann daonna, *a human body*—not colann ḋaonna."—O'Donovan, *Irish Grammar,* p. 351.

§ 242. Obs.—Remember, therefore that adjectives beginning with the dental or lingual consonants, d or t, ought never to be aspirated after d or t, or after the liquids l, n, or the sibilant consonant r. This rule is true under every respect in which these consonants, d, t, l, n, r, may chance to come together, either in agreement, composition, or the like; as, ард-тiġeanna, *sovereign lord;* treun-duine, *a brave man;* ruil dear, *a right eye;* " déan-ta" (past part.), *done.*

"This exception," adds Dr. O'Donovan (p. 351), " is made to preserve the agreeable sound arising from the coalescence of the lingual consonants."

Obs. 2.—(*a*) The letter t, of the past participle passive, has its aspirate or non-aspirate state regulated entirely on this principle of lingual euphony.

(b) All compound terms are regulated by it: (c) The adjective, in its phonetic relation with its noun: (d) The noun or adjective beginning with ḃ, ċ, or ṗ, and governed by a preposition ending with l, ṉ, ꞅ: (e) After the article ᴀɴ, words beginning with ḃ or ċ are not eclipsed.

Hence too, for a similar reason, the letter ᴣ, following the consonant ɴ of ᴀɴ (*the, whether, in*), is not eclipsed, for ɴ and ᴣ form only one sound (see Nᴣ, p. 21.)

See exceptions 1, 2, p. 35 of this treatise; rule ii., p. 38; exception to rule iv., p. 40; § 136, p. 138.

§ 243. ᴅᴀ́, *two*, is a sort of dual number in Irish, partaking of the nature of the singular and the plural, yet neither one nor the other; the article agreeing with it is of the singular number; the noun (feminine) of the dative singular, (masculine) of the nominative singular; while the adjective is plural to agree with the noun; as, ᴀɴ ᴅᴀ́ ᴍɴᴀᴏɪ, *the two* women; ᴀɴ ᴅᴀ́ ᴍɴᴀᴏɪ ᴍᴀɪᴛᴇ, *the two* good women; ᴀɴ ᴅᴀ́ ᴛᴇᴀċ, *the two* houses; its genitive is the same as the genitive plural; as, ʟᴏɴɴꞃᴀ ᴀ ᴅᴀ́ ꞅúʟ, *the brightness of his eyes.*

ᴅᴀ́, when compounded with ᴅᴇᴜᴣ, the decimal ending, governs in the same way the noun placed between them; as, ᴅᴀ́ ꞅᴇᴀꞃ ᴅᴇᴜᴣ, *twelve men*—see § 84, p. 88.

CHAPTER IV.

THE PRONOUNS.

§ 244. *Personal Pronouns.*—Ṫᴜ, *thou*, the second person singular, is still, with grammatical correctness, the only pronoun employed whenever a single person or thing is addressed; as, cɪᴀɴɴóꞃ ᴀ ḃ-ꝼᴜɪʟ "ᴛᴜ?" how are *you?*

You, and *vous*, and *sie*, the second or the third person plural, are, agreeably to the manners of the age, but contrary to strict grammatical truth, now in use; (*you*) in English, (*vous*) in French, and (*sie*) in German, for the second person singular.

§ 245. The personal pronoun, be it the nominative or objective case, comes after the verb; as, ᴍᴏʟᴀɴɴ ᴛᴜ é, you praise *him.*

Ṫᴜ, *thou*, is nom. to ᴍᴏʟᴀɴɴ, *praisest*; é, *him*, is the accusative or objective.

Ꝃᴏʟᴀɴɴ ꞅé ṫᴜ, *he praises you.*

Ṫᴜ (*thee*), is objective on ᴍᴏʟᴀɴɴ; ꞅé, is nominative to it (see pp. 90-1.)

Oʙs.—The *secondary* form of the personal pronouns, in the third person especially (singular and plural), follows:

(*a*) Verbs passive (see p. 135—Obs.)
(*b.*) The assertive verb ɪꞅ, *is*; ʙᴜḋ, *was, may be.*
(*c*) Aċᴛ, *but*; ɴí, *not*; ɴᴀċ? *is not?* ɴᴀꞃ? *was not?* ᴀɴ? *whether?* ᴀꞃ? *whether* (past time)? ᴀᴣᴜꞅ, *and.*

Examples of ᴀᴄᴛ, *but.*—Ηϳon ᴛᴀιnιᴄ ᴀon ᴅυιnᴇ "ᴀᴄᴛ é-ᴦᴀn," no one came but *him ;* é-ᴦᴀn, is the nominative (affected form) to ᴛᴀιnιᴄ understood, or the accusative case on ᴀᴄᴛ, *but.*

Of ᴀ3υᴦ.—Cυιn ᴦᴇ ᴛιoᴦ 'nnᴀ ᴄυιnᴇ ᴀ3υᴦ é ᴀι3 ᴛᴇᴀᴄᴛ, *he sent a message for him, and he coming ;* é, is nom. (affected form) coming after ᴦ in the word ᴀ3υᴦ (see particles, rule v. and vi., pp. 36-7.)

§ 246. *Compound Personal Pronouns.*—In the English expressions, " which *of you,*" " which *of them,*" the phrase *of you* is in Gælic—not ᴅϳb (*deev*), of *you ;* ᴅϳob (*dee-ov*), of *them,* but ᴀ3ᴀιb, *at* you ; ᴀᴄᴀ, *at* them ; as, which *of you* is the best ? ᴄϳᴀ " ᴀ3ᴀιb" ιᴦ ᴦᴇᴀᴦᴦ ? which *of them* is the highest ? ᴄϳᴀ " ᴀᴄᴀ" ιᴦ ᴀιᴦᴅᴀ ?

§ 247. *Idioms.*—Some idiomatic forms arise from the use of the compound personal pronouns with the verb *to be ;* as, ᴛᴀ " ᴀ3ᴀm." *I have* (there is at me): ᴛᴀ ᴦιoᴦ ᴀ3ᴀm, *there is knowledge at me, i.e.,* I know; nι 'l ᴦιoᴦ ᴀ3ᴀm, *I do not know ;* ᴛᴀ υᴀιm, *I have not* (there is from me); ιᴦ mιᴀn lιom (there is a wish with me), *I desire, I intend ;* ᴛᴀ ᴦonn onm, *there is an inclination on me, i.e.,* I am inclined ; ᴛᴀ ᴦυᴀᴄᴛ onm, *there is cold on me,* I am cold; ᴦυb onᴛ ! *your health !*—literally, there it is *on* thee ; ᴛυ3 ᴦé ᴦύm, *he gave under me, i.e.,* he scolded me ; ᴦιᴀn lᴇᴀᴛ ! *fare-thee-well!* ᴛᴇιᴛ lᴇᴀᴛ ; *away with you !* i e., flee *with thee ;* ᴛᴀᴦᴦ υᴀιᴦ, *come on,* come *along*—literally, come *from you, i.e.,* come from where you are ; 3o m-bᴇᴀnnυι3ᴇ ᴅιᴀ ᴅυιᴛ, *God save you, benedicat tibi Deus,* may God give you a blessing, our national salutation, expressive of the religious feelings of our people ; and the reply, 3o m-bᴇᴀnnυι3ᴇ ᴅιᴀ '3υᴦ 𝔐υιnᴇ ᴅυιᴛ, tells how our fathers loved, in the polite interchanges of civility, to unite the name of the Virgin Mother—𝔐υιnᴇ—with that of her divine Son; and in thus asking a blessing through her who is " the channel of all graces," raised the words of civility to the dignity of prayer, and the poverty of mere expression very often to the richness of merit. When compared with this, how cold our English " good morrow," and " how do you do," appear ! (See § 118, p. 115 ; § 229, p. 206 ; § 239, p. 213.

☞ The several idioms which are connected with the use of the compound personal pronouns have been clearly and fully explained by us, in the work lately presented to the Irish reading public in Ireland, America, and Australia—the *Easy Lessons ; or, Self-Instruction in Irish,* of which see part iii. on this subject, pp. 160, 190, third edition. Dublin—published by John Mullany, 1, Parliament-street.

§ 248. The possessive pronouns precede the noun ; as, mo ᴄᴀᴦᴀᴅ, *my* friend ; ᴅo 3ᴦᴀᴅ, *thy* love ; ᴀᴦ n-ᴀᴛᴀιᴦ, *our* father; bυᴦ n-Ðιᴀ (*vur Nia*), *your* God.

For examples of ᴀ, *his, her, their,* see p. 100, § 101.

Obs.—In § 96 of this Grammar, it is clearly shown that the possessive pronouns are the possessive cases of the personal pronouns. On this account they (firstly) are not found in agreement like persoual pronouns in French, Italian, Greek, Latin, German, &c., with the noun ; and (secondly), they exercise a phonetic influence on the initial consonant of the term which immediately follows them (see §§ 24, 27, pp. 34, 40, rule i.)

§ 249. *Relative Pronouns.*—ᴀ, *who, which, in whom, in which;* noc̄, *who, which;* nac̄, *who-not, which-not,* come immediately after the noun or pronoun to which they refer.

Obs. 1.—According to Zeüss the primitive form of the relative pronoun ᴀ, *who,* was ᴀn (kindred in its radical meaning with ᴀn, *the,* ᴀon, *some one*). This being so, it is easy to account for the eclipsing influence of ᴀ (or ᴀn, *who*), which is nothing more than retaining or changing, according to a well known principle in phonetics, the sound of n to suit the cognate character of the consonant following it immediately.

n, before vowel sounds, remains unchanged; before b, a lingual, and ꞅ, a palatal, it remains unchanged; before b, it becomes (m); before ꝼ and r it is lost.—*Zeüss,* p. 348.

Relatives, nom. case.—All the relative pronouns affect with aspiration the initial mutable consonant of the verb.

In the objective case.—ᴀ for ᴀnn ᴀ, *in which time,* or (*place*), is translated, *when* or *where,* for "*when*" means the time *in which*—"*where,*" the place *in which* ᴀ, or ᴀnn ᴀ, *in which,* causes eclipsis; as, ᴀɪꞇ "ᴀn ᴀn" ꞅ-cuɪneᴀꝺ é, *the place* in which *he was interred;* ᴀn ᴀn "ᴀ" ꞅ-cruṫaɪꞅᴀꝺ ᴀn ꝺomᴀn, *the time* (in) which *the world was created.*

From the former example, it is seen that "ᴀ" takes n after it sometimes. It may be asked, is ᴀn a case or inflection of ᴀ, *who, which.* It must be said that it is not. Take this sentence—ᴀn ꝼeᴀn "ᴀn" leɪr ṫu, the man *with whom* thou. *i.e.,* to whom you belong; n, in this instance, is the consonant of no, which usually precedes the tense buꝺ, *may be, was;* buꝺ is commonly omitted, and no remains, which on eliding o, is only a solitary letter. Reduced to this state, it coalesces with the vowel next to it—the relative ᴀ. In like manner, no was formerly, and is even at present, expressed before the perfect passive; the same elision of o arising, n naturally coalesces with the relative pronoun. The theory expounded above by Zeüss, and explained in Obs. 1, proves this point satisfactorily.

Obs. 2.—Ꝺo and no serve in Irish to point out the preterite of verbs, just as the particle "*to*" does the infinite mood in English.

There seems to be no reason for coinciding with another late unphilosophical writer in the opinion that no, before the perfect tense, is an "augment;" if so, "to" in English, and "zu" in German, are augments.

An Instance of Amphibology in Irish.

⁎ Since the relative is indeclinable and found always before the verb, one cannot, unless from the context alone, know when it is the agent and when the object; as, ᴀn Ꝺɪᴀ ᴀ ꞅnᴀꝺuɪꞅɪm, the God *whom I love.* In this, one can know from the verb, which is in the first person, that the relative ᴀ is in the accusative case. But let the proposition be altered, and let the verb assume the relative ending "eᴀr," then the sentence runs, ᴀn Ꝺɪᴀ ᴀ ꞅnᴀꝺuɪꞅeᴀr mé, the God *who loves me.* The sentence is not at all plain. And should one say, ᴀn Ꝺɪᴀ ᴀ ꞅnᴀꝺuɪꞅ mé, it would be difficult to know whether it means, the God *whom* I loved; or, the God *who* loved me.

There is no language, no matter how polished, that cannot furnish instances of amphibology. Take the Latin language, for instance; every schoolboy knows the sayings of the Delphic Oracle :

"Aio te, .Eacide, Romanos vincere posse."
"Ibis, peribis nunquam in bello peribis."

A correct writer can readily avoid this species of writing.

§ 250. The forms, ḋapb, or ḋapab, lepb, mapb, ab, &c., which are nothing more than contractions—ḋapab, for ḋo, to, a, whom, po, ba, was; lepb, for le, with, a, whom, po, ba, was; mapb, for map, po, ba; 5upab, for 5o, that, po, ba; should be written in their simple form, and would accordingly be less puzzling to the young learner; as, bean ḋapb apm Bpi5iḋ, a woman whose name is Bridget—literally, a woman (ḋapb) to whom is (i.e., ḋo, to; a, whom; po, ba, is;) a name Bridget.

The Latin idiom of "est pro habeo," is very like this Celtic turn ; v. g. femina cui est nomen Brigida (see p. 112.)

§ 251. "He who," is translated by "an ṫe;" "they who," by "na ḋaope a; an muipṫip a;" as, an ṫe a 5paḋui5 an ḋomap, He who loved the world; na ḋaope a pinne an coip, they who did the deed; an muipṫip a cuip ip ḋibipṫ na 5aill, they who banished the foreigners.

§ 252. It is usual to omit the relative in familiar language; as, an ṫ-am ṫaipic Patpaic 5o h-Eipipp, the time Patrick came to Ireland.

In English a like omission of the relative is common, but not approved. But in Irish the relative in the *nominative* case imparts to the verb a peculiar ending, by which the omission of the pronoun is compensated (see p. 105 of this treatise).

§ 253. *Is the use of the Preposition in Irish, as in English, at the end of a sentence an error or an idiom ?*

In familiar discourse, prepositions are in Irish, as in English, separated from the *relative* and the *interrogative* pronouns; as, ṫaipic an pean "a" b-puil mpe copamail "lep," the man *whom* I am like *to*, came; "cpa" b-puil ṫu copamail "lep," *whom* are you like *with*. The former could, perhaps, be more gramatically written thus, "ṫaipic an pean "le" b-puil mpe copamail; and the latter, cpa "lep" b-puil ṫu copamail.—*Easy Lessons,* p. 193.

Dr. O'Donovan does not approve of thus separating the relative pronoun from the governing preposition, and of placing the latter at the end of the sentence. He says: "The relative pronoun is often loosely applied in the modern languages, somewhat like the colloquial but incorrect English, 'who does he belong to?'

10

"This form, however, should not be introduced into correct writing, but the relative should be always placed immediately after the preposition; thus, instead of ꞏn é ꞏꞏn ꞏn ꞏeꞏn ꞏ nꞏꞏb cú ꞏꞏ cꞏꞏnꞏ lcꞏꞏ? is that the man *who* thou were talking to? we should say, ꞏn é ꞏꞏn ꞏn ꞏeꞏn lc ꞏ nꞏꞏb cú ꞏꞏcꞏꞏnꞏ? *is that the man to whom thou wert talking?*"—O'Donovan's *Irish Grammar*, p. 376.

Lindley Murray condemns the same practice in the English language; yet the best English writers, from Lord Macaulay to Dr. Faber, obstinately continue to practise it, judging the point to be, it seems, in English as it is in Irish, rather a propriety of idiom than an error of grammar.

"In languages," says Dr. Latham, "a great number of expressions scarcely warrantable in strict syntax become part and parcel of the language. To condemn these at once is unphilosophical. The better way is to account for them."

It can with truth be said that the loose application of the preposition to the relative pronoun in the English language, has come from the parent Saxon dialect. It was a grammatically correct form of phrase in the tenth century, when Saxon was the language of England. In the Irish and Saxon languages there is one striking feature, in this point of view, common to both—that prepositions come after not only verbs, but other terms; as, he went *up*, he went *down*; ꞏo ċuꞏꞏó ꞏé ꞏuꞏꞏ; ꞏo ċuꞏꞏó ꞏé ꞏꞏoꞏ; he went *over*, *under*; again, *herewith* (with this), *therewith* (with that), *thereby* (by that), *therefrom* (from that); and in Irish, cꞏꞏ lcꞏꞏ (whom with), cꞏꞏ ꞏó (whom to). From this it appears there exists a peculiar tendency of having at the close of the sentence the preposition whenever it refers to the interrogative or relative pronoun. Again, the pronoun cꞏꞏ, *who what*, is a more forcible term than a mere particle to hold the first place in a sentence.

☞ Translate accordingly the phrase, *with* whom, whom *with*, cꞏꞏ "lcꞏꞏ;" *to* whom, whom *to*, cꞏꞏ "ꞏó."

Whose, cꞏꞏ lcꞏꞏ (whom with); as, cꞏꞏ lcꞏꞏ é ꞏo? *with whom this (whose is this)*? The preposition lcꞏꞏ, as has been shown in § 229, p. 206, conveys the idea of possession.

∴ Hence the words *mine, thine, his, her, our, &c*, are translated ꞏomꞏꞏ, *with me;* lcꞏc-ꞏꞏ, *with thee;* lcꞏꞏ and lcꞏꞏ-ꞏꞏn (emphatic form), *with him;* lcꞏċ-ꞏc, *with her;* ꞏꞏb-ꞏc, *with you;* lco-ꞏꞏn, *with them.*

Iꞏ ꞏomꞏꞏ ꞏn lcꞏbꞏn ꞏo, this book is *mine.*
Iꞏ lcꞏc-ꞏꞏ ꞏn cꞏpꞏl ꞏꞏn, that horse is *thine.*
Iꞏ lcꞏꞏ ꞏn pcꞏn ꞏo, this pen is *his.*
Iꞏ lcꞏċc-ꞏc ꞏn ꞏubꞏc ꞏꞏn, that ink is *her's*
Iꞏ ꞏꞏnnc ccꞏꞏc Cꞏncꞏnn ꞏ'ꞏ ꞏn ꞏ-cꞏꞏnꞏc,
On *our* side are Eire's right and our friends.

☞ *Whose*, meaning belonging *to whom*, cꞏꞏ lcꞏꞏ.

Whose, of whom; as, *whose* image is this, cꞏꞏ "ꞏo" ꞏn ꞏomꞏꞏꞏ ꞏo, *of whom* is this an image.

§ 254. *The Demonstratives,* So, *this,* Sꞏn, *that.*—The demonstrative pronoun always follows the noun; as, ꞏn ꞏeꞏn "ꞏo," *this* man; ꞏn bcꞏn "ꞏꞏn," *that woman*—literally, *the* man *this; the* woman *that.*

The demonstrative follows not only the noun but the adjectives which accompany it; as, ɴᴀ ᴅᴀᴏɪɴᴇ ᴍᴀɪᴛᴇ ᴅóᴊᴀᴍʟᴀ "ro," *these good, decent people*—literally, *the people, good, decent, these*.

From the foregoing sentences the learner sees that the article *the*, ᴀɴ (and its inflections), goes *before* the noun; ro, or rɪɴ, comes after.

The demonstratives ro and rɪɴ are never used unless the article *the* precedes the noun.

The demonstrative character of these pronouns, ro and rɪɴ, although they come *after* the noun, is fully attained by aid of the article, which must necessarily precede. By this means, the attention of the learner or reader is arrested, while ro or rɪɴ, closing the phrase or sentence, clearly points out the thing to be "demonstrated." Hence, it appears that it is in the combined use of both—namely, the article ᴀɴ and ro, that their demonstrative character is fully shown.

The definite article, from its office of defining, as well as from its root, has a strong demonstrative power.

See § 92, in which the difference between the emphatic particles rᴀ, re, rᴀɴ, and the demonstrative pronoun is shown. The emphatic particles follow the pronoun (personal and possessive), while the demonstrative pronoun always follows, when the article precedes.

CHAPTER V.

VERBS.

Verbs may be viewed in regard (1) to their subject or nominative case; (2) to the relative place they hold in a sentence; (3) the case which they govern denoting the object; (4) moods, the infinitive.

§ 255. The verb agrees with its nominative case (1) in number and (2) person; as, ᴍᴏʟᴀɪᴍ ᴀɴ Ⲧɪɢᴇᴀʀɴᴀ, *I praise the Lord;* ᴍᴏʟᴀᴍᴜɪᴅ ᴀɴ Ⲧɪɢᴇᴀʀɴᴀ, *we praise the Lord;* ᴀʀ ᴍᴏʟᴀɪᴅ "rɪᴀᴅ," ᴀɴ Ⲧɪɢᴇᴀʀɴᴀ? *did they praise the Lord?* ᴍᴏʟᴀᴅᴀʀ, *they did (praise the Lord).*

"Ⲙᴏʟᴀᴅᴀʀ" is *plural* number and *third* person, because its nominative, rɪᴀᴅ, is *plural* number and *third* person.

☞ The student will please to refer to pp. 113, 114, § 117 of this treatise, and read all that is there written on the two forms of the *same* conjugation—the analytic and synthetic.

The form ᴍᴏʟᴀɪᴍ of the verb ᴍᴏʟ, *praise*, in the example just presented, is equal to "ᴍᴏʟᴀɪᴅ ᴍé," *I* praise; the pronoun "ᴍé" is incorporated with the verb "ᴍᴏʟᴀɪᴅ." It is therefore called the *synthetic*, which means *put together, combined*, from συν, *sün*, together, and τιθημι, *tithemi*, I put.

§ 256. Obs. 1.—Hence, whenever the nominative case is not expressed, the verb is in the synthetic form, and conforms to the general rule of agreement in number and person with its subject; as, "b-ꞅuꞁl" ꞃꞁb ꞃláꞃ? *are ye well?* ꞇámuꞁꝺ (*we are*). "B-ꞅuꞁl" is the analytic, because "ꞃꞁb," the nom. case, is expressed; "ꞇámuꞁꝺ," the synthetic, when the nominative is not expressed.

In asking questions, the analytic form is more forcible, it is therefore more in use than the other; but in replying, the synthetic is the fullest and most usual.

OBS. 2.—Whenever the *nominative* case is *expressed*, the verb must be analytically conjugated, and must therefore have only the same ending in all numbers and persons

Exception.—After nouns in the third person plural, the verb follows the general rule and agrees in number with its subject: "In vetusta Hibernica etiam tertiæ personæ pluralis usus est adhuc frequens et communis."—Zeüss.

§ 257. *The place which the verb holds in a Gaelic sentence.*—The verb in Gaelic commonly holds the first place; the nominative, which denotes the subject, the second; the accusative, which points out the object, the last.

"Vox," says Zeüss, "ante alias prædicans verbum est.......... primum inde locum in sententiis Hibernicis obtinet verbum."—*Grammatica Celtica*, p. 881.

In an English sentence the order of construction is, first the noun, next the verb, last the objective case.

This statement regarding a fact it is quite sufficient to make; for, the intelligent student will immediately perceive that the difference of construction in a simple sentence between the two languages is a matter of idiom.

§ 258 *Philosophical analysis of the Irish and English methods of placing the predicate.*

Some may say that the arrangement of an English sentence is simpler and more natural than the arrangement in an Irish one—that the subject, and not the attribute, should be the first enunciated. Let us see. Take a simple sentence; for example, *the sun is bright*. What is it? It is, as logicians say, the expression of a mental judgment—that is, the expression in words of the agreement of two ideas in the mind. As in the example above, the mind conceives the idea of "*sun*," and the idea of "*brightness*," and on comparing the two, it sees they agree, and "judges" accordingly that "the sun is bright." This agreement expressed, is a simple sentence, or what the mind thinks.

That arrangement of words in a sentence is, therefore, natural which follows the order the in which mind conceives the ideas and associates them. The question, then, is reduced to this: what is that order?

First View.—The order in which the mind receives ideas through the medium of the senses is—first, the qualities of things present themselves; next, the things; as the quality *brightness*, for instance, strikes us before we form a notion of the *sun*; the idea of the quality of the thing is called by logicians the *attribute*; of the thing, *the subject*; and the connecting link, "*is*," the *copula*. The natural manner, therefore, of expressing a judgment agreeably to the order in which the ideas arise in the mind is, to enunciate the *attribute* first, the *subject* next. Hence, *bright* is the *sun, fair* is the moon, *pleasant* is wine, *high* is the house, are correct and natural forms of expression; and by analogy, *round* is the world, *terrible* is death [see p. 210 (*d*) supra.]

Now, this is generally the form in which the qualities of things are predicated in Gaelic. In Hebrew it is not an unusual form; as, *great* is God, *mighty* is Jehovah, "terrible is this place," as Jacob said of the place Bethel; "great is Diana of the Ephesians."

Second View.—On the other hand, it is true to say that in every judgment the subject is the leading or primary idea—the attribute, the secondary; and it is only natural that as the quality comes of the substance, so the attribute should follow the idea of the subject, on the principle "*accidentale sequitur principale*" Hence, in comparing the ideas, the subject is the leading concept, the attribute follows. And expressing the judgment in this order, the subject comes first, the attribute next; as, the sun is *bright*, the moon is fair, wine is *sweet*. This arrangement is that observed in English, French, Italian, and the Romance languages.

From this exposition of the matter, it is plain that the Irish idiom is natural, if one regard *the order in which the ideas are conceived*; the English idiom is natural if *one regard the order in which the ideas are compared in forming a judgment*. The former is stronger and more striking; and hence is even in English adopted by poets, and in moments of surprise by persons the most prosaic.

Accordingly, the ancient writers and speakers of Rome and Greece wisely followed neither form of expression exclusively, but availed themselves of either the one or the other as occasion or judgment demanded.

OBS. 1.—After cá, the predicate follows the nominative; as, cá ꞃe ꞃlan, *he is well.*

OBS. 2.—When iꞃ, *is*, the copula which connects the subject with the attribute is expressed first, the predicate immediately follows, and next in order the nominative case; as, iꞃ cléiꞃeac mé, *I am a cleric;* iꞃ, the copula, is first, cléiꞃeac, the predicative, is next, and mé, the nominative case, follows.

☞ A certain writer has said: "That should the definite article come before the predicate, then the nominative case immediately follows the verb, and the predicate comes last; as, iꞃ mé an cléiꞃeac, *I am the* cleric; but even in this instance there is no reason for asserting that cléiꞃeac is not the nominative to the verb iꞃ.

§ 259. The copula iꞃ, *is*, is sometimes omitted; as, cia ꞃé, Dia, *who* (is) *He, God;* cia tu? *who you,* i.e., who (art) thou?

"Leiġeaꞃ ġac bꞃóin comꞃáḋ,"
Cure for every sorrow—converse.

"Liaġ ġac boict báꞃ,"
The physician of every poor man—death.

"Deine loinge a bátað
Deine áic a lorzað;
Deine flaic a cáinzað,
Deine fláince ornað.

The end of a ship—drowning,
The end of a kiln—burning;
The end of a chief—reviling
The end of health—a sigh.

Obs.—Such English sentences as, "who am I? who is he? what is it? what is the matter? is it he? is it not he? this is the man," are translated into Irish by omitting the verb, *is, are, am, was*—cia mire? cia ṙe? caḋ ṙé? caḋ ṙé an nið? an ṙé? (*is it*) he? naċ ṙc? *is it not he?* ní ṙe (*it is*) *not he?* ro ṙc an ṙean.

§ 260. Active verbs govern the accusative case; as, molaim Día, *I praise God;* ṡraðuiṡann ṙé é-ṙein, *he loves himself.*

☞ The accusative and nominative both come after the verb.

§ 261. *Idioms of the Infinitive and Participles of Active Verbs.*

Obs. 1. The infinite mood of active verbs governs the genitive case of those nouns which come immediately *after* it; as,

Do ṡraðuṡað Dé, *to love God;*
Do ðéanað oibre, *to do work.*

Obs. 2.—When the noun goes before the infinitive—which is the usual vernacular form—the noun is governed in the accusative case, and not in the genitive; as,

Le "Día" a ṡraðuṡað;
Le "obair" a ðéanað.

Día and obair are in the accusative case.

After the compound preposition ċum, *towards, for the purpose of,* the gen. and sometimes the accusative is employed; as,

Ċum Dé a ṡraðuṡað;
Ċum oibre a ðéanað; or,
Ċum Día a ṡraðuṡað;
Ċum obair a ðéanað.

§ 262. Obs. 1.—The active participle governs the genitive; as,

Ag oeaṅaḋ oibre, *doing work;*
Ag gráḋuġaḋ Ḋe, *loving God;*
Iar ndeaṅaḋ turuir, *after performing a journey.*

Obs. 2.—Before the infinitive or participle, the gen. case of the personal pronoun is the more common; as,

Le n-"a" gráḋuġaḋ, *in order to love* (a) *him;*
Le n-a gráḋuġaḋ, *in order to love* (a) *her;*
'G a gráḋuġaḋ, *loving him;*
'G a gráḋuġaḋ, *loving her.*

Literally, at his (a) loving; at (her) loving; a, *his*, aspirates the initial or first letter of the infinitive mood; a, *her*, does not; a, *their*, causes eclipsis.

The difference in sound leads the hearer to know their respective meanings.

Note.—The two foregoing idioms in Gaelic are founded on the substantival character of verbs—a principle which is true in all languages, and which is well explained in the following words of Professor Latham, in his work, *The English Language*, p. 290: "A noun is a word capable of declension only. A verb is a word capable of declension and conjugation also..... The infinite mood has the declension of a noun substantive. Verbs of languages, in general, are as naturally declinable as nouns."

If the learner ask, then, why do the infinite active and the active participle govern in Gaelic the genitive case of nouns immediately following them, the reason is, because they are verbal *nouns*, and therefore come under the rule, "the latter of two nouns," &c.—p. 202, § 224.

§ 263. After verbs passive, the noun is in the nominative case; as, déantar olc air, *evil is done to him;* cuirtar ceirt orm, *a question is put to me.*

Olc, *evil*, and ceirt (keshth), *a question*, are nominatives.

§ 264. Observe, however, that the personal pronouns, particularly those of the second and third person singular and third plural, are in the secondary or affected form; as, moltar "iad," *they are praised;* buailtar tu, *you are beaten;* buailtar é (or í, *she*), *he is beaten;* buailtar sinn (or sib), *we or you are beaten.*

Mé, *I*, sinn and sib, the first person singular and the first and second person plural, are in the primary form; tu, second person singular, é, *he*, í, *she*, iad, *they*, are found in the secondary form after verbs passive.

§ 265. *The Nominative and not the Accusative Case of the Personal Pronouns follows Verbs passive.*

Reasons for this opinion.—For a long time, the case of the personal pronoun in these positions was regarded as an accusative, because of its aspirated or accusative character. Dr. O'Donovan, treating this subject, writes: " In Latin and most other languages, when a verb active is turned into the passive, the accusative of the verb active becomes the nominative of the verb passive; but in the Irish, the accusative still retains its form and position; thus, buaιl ιaδ, *strike them*, and buaιlτeaη ιaδ, *let them be struck;* ιaδ has the same form and position, and some have thought that it is the accusative case, governed by buaιlτeaη, like the accusative after the Latin impersonal verbs; as, *oportet me.*"—*Irish Grammar*, pp. 183-4.

And Zeüss appears to have held the same views: " Vix dubium est quin in vetustâ lingua Celtica, per verbi passivi tempora, etiam exstiterit omnium personarum flexio, eo fere modo, ut in serie verborum deponentium. Sed evenit ex usu flexionis impersonalis, inde quod persona prima et secunda utriusque numeri etiam significari poterant per tertiam personam numeri singularis, infigendis tantummodo pronominibus hujus vel illius personæ, ut perierint præter hanc ceteræ personæ, quarum vix rudera quædam adhuc extant.... in vetusta Hibernica etiam tertiæ personæ pluralis usus est adhuc frequens et communis "—*Liber* iii., p. 463.

The pronouns ἑu, é, ι, ιaδ, after verbs passive are nominatives, but nominatives, it is true, in the aspirated or secondary state; for, as has been shown in chap. iv., pp. 90-1, § 88, 89, ἑu is nominative case as well as τu, and é i.e., ŕé, ſ. i.e., ŕι; ŕ, aspirated, loses its force as a consonant (see note, p. 90).

It is plain that ἑu, é, ſ, ιaδ, are nominatives—first, from the immediate connexion in sense, as subject, which the pronoun makes with the verb; secondly, from analogy, for if mé, rιnn, rιb, be nominatives to the verb, so ought τu, é, ιaδ, for a similar reason; thirdly, there are many instances in which, beyond all dispute, ἑu, é, and ιaδ are nominatives; v. g., an Ⅿιċael a ŕιnne é? *was it Michael who did it?* Νſ " ḣ-é," i.e, nι ŕé, not *he;* cιa ŕιnne é? ιaη ŕaη. Now ŕé, or é, and ιaδ-ŕaη seem, plainly enough, in these and similar answers to be in the nominative case, and therefore mere aspiration after a verb in the passive voice does not undo their character as nominatives.

Ⅿo mḟúιŕnιn !
I.
'Sſ blaċ ʒeal na rmeuŕ ſ,
Ir blaċ δeaŕ na ŕub-cŕeab ſ,
'Sſ planδa b' ḟeaŕŕ meιn ſ,
Le h-aιnaιŕc δo ŕúl !

II.
'Sſ mo ċuιŕle, 'ŕſ mo ŕún ſ,
A'r ſ blaċ na n-úbal cúmŕa ſ,
Ir ŕamŕa anŕr an ḟuaċċ ſ
Cιoιn nδolaιʒ aʒur ċaιŕʒ?

She's the white flow'r of the berry,
She's the bright bloom of the cherry,
She's the noblest, fairest maiden
    That ever saw the day !

She's my pulse! my love! my pleasure!
She's the apple's sweet bloom-treasure,
There is summer in her presence
'Tween Christmas and the May!

☞ í in these stanzas is nominative case.

The folowing from Hardiman's collection is like the foregoing:

Ann ra m-baile ro ca an Cuilfionn a'r an maiʒoean breaʒ muince,
'Sí an buinneán ir áine í, o'a b-feicim oíoin mnáib,
'Sí mo reanc í, 'rí mo nún í, 'r í annraċt mo ful í,
Sí raiuna ann ra b-fuaċt í, ioin noolaiʒ a'r cairʒ.

Irish Minstrelsy, vol. i., p. 274.

The personal pronouns coming after ba, *was*, take the objective form, which are only aspirated nominatives; as, buo tu, and not buo tu; buo íc or ó, and not buo ré. It appears that after buó, the aspirated nom. íc, íí, íao, and not é, í, iao, ought to be employed (see *Easy Lessons*, pp. 39, 40).

§ 266. *Do, did, may, can, will, shall*, when denoting time, are expressed in Irish as in French, Italian, Latin, and Greek, by the termination which the verb assumes in each respective tense; as I *do* love, ʒraouiʒim; *I will* love, ʒraoóċtao; I *would* love, ʒraoóċtainn.

When denoting action, power, ability, resolution, wish, are rendered by oéanaim, I *do*, or *make;* ir toil liom, or ir mian liom, I *wish;* tiʒ liom, I *can;* ir féioir liom, I *am able;* or féaoaim, I *am able;* caiḟfio mé, I *must*.

§ 267. The continuative form of the active or passive voice, such as, *I am striking, I am being struck*, is expressed in Irish by the different persons of the verb taim with the present participle; as, ta an cloʒ '5 a bualao, *the clock is striking*, corresponding to the Saxon form, *a-striking*.

In sentences of this kind, oo, contrary to strict etymological propriety, is in much use instead of the particle aiʒ; as,

Ta re o'a bualao, *it is a-threshing;*
Ta re o'a caiteao, *it is a-winnowing.*

Ancient Music of Ireland, vol. i., p. 30.

Faoi banna na ʒ-craob 'r an ʒaot o 'a boʒao,
Under the leaves of the boughs, and tossed by the wind.

Ibid, vol. i., p. 146.

Obs.—He *is* loved, is translated ʒraouiʒtan íé, and also ta ré ʒraouiʒte. The former denotes a continuance of action; the latter a complete action.

§ 268. A verb in the infinitive mood depends for its government on some other verb going before, on a noun, or on an adjective; as,

" 'Ꝃuꞃ ꞇuꝣ ꝺo comaꞏnꞏc 'éꞏꞃꞇeaꞏcꞇ' ꞏe ꞑ-a ꝣꞏóꞃ,"
And *counselled* him *to heed* his voice.
Irish Homer, b. i., l. 32.

" Iꞃ cóꞏꞃ ꞑa ꞃoꞏꞇꞏꝣc ꝣꞏeuꞃ, ꞇa 'ꞑ ꞇꞑaꞏꝣ 'ꞑꞑa ꞏuꞏóc,
'S a ꞃeoꞏꞇa ꞃꝣaoꞏꞏcaꝺ 'baꞏꞏe ꞏeꞏꞃ aꞑ ꝣaoꞇ."
Id., b. i., l. 79.

§ 269. Obs.—The sign (*a* or *do*) of the infinitive mood is omitted in Irish after verbs of commanding, exhorting, ordering, and the like, and after the pronouns or a vowel sound; as, *aꝣuꞃ aꞃ aꞑ ꞇaꞏam ꝺo ꞇuꝣ aꞑ ꞇꞏꝣeaꞑꞑa Dꞏa aꞏꞑ ꝣac uꞏꞏe cꞃaꞑ " ꞃaꞃ,"* and out of the earth the Lord God made every tree *grow*.

O'Donovan says: "When the governed verb is one expressing motion or gesture, which does not govern an accusative, the sign *do* is never prefixed; as, *ꝺúbaꞏꞑꞇ ꞃé ꞏꞏom ꝺuꞏ ꝣo Coꞃcaꞏꝣ*, *he told me to go to Cork*."—*Irish Grammar*, p. 387.

§ 270. When a *purpose* or *end* is to be expressed, the infinite mood is sometimes preceded, like verbs in Italian, or French, by a preposition; such as, *cum*—*pour* (French)=*for*=*per* (Italian); *ꞏe*, *with*, or *with the intention of*; *aꞏꞑ*, *on*.

Aꞏcꞇ ꞃeuc ma " ꞇa" ꞑeac ꞑaomꞇa aꞏꞑ bꞏc " ꞏe ꞃaꝣaꞏꞏ,"
But try is there any person of divine knowledge *to be found*.
Irish Homer, b. i., l. 80.

Le ꝣꞑaꝺuꝣaꝺ=*pour aimer*=*to* love.

Obs.—*Le, with*, preceding the infinitive mood active, gives it a passive meaning, as in the words *ꞏe ꞃaꝣaꞏꞏ, to be found*, in the line just quoted from the first book of the *Irish Homer*. This idiomatic trait should be noted by the student.

Le, going before the infinitive in this way, comes after the verb *to be*, *ꝺo beꞏꞇ*; as, *ꞇa aꞑ obaꞏꞃ ꞏe ꝺeaꞑaꝺ*, the work *is* to be done; *bꞏ aꞑ obaꞏꞃ ꞏe ꝺeaꞑaꝺ*, the work *was* to be done.

§ 271. If the infinitive mood is taken substantively, it is governed in the genitive case by the prepositions *cum*, *ꝺ' éꞏꞃ*, *ꞏaꞃ*, *ꞃeꞏꞃ*, &c., as a noun would; as, *cum a ꞃꞏaꞑuꞏꝣꞇe*, *for their salvation*, or *for saving them*.

☞ The infinite mood is the nom. case to a verb, or the objective case on a verb active, influenced as a noun would be if in the same situation; as,

Do moꞏaꝺ ꞑꞏ cꞏꝣꞏꞑ, 'ꞃ caꞏꞑ ꞇabaꞏꞃꞇ ꝺuꞏꞇ, ꞑꞏ cóꞏꞃ,
To praise you is not needed, to disparage you is not meet.
Irish Homer, book iv., l. 411.

§ 272. The *nominative* absolute in English, or *ablative* absolute in Latin, is translated into Irish by the *dative* case of the noun coming after the infinitive of the verb " to be," governed by *aꞏꞑ, on;*

Example.—" *Aꞏꞑ beꞏꞇ ꝺo'ꞑ ꞇꞏoꞑoꞏꞏ ꞏꞏoꞑmaꞑ ꞏeꞏꞃ aꞑ ꞃꞏuaꝣ,*"
The assembly being filled with the multitude.
Ibid., b. i., l. 74.

" *Ꝃeaꞑꞃóꞏꝺ Nuꞏꞑꞃꞏoꞑꞑ aꞏꞑ b-ꞃaꝣbaꞏꞏ Cꞏꞃeaꞑꞑ ꝺu,*"
Gerald Nugent, *on leaving* Ireland.
Irish Minstrelsy, vol. ii., p. 226.

CHAPTER VI.

ADVERBS.

§ 273. Adverbs are placed nearest the words whose meaning they modify; as, ɼıubᴀl " ʒo beo," *walk quickly* (pr. shoo-il); cᴀɲɼ " ʒo luᴀċ," come *speedily*.

They are placed therefore immediately *after* the verb.

Quite unlike adverbs in English, they cannot in Irish, according to idiom, be placed between the verb cᴀım and the past participle; as, he was very much praised, bɼ ɼe molcᴀ ʒo h-ᴀɲ-móɲ, and not bɼ ɼé ʒo h-ᴀɲ-ṁóɲ molcᴀ.

§ 274. Adverbs beginning with a vowel, in coming after the assertive verb ɩɼ, buó, are, in many instances, distinguished from the adjectives from which they are derived, by taking the aspirate h prefixed; as, b' olc ᴀɲ ɼeᴀɲ é, *he* was a *bad* man; olc, the adjective, has no aspirate prefixed; but if a person say, he did it *badly*, he must put an h before olc; thus, buó h-olc oo ɼıʒɲe ɼé é; b' ᴀɲ-mᴀıċ ᴀɲ ɼeᴀɲ é, he was a very *good* man; buó " h-ᴀɲ-ṁᴀıċ" oo lᴀbᴀıɲ ɼé, he spoke very *well*; b'ᴀoıbɩɲɲ ᴀɲ lᴀ é, *it was a delightful day*; buó h-ᴀoıbıɲ oo ċᴀɩɲcıc ɼɼ, she sang *delightfully*. It is said above, " in many instances," since the remark does not hold true in all cases; for in speaking of a subject of the feminine gender, the aspirate h is employed before the adjective; as, she was a *young*, handsome woman, bᴀ " h-óʒ," ᴀlᴀɩɲ, ᴀɲ beᴀɲ ɼ.

See Etymology, c. viii., p. 152, 160; also § 207, p. 182.

§ 275. *Peculiar use of the Negative Adverb in Irish.*

" It is worth the learner's attention to observe a feature peculiar in some measure to the character of the native Irish people, as reflected in the mirror of their language. The positive worth or merit of an object is expressed not unusually by asserting that it does not possess qualities of an opposite character. It is true that many examples of this style are found in the inspired writings, and that it is not uncommon with other people; yet amongst the Irish the use of this peculiarity of expression is very striking."—From *Easy Lessons, Part IV.*, p. 301. Third edition; Dublin—Mullany.

CHAPTER VII.

PREPOSITIONS, CONJUNCTIONS, INTERJECTIONS.

§ 276. All the simple prepositions govern the dative case.

§ 277. All the compound prepositions govern the genitive (because radically they are nouns).

☞ Some grammarians have taught that ejoin, *between*, governs the accusative.

My observations on the written and spoken Irish for the last ten years, have tended to prove the contrary (see in § 265, the quotation from the song, Ann ra m-baile ro, &c., second line).

'Sı an buınneán ır uıme ſ ò'a b-feıcım "eıoın nynaıb."

"Ánaıb" is the dative case on eıoın.

"Cıoın mac agur ınaoı agur fean."
M.S. Irish.

§ 278. Ons.—Ánn, or ın, signifying *towards* (like *cum, towards, for the purpose of*), governs the genitive case (passim in the writings of Dr. MacHale.)

⁎ O, le, ne, and ıne, take n when going before any of the possessives a, *his*; a, *her*; a, *their*; an, *our*; and h commonly before words whose first letter is a vowel; as, le n-a mac, with *his* son; le n-a mac, with *her* son; le h-eagla, *with* fear; le h-aıngıo, *with* silver; le h-òn, *with* gold.

CONJUNCTIONS.

§ 279. Conjunctions have the same connecting power in Gaelic as in other languages (see all that has been written concerning them in Etymology).

Obs.—A'r, agur, written 'gur and 'r, *and*—like the Latin "ac," *and*, has the meaning of "as." Ex.—cáım "co" maıt agur cıg lıom, *I am as well as I can be.* Co and agur=*as* and *as* in corresponding clauses of a sentence.

The English "than," Latin "quam," after the comparative, is expressed in Irish by 'ná, or ıoná (see pp. 165, 168, Etymology.

INTERJECTIONS.

§ 280. In addressing a person or thing, the vocative case is employed; as, a Cıgeanna, *O Lord;* a mıc na g-cumann, *son of my affections.*

Manz, *woe*, takes the dative case; as, manz ðam, *woe to me.* Cruag, monuaın, mo náıre, and the like, expressive of pity, are nothing more than nouns, forming with the verb ır, expressed or understood, short sentences, which agreeably to their meaning, take a nominative or a dative case; as, mo náıne tu! *fy!* (or) *thou art my shame!* ır cruag lıom tu! *pity!* (*thou art to me a pity!*)

PART IV.—PROSODY

CHAPTER I.

§ 281. Prosody—derived from προς, *to*, ὠδή, *a song, an ode*—treats of the laws of harmony in metrical composition.

Its end is twofold—to direct the harmony of articulate sounds, and to adjust words according to the measure of their rhythmical combination.

§ 282. To direct the harmony of articulate sounds is called *Orthoëpy*, from ὀρθοέπεια,—ὀρθός, *right*, and ἔπεια, *speaking*, ἔπος, *a word*; to adjust the measure of their rhythmical combination is called *Versification*.

Prosody is, therefore, divided into *Orthoëpy* and *Versification*.

§ 283. *Orthoëpy* regards correct pronunciation not only of letters and syllables, but also of terms.

In chap. i., Etymology, pp. 12, 27, directions have been given for the proper pronunciation of vowels, consonants, and syllables.

§ 284. Proper *pronunciation* of words of two or more syllables is regulated by the usage of the learned and intelligent who speak the language, or by some standard authority agreed to by the majority of the nation whose language it is.

The pronunciation of a word of two syllables or more, is regulated by *accent* and *quantity*.

§ 285. Accent is a stress of voice laid on a certain syllable.

Accent is twofold, *primary* and *secondary*. Words of *one* syllable can have no accent; words of two syllables have the primary accent only. Words of three or more syllables may have the primary and secondary accent. As a general rule, the primary accent in Irish is on the *first* syllable.

Obs.—In Connaught, Irish speakers always accent the first syllable; in Munster, the second. This difference in accentuating, causes the verse of Connaught poets to appear harsh to the people of Munster, and *vice versâ*. The written language is not in any way affected by this difference in the pronunciation of the Irish-speaking people of the two provinces. In conversation, however, one readily perceives the dissimilarity. It must be said, that really this difference is far less than many persons who know not the people nor their language have pronounced it to be. Two Frenchmen, say from the borders of the Seine, and the banks of the Garonne, would have greater difficulty in mutually interchanging thought in their own language, than a native of Munster and Connaught would in their native Irish tongue.

§ 286. *Quantity* is the time occupied in pronouncing a syllable: it is long or short. A syllable is long when the stress is on the vowel; short, when on the consonant.

§ 287.
A syllable is long
{
(1) When followed by ḋ (asp.) or ġ (asp.); as, ṙaḋ (pr. *raw*), *a saying*; ṙıġ (*ree*), *a king*; ṙoġ (*sūh*), *happiness*; ṙaġ, *get*; ṁıḋ, *a thing*; ṙuġ, *juice*; beaṅṅuıġ, *bless*; ṙaıḋ, *a prophet*; ṙıġ (*shee*), *a fairy*.

(2) In written language when marked with the grave accent; as, bàṙ, *a boat*; òl, *drinking*; òṙ, *gold*; àṙ, *slaughter*; àċ, *luck*.

(3) The endings àṅ, ìṅ, óġ, expressive of smallness, youthfulness, &c.; as, caṙàṅ, *a path*; ṙuıṙóġ, *a lark*: see the long diphthongs, p. 23; and the triphthongs, p. 26.
}

Obs.—Every long syllable is not an accented syllable.

§ 288.
A syllable is short
{
(1) Whenever, as a general rule, it follows an accented syllable.

(2) When a double consonant follows the vowel; as, coṙṙ, *a crane*—a few words excepted; as, baṙṙ, *top*; ṙeaṙṙ, *better*.

(3) See the short diphthongs.
}

Derivative words follow the accentuation of those from which they are derived.

Note.—The art of making a proper use of *pauses, emphasis*, and tone or *intonation* is called elocution.

※ The foregoing explanations regard Irish, whether in prose or verse.

CHAPTER II.
VERSIFICATION.

§ 289. Versification means *verse making*.
Verse is a measured arrangement of words.
It is of two kinds—blank verse and rhyme.

§ 290. *A* verse is one line of poetry.

§ 291. Rhyme is applied to verse which ends in syllables of the *same* sound. Blank verse is devoid of sameness of sound in the final syllable.

§ 292. Rhythm lends to poetry and to prose the charms arising from rightly adjusted sound.

§ 293. *Metre* is the recurrence within certain intervals of syllables similarly affected in the same line.

Note.—Rhyme and rhythm differ very much. Rhyme regards the same sound in the final syllable; rhythm, the movement by regularly occurring accents.

"Rhythm or cadence is the simplest combination—the lowest measure by which evident order can be given to the sound of either music or speech"— *Mitford*.

Rhythm differs even from *metre*. Rhythm is proportion applied to any motion whatever; *metre*, proportion applied to syllables in a line.

Rhythm is derived from the Greek $\rho\iota\theta\mu\delta s$, *a measured motion*, from $\rho\nu\omega$. *to run;* Irish, ṅiċ, *to run; rhyme*, from the Irish ṅím, *count;* or the Anglo-Saxon *rim, to number*. Ṙım, *count;* is even still in use amongst the people; as, ṅíl ṁṁ leır, there is no *counting* with him, no standing him.

'§ 294. The same kind of stress, or the same lengthening of a syllable, may occur in every second or third syllable. The number of such, inclusively, from one emphatic syllable to another, is called a *measure*. If it happens on each alternate syllable, the measure is dissyllabic; if on every third, it is trisyllabic. Two or more syllables constituting a measure is called a foot.

§ 295. A couplet consists of two lines; a distich, the same; a hemestich is half a verse; a stanza or stave, a number of verses forming a regular division of a poem or song; a stróphé, the same as a stanza.

§ 296. *Certain Essential Properties of Verse.*

In reading a verse, one can note the phonetic accordance with which two or more words in the line begin or end.

A phonetic agreement, or a similarity of articulation in the *beginning* of two or more words in a verse is called *alliteration;* a like agreement at the *end* is called *assonance*.

§ 297. *Alliteration* (from *ad, to,* and *litera, a letter*), requires that two or more words in a verse begin with the same articulate sound.

As, from Lord Byron,

" The bay
Receives the *prow*, and *proudly spurns* the *spray*."

Prow, and *prou* in proudly form an alliteration; *spurns* and *spray* are alliterative.

§ 298. *Assonance* (from *assono*, to correspond to by sound), requires that a certain number of words *end* with a similar articulation.

All rhymes, perfect and imperfect, form assonant metres.

Note.—Alliteration and sometimes assonance are employed in prose writings as an ornament. " Alliteration as an ornament must be distinguished from alliteration as an essential quality of metre."

☞ Showy writers are very fond of alliteration. A moderate use of it renders prose writing very agreeable. But to sacrifice sense to sound, which is not uncommon with young and vain writers, is a sign of silliness and self-sufficiency.

§ 299. *Various kinds of Accented Metre.*

Again, in reading a line of poetry one can note the accented syllables.

In dissyllabic measures the accent falls on the *first* syllable or on the *second*; as,

Dissyllabic. { *a.* Gó where | glóry | wáits thee.
{ *b.* The hárp | that ónce | through Tá | ra's halls.

In trisyllabic measure it falls on the *first* syllable, on the *second*, or *third*; as,

Trisyllabic. { *c.* Próudly the | nóte of the | trúmpet is | soúnding.
{ *d.* Remémber | the glóries | of Brían | the Bráve.
{ *e.* At the clóse | of the dáy | when the hám | let is still

Obs. 1.—The dissyllabic measures are more usual than the trisyllabic.
Obs. 2.—Of the two forms of dissyllabic, the second is the commoner.
Obs. 3.—Of the trisyllabic, the first form (*c*) is the least common.

§ 300. *Nomenclature of Modern Metre.*

1. *Octosyllabics*, or eight syllable metre, with the accent on the second syllable; as,

The hárp that ónce thróugh Tára's hálls.
Melodies, by Thomas Moore.
The wáy was lóng, the wínd was cóld.
Lay of the Last Minstrel,
by Sir Walter Scott.

2. *Heroics*—ten syllables, or five feet of the same; the accent on the second syllable. *Blank Verse*—heroics without rhyme.
3. *Elegiacs*—heroics in four-line stanzas, with alternate rhymes.
4. *Rhyme royal*—seven lines of heroics, with five lines having either alternate or periodic rhymes, and the two last lines successive rhymes.
5. *Ottava rima*, or eight lines of heroics, employed in narrative poetry. The first six rhyme alternately, the last two in succession.
7. *Spenserian stanza*—eight lines of heroics, like the foregoing, but closed by an Alexandrine.
8. *Alexandrines*—twelve syllables of the dissyllabic (class *b*).
9. *Service metre*—fourteen syllables of this same measure (*b*).
10. *Ballad metre* is service metre divided in twain; it consists of stanzas of four lines—the first and third lines have eight syllables, the second and fourth, six, with alternate rhymes; as,

Thus freédom nów so séldom wákes,
The ónly thrób she givés,
Is whén some héart indígnant breáks,
To shów that still she livés!

☞ In trisyllabic measure, a dissyllabic foot is introduced; as,
Próudly the | nóte of the | trúmpet is | soúnding.
The line closes with a dissyllabic foot.

Obs.—Although one measure predominates, it is rarely unmixed.

Note.—The different species of *accented* verse now in use, are pointed out in the two foregoing paragraphs.

§ 301. *The Metrical System founded on Accent differs widely from that founded on Quantity.*

"Accent and quantity differ," says Latham, "and the metrical systems founded on them."

(*a*) With metres founded on quantity, *accent* is combined; but with those founded on accent, *quantity* is not combined.

(*b*) On this account Latin and Greek poetry, even to people of this country who read it chiefly according to accent, sounds euphonious.

(*c*) The ancients of Greece and Rome read their poetry in a manner quite unknown to moderns. They expressed the quantity and the accent perhaps in a kind of musical strain, much in the same manner that the Jews read the Sacred Scriptures, or religious in the Catholic Church recite the psalms.

(*d*) Accented verse cannot, properly speaking, be read according to quantity.

"*Certain classical feet have no English equivalents*"—*Latham*, p. 515.

"*No English measure can have either more or less than one accented syllable*"—*Ibid*.

On this account the learner now sees why, in the foregoing paragraphs, no mention is made of Greek or Latin measures, *Iambus*, *Trochee*, *Spondee*, *Dactyl* or *Anapæst*.

§ 302. The Irish language, however, in the plastic hands of poets like His Grace the Most Rev. John MacHale, Archbishop of Tuam, has been moulded into all the graceful varieties of which accented metre is capable.

Example of a.

Teié 'nẛ |: ηȝeıbfın ȧnt-ṫuaṫ,
'S ṫnaṫ bejȯar b' ṗeım 'ȝa lan-luaḋ,
Fór oṅm cuıṁneać bf.

Go where glory waits thee,
But while fame elates thee.
Oh! still remember me.

Example of b.

THE HARP THAT ONCE THROUGH TARA'S HALLS.

I.

An ċnuıṫ, ḋo ṫeap ṫnf ṫallaıȯ 'n nıȝ
Na ȝaeṫe ceolṫa bınn',
Ṫa 'n ballaıȯ Ṫeaṁna 'nóıṫ 'nn a luıȯe
Ȝan feanrȧṫ ceoıl, no ṗınn:
Man fúḋ ṫa 'n ṫ-am, ċuaıḋ ṫanṫ, faoı ċeo,
Ṫa 'caıl, 'r a ċlu faoı fuan;
A'r cnoıḋṫe, 'fanṫuıȝ molṫa ceo,
Nı aınıȝeann ıaḋ ȝo buan.

II.

Ní cluinfear cruit na Teamra : freun
Mearg cruinniúgad ban, no faoi,
Óir, ruagnann i beit feadta, faon,
Fuaim bricte teud 'ra n-oidce!
Mar rud do 'n t-raoinract, 'r anam cra
A dúrgtar í go deo,
Act 'nuair a brirtar croide 'g a cnadad,
Aig foilrúgad í beit teo.

Irish Melodies, by Dr. MacHale.

Example of c.

I.

Ta binn gut an adairc go glórac a géimnugad,
'Gur gairc-éac a rínead go h-ard air an gaot;
Tar loc Suiligh ta 'n treun laoc go luatmar a léimnugat
Aig na rluagta 'nglean t-Samair a deifnugad gan rgic.
  Sior ó gac rleib go beó,
  Treun-fir nac teifead gleo
Brurtigid faoi glar-bnat bur ngairgide Aoid Ruaid
  Buanact 'gur galuglaid
  Deifnigid go claon aig cac,
Suar fa bur n-oil-tir!—Uí Domnaill Abú.

II.

Feuc Ua Niall, rgiac na b-flat, cum cabair a claonad,
Le mór-rluad gairgide, 'gur toga na b-Feadann,
Ta mile eac burb ann a roim-rann a rínead
  Faoi na marcaigib ó'n g-cluan a b-fuil riue banna ann,
  S' ionda an croide beideas fann,
  Faoi rgat a culaid lean',
Béid geur-brón air namaid, iad-rein bí gan truag,
  Nuair cluinfear air 'n gair-gleo
  'Sgniad air an t-rínean teo
A brurtugad cum diogaltair Uí Domnaill Abú.

III.

Ta 'n facl-cu ann Dearmuin aig ailleas go faocnac,
'S an iolra gan eagla a rgniac air an maig;
Ta'n rionac air inaidte a fairrne go caocrac,
Níl duine le bagairt air, beo air an fait!
  Fairg' uile lam go teann,
  Tuad-cat 'gur faobnac-lann,
Tóig onéa tnom-diogaltar ceant agur luat
  Béid aca cnaiótead-rgeul,
  Air óil clair na Gaél,
S' air treun-clan Uí Conaill, Uí Domnaill Abú.

IRISH GRAMMAR. 235

iu.

'Sé 'n fíon-ċeapt ca Clap Ċonaill, coraṁt do toiltead,
Na teallaiġe 'r 'na h-altoip' ca anra b' an g-cnoiḃe,
Ca lonġ an namaid 'nna ḃan-ḟaraḋ fuilteaḋ,
Le laraṁ a b-teinte ca roilreaḋ 'meaḋon oiḋċe
'Suar, le raḋ laoḋ, man riṗ,
'N g-crár gleó, bi agaiḃ noinn,
A ċlap Ċonaill oiḃir all-neantṁan faoi ḃnuḋ,
Aṁniġa, an Sacrap reall,
Tnom ḃuillioḋ clain na nGaél,
buail fa bun glar-ṫin Ui Ḋoṁnaill Aḃú.
Song—O'Ḋoṅnaill Aḃú—*O'Donnell Abú.*
Translated by a Maynooth Student.

Example of d.

Third stanza of the song by Moore—*Remember the glories of Brian the Brave.*

Forget not our wounded companions who stood
  In the day of distress by our side;
While the moss of the valley grew red with their blood,
  They stirred not, but conquered and died!
The sun, that now blesses our arms with his light,
  Saw them fall upon Ossory's plain.
Oh! let him not blush when he leaves us to night,
  To find that they fell there in vain!

Na beanṁaḃaiḋ na có-laoċna oiḃre, tug toil
  Beiḋ farcuigte go calṁad 'rap gleo;
Giḋ bi caonaḋ an ġleanna ḃeang le n-a b-fuil,
  Nion teiteaḃan, aċt tuiteaḃan réir clót.
An grian, a ta h' an roilriuġaḋ, do ċonairc iaḋ 'na luiḋe
  Ain ḃaiṁreaḋaiḃ Orruiḋe ta lan,
Na bioḋaḋ rṁuiḋ ain, na ḃnat-ḃnoin a noċt aig ḋul faoi,
  Fa gun tuiteaḃan gan cuitiugaḋ 'ran ap.
      Translation by Dr. MacHale.

Another Example of d.

THE EXILE OF ERIN.

1.

Do tainic ċum an ċuain fean deonaiḋ ó Ċininn,
  Bi 'n ḋnúċt ain a lom-ċulaiḋ fuan agur tnom;
Ain a ḋin tug ré orna aig maiḋin aig einiġ,
  Ḋul' riuḃal taoḃ au ċnoic b'fag na gatta no-lom.
Ain neult geal na maiḋne bi a rúile aig faine,
Bi aig eiriġ tan Cininn—bean-niġan na mana,
Ain aic ann a b-toigaḋ é 'r a b-tug ré rót aine,
  Do finiṁ binn-ṗanta a Ċineann gu bnat.

II.

Oċ! is tuaiṡ e mo ċas saoi ansóṡ a ḃúsaċt,
Ta an sionnaċ 'san siaḃ ṡo ruamnaċ 'nn a ulóċ;
Aċt aṡam-sa ní'l coinne ó oċnur a'r ṡuarċt,
Mo ċeaċ, nó m' ċín seln ní seicsaḃ a ċoiḃċe.
Ní seicsaḃ a ċolóċe na ṡleanta a'r na rṡaċa,
Ann a ṡ-caiċnaṅ mo ṡinsean a saoṡal a'r a m-ḃeaċa,
Mo ċruis ċaoin ní ċróinsaḃ ṡo h-euṡ le na m-ḃlaċa,
'S ní ḃualsaḃ ruas ḃioṡ-ċeolta Ċineann ṡo ḃsaċ.

III.

Ċine, mo ċin séin, ṡiḃ tnéiṡċe ṡo h-iomlan,
Ann mo aisling' ní raṡaim ḃo ċalam ṡo ḃeó,
Aċt, sanaoin! 'nuais a ḃúsaim, tain a ḃ-saḃ uais ain
reaċnaḋ,
Aiṡ rmuaineaḃ ais mo ṁuintis náċ seicsaḃ níos mó.
Ḃ-Fuil sé 'nn han ḃam, a ċineaṁuin ċruajḃ seaḃ mo saoṡail,
ḃeié ais ais ann mo ċiṡ séin ṡan ḃoċan no ḃaoṡal,
Faice a ṡ-cuinsaiḃ onm clan m' aċar a'r mo ṡaoil?
D'euṡ siaḃ le mo ċorainč no m' ċaoineaḃ čais ḃeo.

IV.

Donas no čiṡe ḃí aiṡ coill ṡlas an ḃ-tnéiṡaḃ?
Deinluṅaċa an ċaoin siḃ a čuiċin 'sa čnaċ?
Ca ḃ-fuil m' aċain 'r mo ṁaċain ḃí 'ṡ-comuiḃe a ḃneaṡúṡaḃ
A ṁic sein—a'r ca ḃ-fuil rí, mo ċeile a'r mo ṡnaḃ?
Oċ! is ḃuḃ ta mo ċnolḃe 'rtiṡ saoi amṡan aiṡ cniċe,
Fa ṡnaḃ tab'nt ḃo 'aon ionnur ċo luaċ uaim a niċe,
Ta ḃeóna.no síile aiṡ tičim man cioča.
Aċt san.ḋ! ní leiṡ'sóċaiḃ mo ċneaċ a'r mo ċnaḃ.

V.

Ṡo ḃeine mo saoṡail a'r mo ḃeaċa annóčaiṡ,
Mo seanc ṡean ont, Ċine, a ṡnaḃuiṡim ċan caċ—
Aṡaḃ-ra ča ḃeannaċt is ḃeiṡionaiṡe ḃo ḃeónaiḃe,
A ċín ṡil mo sinsin, a Ċine ṡo ḃnaċ.
Ṡiḃ smiṡċe ḃo óiḃinčeaċ a'r na ḃeona a sil sé,
Ḃioḃ ḃlaċ ais ḃo ṡontaiḃ ṡlas-innis is mlse,
Ṁolta ṡo naiḃ tú aiṡ siliḃe níos ḃírse,
Ċine, mo ṁuinnin! Ċine ṡo ḃnaċ!

Translated by the Rev. James Casey C.C., Sligo, Diocese of Elphin while he had been a student of Maynooth, March, 1856.

In the first edition of the Grammar it has been remarked in regard to this song that it was a translation and not the original; and that of course, the writer did not in any way interfere with the rival claims of our countryman, George Nugent Reynolds, and Mr. Campbell. The version differs from that furnished by Collins—which is in blank verse.

§ 303. The following beautiful hymn, *Jesu dulcis memoria*, composed by St. Bernard, and sung by the Church in the office of the Sacred Name, has been translated into Irish verse of the same metre as the original by the author.

IRISH GRAMMAR.

The translation is very literal, yet idiomatic, preserving the dignity, simplicity, and beauty of the Latin hymn, together with that necessary elegance—in order to be a suitable translation—its capability of being adapted to the same musical notes:

Jesu dulcis memoria,	Suaincⁱ linn, Íora, meamnużaḋ a ċoiḃċe
Dans vera cordis gaudia,	Ḃronnar onainn ḟíon-aoiḃnar cnoiḋe;
Sed super mel, et omnia,	Aċt tan mil a'r żáċ uile ní,
Ejus dulcis presentia.	Tá ċuiḋeaċt cáiḃ linn annr a t-rlíże.
Nil canitur suavius,	Ní cluinteaṅ ceol níor luíne,
Nil auditur jucundius,	Ní cainteaṅ focail ir binne,
Nil cogitatur dulcius,	Ṡuċ ar ċnoḋaḋ ní ṫíż ó ḃuine,
Quam Jesus Dei Filius.	Man ainṁ ruaiṫe Aíc Dé na cnuine.
Jesu spes pœnitentibus,	Íora ḃóċċuir luíċ an żeun-ċaoiḋe,
Quam pius es petentibus!	Naċ ḃil ḋo'n ḋneaṁ tá ont a 'ḃlaoiż!
Quam bonus te quærentibus!	Naċ ḟial ḋón ċé tá ḋó long ra t-rlíże
Sed quid invenientibus?	Aċt cirḋe ḟein, ḋo ḟeilḃ a ż-cnoiḋe?
Nec lingua valet dicere,	Ní ḟéiḋin le teanża a luaḋ,
Nec littera exprimere;	Ní ḟéiḋin le leitin a ċloḋ;
Expertus potest credere,	'S aiż an ḋuine ḃiaḋa a ta,
Quid sit Jesum diligere.	Caḋ é żiali. iḋ Íora, a ṅáḋ.
Sis, Jesu, nostrum gaudium,	Íora, ir tu ar luat-żáin,
Qui es futurus præmium,	An n-ḃuair annra t-raożal eile, cain;
Sit, nostra in to gloria,	An nżloin ḃiaḋ ionnaḋ-ra, a ṅún,
Per cuncta semper secu a.	Tré raożal na raożal, żo buan.
Amen.	Amen.

An Example of Accented Heroic Metre, from the Irish Iliad by Dr. MacHale.

An ceuḋ leaḃan ḋe 'n Iliaḋ.

Ḃnuṫ Aċuil, ṫéin, óiż néaṁḋa, 'żur buan ḟeanż,
Aċuil mic Ṗeil, an żairżiḋeaċ céimteaċ, żanż,
Ḋo rcap tníḋ ḟluaż na nżneuż cnom leun a'r án,
'S ḋ' ḟáż mónan laoċna tneun, ḋo luaṫ ain lán,
Raḃ n-aḃlaiż ḟuilteaċ, ṫnaċéa ain a' ḃ-ṫeun,
Aiż maḋnaiḃ reanża, 'r ḟanżaiḃ żonteaċ, żeun.
Ḃuḋ 'n' ḋan néin tola Íoḃ żo ḃ-tiocṫaḋ an t-euż
O ċuaiḃ cum iṁnir Aċuil 'r tlaiṫ na nżneuż.
'Ceolnaiḃe an ḃirnir, cnaoḃrżaoil, ḋe na Ḋéa,
Ce 'n neaċ ḋo tionrżnaiḃ żleo ó'n ḟjoinuiż an cnaḋ?
Ḋo rżaoil mac Ionnaċ Íoḃ a żaete tec,
Żur ḟeoil żo níżáċt an ḃair na ṫluaiżte ḃeo:
Man żeall ain óiṁear ḋiḃliż tuż an níż
Ḋ'a ṫażant naoiṁea; ḃeant an leun żan róiſé,
Aiż teaċt żo tiuż 'r żo h-oḃan ain a lonż.
Man ḃrożaltar ceant ain Ċeantant uailleaċ, ḃonḃ,

Cum luinge na nGreag, do chiall an ragant raim,
Le tabantar trom 'gur rooide ann gac lain;
Man bi tlearg cnaob, bfo fillte ain a cean,
'Sur bacull oin, gnat-bnata Pheuba ceann:
Do suio an rluag go lein, act for go buan,
Suio bir clain Aiteinoc, caoirig ano na luan.

§ 304. There are some few who imagine that the foregoing and similar specimens are not real Irish poetry, because not fashioned according to the rules of the ancient Irish grammarians. The excellence of the specimens, and their exact conformity with the requirements of the accented measure is sufficient answer. Still we shall give authority to support this truth.

"Poetry," says Lord Macaulay in his essay on Moore's life of Lord Byron, "as the most acute of human beings, Aristotle, said, more than two thousand years ago, is 'imitation.' It is the imitation of nature, and the more closely it approaches that great pattern, the more perfect it becomes."

"The heart of man," continues the celebrated author, "is the province of poetry, and of poetry alone." And can the heart of man be governed by any unsentimental regulations—no matter how fixed, or how ancient soever? Why then have poetry, whose province is the heart, fitted and trimmed out by rules which have no foundation in nature, nor in those principles by which the movements of the heart are often more or less regulated? Hence, "an art essentially imitative," says the same writer, "ought not, surely, to be subjected to rules which tend to make its imitation less perfect than they would otherwise be; and those who obey such rules ought to be called—not correct, but incorrect writers."

> "You who would dull the poet's fire
>   With learning of the schools,
> Gay fancy's feet with fetters's tire,
>   And give to genius rules;
> Had bounteous nature's counsel hung
>   Upon your will severe,
> Tom Moore had ne'er green Erin sung,
>   Nor Burns the banks of Ayr.
>   O'erawed, I ween,
>   Both bards had been,
> Nor dared to strike the simple lute,
> In your majestic presence mute."
>   *Poems and Lays* by Gerald Griffin, p. 123.
>   Dublin, Duffy.

The principles of versification, which is founded on *accent*, have been thus briefly yet fully explained in the two preceding chapters.

⁎ The conclusion to be drawn from the theory, reasons, and examples furnished is, that Irish, *in accented metre*, is at least as rhythmical and euphonious as English, French, or Italian.

CHAPTER III.

VERSIFICATION AS PRACTISED BY THE IRISH BARDS.

§ 305. Every scholar who has read Hebrew, Greek, Latin, and any of the European languages, knows that the phonetic framework in which the poetry of a people is usually fashioned, differs with each of the great national families, much in the same way that their languages and their genius differ. The Greeks, for instance, and the Latins of old, framed the language of poetry in metre consisting *essentially* in the recurrence of similar quantities; the Indians make it consist in measure alone, or in a specific number of syllables; the Hebrews thought that poetry without *parallelism*, or a recurrence of similar ideas in certain parts of the verse, would be like the body without the soul; the Germans, Swedes, and the Norse generally thought, that poetry could not be expressed without *alliteration*—a quality which, to their mind, constituted the essential characteristic of versification; and moderns—as well Irish as English, French, and Italian—embody poetry in *metre* founded on accent, rendered symphonious by the use of assonance and alliteration. Amidst these varieties, no mention has here been made of the metrical system of the ancient Irish bards. Was their versification founded on quantity or on accent—on measure alone, on assonance, alliteration, or parallelism? It was founded on none of these exclusively: not on quantity, as practised by the Greeks and Latins, which any one skilled in Latin prosody may readily learn by analyzing an Irish quatrain; nor on accent only, for Zeüss puts the question and answers it: "Queritur, an syllabarum majoris et minoris accentus in versuum membris alternantium *certa* fuerit regula? Conjici possunt. . . . pro diversa locatione accentûs duo diversa schemata. Attamen nec in hoc membro nec in aliis plurium vel pauciorum syllabarum *certus* usus statuendus videtur."—*Grammatica Celtica*, pp. 914, 915. Of course, it is true that accent plays a part in all kinds of versification. Nor was the ancient Irish metre one merely of measure, of assonance, or parallelism. It embraced all these qualities, some one of which was considered by other people specially essential in constituting verse. It is no wonder then that it has been pronounced by O'Molloy "the most difficult kind of composition under the canopy of heaven"—"*Maxime autem de metro, omnibus quæ unquam vidi, vel audivi, ausim dicere quæ sub sole reperiuntur difficilimo.*"—*Grammatica Latine-Hibernicâ*, p. 114.

§ 306. In reading the poetry of the ancient bards, either published or still in MSS., one cannot fail to perceive in Irish verse composition, that the following requisites have been deemed either essential or necessary:

Requisites for Irish Verse Composition.

1. Each stanza is a quatrain or a stave of four lines.
2. In each line there are seven syllables, generally.
3. Of these some must necessarily be *alliterative*.
4. Assonance is indispensable.
5. Rhyme therefore, if the assonance be perfect, is found in Irish verse.

6. Rhythm, as well as rhyme, lends its symphony.
7. Parallelism of thought is often—of words, usually employed.
8. Each line expresses a judgment. The same word in the same sense is never used twice in a stave.
9. Special kinds of verse require (1) a syllable to be annexed to the prescribed member; or that (2) the final term in the second and fourth lines, or first and second lines, consist of one syllable more than that of the other verse in the same couplet ; or that (3) there exist a certain alliteration or assonance. These specialities Irish bards and grammarians have distinguished by specific names.

Obs.—1, 2 regard the metre and mould of verse; 3, 4, 5, 6, 7, its ornaments, its symphony, and phonetic effect; 8, the thoughts; 9, special kinds of verse-making.

Obs. 2. The first four—number of lines, number of syllables, alliterations, and assonance—are indispensable in ḃán ḃíṗneaḋ, or direct metre ; the others only for particular kinds of Irish verse.

The requisites for Irish Versification more fully explained.—The Irish prosodical nomenclature—their modern equivalents.

§ 307. *First Requisite.*—The Irish stave or stanza is called in the Gaelic language ceaṫruġaḋ (pr. *kah-roo*), from ceaṫan (*Kah-har*), *four*. Grammarians have given it in English the name *quatrain*, because like the Irish term, its root, *quatuor*, means four. It consists of two couplets—the one called from its office reolaḋ, *leading* or *guiding;* the other comṡaḋ, or *closing* (see § 295, p. 231). A stanza is called also Rann, from rann, a *division;* because it is the common division of a poem. Rann iomlán is a complete stanza; rann briṫe, an incomplete stanza. Every rann must express completely and absolutely the sense intended to be conveyed, and must not depend for any of its special meaning on another rann.

§ 308. *Third requisite —Alliteration* has been defined in § 297, p. 231. Its Gaelic name is "uaim," which means (like fuaim)—first, either *sound, symphony, accord;* or, secondly, *framework, gear.* In the former sense it tallies exactly with prosodical alliteration, which, like the sound arising from the same note repeated, produces a pleasing symphony ; in the latter, it shows that alliteration was considered by the Irish bards, as it was by the Germans, a quality essential in verse—the frame as it were in which it should be wrought. Modern Irish grammarians give it the name of *concord*, from the accordance of sound. The term *alliteration* conveys more fully than that of *concord* the idea of which uaim is the expression.

" Uaim " is of two kinds :

1. { Fíor-uaim=true-alliteration, or,
    Uaim cluaire=ear-alliteration.

2. { Uaim ġnúire=alliteration-of-appearance, or,
    Uaim ruile=alliteration-of-the-eye.

Fíor-uaim requires the *last two words* of a line to begin with a vowel, or the same consonant; uaim ġnúire requires only that any two consecutive terms in a line be alliterative. The latter, or eye-alliteration, can be used for the former in the leading couplet of the rann, but not in the closing couplet.

IRISH GRAMMAR.

NOTE.—On this subject of alliteration, which so abounds in Irish poetry, many pages could be written. The writer has culled several beautiful alliterative examples from ancient poems. Their insertion here would not harmonize with the other parts of prosody, and would mar the symmetry of the work as a whole. The poor Irish people who ask for alms speak in alliterative strains. It is not uncommon to hear, as the writer of these lines has often heard them say:

Ouȷne boċṫ mé—a ċú.
Ꝛan bṛaó, ꝛan beaċa.
Ꝛan cuȷb, ꝛan cuṛṫaṛ.
Ꝛan buȷne, ꝛan beopaȷó.
Ꝛan maoȷn, ꝛan muȷnꝛȷn.
Ꝛan ṫeaċ, ꝛan ṫéaꝛan, &c.

Such is the alliterative phonetic flexibility of the Irish language, even with the illiterate.

§ 309. Fourth requisite, *assonance*.—This quality is called by the Irish bards, comanoa (from com, *together*, and anoa, *elevating*), a term which has been translated "correspondence" by modern grammarians, because they perceived that two or more final syllables were identical, and, as it were, responded one to the other in phonetic effect. From this it is plain that the quality called comanoa requires that a certain number of words end with a similar articulation.

This definition is the same as that of *assonance*, see § 298. Now, assonance is twofold—vowel assonance and consonantal assonance. Vowel assonance consists in identity of phonetic effect arising from vowel sounds; as, bold, note; consonantal assonance consists in identity of sound of the same consonants; as, *ld* in bo*ld*, mi*ld*. All vowels are assonant: "Hæ omnes (vocales) sibi assonant, nec necesse est esse easdem."—Zeüss, *Grammatica Celtica*, p. 911.

Comanoa, or assonance, in Irish also has been by the bards divided into two sorts—ṛlan, *perfect*; bṛȷṛṫe, *broken*—the former is vowel assonance; the latter, consonantal. Perfect consists in the chiming of the closing terms in each line of a couplet; broken consists in their agreeing in vowels only, and not in consonants.

In comanoa bṛȷṛṫe, or consonantal assonance, it is not necessary that the consonants should be identical; it is enough that they be of the same class.

§ 310. *Classification of Assonant Consonants by Irish Bards.*

In page 39 there is a "Table of the Cognate Consonants." The consonants in the perpendicular line in that table are homorganic, or belonging to the same organ; those in the horizontal line, homogeneous, or of the same genus or class. Now, consonantal assonance only requires that they be of the same class. They are:

Common classification by linguists.
1. Tenues, or smooth, c, p, ṫ.
2. Mediæ, intermediate, ꝛ, b, ɒ.
3. Aspiratæ,ċ, ṗ (*i.e.*, f), ṫ, with the liquids l, m, n, ṛ, and the sibilant ꞅ.

11

The division by the Irish bards (see O'Molloy, p. 160; Halliday's *Irish Grammar*, p. 159, Dublin, 1808; O'Donovan, p. 416) is the following:

Classification by the Irish bards.
1. Three *soft*, i.e., smooth, c, p, т.
2. Three *mediæ*, ʒ, b, ᴆ.
3. Three *rough*, i.e., *aspiratæ*, ċ, ṗ (i.e., f), ṫ.
4. Five *strong*, or double, ll, nn, ɲɲ, ŋʒ, ɲ (nasal).
5. Seven *light* (*aspirated* mediæ and the liquids), ʒ̇, ḃ, ḋ. l, m, n, ɲ, and the sibilant r, called by them the queen of of consonants, for it is bound by no rule, nor influenced by those laws which direct the use of the other consonants.

Obs. 1. comȧnɒa bnɪrᴄᴄ requires, then, a phonetic agreement in consonants of the same class; e.g., ɲ) and ɲ (class 5), ċ and ṫ (of class 3).

The terms uaɪm and uaɪɲ } make an assonance
ɲaċ and ʒaċ

Obs 2. Perfect assonance is imperfect rhyme.

"In eâ assonantiâ, origo prima assonantiæ *finalis* est, cultæ præsertim a populis recentioribus Europæ quam dicunt rimum."—*Zeüss*. And he shows in a note that the word *rimum*, rhyme, is of Irish origin: "Quamvis ea vox computationem poëticam indicans in vetustis libris Hibernicis non occurrat, frequentissimi tamen est usus. Simplex Hibernica substantiva *rim*, inde derivatur ɲɪmɪné, *rimirć*, computator," p. 912—Zeüss.

§ 311. The fifth requisite.—*Rhyme* is, therefore, a quality of Irish verse.

Rhyme consists in the combination of *like* and *unlike* sounds; as, *told*, *bold*; the sound *old* in each of these words is like; the sounds of *t* and *b* unlike.

Rhyme is perfect or imperfect.

In *perfect* rhyme mere chime is not enough—the *accent* must fall on the chiming syllables; in *imperfect*, the accent does not fall on the chiming syllables. To couple an accented syllable with an unaccented one (as the words *fly* and speed*ily*), or two unaccented syllables (like *ty* in fligh*ty*, and *ily* in merr*ily*) is *im*perfect rhyming. In order, therefore, to form a *perfect* rhyme, the chiming syllables must be accented.

It happens very rarely that perfect rhyme is found in Irish verse. It is only whenever some very perfect assonances occur. In Irish, as in Spanish poetry, assonance was more attended to than mere rhyme.

§ 312. The sixth requisite is uaɪċno, *union, symmetry, symphony*. The term uaɪċno is applied to a hinge, because it is the sole point which unites and binds the whole hanging framework—and to a column which supports a superstructure.

From the meaning of the term, therefore, and from its use, as defined by grammarians, uaɪċno is that quality in Irish verse which fashions and frames the parts, and which imparts symmetry and symphony to the entire stanza—the charms of mould and melody to each couplet.

Hence this sixth requisite includes the two qualities known by scholars as *rhythm* and *verbal parallelism* (see Rhythm, as defined in p. 230). *Parallelism* requires that two or more terms in the second line of a couplet should form a symphony with others of the same articulate character in the first or leading line. Assonance is also employed as a subordinate kind of parallelism, or balancing of words and syllables.

"Iomuin runaó, blaté-ṡeal a bnac;
A'r a rluaṡ 'nna nṡalé-beanc ṡlec,
Séir neanóuióe caine a cneé,
'S raióe a rcoc mbennbuióe bncc."

E. O'Hussey.

In the leading couplet runaó and rluaṡ, and blaṡéṡeal and ṡalé beanc form a parallelism; in the closing couplet neanóuióe and bennbuióe another. Then cnoc (final) and rcoc, in the middle, are assonant. In like manner, bnac and ṡlec, cnoc and bnec are assonant.

The rhythmical element, like latent electric fire, permeates and combines the whole.

To illustrate this plainly, let us analyze the first stanza of that hymn composed by our countryman, Sedulius, A.D. 430, and sung in the Divine Office on the feast of Epiphany, beginning with the words *Hostis Herodes impie:*

"Hostis Herodes impie,
Christum venire quid times?
Non eripit mortalia,
Qui regna dat cælestia."

Impie and *venire*, having the same vowel sounds, form a correspondence; so do *Herodes* and *times; mortalia* and *regna* correspond; *non eripit* forms a parallel symphony with *qui regna dat; mortalia* and *cælestia* chime.

So natural was it for Irish bards to compose couplets in this strain, that many of the ballad-writers of the last century who knew only a little English "made the attempt," as Dr. Petrie remarks (*Ancient Music of Ireland*, vol. i., p. 2), " to transfer to the English language the constantly occurring assonantal or vowel rhymes of the original Irish songs." Mr. Millikin of Cork, in the song, " The Groves of Blarney," has introduced the Irish style :

"Kind sir, *be easy*, and do not *tease* me,
With your false *praises* most jestin*gly ;*
Your dissim*ulation* of invo*cation,*
Are *vaunting praises* seducing *me.*
I'm not *Aurora* nor beauteous *Flora,*" &c.

Father Prout has imitated it in his

"Bells of *Shandon*, that sound so *grand on*
The pleasant waters of the river Lee."

Every one knows how Turlough O'Carolan, in his first and only composition in English—the song on Miss Fetherston—could not avoid introducing into English versification what he practised so much in Irish :

" Though the mass was my *notion*, my *devotion* was she."

Hardiman's *Irish Minstrelsy*, vol i., p. 54.
Historical Memoirs of the Irish Bards,
by Joseph C. Walker, vol. i., p. 303.

§ 313. *Other requisites.—(a)* Rinn, or *termination*. Rinn, which means literally a pointed end, a promontory, requires that the closing terms in the second and fourth verses exceed the final words in the first and third verses of the stanza, by one syllable; so that if the last word in the first line contain only one syllable, the last word in the second line should contain two; and if the last word in the third line consist of two syllables, the ending one in the fourth must have three syllables. The first is called simply ꞃinn, or *minor ending;* the second, ꞅꞃo ꞃinn, or *major ending.*

§ 314. (*b*) Ceꞃnn, which means *head,* or an *unit,* consists in having the last word in each distich a monosyllable.

§. 315. (*c*). Ꞃmuꞃ, means *leisure, time-measure* (from ꞃm, *time*), and requires that the final words which correspond be assonantal and parasyllabic.

☞ Those just pointed out are the requisites which Gaelic bards demand that every versifier should understand and practise.

CHAPTER IV.

Ꞇán Ꞇíꞃeꞃḋ, Oꞅlꞃcꞃꞃ, Bꞃulꞃꞃꞅcc, Ꞇuoꞃꞅꞃeꞃḋ.

§ 316. Ꞇán Ꞇíꞃeꞃḋ, *i.e., direct metre,* is the principal and prevailing kind of Irish versification. In writing Ꞇán Ꞇíꞃeꞃḋ, the first six qualities just now explained must be attended to.

Its general subdivisions are—Ꞇeíbíde, ꞃéꞃdꞃꞃ, ꞃꞃꞃꞃꞃꞅcꞃḋ móꞃ, ꞃꞃꞃꞃꞃꞅcꞃḋ beꞃꞅ, Cꞃꞃbꞃꞃꞃꞃ, and ꞃꞃꞃ ꞅꞃo.

The first, called Ꞇeíbíde (from Ꞇeíbeꞃó, *to hasten*), is such a form of Ꞇán Ꞇíꞃeꞃḋ, that the last word in the second and fourth lines exceed the final word in the first and third by one syllable, *i.e.,* that the seventh requisite be perfectly carried out.

The second, called ꞃéꞃdꞃꞃ (*i.e., extending*), is the reverse of the last in ꞃꞃꞃ, having two syllables in the last word of the first and third lines, which besides must contain eight syllables; the second and fourth lines end in a word of one syllable.

Every second and fourth line rhyme, or form a perfect correspondence; and every first and third may make a perfect or imperfect one, that is, they may or may not rhyme.

Of this there are three kinds, ꞃéꞃdꞃꞃ móꞃ, ꞃéꞃdꞃꞃ coꞃcceꞃꞃꞃ, and ꞃéꞃdꞃꞃ ꞃeꞃdoꞃꞃꞃḋ. Móꞃ requires every distich to terminate—not in a monosyllable, but in a trisyllable; the coꞃcceꞃꞃꞃ is that already described; and the ꞃeꞃdoꞃꞃꞃḋ must have the first line of every couplet ending in a trisyllable.

Rꞃꞃꞃꞃꞅcꞃḋ.—This species of Ꞇán Ꞇíꞃeꞃḋ is of two kinds, called móꞃ and beꞃꞅ, or *great* and *little.*

Rꞃꞃꞃꞃꞅcꞃḋ móꞃ requires all that is necessary for Ꞇán Ꞇíꞃeꞃḋ, and is distinguished by its requiring that every line in each stanza end with a word of one syllable.

Rꞃꞃꞃꞃꞅcꞃḋ beꞃꞅ differs from this in having the last word in each line consist of two syllables.

Cꞃꞃbꞃꞃꞃꞃ is another division of Ꞇán Ꞇíꞃeꞃḋ and differs from ꞃꞃꞃꞃꞃꞅcꞃḋ beꞃꞅ, in requiring the final word of each line to be a trisyllable and not a dissyllable. There is a vulgar kind of Cꞃꞃbꞃꞃꞃꞃ, in which every line ends with a word of four syllables. This, from the weight of its head, is called *heavy-headed* carbánn. Carbánn is from car, *turning, closing,* and bainn, *coming to a* (bán) *top, i.e.,* increasing at the close of the line.

Each of these enumerated as being species of bán óineać, must have the requisites of bán óineać. Indeed, the different names seem to have been given *from a mere change* in the ending of each line or couplet.

Haliday speaks of another species of this " direct measure," called nínn ann, of which there are four kinds, in one of which—that consisting of six syllables in each line—Aengur céile Dé, or, *The Culdee,* he remarks, wrote his " Festiology."

§ 317. Oglaćar is an imitation of bán óineać. Oglaćar means *servile metre* (from oglać, *a slave*).

Because it is servile, a strict adherence to the perfections of bán óineać is not required.

Example.

Truaż rin, a leabrin biż, báin,
Tiocfaió an lá a'r buó fíon;
Déarfaió neać or cionn do cláin,
Ní maireann an lám a renfob.

> How sad it is, fair little book;
> The day shall sure arrive,
> When o'er thy page it shall be said,
> Thy author's not alive.

All the requisites for bán óineać are not here found. Still there are some—for instance, alliteration in the first and third stanzas: biż, báin; and cionn, cláin. And báin and cláin; fíon and renfob are assonant.

§ 318. Bruilngać, *fullness, plumpness* (bru and líon), requires the final term in each line to consist of three syllables.

In bruilngać the requisites of the bán óineać are not essential.

§ 319. The species of poetry called droigneać is not imitative. It is called droigneać from droigean, the *black-thorn,* on account of the difficulty attending its composition. It will admit of from nine to thirteen syllables in each line; each line must end in a word of three syllables; it must have the sixth requisite, uaiṫne, or rhythm, parallelism, and assonance; and, lastly, the final words in the lines of the closing couplet must form perfect or imperfect rhyme.

An Example of mixed oṗoiġneaċ.

Ḋuine ᵹan ainim, ccc.

I.

Iſ áluin rᵹáiṫ, ᵹaċ flaiṫ a Ṁúṁain,
Aᵹ coſaint cṙíċe ᵹaċ anḃfann,
Iſ tiſ lionta i ḃe ṁil a'ſ ḃe ḃcoin,
A'ſ fion-óiḃean ᵹaċ óiṫleoin!

II.

Iſ iomḃa ᵹuṫ a ᵹ-cláſ Laiᵹean ᵹo mean,
Steuḃ luaṫṁaſ, aᵹuſ tſeun-ḟeaſ,
Iſ óiᵹ-ḃean roineanḃa ſáiṁ ċeóil,
Ann a h-iomaḃ uaiſle a'ſ onóiſ!

III.

Ní liaċtaiḃ fuintin aᵹ faſ ain faiṫ,
Na maiᵹḃean álain, a'ſ aṅḃ-flaiṫ,
Aᵹ ᵹ-cṙioċaiḃ Ullaḃ na lann mean,
Na rᵹiaṫ, na n-eaċ, iſ na ḃ-tſéin-ḟeaſ!

IV.

Tá Connaċt molta, ḃá m-beiḃin mo ċoſḃ,
Connaċt aoiḃinn—ᵹan aon loċḃ,
Tá óiſ le faᵹail ann aᵹ luċt aiṫiſ ſann
Aᵹuſ 'ſí Connaċt cniṫneaċt Éiſeann!

[Translated from the Irish.]

I.

Each Munster chief is a beautiful flower,
The weak man's dauntless, defending power;
'Tis a land o'erflowing with honey and beoir—
It shelters and succours the poor evermore!

II.

On Leinster's plains what voices of revelry!
What fleet-footed steeds! what pillars of chivalry!
How musical, mirthful, and gentle each maiden,
Whose heart is with honour and nobleness laden.

III.

'Twere easier to reckon the leaves of the lea,
Than the beautiful maids and high chieftains that be
In Ulster! Grand home of brave steed-warriors,
Thy shields and thy quick swords are Liberty's barriers!

IV.

Fair Connacht were praised, tho' hushed in the tomb I lay;
Oh, land without fault, thou never lookest gloomily!
For the children of song, gold, and honour are therein,
And 'tis Connacht's the wheat of our green, pleasant Eriun!

Erionnach

Observe in each stanza how alliteration, assonance, uаιcηe, *i.e.*, rhythm, and parallelism—with ηηη, or the prolonging by an additional syllable the last term in a couplet (bcoιη and oιċleoιη), and rhyme, have all been observed in these verses.

§ 320. Conаċloη is a kind of versification in which the same word which ends one line begins the next. This species of verse is very ancient. The oldest specimens in the language are composed in this metre (see § 324, *infra*, p. 251).

§ 321. There are several other kinds of metre; but all may be conveniently classed under three heads, аbrаn, or *song*, bunбún, and cаoιne, *elegy* (see Hardiman's *Irish Minstrelsy*; O'Daly's *Poets and Poetry of Munster*; *Reliques of Irish Jacobite Poetry*; *Ancient Music of Ireland*, vol. i. ii. (by the Society for the preservation and publication of the ancient songs of Ireland); *The Transactions of the Royal Irish Academy*; the vols. i. to vii., published by the Ossianic Society; *Irish Melodies* by Dr. MacHale; *Irish Homer*, *ibid*; *The Language and Poetry of the Highland Clans*, by Donald Campbell, Esq.

"According to some writers," says Denis Florence M'Carthy in his introduction to *The Poets and Dramatists of Ireland*, vol. i., p. 53, " Irish poetry was as abundant in the variations of its lyric measures as the language itself was copious, flowing, and harmonious, there being anciently, according to them, one hundred varieties of verse among the Hibernian bards. On the other side it has been stated by Dr. Drummond, that in all the more ancient specimens which have reached our times, there is a great simplicity and uniformity."

From the little that has been here shown, the reader cannot but perceive what astonishing command our ancient bards had over all the sources of melody and song; and how thoroughly conversant they were with *every* kind of rhythmical elegance, and hence how utterly false, to use the language of the gifted poet whose words we have just cited, "is the opinion that attributes the introduction of rhyme to the Saracens in the ninth century."

§ 322. *The utter absence of truth in the assertion.*—How utterly opposed to historic truth is the assertion, that it is to the Saracens in the ninth century is due the introduction of that poetic quality—rhyme—into Europe, s)all be seen in the next chapter. Rhyme was known and practised in the fourth century even by Latin poets. Those from whom the writers of the

Latin hymns borrowed or learned the practice, must have known it at a much earlier period.

§ 323. In order to show the young learner how the several requisites just now explained were attended to in verse-making by the Irish poets, a few stanzas must be analyzed. A poem just now at hand, composed in the last century by Hugh MacCurtin (died 1750), the poet and historian, will serve the purpose. It is written in the leading kind of versification, called Dán díreac, and must necessarily have those qualities which have been just now enumerated and explained, and which had been by poets considered essential in that kind of poetry.

Example I.

Dán díreac

I.

A uaiṡle Éireann áilne,
A cṅú na g-céimeann comḃáiḋe,
Treiġiḋ buṙ d-ṫroimṡuan gan ón;
Céimiḋ lomluaḋ buṙ leaḃaṙ.

II.

Trom an téiḋin ṡo ṫarlaiḋ daoiḃ;
Idiṙ mnáiḃ aguṡ macaoimh,
Aṙ ṙéanaḋ ṡeanṙáḋ buṙ ṡean,
Coṁṙaḋ ṡoluiṙ buṙ rinnṙeaṙ.

[Literal translation.—Oh, ye nobles of fair Ireland—blood of the generations of friendship—fling off your deep slumber without delay; aspire to ready-reading (of) your books. (2.) Heavy has been the trance which came on you—as well on women as on the young men—in eschewing the old sayings of the sages, that language of light, from your ancestors.]

In each of the two foregoing stanzas there are seven syllables. Each line is *alliterative*—not only in part, but throughout:—Cnu, and céimeann, and comḃáiḋe. 2nd stanza.—Trom, téiḋin, and tarlaiḋ; mnáiḃ and macaoiṁ; ṙéanaḋ, ṡeanṙáḋ, and ṡean. Assonance abounds:—Éi and ea in Éireann; éi and eá in céimeann; uaiṡle and áilne; treiġiḋ and céimiḋ; troim-ṡuan and loim-luaḋ. 2nd Stanza.—Ai, in tarlaiḋ, daoiḃ, mnáiḃ, macaoiṁ, is a continued strain of assonance. The closing couplet of the second stanza is, if possible, more full of assonant beauty. The words daoiḃ and macaoiṁ rhyme. Rhythm smooths and completes the whole. Parallelism is not forgotten; as, "A uaiṡle Éireann," and "a ċnu na g-céimeann;" "treiġiḋ buṙ d-ṫrom-ṡuan," and "céimiḋ lom-luaḋ buṙ." Rinn, or the increasing by one syllable the final word over that of the line preceding it; as, ón and leaḃaṙ; ṡean and rinnṙeaṙ.

IRISH GRAMMAR.

Two Stanzas in double lines.

III.

[Irish text in Gaelic script:]

Níor ḋealḃ an ḋomán uile ; teangaíḃ is milḃe mórċuile ;

De ḃriaṫraiḃ is ḃrioċernuiṫe ḃlas ; caint is ciainṫilte

cuntur.

IV.

Aḋa tnaigteair ṫiobruiḃ an fír : Leaḃair uama a'r inir

Falaċ ḃun rgeul ní rgníor gan : Gan fíor ḃun g-céimeann coṫrom.

Literally thus—The whole world never fashioned a language sweeter or more abounding in words—of a more finely formed accent; a speech, of ancient story the faithful vehicle.

If the fountains of knowledge be dried up, books, records, and chronicles become neglected, the concealing of your history is not a small loss; nor is it small to be without a knowledge of your progenitors.

NOTE.—The strokes under the words denote alliteration; those over, assonance.

Example II.

(Taken from a collection of poems by Angus O'Daly Fionn, surnamed The Divine, died A.D. 1570.)

[Irish text:]

Na déan díomas, a ḋuine ; deimin gur fuit fíor ḃ oċt

Fogur daoiḃ, faraoir ! an t-uar ; na ḃideaḃ ḃ' a ṫaoḃ
uaḃar oit.

☞ The writer has in his possession more than twenty poems by the "divine" bard in this measure.

Example III.

St. Kiaran composed, A.D. 541, a poem on the three Marys, of which the following is the first stanza :

[Irish text:]

Sagart do ḃi, feaċt eile ; do ḃ' é ainm gan ainḟeine

Iracain an fíon-ḟlaiṫ fial ; ḃ' uairliḃ clainne Inrail.

[A priest there was, another time, to whom was the name without mistake, Isacar, the fair, freely giving-prince, of the nobles of the children of Israel.]

Example IV

§ 324. The following is taken from the second volume, p. 7, of the "Transactions of the Royal Irish Academy," a Roṙg cáċa, or martial ode, sung at the battle of Cnuca by Feargus, son of Finn (not Finn MacCumhal), and addressed to Gall, the son of Morna (A.D. 150):

Roṙg Ṡuill ṀacṀoṙna.

Ṡoill mear, mileaḋta; ceap na cṙoḋaċta,
Laiṁ fial, arṙaċta; mian na mṙaċta.
Ṁar léim lan-teinne; fṙaoċ naċ ffuaṙtaṙ
Laoċ go lán nocabnaiḋ; ṙéim an ṙiċuṙaiḃ;
Leċman luaṫaṙmaċ; a leonaḋ bioḋbaiḋ;
Toin ag tṙeun tuaṙgain, Ṡoill na ngnaṫ iarguil,
Naṙ tṙaoċ a dtṙeun taċaṙ. . . . .

Again—

Fial le filiḋiḃ; rgiṙ aiṙ cuṙaiḋiḃ,
Cioṙ aiṙ cineaḋaiḃ; ḋiṫ aiṙ danaṙaiḃ;
Flaiṫ noc fioṙ ḋiaṁuṙ; gaċ tiṙ' tṙeun leonaiḋ;
Riġ go ṙiġ ṙiaġail; feaṙ fuiġle ailgeana.

Goll, vigorous and warlike; chief of heroes;
Generous and brave of hand; the choice of chivalry.
Like the bound of full-fed flame; a blazing which cannot be quenched.
A hero in many encounters; the sway of the royal knights;
A lion rapid to the attack; disabling the foe;
Bulwark to the brave; when under blows;
Valiant hero in constant after-battles; who never yielded in a battle of the brave.

Generous to poets; rest to knights;
Tax on nations; ruin to invaders;
Prince of true tutelage; subduer of every country;
King to the king of laws; a man of firm judgments.

Example V.—Conaclon.

In this kind of versification, the same word which closes one line commences the next (§ 320, p. 247.)

Ailin ιαċ n-Ĉpeann
Ĉp mac muip moċaċ
Aḃōċaċ pliaḃ ppeaċaċ,
Speaċaċ coill cioċaċ.

[Lines by Amergin the poet-warrior, and brother of Milesius, who flourished, according to O'Flaherty's " Chronology," the year 1015 before the Christian era, A.M. 2934 (see vol. i. *Annals of the Four Masters; Transactions of the Hiberno-Celtic Society,* vol. i., p. 13, 14.]

§ 325. From those examples now furnished—drawn as they are from the best authenticated sources—it is very evident—first, that in the second, third, sixth, and subsequent centuries, the Irish bards and *filidh* composed verses in which (1) *assonance*, (2) *alliteration*, (3) *rhyme, parallelism,* were essential qualities; that versification without some of these essential requisites was never tolerated by the bards. And bearing in mind that the bardic laws and regulations were very binding, and that all the Keltic races have tenaciously adhered to the traditions and teaching of their progenitors, as Zeüss remarks— " Morum priscorum semper tenacissimi fuerint Celtici populi" (p. 915, *Grammatica Celtica*), we must infer, secondly, that the Irish *bards* and *filidh* who flourished several centuries before the Christian era, practised, as our historic annals testify, the same kind of versification which was in use in the early Christian ages. And the third conclusion to be drawn is, that which Zeüss attests—the druids and bards of Wales and Gaul practised the same kind of versification in which the bards and filidh of Eire composed their hymns and elegies.

" Apud Hibernos vetustos et Cambros constructio poeticæ orationis, in genere est *eadem.* Facile inde statui poterit, cum morum priscorum semper tenacissimi fuerint Celtici populi, etiam apud veteres Druidas et Bardos Gallicos *carminum constructionem non fuisse diversam.*"

Another inference is this, that the Keltic inhabitants of Gaul, Cambria, and Eire knew quite enough about rhyme and its use—that the Keltic bards, at least of Gaul, put that knowledge into practice two thousand years, perhaps, before the Saracens came to enlighten Europe.

CHAPTER V.

VERSIFICATION OF LATIN HYMNS.

§ 326. *Latin hymns.*—In the divine offices of the Church, the hymns sung throughout the year, and found in the Roman Breviary, are about one hundred and twenty. In the pontificate of the most holy Father, Urban VIII. (A.D. 1629), the hymns known at the time were collected and re-edited in an improved form. That collection consisted of ninety-six. Since then, more than twenty others have been added to the number, composed in honor either of saints enrolled in later years on the calendar, or in commemoration of some great event—like the victory over the Turks at Lepanto, and the unexpected and sudden triumphal return of Pope Pius VII., from his imprisonment in Sevona, to the Capital of the Christian world.

§ 327. *Their metrical character.*—Of these hymns (1) some are composed in the metre of the poetic prototypes according to which Horace and Terence wrote—(a) iambic trimeter, (b) iambic tetrameter, (c) sapphic, with a closing adonic to complete the strophé.

(2). Others have been composed irrespective of the laws of Latin versification. Their authors attended, as St. Bernard remarks, more to the sense of the words than to their classical completeness. As a matter of fact, however, the whole of this latter class, and a great many of the former, are written in verses of the same number of syllables, and adorned with the same phonetic qualities in which the bards of Keltic Gaul, of Cambria, and Eire composed.

§ 328. Composed in the manner and measure usual with the Keltic bards:—How account for this fact? Did it happen by accident? No; for nothing bearing the impress of knowledge and wisdom can happen by accident. The hymnologists must then have learned of the Keltic bards, or the Keltic bards learned of them. The latter part of this proposition cannot be admitted—chronology and facts are against it. Again, Zeüss says this form of versifying was unknown and entirely foreign to poets of classic antiquity: "Formam incognitam poetis classicæ vetustatis et *peregrinum certe.*"—*Grammatica Celtica*, p. 918.

§ 329. *Latin hymnologists.*—The hymns sung in the Church prior to the period in which Urban VIII. flourished, were composed either by (1) Irishmen, such as Sedulius, Columbanus, Columba,Secundinus; or (2) by men of Keltic origin, as St. Ambrose; or (3) those who, like St. Augustine, were of the same metrical school with St. Ambrose; or, lastly (4), those who flourished between the fourth century and the fourteenth, and followed, in the composition of hymns, the metre and the melody of the great master of hymnology, St. Ambrose.

§ 330. *The hymns written by Irishmen* —With regard to the first, they, like St. Fiach Bishop of Sletty, wrote in Irish ban ojncac, and in that species of it called réabna, which contained eight syllables, and required necessarily the employment of those requisites spoken of in p. 239. For men who understood Latin so well, that in all the ancient manuscripts we find they wrote alternately in Latin and Irish, the transition from Irish to Latin versification was quite natural and easy. When, therefore, one finds such hymns as those which Sedulius composed,

"*A solis ortu carmine,*"

And

"*Hostis Herodes impie,*"

written like the Irish odes of the time, the proof is complete that that manner of composing hymns was borrowed from the Irish bards.

§ 331. *The hymns written by St. Ambrose.*—But what of St. Ambrose, who lived in the fourth century? How did it happen that he wrote poetry like the Keltic bards? Because he was a native of Gaul (born A.D. 333, died 397), and before his conversion to Christianity he understood the manner of versifying which the bards of Keltic Gaul practised. "Non nimium audere mihi videbor, si affirmavero jam prima religionis Christianæ ætate in Gallia, eam Gallicam carminum formam in carmina Christiana translatam esse." If I should affirm now, that in the first age of the Christian religion in Gaul, that Gaulish form of composing odes was transferred to the composition of Christian hymns, it would not appear to me, says Zeüss, that I stated too much. He—and no living writer of this century knew better, or could know better—is of opinion, that the form of ode-writing in Gaul was handed over to the Christian poets of the first age of the Church. Now, of these St. Ambrose was the first and the greatest. He was the first, for although hymns were sung before his time, as we know from the evangelists' account of the night before the Passion, and from the words of St. Paul to the Colossians. nevertheless St. Ambrose is justly regarded as the first hymnologist in the Church, because he composed seventy-seven hymns of those now sanctioned by the Roman ritual, and because, as his commentator Paulinus testifies, "Hymns began first in St. Ambrose's time to be sung in the church of Milan, a devotion which continues at the present day to be practised, and which has spread throughout all the provinces of the west." "Cultus divini publici hymnis, celebrandi primus auctor fuit."—*Zeüss*. "Ambrosius plures hymnos et ipse conscripsit, adeo commendatos Ecclesiis, ut pleræque illos adoptare non dubitaverunt."—*Thesaurus Sacrorum Rituum*, by Rev. D. Bar. Gavanto, with a commentary by P. D. Merati, tom. ii., p. 105—Venetiis, 1744. St. Benedict called the hymns of the Church by the name *Ambrosiani*, for nearly all the hymns known in his time were written by the sainted bishop of Milan.

§ 332. St. Augustine and others of his time—St. Paulinus, for example, learned in the school of the great St. Ambrose.

§ 333. All the hymns of that time, whether written by St Ambrose or by the Irish missionaries, were looked upon by every hymnologist in after times as the prototypes according to which new hymns should be written.

☞ It is plainly seen, then, that all the hymns which are sung in the divine office of the Church, are moulded in the form of the Irish poetry of the earliest ages. How very few of the young ecclesiastics think of this, when reciting the hymns sung daily at prime, terce, sext, none, complin, and those at matins. lauds, and vespers.

§ 334. A few examples of Latin hymns written in the style of, and possessing the qualities required for Irish versification are here presented:

Example I.

Hymns by Caius Cœlius Sedulius.

He flourished in the middle of the fifth century. His original name was Siadal (hence the family name, Sheel). He left Ireland in early life; travelled through France, Greece, Asia, settled at Rome. He wrote commentaries in more than fifty books, on the Sacred Scriptures and on the life of our Lord. Besides the following hymns, he wrote several others not extant, and the *Carmen Paschale*, or a poetical life of our divine Lord, in four books.

| A solis | ortus cardine
| Ad | usque terræ limitem
| Christum | canamus principem
   Natum Mariá Virgine.

In this stanza, all the qualities required for composing in the metre and molody of oán bjneác are found.

Second Stanza:

Beatus auctor seculi ‖ servile corpus indu*it*
Ut carne carnem liberans ‖ ne perderet quos condid*it*.

The foregoing hymn is sung in the divine office at lauds on the festival of Christmas.

Second Stanza of the hymn *Hostis Herodes Impie.*

Ib*ant* Magi, qu*am* vider*ant* ‖ stell*am* sequentes præv*iam*,
Lum*en* requir*unt* lum*ine*: ‖ de*um* fatentur mun*ere*.

[Sung at vespers on the festival of Epiphany.]

Example II.

Take an example from the writings of St. Columbanus, the founder of the monastery of Bobio. These monosticha (or epigrams consisting of a single line) are selected from a collection of the saint's pithy sayings, copied by Zeüss, p. 920.

11.   Omnib*us* est | mundi | melior sapientia gaz*is*.
16.   Morb*i* causa mal*i* nimia est quaecunque voluptas.
52.   Inclita | perpetu*am* | præstat | patientia | vit*am*.
88.   Quod tib*i* non | optas | al*ii* ne feceris | ull*i*.
100. | Disce sed à | doct*is*, | indoct*os* | ipse | doceto.
102. | Sermo datur mult*is*, animi | sapientia pauc*is*.
159. Alma | di*es* noctem sequitur sic | dona labor*es*.
165. Qui | modica spern*it* | minu*it* | majora per horas.
170. | Cui secreta | quidem | credas | cautissime cerne.

₊ Assonance is shown by the italics; alliteration, by means of the perpendicular strokes.

Internal assonance is plainly seen in the following lines, by the same author.

59.   T*antum* | verba | val*ent* quant*um* m*ens* s*ent*iat illa.
61.   Non erit | *anti*quo nov*us* | *ante*ferendus amic*us*.

In the following, assonance between the radical parts of the words—so peculiarly Irish—is observed:

128. | Semper in ore tuo re- | sonent bona verba | salutis.
174. Ob- | servat | sapiens | sibi tempus in ore loquendi.
175. In- | sipiens loquitur | spretum | sine tempore verbum.

The foregoing monosticha of St. Columbanus are not only assonant and alliterative, but are withal composed in heroic hexameter.

Example III.

The following is from Secundinus, or Seaċnall, anotherIrish saint, the son of Darerca, the sister of St. Patrick, and therefore the nephew of our glorious Apostle. The hymn written in his honour, is not in hexameter; it is after the Irish models, and accordingly abounds in assonance and alliteration.

See *Book of Hymns*, part i.. p. 44, edited by Dr. Todd, and published for the Irish Archælogical and Celtic Society—Dublin, 1855. Vide Vitam S. Patricii apud Boll.

| Audite | omnes | amantes || Deum sancta merita.
Viri in Christo beati   Patrici episcopi.
  Quomodo bonum ob actum ˌ similatur angelis.
  Perfectamque propter vitam ⁞ æquatur apostolis.

Example IV.

The most wonderful specimen of this kind of versification, abounding in assonance and alliteration, and not constructed with any regard at all to the usual Latin metre of the prosodical prototypes of the Roman poets, is the Catholic carmen of St. Augustine, written against the Donatists of his time. Everyone knows that the great doctor of the Church was bishop of Hippo, in Africa, and had been, before he embraced the Catholic faith, for many years professor of rhetoric at Milan. On the occasion of his conversion, St. Ambrose and he composed the celebrated canticle, " *Te Deum Laudamus*." Subsequently he composed the following. He died A.D. 430. Each line or verse is composed of two members, each consisting, like that species of Irish ḃán ḋíneaċ called réaḃṅa, of eight syllables (see p. 244.)

The following *strophé* is taken from the works of St. Augustine, printed at Lyons, 1586.

Abundantia peccatorum || solet fratres conturbare ;
Propter hac dominus noster ⁞ voluit nos premonere,
Comparans regna cælorum ⁞ reticulo misso in mare,
Congregante multos pisces, omne genus hinc et inde.
Quos cum traxissent ad litus, ⁞ tunc cooperunt separare,
Bonos in vasa miserunt, ⁞ reliquos malos in mare.
Quisquis recolit evangelium, ⁞ recognoscat cum timore,
  Videt reticulum ecclesiam, ˌ videt hoc sæculum mare,
  Genus autem mixtum pisces ⁞ justus est cum peccatore.
  Sæculi finis est litus, ˌ tunc est tempus separare,
  Quando retia ruperunt, ˌ multum dilexerunt mare.
Vasa sunt sedes sanctorum, quo non possunt pervenire.

The entire piece consists of twenty strophes, consisting like the foregoing of twelve double lines

On this Zeüss makes the following remark : " Magis inauditam formam offert, novam quasi terram aperit novumque ævum annuntiat psalmus abecedarius S. Augustini—The abecedarian psalm of St. Augustine presents a more unheard of form, opens, as it were, new ground, and proclaims a new era in the annals of verse-making."

Example V.

The following is one of the many which St. Ambrose wrote. It is sung at matius in the office of Monday (feria secunda) :

| Somno refect*is* artub*us* ‖ spreto cubili surg*imus*,
Nobis | pater, canentib*us* ‖ adesse te deposc*imus*.
*T*e lingua primam concin*at*, ‖ *te* mentis ardor ambi*at*,
Ut actu*um* sequent*ium* ‖ tu, sancte, sis exord*ium*.

It is true that it is an iambic tetrameter—a metre consisting in each hemestich, as it now stands, of four feet, chiefly iambics, or eight-syllable measure. In it, however, are carefully wrought all the required artificial elegancies which the Keltic bards deemed essential in versifying. "Assonantia etiam vetusta *Hibernica* induta sunt," says Zeüss.

In the same metre, and with the same assonant qualities, are composed most of the hymns which St. Ambrose wrote; these, for example, recited at prime—" Jam lucis orto sidere ;" at terce—" Nunc sancte nobis spiritus ;" sext—" Rector potens, verax Deus ; at none—Verum Deus tenax vigor."

Example VI.

From the poetic pieces of Aldhelm, bishop of the Western Saxons (A.D. 709) :

| Summi | satoris | so*lia* ‖ sedit qui per cathr*alia*
| Alti | olympi | arc*ibus* ‖ obvallatus min*acibus*
| Cuncta | cernens | cac*umine* ‖ cœlorum summo lu-
mine.

Again—

| Vale, | vale, | fidiss*ime* ‖ phile Christi cariss*ime*
| Quem in | cordis | cub*iculo* ‖ cingo amoris v*inculo*.

The assonance occurs in two or more syllables in each half line ; as, *arcibus, minacibus, cacumine, lumine, fidissime, carissime*—a form very usual in Irish metre. Observe, too, that the Latin metre and quantity are in this sixth example entirely overlooked.

Example VII.

But that noble piece by St. Thomas Aquinas (born 1227, died 1275), sung in the mass of this day (feast of Corpus Christi, 1864), is by far the most magnificent of all—full of celestial solemnity, and sonorous with all the phonetic forms which can charm the ear or affect the heart.

1. Lauda, Sion, salvat*orem*:
 Lauda ducem et past*orem*,
    In hymnis et cant*icis*.

2. Quantum potes, tantum *aude;*
 Quia major omni *laude*,
    Nec laudare suff*icis*.

11. Dogma datur christi*anis*,
 Quod in carnem transit p*anis*,
    Et vinum in sang*uinem*.

12. Quod non capis, quod non v*ides*,
 Animosa firmat f*ides*,
    Præter rerum or*dinem*.

23. Bone pastor, panis v*éré*,
 Jesu, nostri miser*ére;*
    Tu nos bona, fac vid*ére*
    In terra viventium.

*** The other hymns of which St. Thomas was the author, embrace, though not composed in the same kind of metre, all the qualities of the ancient Irish poetry.

The splendid hymn which is the admiration of all—the " *Stabat Mater Dolorosa*"—written in the fourteenth century, as is commonly supposed, by the blessed Jacopone di Todi, is wrought in the same rhythmical mould as the *Lauda Sion*.

Thomas Celano, the friend and disciple of St. Francis (beginning of the thirteenth century), and the now acknowledged author of the incomparable *Dies Iræ*, composed a hymn, of which the following is the first strophé, in honour of the seraphic saint (see the other twenty-nine stanzas in the copy of the *Rambler* for November, 1853):

Fregit victor virtualis, hic Franciscus triumphal*is*,
    Crucis adversarium :
Crucis lator cordial*is*, princeps *pugnæ* spirital*is*,
    Insignis amantium.

This hymn had been for a long time lost, " but has been lately," says the *Rambler* of November, 1853, p. 357, "published in the *Sequentiæ Ineditæ* of the Ecclesiological Society. It was found in a small octavo MS., of date about 1400, in the National Library at Lisbon."

APPENDIX I.

The annexed specimens of the Irish language from the fifth to the seventeenth centuries, selected from authentic works, published either by individuals whose names are illustrious in Irish literature, or under the direction of learned and patriotic bodies, such as *The Archæological and Celtic Society*, will serve to show what changes the language has undergone from the days of St. Patrick to the present time.

The first specimen, which has been selected, with the author's kind permission, from Dr. Petrie's work (*History and Antiquities of Tara Hill*, p. 33), is the hymn composed by our Apostle on Easter Saturday, A.D. 433, on his way from Slane to the royal palace of Leogaire, at Tara, with seven clerical companions and the youthful St. Benignus, to shield himself and them against the wiles and plots of the druids and assassins appointed to compass their destruction.

"Tunc vir sanctus composuit illum Hymnum patrio idiomate conscriptum, qui vulgò *Feth-fiadha*, et ab aliis *lorica* Patricii appellatur; et in summo abinde inter Hibernos habetur prætio; quia creditur, et multa experientiâ probatur, piè recitantes ab imminentibus animæ, et corporis præservare periculis." Colgan—*Septima Vita Tripartita S. Patricii*, par. i., cap. lx., Tr. Th. p. 126.

The Irish version furnished by Dr. Petrie, and published in the first edition of the *College Grammar*, is in the *Bearla Feine*, an old form of the language in which, for instance, the Brehon laws are written. In the present edition the old form is excluded, for it can be found by the curious in Dr. Petrie's work; the modern version is considered preferable.

A modern-Irish version of it, with an English poetical translation by J. Clarence Mangan, is here given for the benefit of many who may wish to see it either in modern Irish, or in an English *poetical* dress. The poetical version, taken from *Duffy's Magazine*, is extremely literal, yet lighted up with the same devotional glow that pervades the original.

The same protecting power which, according to St. Evan, who flourished in the sixth century, this hymn was known to possess in and before his time, is with reason ascribed to it even to this day. "The *Luireach Phadruig*," says Dr. Petrie, "is still remembered popularly in many parts of Ireland, and a portion of it is to this day repeated by the people usually at bed-time."

An instance of this popular devotion towards our holy Apostle came under my own notice in the year 1848, when a peasant from my native parish, who was preparing with his family to go to America, asked me to procure for him, if possible, a copy of St. Patrick's hymn. How exactly this practice accords with the words read in the *Book of Armagh* (which, according to Dr. Graves, was written A.D. 807), transcribed from "Tirechan's Annotations on the Saint's Life, written in the seventh century."—*Canticum* ejus *Scotticum* semper canere, *Book of Armagh*, fol. 16. p. a, col. 1. See Dr. Petrie's *History and Antiquities of Tara Hill*, and the *Liber Hymnorum, Fasciculus*, i. p. 50.

21 ɒ-Ceaṁpaiʒ a ḃ-ɔiu atċuiŋʒim ṅeapc cṙeuṅ ṅa Cṅionóiɒe,

APPENDIX.

Creidim 'sa Tríonóid faoi aondacht Chrutuighteoir na n-dúl.

A d-Teampall a n-diu, neart Zeine Chríost go n-a baisde; neart a ceusda go n-a adhnacal; neart a eiseirghe go n-a dear-gabáil; neart a teachta chum an bhreithearhnair deighéanaigh liom.

A d-Teampall a n-diu, neart grádh Serapim; an neart atá ann umhalóid na n-aingeal; ann dóchur eiseirghe chum luach-saothair; ann urnaighthibh na n-uasal aithreach; a d-tairngirteacht fáidheadh; ann seanmóintibh na n-apstal; a g-creideamh na g-coinfeoiridh; a n-geanmnuidheacht naoṁ-ṁaighdean: ann gníoṁartaibh fíreun.

A d-Teampall a n-diu neart neiṁe; soillse gréine; gilleacht sneachta; brígh teinidh; déinneacht larrach; luaite gaoite; doiṁneacht mara; taisisceam talṁan; cruaidheacht carraigeach:

A d-Teampall a n-diu, neart Dé do m' threórughadh; cúṁacta Dé do m' congbháil; eagna Dé do m' ṁúineadh; rúil Dé do m' roiṁ-feacain; cluas Dé do m' eisdeacht; briathar De do m' úrlabhradh; láṁ Dé do m' choimirceadh; slighe Dé do m' reṁrúghadh; sgiath Dé do m' dídin; sluagh Dé do m' anacal ar inleogaibh deaṁon; air cathuighib dubailceadh; air droichtoil na h-aigne; air gach duine a smuainigear droghbáil dam a b-fogar nó a g-céin; an aonar nó a g-cuideachta.

Cuirim a m' timcheall na h-uile neart so, ann agaid gach neart naṁaideach, eadtrócaireach fuirighte do m' chur agus do m' anam; a n-agaid tinceartla saobh-faid; a n-agaid dubh-dlighte pagantachta; a n-agaid saobh-reachta eiriceachta; a n-agaid gach colair a dallar anam an duine.

Críost dom' choimirceadh a n-diu air nith; air lorcadh; air báthadh; air guin nó go d-tuillfeadh mórán luachsaothair. Críost liom; Críost romham; Críost a' m' dhiadh; Críost ionnam; Críost foram; Críost uaram; Críost dearam; Críost tuatham; Críost do 'n taobh so; Críost do 'n taobh rin; Críost do m' cúl; Críost a g-croidhe gach duine le a labhraim; Críost a m-beul gach aon a labhras liom; Críost ann gach súil a dhearcar orm; Críost ann gach cluais a chluinear mé.

A d-Teampaiġ a n-oiu aċċuingim neaṗc cpeun na Tpionoide: Cpeidim ṗa Tpionóid ṗaoi aondaċc Cpucuiġċeoṁa na n-dul.

Domini ert ṗalur, Domini ert ṗalur, Chṗirti ert ṗalur, ṗalur, tua, Domine, rit rempeṗ nobircum. Amen.

ST. PATRICK'S HYMN BEFORE TARA.
(From the original Irish).

I.
At Tara to-day, in this awful hour,
   I call on the Holy Trinity!
Glory to him who reigneth in power,
The God of the elements, Father and Son,
And Paraclete Spirit, which Three are the One,
   The everlasting Divinity!

II.
At Tara to-day, I call on the Lord,
On Christ the Omnipotent Word,
Who came to redeem from death and sin,
    Our fallen race;
    And I put and I place
The virtue that lieth in
    His incarnation lowly,
    His baptism pure and holy,
His life of toil, and tears, and affliction,
His dolorous death—His crucifixion,
His burial, sacred, and sad, and lone,
   His resurrection to life again,
His glorious ascension to heaven's high throne,
And, lastly, His future dread,
   And terrible coming to judge all men—
Both the living and dead. . . .

III.
At Tara to-day, I put and I place
   The virtue that dwells in the seraphim's love;
And the virtue and grace
    That are in the obedience
    And unshaken allegiance
Of all the archangels and angels above;
And in the hope of the resurrection
To everlasting reward and election;
And in the prayers of the fathers of old;
And in the truths the prophets foretold;
And in the Apostles' manifold preaching;
And in the confessors' faith and teaching;
And in the purity ever dwelling
   Within the Immaculate Virgin's breast;
And in the actions bright and excelling
   Of all good men, the just and the best.

IV.

At Tara to-day, in this fateful hour,
I place all heaven with its power,
And the sun with its brightness,
And the snow with its whiteness,
And fire with all the strength it hath,
And lightning with its rapid wrath,
And the winds with their swiftness along their path,
And the sea with its deepness,
And the rocks with their steepness,
And the earth with its starkness—
    All these I place,
    By God's almighty help and grace,
Between myself and the powers of darkness.

V.

    At Tara, to-day,
    May God be my stay!
May the strength of God now nerve me!
May the power of God preserve me!
May God the Almighty be near me!
May God the Almighty espy me!
May God the Almighty hear me!
    May God give me eloquent speech.
May the arm of God protect me!
May the wisdom of God protect me!
    May God give me power to teach and to preach!
May the shield of God defend me,
May the host of God attend me,
    And ward me,
    And guard me
Against the wiles of demons and devils;
Against the temptations of vice and evils;
Against the bad passions and wrathful will
    Of the reckless mind and the wicked heart
Against every man that designs me ill,
    Whether leagued with others, or plotting apart.

VI.

    In this hour of hours,
    I place all those powers
Between myself and every foe
    Who threatens my body and soul
    With danger or dole;
To protect me against the evils that flow
From lying soothsayers' incantations;
From the gloomy laws of the gentile nations;
From heresy's hateful innovations;
From idolatry's rites and invocations.

> By these my defenders,
>> My guards against every ban—
> And spells of smiths, and druids, and women;
>> In fine, against every knowledge that renders
> The light heaven sends us, dim in
>> The spirit and soul of man!

VII.

> May Christ, I pray,
> Protect me to-day,
>> Against poison and fire—
> Against drowning and wounding;
> That so in his grace abounding,
>> I may earn the preacher's hire.

VIII.

> Christ, as a light,
>> Illumine and guide me;
> Christ, as a shield, o'ershadow and cover me;
> Christ be under me; Christ be over me;
>> Christ be beside me—
> On left hand and right;
> Christ be before me, behind me, about me;
> Christ, this day, be within and without me!

IX.

> Christ, the lowly and meek,
>> Christ, the all-powerful, be
> In the heart of each to whom I speak,
>> In the mouth of each who speaks to me—
>> In all who draw near me,
>> Or see me, or hear me.

X.

> At Tara to-day, in this awful hour,
> I call on the Holy Trinity;
> Glory to Him who reigneth in power,
> The God of the elements, Father and Son,
> And Paraclete Spirit, which Three are the one,
>> The everlasting Divinity!

XI.

> Salvation dwells with the Lord,
> With Christ the Omnipotent Word,
> From generation to generation;
> Grant us, O Lord, thy grace and salvation.—J.C.M.

The following extract is from the preface in the *Lealhar Breac* to the hymn composed by St. Sechnall, or Secundinus, in honour of St. Patrick. According to the Rev. Dr. Todd (*Book of Hymns*, part i., p. 44), it "is supposed by the best Irish scholars, judging from its language and style, to be a composition of about the seventh or eighth century." This preface is found in the published *Fasciculus* (p. 31) of the Leabap Imuinn, as edited (Dublin, 1855) by the learned doctor for the *Irish Archæological and Celtic Society*, as a historical commentary on the first hymn.

APPENDIX.

II.—Ir ann rin arbept an t-aingel fria Patraic, bid latra rin uile. Do ronrat cra ric anrin, Patraic ⁊ Sechnall, ⁊ cen batan [ac] tiactain timchell na relgi ro chualutan clair aingel oc cantain immon jobairit ir in eclair, ⁊ irred ro canrat in n-immon bia ban torrach:—

"Sancti uenite Chpirti conpur," etc. Conid o rein

Then the Angel said to Patrick: "All these shall be thine." They made peace then, Patrick and Sechnall. And as they were going round the cemetery,(a) they heard a choir of angels chanting a hymn at the Offertory in the church, and what they chanted was the hymn whose beginning is:

Sancti venite, Christi corpus, &c.(b) So that from

(a) That is, at Sechnall's place—the church of Dunshaughlin, near Maynooth.

(b) The hymn is entitled, *Hymnus quando communicarent Sacerdotes*, and is as follows:

Sancti venite,
   Christi corpus sumite;
   Sanctum bibentes,
   Quo redempti sanguinem.

Salvati Christi,
   Corpore et sanguine,
   A quo refecti,
   Laudes dicamus Deo.

Hoc sacramento,
   Corporis et sanguinis,
   Omnes exuti,
   Ab inferni faucibus.

Dator Salutis,
   Christus filius Dei,
   Mundum salvavit,
   Per crucem et sanguinem.

Pro universis,
   Immolatus Dominus,
   Ipse Sacerdos,
   Existit et hostia.

Lege preceptum,
   Immolari hostias,

Quæ adumbrantur,
   Divina mysteria.

Lucis indultor,
   Et salvator omnium,
   Præclaram sanctis,
   Largitus est gratiam.

Accedant omnes,
   Pura mente creduli,
   Sumant eternam,
   Salutis custodiam.

Sanctorum custos,
   Rector quoque Dominus
   Vitæ perennis,
   Largitur credentibus.

Cælestem panem,
   Dat esurientibus,
   De fonte vivo.
   Præbet sitientibus.

Alpha et omega,
   Ipse Christus Dominus,
   Venit, venturus
   Judicare homines.

ille cantain in Erinn in imunro in tan tiazan do chuinn Cairt.

Ocur no faid Patraic iar rin Sechnall co Róim for cend neich do thairrib Poil ⁊ Petair ⁊ martire aile, ar in cuiracud do pat fair, ⁊ ite rin cairre filet in Ard Macha h-i rcrin Poil ⁊ Petair.

O ru rcaich tra do Sechnall in molud-ra do denam, luid dia tairpenad do Patraic. In tan no riact Sechnall co Patraic arbert friss, Molad do digner dia anaile mac bethad. Ir ail dam etrect duictiu friss. Arbert Patraic, mochen molad fir muintire De. Iro tra torrach do pat Sechnall for a immon .i. beata Christi curtodis, ar na no tucad Patraic [dia aine] cia dia n-dernad in t-immon co tairced a zabail.

that time to the present, the hymn is chanted in Erinn when the Body of Christ is received.

And Patrick, after this, sent Sechnall to Rome for portions of the relics of Paul and Peter, and other martyrs, in consequence of the accusation he had made against him. And these are the relics which are now in Ardmacha, in the shrine of Paul and Peter.

Now, when Sechnall had finished this hymn, he went to show it to Patrick; and when he had reached Patrick, he said to him, "I have composed a hymn in honour of a certain Child of Life—I wish that thou wouldst listen to it." Patrick answered, "I welcome the praise of a man of the people of God." But the beginning that Sechnall gave to the hymn was, *Beata Christi Custodit*, in order that Patrick should not know in whose honour the hymn was made, until he had finished it.

Obs. In this hymn (*Sancti Venite*), the first and third lines consist of five syllables; the third and fourth of seven; or in double lines—the first member of five, the latter of seven syllables. It has all the qualities which in Irish poetry the *filidhe* considered essential.

Its authenticity is undoubted. It is therefore a proof of the Catholic faith and piety of the Christians of the early Irish Church.

*** It was published in the first edition of this work in 1856.

The six following verses were composed in the seventh century by St. Colman O'Clusaich, tutor of St. Cummine Foda, A.D. 661. See O'Reilly's

"Catalogue of Irish Writers," p. 45; also "The Book of Hymns," part i., p. 86. This selection is made from the "Four Masters," translated by Dr. O'Donovan, vol. i., p. 272; Dublin, Hodges and Smith:

III.—Aoir Criost, ré céd perccat a haon. An caicceaḋ bliaḋain do Ḋiarmaic ⁊ Blaṫmac. S. Cummine Foda, mac Fiaċna, epscop Cluana Feapta Breanoinn, décc in dapa la dég do Nouember. Colman Ua Claraiġ, oide Cummine, ro raiḋ na roinn ri:

"Ni bein Luimnech ror a druim: de ril Muimnech il Leṫ Cuinn,

Marban in noi ba riú do: do Cummine mac Fiaċno. Ma do ceiġeaḋ neaċ tan muir: reireaḋ hi ruiḋe n-Griġair, Maḋ a ḣEri di bui dó, inse Cumine Foda.
Mo ċuṁa-sa iar cCumine, on lo ro foilseḋ a arċ; Coi mocuil nir ninġaireaḋ: dond ġaill iar ndeanaċ a bapc."

The age of Christ, 661. The fifth year of Diarmaid and Blatmac. St. Cummine Foda, son of Fiachna, bishop of Cluainfearta Breanain (Clonfert), died on the 12th day of November. Colman Ua Cluasaigh, the tutor of Cummine, composed these verses:

The Luimneach did not bear on its bosom of the race of Munster, into
 Leath Cuinn,
A corpse in a boat so precious as he. as Cummine, son of Fiachna.
If any one went across the sea to sojourn at the seat of Gregory (Rome),
If from Ireland, he requires no more than the mention of Cumine Foda.
I sorrow after Cumine; from the day that his shrine was covered
My eyelids have been dropping tears;
I have not laughed, but mourned since the lamentation at his barque.

The following extract is taken from "The Irish Charters in the Book of Kells," translated by Dr. O'Donovan, and published (1846) in a copy of *The Miscellany of the Irish Archæological Society*. The learned translator says that the "splendid MS. of the Gospels, called the "Book of Kells," preserved in the Library of Trinity College, Dublin, was, there is every reason to believe, executed in the time of St. Columhkille. The existence of the charters which have been copied into it, is sufficient to connect it with the Monastery of Kells; and that it was in existence there in the year 1006, and then regarded as one of the most splendid relics of the western world, will appear from the annals of Ulster under that year." He then quotes the annals of Ulster, and of the Four Masters.

From internal evidence even, it is manifest that it was written before the tenth century:

IV.—Do raine cille delga inro.

Feċtar táinic Conchobor ua Maelseċlainn do riċnaḋa ui Aeḋa .i. nia ġilla coloim. . . . coaltan ce-

nanora co tapat comanba colaim cille (.i. maelmoire ua
Uchtan) co na ramud ┐ co na minnaib . . . noct
chommaince rrui, ┐ conarriagaib roir a muin do altoir
coluim cille ┐ conarnuc leir co ler luigdech ┐ co nor
dall ir in glind ni dun meic cennan a ndes. Conid i
cinaid in trapaigthe rein do rat concobor ua mael-
reclaind cill delga co na crich ┐ co na rerund do dia
┐ do culum cille co brat cen cir cen cobac cen rect
cen luaged cen coinnim rig na toirig ruirri man . . .
ba naeimi ar ni laimed tairec a tadall etir cein no
bai i cric. Ocur a teat ro inna commaince ┐ inna
rlana do rata and .i. amalgaid comanba patraic co
mbachaill iru ┐ comanbu rinnen ┐ comanba ciaran
cona minnaib o cleirceib, ni inorra telca aipod .i. oen-
gur ua caine bain, ┐ ni telca cail .i. maelisu mac
cointen, ┐ ni maige laca .i. gilla grigur ua dummaigc,
┐ ni tuat luigne .i. laidgnen mac maelan, o laecaib, ┐
mor ingen meic concobair ind rigan cen nach nathcor
na commaince ren co brat.] riadnaire reir mide eter
laecu ┐ cleirciu do rata na rlana rein ┐ na commaince,
┐ tucrat uile etcr laecu ┐ bleirciu a mbennactain do
cac rig na tairigad dar in raire rein co brat, ┐ tucrat
uile a mallactain do cac rig do roired tairir rein. ┐
gid guaract do cac ni rariugad coluim cille ir guarac-
tuca do rig tempach, uair ir bratair he do columcille.

OF THE FREEDOM OF CILL DELGA.*

One time that Conchobhar O'Maelsechlainn came to a peaceful conference with the grandson of Aedh (*i.e.*, Gilla Columb . . . alumnus of Kells), so that the comharba of Columbkille (*i.e.*, Maelmuire O'Uchtain), with his congregation and reliques . . came to give them protection. But he (Conchobhar) took him (Gilla Columb), on his back from the altar of Columb-kille, and carried him to Les-Luigdech, and deprived him of sight in the valley which is to the south of Dun-mic-cennan. It was in atonement for this violation that Conchobhar O'Maelsechlinn gave Cill-delga with its terri-tory and lands to God and to Columbkille for ever, as king or chieftain having rent, tribute, hosting, coigny, or any other claim on it as . . before, for no chief durst touch it while (staying) in the territory. Now these were the

---

* "*Cill delga*, now Kildalkey, a parish situate in the west of the town of Trim, in the barony of Lune, or Luighne, and county of Meath, where the festival of the celebrated virgin, St. Damhnat or Dympna, is still celebrated on the 15th May."

APPENDIX.

sureties and guarantees given in it viz., Amalgaidh, Comharba of Patrick, with the staff of Jesus ; the Comharba of Finnen ; the Comharba of Ciaran, with his reliques of the clergy ; also the King of Telach-ardd, Oengus O'Cainelbain ; the King of Telach-Cail, Mael Isu Mac Cairthen ; the king of Magh Locha, Gilla-Griguir O'Dummaig; the King of Tuath Luigne, Laignen Mac Moelain, of the laity ; and also the Queen Mor, the daughter of the son of Conchobhar, without any revocation of this for ever. In the presence of the men of Meath, both clergy and laity, these sureties and guarantees were given ; and they all, both laity and clergy, gave their blessing to every king who should not violate this freedom for ever ; and though it is dangerous for every king to violate Columbkille, it is particularly dangerous to the king of Tara, for he is the relative of Columbkille.

The next is a specimen of the language as it was written and spoken in the tenth century. It is taken from the "Annals of the Four Masters," vol. i., p. 619. Dublin, Hodges and Smith, 104 Grafton-street, 1851.

V.—Aoir Chiort, naoi cceb, ᵹice a ré. An naomhaḋ bliaḋan do Ḋonncaḋ. Baoiṫhine, abb Binnae, Fionn-acta, abb Corcaiġe, ceand piaġla eirmoiri Ereann, Ciaran, abb Achaiḋ bó Caindiġh, Celedabail, mac Scannail, do ḋol co Rómh dia ailiṫre a haḋdaine Beandcain, ⁊ atbert na painnri* occ imteċt dó :

Aiṫiġ dámhra tairir do ṫriall o ċorhaiḃ teaġlaiġ,
Do arccnamh imin ailiṫer, tar tuinn mara muaiḋ mean-
   mnaiġ.
Aiṫiġ anaḋ dinntlaḋaḋ collna co lion a caine,
Aiṫiġ iaram imriaḋaḋ co ro ᵹiṡċ Aiac móir Aaine.
Aiṫiġ arccnamh rualac, ráltnaḋ ror toil co tneamhon,
Aiṫiġ ᵹreiteach ndualcha, aġur derna ᵹri deamhon,
Aiṫiġ corp do ċairiuccaḋ, daiġ ira cion ion brena,
Aiṫiġ ᵹorr iar ttairirniud airm ⁊ ttelcomir ar ndéra
Aiṫiġ rocuil tiġlaiṫi, terḃaḋ ᵹri ġuniri ġnáta,
Aiṫiġ omhan iudnaiḋe tneara luain láiṫe bráṫa.
Aiṫiġ lámh corp creḋḃaiḋe, cortaḋ im ċriaḃaiḋ nġlinne,
Aiṫiġ reic na neariċriaiḋe ar ṫir na ᵹlaṫa ᵹinne.
Aiṫiġ lámh ᵹri turḃaiḋe domhnain ce cétaiḃ caingean,
Aiṫiġ ġner ᵹri hirnaiġe, icc aḋraḋ airdriġ ainġeal.
Act inġe di aen bliaḋain, ni ċearta dom tri ᵹiċte.
Airiream ro naomh riaġail in raċ maiġin ba nicṫiġ.

---

* It is worthy of remark that the rhyming in these stanzas is quite as perfect as any that can be found in modern English poetry.

APPENDIX.

Ní maparr mo comaeirri, biccir fiú cpábaió cpichió,
Auaó do piot pó baoirri inuac maigín bá miéig.
Bá liach Copbmac cuipeadach zaeze zo rleagaib riéib,
Iodreaécach muaó, Maipeadach, Maonach, Maol molb-
éaé miéhig.

Literal Translation.

The age of Christ, 926. The ninth year of Donnchadh. Baeithine, abbot of Birra; Finnachta, abbot of Corcach, head of the regulars of the most of Ireland; Ciaran, abbot Achadhbo-cainnigh; Celedabhaill, son of Scannal, went to Rome on his pilgrimage from the abbacy of Beannchair; and he composed these quatrains at his departure:

> Time for me to prepare to pass from the shelter of a habitation:
> To journey as a pilgrim over the surface of the noble, lively sea.
> Time to depart from the snares of the flesh, with all its guilt.
> Time now to ruminate how I may find the Great Son of Mary.
> Time to seek virtue, to trample upon the will with sorrow.
> Time to reject vices, and to renounce the demon.
> Time to reproach the body, for, of its crime it is putrid.
> Time to rest after we have reached the place wherein we may shed our tears.
> Time to talk of the last day, to separate from familiar faces.
> Time to dread the terrors of the tumults of the day of judgment.
> Time to defy the clayey body, to reduce it to religious rule.
> Time to barter the transitory things, for the country of the kingdom of heaven.
> Time to defy the ease of the little earthly world of a hundred pleasures.
> Time to work at prayer, in adoration of the High King of angels.
> But only a part of one year is wanting of my three score.
> To remain under holy rule in one place, it is time.
> Those of my own age are not living, who were given to ardent devotion:
> To desist from the course of great folly in one place, it is time.
> It was grievous that Cormac the hospitable was wounded with long lances,
> Indreachtach the noble, Muireadhach, Maenach, the great Maelmithigh.

LAY OF CALADABHAILL, SON OF SCANNAL.

On his starting as a pilgrim for Rome, A.D. 926.

> The time is come, I am doomed to part
>   From the land that is dear to me;
> From the home that is wreathed round my heart
>   I must cross o'er the level sea,
> In a pilgrim's guise I must rise and start
>   O'er the waves of the deep, green sea.
>
> It is time I should fly from the ills of life,
>   From its guilt and its deep laid snares,
> That I leave behind me the wretched strife,
>   That I part with its thousand cares,
> To seek the shelter of Mary's Son,
>   And the heavenly smile He wears.

To trample down on the worldly will
    That is wedded to earthly lore ;
To turn my back on the golden strand,
    Of that bright, mammonic shore ;
Till I find the home in which virtue reigns,
    And dwell there for evermore.

I will weep for the days that for aye are fled—
    I will weep them with sea-salt tears,
Till my heart is sore with the floods it shed,
    As if pierced by a thousand spears ;
Till my soul is sad and my eyes are red,
    I will weep for my mis-spent years.

I will muse on the awful day of the Lord—
    That day of doom and dole,
When the earth shall quake and the hills shall shake,
    And the mighty trumpet roll ;
When the sun shall fail and the sky shall pale,
    And shrink like a blazing scroll.

It is time to look towards the spirit land,
    Where bliss ever reigns supreme—
Where the golden gates of that city stand,
    Whose walls are of diamond gleam ;
'Cross the bridge of death, which the Lord hath spanned,
    Over life's ever-rolling stream.

It is time to pray, for we know not when
    There cometh that night of gloom,
When the hopes, and the cares, and the crimes of men,
    Shall be wrapped in a shroud of doom ;
When the pride of rank will be grimly caged
    By the bars of the lampless tomb.

My thread of life has been kindly spun,
    And my hair is as white as snow ;
Three-score years of my time have run—
    Ah ; they flash like a lightning glow,
O'er the darkened face of the noonday sun,
    For I spent them in reckless woe.

Oh ! friends of my heart, and my youth's compeers,
    Whom I'll bless with my latest breath,
You have passed, alas ! thro' the gate of tears,
    You are cold in the clasp of Death—
Cut down by the blade of that mighty chief,
    The reaper whose name is Death.

APPENDIX.

Cormac, the chieftain, whose heart and hall
To the world were opened wide,
Indreactach the noble in fight did fall,
With a lance in your gaping side;
Muireadhach, Maenach, the great Maelmithigh,
God grant that with Him ye bide.

So my time is come, and, alas! I part
From the hills that are dear to me;
From the flowers that are planted within my heart,
I must cross o'er the dancing sea:
Like a lonely palmer, I rise and start
O'er the waves of the ridgy sea.

Boz.

The following short poem was written about the middle of the sixteenth century by Angus O'Daly Fionn, surnamed the Divine. He composed many religious pieces, twenty-eight of which are now in a collection of poems transcribed by Professor Eugene O'Curry for the late Rev. Matthew Kelly, D.D., Professor, St. Patrick's College, Maynooth, from whose MS. these stanzas have been copied. For a short account of this writer, and the poems he has left, see "Transactions of the Iberno-Celtic Society for 1820," vol. i., part i., p. cxl; "A Chronological Account of Irish Writers," by Edward O'Reilly, author of the "Irish-English Dictionary."

VI.—Soıżċeaċ baſraım bŗú Ⱥıŋŋe,
    Coŋŋ làŋ aŗ ļıa cŋócaıŋe;
    Soıżċeaċ ŋa ŋżŋáŗ a'ŗ żlaŋ ḃeoċ,
    Nıŗ ŧáŗ ŗal aıŋ aŋ ŗoıżċeaċ.

Soıżċeaċ ıŗ mıļŗe 'ŋa mıļ,
    Ⱥŋŋ ḃo cuıŗeaḃ ŗıż ŋa ŗıċıḃ;
    Soıżċeaċ aŗ ıoŋċuıŗ ŧa ŧıoŋ,
    Soıżċeaċ ıomċuıŗ aŋ aŋḃŗıż.

Nıŗ ċum ceaŋḃ ŗoıżċeaċ moŗ ŗıŋ,
    Coŋŋ aŗ uaıŗle leaż ļożmaıŗ;
    Roŗż żoŗm ŋa ŋ-żıuaḃ ċŗoċ ŋżaıŗċe,
    Coŋŋ ŋa m-buaḃ ċloċ m-beaŋŋaıżċe.

Soıżċeaċ óıŗ aŗ uaıŗle ŧleaż,
    Ⱥŗ ċaıŋıċ cŗıaċ ŋa ŋ-aıŋżeal;
    Żaolċoıl aŗ żıle 'ŋá aŋ żŋıaŋ,
    Ⱥıŋŋe ŋáŗ aoŋċaıż aıŋmıaŋ.

Copn beaṅg óiṅ na n-beoċ m-blaṅba,
   Fleaġ ṅiṁe aṅ an ṅobaṅṅa;
Copn áluinn aṅ aoiḃne beoċ,
   D'aḃaill an ṅaoinne an ṅoiġċeaċ.

An ḃṅu glan ó'ṅ buineaḃ Dia,
   Eiṅṫi ċainic Ṁac Ṁaṅia;
Do ḃ'í ionaḃ a alṫa,
   Cli ioḃan na h-umlaċṫa.

Ní h-ionann aon ḃean eile,
   Iṅ maċaiṅ meic na maiġbine;
Beag bo ṅaṅṫaiġ mo ṅiuṅ gaoil
   Jul an anṫoil 'na aṅ anaoiḃ.

Ní maiṫ ċuillim ṫeag ṅime,
   D'ṗagail aċṫ le a h-impṅbe;
Ṙiġ an ṫiġe ṅáṅ ċṅeigib mé,
   'Snáṅ ċṅeigib Muiṅe meṅe.

Maṫaiṅ ṗṅionṅa an puiṅṫ neaṁba,
   Bean aguṅ buime an Ṫigeaṅna;
Biob ṫean aṅ mo ṫeaċṫ bo'n ṫoiġ,
   Ní ceanṫ aṅ ṅeaṅṅ baṁ b'iaṅṅaib.

Muna ḃ-ṅuil aon ċaoi eile,
   Le a ṫṫuilṅinn an ṫṅócaiṅe;
Lóṅ goiṅe mo gaoil bo ṫ'ṅeaṅ,
   Ab ṫaoiḃ a Muiṅe, a ṁaiġbean.

Da n-beaṅnab maoṅ ṅiġ na ṅiog,
   Coṁċṅom ag meaṅ mo ṁiġniom;
Mo baonab aṅ é aṅ uṅa,
   Baogal a Dé an biomuṅ ṅa.

Angus O'Daly Fionn, cecinit A.D. 1570.

A vessel of balsam is Mary's womb,
An urn full of plentiful mercy,
Vessel of graces, and of the purest draughts—
A vessel which never bore a stain.

A vessel sweeter than honey,
In which was placed the king of kings;
A vessel most fit to bear wine—
A vessel that carried the sovereign King.

APPENDIX.

No artizan ever fashioned a vessel like to this;
Urn most noble, of the richest pearls;
Blue eye of the graceful, smiling form;
Urn of the choicest blessed gems.

Vessel of gold of the noblest feast,
Whence came forth the Lord of angels;
Pure will, brighter than the sun,
(Is) Mary's, who never yielded to temptation.

Urn of lurid gold—of exhilarating draughts;
Banquet of heaven from which I shall drink;
Rich goblet of most delightful beverage;
Vessel that saves us from death.

The chaste womb in which God was enclosed,
Whence sprung the Son of Mary;
That was the place of her nursling,
The pure breast of humility.

There is no other woman like
The Mother of the Virgin's Son;
My female relatives have little desired
To curb the stubborn will or check pleasure.

I do not well deserve to obtain the home of heaven
But through her intercession;
May the king of the household abandon me not,
And may Mary not forsake me.

Mother of the Prince of the heavenly citadel,
Spouse and nurse of the Lord,
Be powerful to aid my coming to the house,
(For 'tis) not justice I am better ask.

If there is no other way
By which I can obtain mercy;
My connexion with your divine spouse is sufficient
For thee, O Virgin Mary.

If the steward of the King of kings
Should act with equity considering my misdeeds,
To condemn me would be easy;
Avert, O God, this displeasure.

These two ranns or stanzas are the first and last of another poem written by the same poet, and transcribed from the same manuscript, now (1856) in the possession of the Rev. Matthew Kelly, D D.:

ɟab mo comaınc a cuırp Iora,
A ablaınn naomċa ar mo maoın;
Saon mo člı ó čıc na b-peacaḋ,
Nı ran bıoč nı beacaın baoıb.

A Ṫiċil, a ainġeil naṙail,
An t-ṙúl ḃiṗeaċ ḃéana ḃam;
Tu mo ċṗeiri iṙ mo ċop ḃiona,
Ṫeiri aṗ pon mo ġniomá ġaḃ.

Be my protection, O body of Jesus!
O holy host, and my treasure!
Free my body from the disease of sin,
A thing which in life is not a difficult thing for you.

O Michael! O noble angel!
Render safe the judgment for me,
Thou art my strength and tower of defence;
Take me for my deeds' sake under thy care.

The following stanzas are from a poem called An Sfoġaiṡe Rómánaċ (*The Roman Vision*), composed, as the last quatrain shows, in the middle of the seventeenth century, A.D. 1650.

"The author," says Hardiman (from whose work, "The Irish Minstrelsy," pp. 306, 336, 338, I copy these verses), "supposes himself at Rome, aiṗ ón cnoic Ċéṗaiṙ, where the vision appears to him over the graves of two exiled descendants of the Gael. These were the famous Hugh O'Neill, Earl of Tyrone—the Irish Hannibal—whose signal successes against the forces of Queen Elizabeth in Ireland, embittered the latter years of that princess; and Rory O'Donnell (brother of the celebrated Hugh Ruadh), the first Earl of Tyrconnell," note, p. 430. The language is so simple, that really a translation does not seem necessary:

VII.—Lá ḃ'á ṗabaṙ aiṗ maiḋin a' m'aonaṗ,
Iṙ an Roiṁ aiṗ óṗ-ċnoċ Ċéṗaiṙ,
Sinte aiṗ leic aġ ṙilleaḋ ḃeopa,
Lán ḋe ġṙuaim aiṗ uaiġ na nġaeḋal-ḟeaṙ.

Biaḋ a ġ-cṗeiḋeaṁ ġan ṁilleaḋ ġan cṙaeċaḋ,
Biaḋ an Eaġluiṗ aġ ṫeaġaṙġaḋ a ḃ-cṙeuḃa,
Bṙáiṫṗe, eaṙboiġ, Saġaint a'ṙ Cléiṗ'ċaiḃ,
S' beiḋ ṙíṫ ġo ḃeoiġ 'n a ḃeoiġ aġ Éiṗinn.

76th Stanza.

Ġuiḋim-ri Dia, má'ṙ mian leiṙ m'éiṙṫeaċṫ,
Ġuiḋim IOSA a ċiḋeaṙ an méiḋ po,
A'ṙ an Spioṙaḋ naomṫa, a ṗiṙ ḃ' aen-ṫoil,
Ṫuiṗe ṁáċain a'ṙ Paṫṗuic ḃeiḋ-ġeal.

Noiṙ an Tiġeaṙna a' m-bliaḋnaiḃ ḃeaṙṗaḋ,
Tṙáṫ biḋeaṙ 'ṙan Roiṁ am ḃeóṗaiḋe ḃeuṗaċ,
Ṁile ġo leiċ, cuiġ ḃeiċ a'ṙ ceuḋ leiṙ,
Aġ ṙin ḃaoiḃ-ri cṙioċ mo ṙġeil-ṙa.

APPENDIX II.

IRISH PROVERBS.

It is well known to every student who hasbeen in college, or who has devoted any time to the study of languages, how extremely difficult it is for a person to speak with a ready utterance in a tongue with which he has not been familiar from his youth—no matter how well he may have studied it in books; nay, that it is only by repeated attempts from time to time in oral exercises, that he can finally succeed in speaking any language fluently. The reason of this is obvious; that organ which is the best exercised in any language, is the one which, in the same, is most ready at our command. Hence, in many colleges the practice exists of committing and repeating, over and over again, some of the best passages in the Greek and Latin classics. And is it not a fact that we can easily call to mind, when we wish to express a thought that requires their aid, those words that we have got by rote in the stanzas of some charming lyric, some striking apophthegm, or some favourite proverb? Even that wonderful polyglot, the illustrious Cardinal Mezzofanti, never learned to speak any language without first essaying in this way.

If, therefore, Ireland's sons wish to speak their mother tongue, they must, until it be popularized, if it ever be, use means such as those just suggested. The language cannot be learned thoroughly any other way. And what can be more readily impressed on the memory, and more easily retained, than a nation's proverbs, in which the language is at once pure, idiomatic, and classical? Hence, the following collection of Irish proverbs, which are at present most in use among the people, has, for this end, been compiled. And further, to enable the student to learn more easily the meaning of the words, a literal translation of each proverb is subjoined, and occasionally annexed to it is a corresponding English, Scotch, French, Latin, Italian, or Greek adage of the same import. Every one knows that there are some leading ideas, common to every people, thrown into a proverbial form in each country. It is only in proverbs of this class, we can often meet in other languages sayings similar in meaning to those spoken in our own. Some may be inclined to think that it is going beyond the limits of a simply national work, such as a grammar of a particular language is, to be thus borrowing from the torch of foreign dialects sparks of knowledge to illustrate our own. Such a notion, if entertained, is too puerile to deserve notice. For what is rare and good receives additional lustre from the light of contrast.

This small collection will show many, that Ireland is not, to say the least, inferior to any other country in proverbial lore. Nay, perhaps, it would be more just to say, that had all her national proverbs been published, the volume containing them would equal in size the "Handbook of Proverbs," lately edited (*Antiquarian Library*, London, Henry G. Bohn, 1855), being an enlarged re-publication of Ray's collection, and the fullest that has yet been given to the public. In this volume of the *Antiquarian Library* are Scotch, British or Welsh, Irish, Danish, Eastern, and Hebrew proverbs.

The collection called Irish is really laughable. The miserable slang, unmeaning productions caricaturing Ireland and her sons, sung and acted on the English stage, representing us as blunderers, bullies, drunkards, have already done much, very much, to degrade us in our own eyes and in those of others. This collection, furnished as Irish, is something of the same kind. The sayings are as un-Irish in sentiment as they are un-Celtic in dress, and partake as much of the ribald nonsense of the stranger and the low adventurer, as the words in which they are expressed partake of the dappled jargon of the Saxon and the Norman.

A desire, then, to remove in some measure this slur thrown on our proverbial genius—so to speak—has, in addition to the other motives already given, mainly influenced the writer in submitting this collection to the public. The selection has been made—some from a manuscript collection of proverbs in the possession of Mr. John O'Daly; some from the list printed by Hardiman ("Irish Minstrelsy," vol. ii., p. 397, 4: 9); some from other sources. I have here inserted those only which I thought were best known among the Irish-speaking people. Had Mr. Bohn been furnished with a collection even such as this, it is likely he would do us the justice of inserting them. Indeed, there are many proverbs given in the "Handbook" as Scotch and Gaelic which are really Irish. This appears from their being current among our people; and secondly, from the fact of their running in rhyme :

Áilneact mná ionnaice ṡníðeann cuntur cruaið.
The beauty of a chaste woman excites hard dispute.

Aimideact ṡeann ir rí ir feann.
The less of folly the better.
The less play the better.—Scotch.

Air li ní breiċ fean ṡan ruiliḃ.
A man without eyes is no judge of colour.

Aiċnịṡcean caortoṡ caortoṡ eile.
One chafer knows another chafer.
Chacun cherche son semblable.—French.
Ogni simile appetisce il suo simile.—Ital.
Cada ovelha com sua parelha.—Port.

Aiċnịṡcann mórḃact moðamlact.
Greatness knows gentleness.

Aiċnịṡcann ójnṁið loċt amaðáin.
A foolish woman knows the faults of a man fool.

Aiċnịṡcear carað a ṡ-cruaðtan.
Friends are known in distress.
A friend in need is a friend indeed.—Eng.
Mas vale buen amigo que pariente primo.—Span.
Amicus certus in re incertâ cernitur.—Cic. ex Ennio.

A n-am na briabe braiceap do congnam.
In the time of trial your help (however little) is felt.
In time of prosperity, friends will be plenty;
In time of adversity, not one amongst twenty.

An dub gné ní h-aicruigcear é.
The black hue is not changed.
Lanarum nigræ nullum colorem bibunt.—Lat.

An rud a coigleap na mná iceann na caic é.
What the housewives spare, the cats eat.
What the good wife spares, the cat eats.—Eng.

An rud nac b-fagcar ré foinear.
What cannot be had is just what suits.
[Said of a person who is not content with what he has, but is always wishing to have what he cannot get.]

Air aon ir anam bíd coidce dearmad.
About one matter there is seldom a forget.

Air ceact na b-focal bonb ir binn beul iadta.
When wrathful words arise, a closed mouth is soothing.

An boctanact ní molfad a'r ní cainfad í;
'S ní'l neac a m-beidead d'a molad nac aige do b'feair liom í.
**Poverty I shall not praise, nor shall I dispraise;
But I'd wish him who praises it to be its subject, rather than myself.**

An té nac truag do cár na déan do gearán leir.
To him who has not pity for your state tell not your complaints.

An té ólar acc uirge ní beid ró air meirge.
He who drinks only water will not be drunk.

An té ta suar óltar deoc air,
An té ta síor buailtear cor air.
**He who is up is toasted,
He who is down is trampled on.**
Up the hill favour me, down the hill beware thee.
Vulgus sequitur fortunam et odit damnatos.—Juvenal.

An t-slat nac n-glacann snion.
The rod that admits no twisting.
It is not easy to straight in the oak the crook that grew in the sapling.—Gaelic.

APPENDIX.

An t-reód do-ḟáȝala 'r í ir áilne.
The rare jewel is the most beautiful.
A rare jewel a fair jewel.

An t-uan aȝ munaḋ méiḃleaċ d'a máċaill.
The lamb teaching its dam to bleat.

An uair ir dorċa roiṁ lae.
The darkest hour is before day.

Atá Dia tioḋlaċtaċ, tabartaċ,
Atá Dia fairrinȝ a ȝ-cumȝaċ;
Aċt ní h-ionan bur n-Dia a ȝ-Connaċt,
A'r Dia fairrinȝ na n-Ullteaċ.
God is bounteous and generous,
God is liberal in scarcity;
But the God whom you have in Connaught
Is not like the liberal God of the Ultonians.

Aṫruiȝṫear ȝné na h-aimrire.
The appearance of the times is changed.
Tempora mutantur et nos mutamur in illis.—Lat.

Beaṫaḋ an rtaraiḋe fírinne.
Truth is the historian's food.

Beaṫa duine a ṫoil.
One's own will is food.

Beul éiḋin a'r croiḋe cuilin.
A mouth of ivy and a heart of holly.

Bíḋ aḋ air amaḋán.
Even a fool has luck.
Fortuna favet fatuis.—Lat.

Bíḋ borb faoi rȝéiṁ.
A fierce person is often in beauty's dress.
A fair face often hides a fierce heart.

Bíḋ boirbeaċt ann ȝeal ȝáire.
There is anger in an open laugh.

Bíḋ cluiḋ fearcair aȝ an t-raiċnaiḋe.
The man of plenty has a quiet homestead.

Bíḋ cluanaiḋe a n-deaȝ-ċulaiḋ.
A deceiver is often in a fine dress.
A varlet is a varlet, though he be clad in scarlet.—Eng.

Bíoeann blaf aip ann m-beaʒan.
The smaller the sweeter. Literally—there is taste on what is scanty.

Bíoeann pač aip an t-ppuimileačt.
There is prosperity attending slovenliness.

Boċt an eaʒlaip a bíocar ʒan ceoil.
Poor (is) the church that is without music.

Bpeaṫnuiʒ an aba pul a b-teióip 'nna calait.
Look at the river before you go to the ferry.

Bpóʒa 'pa ʒ-cliabán; laʒap 'pa laṫaiʒ.
Shoes in the cradle; the foot in the mire.
Shoes in the cradle, and bare feet in the stubble.—Eng.

Buaiópió an t-eaċ no cailpió an ppian.
The horse shall win, or lose the bridle.

Buaine clú 'ná paoʒal.
Fame is more enduring than life.

Caileann buine pub le n-a ṁuineað.
A person loses something to teach himself.
Bought wit is best.—Eng.
Duro flagello mens docetur rectius.—Lat.
Παθήματα μαθηματα.—Gr.
Σκληρὰ δὲ μάστιξ παιδαγωγεῖ καρδίαν.—Nazianz.

Caill ré annpa ʒ-carað é.
He lost it in the turning.

Caoin le ceannpaiʒ.
Gentle with the meek.

Caoṁann bóċar an t-inʒpeamac.
Hope soothes the persecuted.

Captap na baoine le céile,
Aċt ní ċaptap na cnoic ná na pléibte. Short form—
Captap ba baoine aċt ní captap na cnoic.
People meet each other,
But the hills and mountains never.
Deux hommes se rencontrent bien, mais jamais deux montagnes.—Fr.
Mons cum monte non miscebitur.—Lat.

Ceann mór na céile bige.
Big head, little sense.

Coigilt teine le loc.
No catam cloc le cuan.
Comairle cabairt do mnaoi boirb,
No buille de iuibe air iarrian ruar.
To rake a fire by a lake,
To cast stones by the coast,
(Is) to give an advice to a wily woman,
Or a blow of a locket on cold iron.

Ceannuig droc rud a'r beidir gan aon rud.
Buy a bad article, and you will be without anything.

Cia air bic duine ólar 'r é Domnall a íocrar.
Whoever drinks, Donald shall pay.
Quidquid delirant reges plectuntur Achivi.—Hor.

Claoióeann neart ceart.
Might subdues right.

Cnuaruig a t-am oireamnac.
Provide in a seasonable time.

Cnuarac na gráineóige.
The provision of the hedge-hog.

Conairc ré Murcad, no cuid d'a cuideacta.
He saw Morogh or some of his associates.

"Which implies," says Mr. O'Daly, "that if a man should meet bad company and escape even partially hurt, he would be as fortunate as if he had got safe from the vengeance of Morogh, whose name in Munster is, among the peasantry, a word of terror. The adage has its rise from Morogh O'Bryen, surnamed Murcad an Tótáin (from the number of houses he set on fire during the troubles of 1641). He was sixth Baron of Inchiquin."

Cormac breiceam na m-breat fíor.
Cormac judge of just judgments.

Cuairt geárr 'rí ir fearr.
A short visit is the best.

Again

Cuairt geárr a'r a déanad go h-anam a d-teac do caraid.
A short visit to the house of a friend, and even that seldom paid.

Cul le ɡaoc a'ɼ aɡaɪo lc cear.
Rear to the wind, and front to the (sun's heat.
[A proverb pointing out the situation which a house intended for comfort and warmth should hold].

Dá d-cɼɪaŋ ɼŋeacca le ɼléɪbcɪb,
Dá d-cɼɪaŋ ɡɼéɪŋe le ɡleaŋŋcaɪb,
Dá d-cɼɪaŋ cɪŋŋɪɼ aɪɡ lucc aoɪɼe,
Dá d-cɼɪaŋ baoɪɼe aɪɡ óɪɡe,
Dá d-cɼɪaŋ ɼaɪŋce aɪɡ ɼeaŋduɪŋe,
Dá d-cɼɪaŋ ɡaoɪce le cɼaŋŋaɪb,
Dá d-cɼɪaŋ caɪŋce aɪɡ lucc póɪce,
Dá d-cɼɪaŋ cóɼac aɪɡ lucc céɪlle,
Dá d-cɼɪaŋ luɪŋɡ aɪɼ bóɪcɼɪb,
Dá d-cɼɪaŋ ɼeoɪce aɪɡ aoɼda.

Two thirds snow in mountains,
Two thirds sun in valleys,
Two thirds sickness with the aged,
Two thirds folly with the young,
Two thirds covetousness among the old,
Two thirds wind among trees,
Two thirds talk among those drinking over their cups,
Two thirds justice among those of sense,
Two thirds foot-prints on roads,
Two thirds feebleness amongst the aged.

Dall aɪɼ lɪ ŋɪ bɼeɪceaṁ ɼɪoɼ.
A blind man is not a true judge of colours.

Deacaɪɼ dɼeɪm leɪɼ aŋ ṁuɪɼ ṁóɼ.
Hard to contend with the wide ocean.

Dealɡ múŋlaɪɡ, ɼɪacal coŋ, a'ɼ ɼocal amadáɪŋ; ɪɼ cɼɪ ŋeɪce ɪɼ ɡéɪɼe aɪɼ bɪc.
A thorn in mire, a hound's tooth, and a fool's retort, are the three most pointed things at all.

Déaŋ ruaɼ leɪɼ aŋ uaɪɼleacc a'ɼ déaŋ cuṁaŋ léɪce, acc aɪɼ do clua ɼ ŋa bí ɼuaɼ le do duɪŋe bocc ɼéɪŋ.
Associate with the nobility, and be in favour with them; but, on no account, be cold with your own poor people.

Déaŋ aŋ oɪbɪɼ acc ŋa bac le do dícɪoll.
Do the work, and heed not your (boasting) endeavour.
[Said to those who say they could (if they only wished it) do much, but who as a matter of fact don't do the work].

Deaṙḃ caṙaḋ ṗoiṁ ṗiaċċaŋŋaṙ.
Prove a friend ere necessity.
Μέννσο απισθειν.—Gr.
Prove thy friend ere thou have need.—Eng.

Deaṙḃṙáċaiṙ leaḋṙáṅaċċ' ólaċaŋ.
Drinking is the brother (of) robbery.

Deaṙḃṙaċaiṙ ḋo Ṫaḋg Ḋoṁṅall.
Donald is brother to Thady.—(Chip of the same block.)
Arcades ambo.—Lat.

Deaṙc ṙul léiṁ a ṫaḃaiṙṫ.
Look before giving a leap.

Déiṙc ḋ'a ċuiḋ ḟéiṅ ḋo'ṅ aṁaḋáṙ.
An alms from his own share is given to a fool.

Déiṙc aŋ ṁáiliŋ láiŋ.
An alms into the full bag.

Diomaoiṅeaṙ miaŋ aṁaḋáiŋ.
Idleness a fool's desire.

Dlíġe ṅa h-iaṙaċḋa ṅa h-eaṙṙaiḋe ḋo ḃṙiṙeaḋ.
The law of lending is to break the ware.

Dóċaṙ liaiġ gaċ aṅṙó.
Hope, the physician of all misery.
If it were not for hope, the heart would break.—Eng.
Spes alunt exules.—Lat.
'Ανὴρ ἀτυχῶν σώζεται ταῖς ἐλπίσι.—Gr.

Doilġe aŋ ṫ-uaiḃṙeaċ ḋo ċeaṅṅṙúġaḋ.
It is difficult to soothe the proud.

Eaḋṫṙom óṙ aiġ aṁaḋáŋ.
Gold is light (with) a fool.
A fool and his money are soon parted.—Eng.

Eaṅlaiṫ ṅa h-aoŋ-ċleiṫe ḟaoi aoŋ ṙgeaċ.
Birds of a feather under the same bush.
Birds of a feather flock together.—Eng.
Pares cum paribus facillime congregantur.—Lat.

Éiṙe óg oileaŋ ṅa ṅaoṁ.
Youthful Eire, isle of saints.

Fada cuimne rean-leinb.
Lasting is the recollection of an old child.

Fág an Céir mar tá rí.
Leave the Keish as it is.
[Applied to a person who cannot be changed, just as the mountain named Keish cannot be moved.]

Fágann na ba bár fad a'r bjdeann an feur a' fár.
The cows die while the grass is growing.
Caval non morire che herba de venire.—Ital.
Live horse, and you'll get grass.—Eng.

Féadaim ór do ceannaċ go daor.
I can buy gold at a great price:—the dearest thing can be had for money.

Féadann cat dearcad air rig.
A cat can look at a king:—the light of day, and the air we breath, and the exercise of his faculties belong to the lowest and poorest.

Fearg a'r fuat namuid un deag-grajd.
Anger and hatred are the foes of pure love.

Fear na h-aon bó fear gan aon bó.
The man of one cow—a man of no cow.

Fearr fuin fleide 'na túr gioraic
The end of a feast is better than the beginning of a shindy.
And,

Fearr deire fleide 'na túr bruione.
The last of a feast is better than the first of a fight.
Better come at the end of a feast than the beginning of a fray.—Eng.

Fearr dneoilin ann doin 'na corr air cairde.
A wren in hand better than a crane yet on loan—*i.e.*, yet to be caught.
Mas vale paxaro en la mano, que búytre volando.—Spanish.
A sparrow in the hand is worth more than a vulture flying.

Fearr mada beo na leon mairb.
A living dog is better than a dead lion.

Fearr a oileamain 'na a oideaċar.
His feeding (has been) better than his education.
Better fed than taught, said the churl to the parson.—Eng.

Fearr da ṡúil 'na aon t-ṡúil.
Two eyes are better than one.
Two heads are wiser than one.—Eng.

Feaṗṗ clú 'na conáċ.
Character is better than wealth.

Feaṗṗ coiṡilt aiṗ b-túṗ 'na aiṗ deiṗe.
Better to spare in the beginning than at the end.

Féile daṗtaċáin.
A niggard's generosity.

Feiṗ Teaṁṗaċ ṡaċ tṗeaṗ bliaṡain.
Tara's parliaments were every third year.

Fóṡlam mian ṡaċ eaṡnaiṡ.
Learning is the desire of every wise man.

Foiṡid leiṡeaṗ ṗeanṡalaiṗ.
Patience is the cure for an old complaint.
Patience is a plaster for all sores.—Eng.
Sale della patienza condisce all tutto.—Ital.
The salt of patience seasons everything.

Foillṗiṡteaṗ ṡaċ niḋ le h-aimṗiṗ.
By time everything is revealed.

Fuṗaṗ fuinneaḋ 'naice na minne.
It is easy to bake with meal at hand.

Fuaṗ cuman caillṡe.
Cold is an old dame's affection.

Fuaṗuiṡeann a ċuiḋ.
His portion cools—more fully thus, an te a ta aṁuiṡ fuaṗuiṡeann a ċuiḋ, the portion of him who is out, grows cold.
Sero venientibus ossa.

Ṡaċ am ní h-eaṡnaċ ṗaoi.
At all times a sage is not wise.
Nemo mortalium omnibus horis sapit.
Obdormivit Homerus.

Ṡaċ leanḃ maṗ oiltteaṗ; ṡaċ oiṡt maṗ aḃḃaṗ.
Every child as nursed; every web as its materials.
As the tree so is the fruit.—St. Matt.
Telle recine, telle feuille.—Fr.

Or, Ṡaċ ḋalta maṗ oiltteaṗ.
Every nursling as he is nursed.
Quæ enim seminaverit homo, hæc et metet.—Epis. ad Gal. vi. 8.
Quonium qui seminavit in carne sua, de carne metet et corruptionem.

Ʒac deaṁan ṗiceann a ṙae.
Every demon runs his course.
Every dog has its day.—Eng.

Ʒac a b-faẓtar ʒo h-olc imtiʒeann ʒo h-olc.
What is got badly, goes badly.
Ill got, ill spent.—Eng.
Acquerir mechamment, et depenser sottement.—Fr.

Ʒac niḋ daor mian ʒac mnaoi.
Every thing dear is a woman's fancy.

Ʒac corr réir a íota.
Every crane according to its thirst.

Ʒac coineal a ʒ-cóṁluadar.
Every candle in company.
Numquid venit lucerna ut sub modio ponatur, aut sub lecto? nonne ut super candelabrum ponatur.—S. Marcus 4. 21.

Ʒac aon réir a ṁiain.
Each one according to his taste.

Ʒac uile nac réir a ʒné.
Every person according to his cast of mind.
Every man in his way.—Eng.

Ʒalar fada ní abrann ríorruiḋe breuʒ.
A long disease does not always tell a lie, *i.e.* will kill at last.

Ʒan lón, ʒan carajd.
Without store, without friend.

Ʒan oileaṁain, ʒan ṁod.
No rearing, no manners.

Ʒan circe ir fuar an clú.
Without a treasure, fame is dull.

Ʒean ʒac leantac a cuid anracc'.
The affection of every follower is for his own coziness.

Ʒeibeann lonʒanac ʒeiṁre ʒortac.
The sluggard finds a famishing winter (lonʒanac from lonʒan the shin bone—one who favors the fire).

Ʒlóir nac t-tuilleann a ʒ-ceann, ní fearr a beiṫ ann na ar.
The glory which the head cannot bear, it is better it should not be there.

Ġnaċ ocṗaċ ṗaoċṁaṗ.
The hungry man is usually (ġnaṫ) fierce.

Ġiníḋeaṅṅ cıṗce caċṗaıṅṅaċṫ.
Wealth creates friendship.

Ġiníḋeaṅṅ leıcé leıceaḋaċṫ.
Diamonds engender elegance (rich attire, &c.)

Ġiníḋeaṅṅ maıṫ maıṫeaṡ.
Good begets goodness.
Χάρις χαριν τίχτει.—Sophocles.

Ġiníḋeaṅṅ olc olc.
Bad begets badness,
Money begets money.—Eng.
Danari fanno danari.—Ital.

Ġiníḋeaṅṅ ṡaıṫḃıṗ ṗéıṅ a ḋoṅṫa.
A rich man acts according to his wish.
Money makes the mail go.—Eng.

Ġiníḋ ṫaṗṫ ṫaṗṫ.
Thirst produces thirst.

Ġiníḋeaṅṅ blaḋaṗ caṗaḋaṡ.
Flattery begets friendship.

Ġo ṗéıḋ a ḃeaṅ ṅa ḋ-ṫṗı mḃó.
Easy, O woman of three cows.

Ġo ṡġaṗaıḋ aṅ laċa le lıṅṅ ḋo ṡṅaṁ;
Ġo ṡġaṗṗaıḋ aṅ eala le ṅ-a cluıṁ ḃáıṅ,
Ġo ṡġaṗṗaıḋ aṅ maḋṗa le cṗeıḋeaṁ ṅa ġ-cıṅaṁ,
Ṅı ṡġaṅṡaıḋ aṅ ġaṅġaıḋ le ıṅṫıṅ mṅa.
Till the duck cease on the lake to swim.
Till the swan's down asume a darkish hue,
Till the canine race cease to snatch and fight,
Woman's mind shall not lack guile.

Iṡ bıṅṅ é beul ṅṅa ṫoṡḋ.
A silent mouth is melodious.
A wise head makes a close mouth.—Eng.
Vir sapit qui pauca loquitur.—Lat.
Le plus sage se tait.—Fr.
Silence is wisdom and gets a man friends.—Eastern proverb.

Iomad glóir aig neac, do beir rin neamciorn air a ceill.

Deanann duine le iomad glóir rraidean de' n cóir féin.

Much noise (of words) in a man, brings disregard for his good sense.
A man with much loud talk makes fudge of truth itself.

Ir caol a tigear an t-ád act 'nna tuilte móra tigear an mio-ád.

In slender currents comes good luck, but in rolling torrents comes misfortune.

Apres perdre perd on bien.—Fr.
Fortuna nulli obesse contenta est semel.—Latin.

Ir ciún agur rortac rruit na linnte lána,
Ní h-é rin do'n t-rruit eadtrom rí bagrar go dána.

Still and silent is the stream of full deep waters;
Not so with the light, little stream—it is it that bellows boldly.

Deep waters run smooth: a shallow stream makes most noise.—Eng.

Ir coim cabán do boict.
A hut is a palace to a poor man.

Home is home, though it be never so homely.—Eng.
Οἶκος φίλος οἶκος ἄριστος.

Ir dall an gnád baot.
Self-love is blind.

Ir dall ruil a g-cuil duine eile.
Blind is the eye in the private abode of another. That is—a man is silent in a strange place.

Ir eagnac beag-duine.
A person of virtue is wise.

Ir fada ó'n láim a tá a g-cian.
Far from the hand which is in a distant (land).

Ir fearr an mait atá 'na an mait a bí.
The good that is, is better than the good that (once) was.
Quod est, melius est.—Lat.

Ir fearr a oileamain 'na a togbail.
His living is better than his education.

Birth is much, but breeding more.—Eng.

Iꞃ ꝼeaꞃꞃ beaʒán de'n n-ʒaoıl 'ná móꞃán de'n caꞃ-
tannaꞃ.
A little relationship is better than much friendship.

Iꞃ ꝼeaꞃꞃ caꞃad 'ꞃ a ʒ-cúıꞃt 'ná bonn ꞃa ꞃꞃaꞃán.
A friend at court is better than a groat in the pocket.
A friend at court is better than a penny in pocket.—Eng.
Bon fait avoir ami en cour, car le proces en est plus court.—Fr.
Good favour is above silver and gold.—Proverbs, xxii. 1.

Iꞃ ꝼeaꞃꞃ coıʒılt a n-am 'ná ann ann-tꞃát.
It is better to spare in time than out of time.
'Tis too late to spare when all is spent.—Eng.
Sera in fundo parsimonia.—Seneca, Epist. 1.
Δεινὴ δ' ἐνὶ πυθμεν φείδω.—Hesiod.

Iꞃ ꝼeaꞃꞃ é 'ná a eaꞃbaıde.
It is better than its want.
A wooden leg is better than no leg.—Eng.

Iꞃ ꝼeaꞃꞃ é 'ná an ıaꞃact, nac b-ꝼuıʒteá.
It is better than the loan you could not get.

Iꞃ ꝼeaꞃꞃ ʒꞃeım de cuınín 'ná dá ʒꞃeım de cat.
One morsel of a rabbit is better than two of a cat.
A piece of kid is worth two of a cat. And *One leg of a lark's worth the whole body of a kite.*—Eng.

Iꞃ ꝼeaꞃꞃ ımꞃeaꞃ 'ná uaıʒneaꞃ.
Contention is even better than loneliness.

Iꞃ ꝼeaꞃꞃ mıne 'ná boꞃꞃbe móꞃ,
Iꞃ ꝼeaꞃꞃ cóıꞃ 'ná dul cum dlıʒe;
Iꞃ ꝼeaꞃꞃ teac beaʒ a'ꞃ teann lón,
'Ná teac móꞃ a'ꞃ beaʒán bıde.
Better gentleness than great haughtiness.
Better adjustment than going to law;
Better a small house and full store
Than a large house and little food.

Iꞃ ꝼeaꞃꞃ neac eıle a mólad duıne 'ná é ꝼéın.
It is better that another and not oneself should praise.

Iꞃ ꝼeaꞃꞃ ꞃtuaım 'ná neaꞃt.
Cleverness is better than strength.

Iꞃ ʒıoꞃꞃa cabaıꞃ Dé 'ná'n doꞃuꞃ.
God's aid is nigher than the door.

Is glas iad na cnoic a b-fad uainn.
The hills seen afar off look green.
'Tis distance lends enchantment to the view,
And robes the mountain in its azure hue.
Pleasures of Hope—Campbell.

Is treise gliocar 'ná neart.
Cunning is superior to strength

Is gnác ranntac a blactanar.
The covetous (man) is always in want.

Is mall 'r ir direac diogaltar Dé.
Late and sure is the justice of God.
God stays long, but strikes at last.—Scotch.

Imigeann an breug agur fanann an fírinne.
The lie passes away—truth remains.
Magna est veritas et prævalebit.

Is milir fíon, ir searb a íoc.
Wine is sweet—sour its payment.

Is dona an giolla act ir meara gan é.
Bad is a (bad) servant, but it is worse to be without him.
Better a mischief than an inconvenience.—Eng.

Is iomda lá 'ra g-cill orainn.
Many a day shall we rest in the clay.

Is mairg do bíoear ran tír nac aiteantar é.
It is a poor thing to be in a country where one is not known.

Is mairg a m-bíoeann a cairde fann,
Is mairg a m-bíoeann 'clann gan rait;
Is mairg a m-bíoeann botán gann,
Is mairg a bíoear gan olc no mait.
'Tis sad for him who has few friends,
'Tis sad for him who has unfortunate children;
'Tis sad for him who has only a poor cot,
'Tis sad to be without any thing, good or bad.

Is mairg a bíoeann go h-olc 'r a beit go boct na díaig.
It is a poor thing to be stingy, and to feel troubled after the little that is given.

Is mairg aig a m-bíoeann bean mi-cainbeac bonb.
It is a source of regret to have an unthrifty, disdainful wife.

APPENDIX.

Ir maiṫ an ṫiomanaiḋe an té biḋeap aip an ṫ-cloiḋe.
He is a good hurler who is on the ditch. *A proverb against critics.*

Ir maiṫ an mapcaċ ṗean aip talaṁ.
A good horseman the man on the ground—*i.e.*, on foot.

Ir minic a bi ṫṗana ṫeanaṁail, aṫup daṫaṁail dona.
Often was Ugly amiable, and Pretty sulky.

Akin to this is the Spanish proverb:—*Not so ugly as to be frightful, nor so beautiful as to kill.*

Ir minic do rinne duine ṫre mioċṫ, beapt ap a d-ṫiṫ an uile olc.
Oft a person commits through impulse (or passion) an act from which flows much evil.

Ir mo d' eaṫla 'na d' aḋḃap.
Thy dread is greater than thy reason (for it).

Ir raṁpaḋ ṫaċ pion ṫo noḋlaic,
'S ṗapaċ ṫo ḋóippe.

Every state of weather is summer till Christmas, and grass to the doors. Meaning that the worst weather does not appear till after that season.

Janiveer freeze the pot by the fire.
February doth cut and shear.—Eng.
Pluye de Februier vaut egout de fumier.—Fr.

Ir reaṁḃ an ṗirinne, aċt ir milir an ḃṗeuṫ aip uaiṗiḃ.
Truth is bitter, but a lie is savoury at times.
The truest jest sounds worst in guilty ears.—Eng.

Ir taiḋḃapaċ iad aḋapca na m-ḃó ṫap leap.
Prodigious are the horns of the cows beyond the seas (taiḋḃap, means a spectre, from taḋ, *an apparition*; ḃap, *death*).
They are ay gude that are far awa'.—Scotch.
Omne ignotum pro magnifico.—Lat.

Ir tuipce deoċ na ṗṫéal.
A drink comes before a story.

[A proverb suggested by the ancient practice of giving *story-tellers* a drink before they began to rehearse their tales].

Laṁ a ṗcapaḋ aṫup laṁ a taippċail.
A hand scattering and a hand saving.
Altera manu fert aquam, altera ignem.—Lat.
Il porte le feu et l' eau.—Fr.
Altera manu fert lapidem, altera panem ostentat.—Plaut.

13

APPENDIX.

Lám láidir ann uaċdar.
The strong hand in the ascendant.—*Motto of the O'Briens.*

Leanḃ loirgṫe ḟuaċuiġeann teine.
A burned child dreads the fire.

Leiġeas gaċ bróin comráḋ.
Conversation is a cure for every sorrow.

Liaġ gaċ boiċt bás.
Death is every poor man's physician.

Loiteann aoraḋ mór-ċlu.
Satire injures great fame.

Lom gaċ a leun.
Every one in misfortune is destitute.

Luiḋeann roḋnar air amaḋán.
Good-fortune abides with a fool.

Má táim buiḋe tá croiḋe geal agam.
If I am yellow, I have a fair heart.

Mairg d'ar b' céile baoċán bonb.
It is sad for the person whose partner is a haughty varlet.

Mairg ṫréigeas a Ṫigearna.
'Tis an evil thing (for him who) forsakes his Lord.

Mairg ṫréigeas a ḋuine gnáṫ air duine dá ċráṫ no trí.
'Tis a sad thing for one to forsake a bosom friend for a person of two or three days' (acquaintance).
Be not ungrateful to your old friends.—Heb.

Mairg do gniḋ eiteaċ a'r goid.
It is evil to refuse and steal.

Mairg ḟeallas air a ċarajd.
It is a sad thing to disappoint a friend.

Már cam no díreaċ an ród 're an bóṫar mór an t-aṫġiorra.
If the road is crooked or straight, the high-way is the short cut.
The farthest way about is the shortest way home.—Eng.

Ḃaʼr ḟaḋa la tiʒ oiḋċe.
If the day is long, night comes (at last).
The longest day must have an end.—Eng.
The oldest man that ever lived died at last.—Gaelic.
Il n'est si grand jour qui ne vienne à vespre.—Fr.
Non vien di, che non venga sera.—Ital.

Ḃaʼr ionṁuin liom an ċráin ir ionṁuin liom a h-ál.
If I like the sow, I like her litter.

Or,

Ḃaʼr ionṁuin leat me, ir ionṁuin mo péim.
If you like myself you like my sway (all connected with me).
Love me, love my dog.—Eng.

Na creiḋ fionn, 'r na creiḋ fiaċ, 'r na creiḋ briaċra mná;
Ḃaʼr moċ, mall, eiróċtar an ʒrian, ir mar ir toil le Ḋia beiḋear an la.

Do not credit the buzzard, and do not credit the raven, and credit not the words of woman (sorceress);
Whether the sun rise early or late, the day shall be as God pleases. (A Christian proverb against pagan prognostics).

Ḃaʼr maiṫ leat a beiṫ buan caiṫ fuar aʒur teiṫ.
If you wish to live old, make use of hot and cold.

Or thus,

Ḃar maiṫ leat a beiṫ buan caiṫ uaiṫ aʒur teiṫ.
If you wish to live long, fling off and flee.

["This sentence was uttered," says Mr. O'Daly, "by a waiter at Mullaghmast, who, being aware of the plot against the lives of the guests, wished in these words to convey an intimation to one of them to fly for his life from the danger that was impending over him and his friends."]

Ḃaiṫ an t-anlan an t-ocrur.
Hunger is good sauce.
Fames optimum condimentum.—Lat.
Apetito non vuol salse.—Ital.

Ḃilleann tairnʒe eaċ, 'ʒur milleann eaċ réirreaċ.
One nail spoils a horse, and one horse spoils a team of six.
One scabby sheep infects a flock.—Eng.

Milis glór gach fir aig a m-bío cuid agus rphéid;
Searb glór an te bídeas lomm, buy-or-cionn do
labhann re.

Sweet is the voice of every man who has means and fortune;
Harsh is the voice of him who is penniless—he speaks quite out of place.

Mol an óige a'r tiocfaid rí.

Praise youth, and it will progress.

Molad gach aon an t-át mar do geabfaid.

Let each man praise the ford as he finds it.

Na bíodad do gníom ó do teangain.

Let not thy act be from thy tongue.
Be slow of giving advice—ready to do a service.—Ital.

Comairle an t-Seanduine.

Na bí caintead a d-tig an óil,
Na cuir anfior air feanóir,
Na h-abair nad n-déantar cóir,
Na h-ob agus na h-iarr onóir,
Na bí cruaid agus na bí bog,
Na tréig do caraid air a cuid,
Na bí mi-modamail, na déan troid,
A'r na h-ob í ma'r éigin duit.

Do not be talkative in a drinking-house,
Do not impute ignorance to an elder,
Do not say justice is not done,
Do not refuse and do not seek honor,
Do not be hard, and do not be liberal,
Do not forsake a friend on account of his means,
Do not be impolite; and do not offer fight,
Yet decline it not, if necessary.

Na mol a'r na cain tu féin.

Neither praise nor dispraise thyself.
Neither speak well or ill of yourself.—Eastern Proverb.

Na tabair do breit air an g-céad rgeul,
Go m-beirid an taob eile ort.

Do not give your judgment on (hearing) the first story,
Until the other side is brought before you.
Every man's tale is gude till anither's be told.—Scotch.
Audi alteram partem.—Lat.

APPENDIX.

Ná mol azur ná di-ṁol daoi,
Aḋar ni ḟáżṫar raoi zan loċt.
Do not praise nor dispraise a dolt
As a sage even is not found faultless.

Ní b-ḟuil glóir aċt glóir neiṁe.
There is no glory but the glory of heaven.

Ní cara zaċ bladaire.
Every flatterer is not a friend.
All are not friends that speak us fair.—Eng.

Ní buan cogaḋ na z-carad.
The fighting of friends is not lasting.
Amantium ira amoris redintegratio est.—Lat.

Ní b-ḟuil róḋ zan ann-róḋ.
There is no joy without affliction.
There is no joy without alloy.—Eng.

Ní b-ḟuil níḋ níor zile na an żeanamnaiżeaċt.
There is nothing fairer than virginity.

Ní b-ḟuil gaol aig aon le raoi zan reun.
No one is related to a sage in misfortune—*i.e.*, no one cares for a man in reduced circumstances.

Ní b-ḟuil diiże aig riaċtanar.
Necessity has no law.

Ní bíḋeann airgiod a'r amadán a b-ḟad le céile.
A fool and his money are not long together.

Ní ḟázann láṁ iaḋta aċt doirn dúnta.
A closed hand gets only a shut fist.

Ní ḟázan an ṁinic onóir.
A constant guest is never welcome.
Nimia familiaritas contemptum parit.—Plutarch.

Ní ḟáiḋ go m-buḋ ḟíor-colaċ.
Not a sage till he be truly skilful.

Ní zaċ am a ṁairbuiżeann Pádruic ḟiaḋ.
It is not on every occasion Patrick kills a deer.

Ní leun go díé tigeanna.
No misery like the want of a lord.

Ní h-ionnan dul do'n baile mór a'r teacé aír ar.
It is not the same thing to go to town and come from it.

Ní lia an ronar 'ná an donar ann orlaib éinn.
Fortune comes not without misfortune inch for inch.

Ní file go flaié.
No poet till a prince.

Ní iad na fir móra uile a bainear an fógmar.
It is not all big men that reap the harvest.
The greatest things are done by the help of small ones.—Eng.
Multis ictibus dejicitur quercus.—Lat.

Ní'l níó níor géire 'na teanga mná.
There is nothing sharper than a woman's tongue.

Ní múinte go coigcríoé.
Not accomplished till one has travelled.
He that travels far knows much.—Eng.

Ní náire an boétannaét.
Poverty is no shame.

Ní saor go m-beió gan ciontaib.
Not free till without faults.

Ní tearaigeaét go náire.
No heat like that of shame.

Ní uairleaét gan rubailce.
No nobility without virtue.

Ní fagann cor na connraió aon níó.
The foot at rest meets nothing.
A close mouth catcheth no flies.—Eng.
A goupil endormi rien ne tombe en la geule.—French.
Bocca trinciata mosca non si entra.—Ital.
En bocca cerrada no entra mosce.—Spanish.

APPENDIX.

Ní cuigeann an rácac an reang,
An uair do bjócann a bolg féin teay,

The man who has enough, does not, with his stomach full, understand the wants of the hungry.

Ní cuimnigeann an cú goptac air a coiláin.

The hungry hound thinks not of her whelps.

Ní beata go bul air neam.

No life till going up to heaven.

Ní h-annfað go gaoit a n-dear.

No heavy fall of rain till the south wind blows.

Ní h-olc aon beart go m-buð feall.

No action is malicious but treachery.

Ní h-ealaða go léigtear rtair.

No science till history be read.

Ní ó 'n gaot do tóig re é.

It is not from the wind he derived it. [A negative way for praising one's hereditary greatness, or natural ability.]

Ní treun go tuitim tuile.

No force like the rush of a torrent.

Ní beatuigeann briatra na braiére.

Mere words do not support the friars.
Men cannot live on air.—Eng.

Ní roga go rig na cruinne.

No choice like the King of the universe.

Ní réim neac go m-buð oilte.

No one is gentle till well bred.

Ní briújte go bul ann aoir.

Not broken till advancing in age.

Ní boct go bul go h-iffrionn.

Nothing so poor as going to hell.

Ní h-é lá na gaoite lá na rcolb.

The day of storm is not the day for thatching. [Said of a person who defers to an untimely hour what he should do in season].

Ní tormann treun go tóirneač.
No roaring noise like thunder.

Ní ancrað go h-éiteoč.
No pain like to refusal.

Ní daoi go mnaoi droič mèine.
No wicked being like a woman of bad temper.

Ní mairuíðc go fear rtiuire.
No navigator till (he is) helmsman.

Ní luač go aifrionn Dé éirteačt.
No reward to that of hearing God's holy mass.

Ní daor go breit an breitim.
Not condemned till (one hears) the judge's judgment.

Ní earba go díť cáirde.
No want compared with the loss of friends.

Ní'l fior aig duine cía ir fearr—an luas 'na 'n moill.
One does not know whether speed or delay is the better.

Ní fearða go rórða,
Ní céarað go rórað.
No feast till there is roast;
No galling trials till one gets married.

Ní'l nío 'ra dóman ir meara le n-inrinn,
'Ná eug na g-carað a'r rgarrað na g-compánac.
There is nothing in the world so bad to announce
Than the death of friends and the separating of companions.
[Said by Carolan on the supposed death of Charles M'Cabe].

Ní'l 'ra t-raogal ro ačt ceo.
This life is but a vapour.

For what is your life? It is a vapour which appeareth for a little while and afterwards shall vanish away.—St. James, iv. 15.

Níor čuaíð fear an eidirgáin ar.
The peace-maker never lost. [Eidir-gáin from eidir, *between*, and gát, *a cover—protector*].

Níor druid Dia beárna ariam nác b-forglóctad ro ceann eile.
God never closed a gap that He would not thereupon open another.

Níor tug an bár, rpár do duine air bit a riam.
Death, when its hour arrives, never granted any one a respite.

Ní tig leat d'arán a beit agad agur a ite.
You cannot have your bread and eat it.
You cannot eat your cake and have your cake.—Eng.
Vorebbbe mangiar la forcaccia e trovar la in tasca.—Ital.

Ní uabar uairleact.
Nobility is no pride.

Ní rún é ó tá fior aig triur é.
It is no secret when it is known to three.

[The Italians say, *Three may keep counsel, if two be away.*—*Trè taceranno, se due vi non sono.* The French : *Secret de deux secret de Dieu, secret de trois secret de tous.*]

Óg gac neac 'ran aoir óige,
Óg arir gac reandine;
Óg deire aoire gac n-duine,
Deire gac rean aoire óige.

Young each person is in youth,
Young again every old man;
Young the close of each person's age,
The close of every old age is (still) youth.

Olc ann agaid maiteara.
Good against evil.

Olc rion nac mait d'aon.
Bad blast that is not good to (some) one.

Oct n-amairc oct g-cuimne.
Eight views, eight recollections.

Otract rod an leagaid.
Distemper is the physician's luck.

Rig mifoglamta ir aral coróinta.
An illiterate king is a crowned ass.

Ríoġaċt ġan ḋuaḋ, ní ḋual ġo ḃ-faġtar.
A kingdom is not usually got without trouble. Without pains, without gains.

Rún ġaċ reapc an ríġ ceart.
The desire of every lover is the rightful king.

Rór cúpa fial, rean ruḋaċ.
A good-humoured man is like a fragrant rose.

Riaġail péir oiḋeaċair.
Rule (is) according to learning.

Rúnaiḋe cealġaċ.
A deceitful secret-searcher.

Saiḋḃreas ríor ruḃailce.
Virtue is everlasting wealth.

Saint ḃun ġaċ uilc.
Avarice is the foundation of every evil.

Saoirse a laetiḃ ḋíomaoine.
Freedom in days of idleness.

Seaċain cluanaiḋe a'r cealġaire.
Shun a prying thief and a deceiver.

Saoiġeann eaġnaċt ġaċ raiḋḃreas.
Wisdom excels all riches.

Saoiġeann críonaċt léiġean.
Wisdom excels book learning.
An ounce of sense is worth a bushel of learning.

Searḃ an t-arán a ítear.
Eaten bread is sour.

Searḃ na rutiḋ traċnona.
Kernels taste bitter in the evening.

[The meaning is, that when satiated with sweets—such as the kernels of nuts are—all day long, we begin at eventide, when tired, to find them tasteless, and even sour].

APPENDIX.

Sgeiteann fion firinne.
Wine reveals the truth.
In vino veritas.
When wine is in, wit is out.—Eng.
Quod est in corde sobrii est in ore ebrii.—Lat.
Τό ἐν καρδίᾳ τοῦ νήφοντος ἐπὶ τῆς γλώττης ἐστὶ τοῦ μεθύοντος.—Plut.
Οἴνου κατιόντος ἐπιπλέουσιν ἔπη.— Herodotus; *i.e.* when wine sinks, words swim.
Quid non ebrietas designat? operta recludit.—Pliny.

Sgeul fior e cia air bic luad e,
Buain de rior e agur cuir air ruar e.
**A true saying by whomsoever said—
Cut of the end what you add to the head.**

Sionnac a g-croicean an uain.
The fox in lamb's clothing.

Soigteac folam ir mo tonann.
An empty vessel has the greatest sound.
Empty vessels make the greatest sound.—Eng.
A fool's voice is known by multitude of words.—Solomon.
The shallowest stream makes most noise.— Eug.

Sona dail gnianda.
A sunny meeting is lucky.

Sona adluic fliuc.
A wet burying is lucky.

Sult gan ceo rod neime.
Delight unclouded is the happiness of heaven.

Tafan gadair a n-gleann glar,
Beit cainc le ceann gan eolur.
('Tis like the) barking of a hound in a verdant valley, to address a head without knowledge.

Ta fo laim an mangaine.
The smile is under hand—*i.e. to smile in one's sleeve.*

Ta fac le gac nid.
There is reason for every thing.
Too much of one thing is good for nothing.—Eng.
Est modus in rebus.—Horace.
Assez y a, si trop, n'y a.—Fr.

Táirne ann beó.
A nail in the quick.

Tig geimre for an fallsa.
Winter comes on the lazy.

Tig iomcar le foglaim.
Good deportment comes with education.

Tig grian a n-diaig na fearcana.
Sun comes after rain.
Sunshine after storm.—Eng.

Tionrganann cur mait crioc mait.
A good beginning leads the way to a good end.

Toirbeart fann ir airig gann.
A small offering and a slender return.
He that soweth sparingly shall reap sparingly.—2 Cor. ix. 6.
Qui parce seminat, parce et metet.—Ibid.

Toil gac aon reir mar gnío.
Each person's wish according as he acts.
Every one to his fancy.—Eng.

Tor eagnaid uaman Dé,
Ní b-fuil eagna mar í;
Mait an gné do'n té,
Eagla Dé cia air a m-bío.
The fear of God is the beginning of wisdom—
There is no wisdom like it;
It is a good sign for the person
Who is filled with the fear of the Lord.
Initium sapientiæ timor Domini.—Psalm cx.

Treid bodaig le sluag.
A clown's fight against a host—an useless effort.

Tóirigeact a gadair a'r gan fior a dat.
Looking for one's hound without knowing its colour.

Torac loinge clár,
Torac ait clocad;
Toraċ flaṫa fáilte,
Toraċ sláinte codla.
The beginning of a ship is a board,
The beginning of a kiln is laying the (first) stone;
The beginning of a prince's reign is greeting,
The beginning of health is sleep.

Torac coille a'r beine mona.
The beginning of a wood and the end of a bog
First in a wood and last in a bog.—Eng.

Tpeid na m-bó maol.
Fighting of the hornless cows.

Triur zan riazal—bean, muile azur muc.
Three without rule—a woman, a pig, and a mule.

Trom cearc a b-fad.
A hen carried far is heavy.

Tuizeann fear leizin leat-focal.
A man of learning understands half a word, *i.e.*, will know what the speaker means before the sentence is fully uttered.
Send a wise man on an errand, and say nothing to him.
Accenna al savio et lascia far a lui.—Ital.

Tuirleann saoi.
A sage slips.
Quandoque bonus dormitat Homerus.—Lat.
Wise men are caught in wiles.—Eng.
A good garden may have some weeds.—Eng.

Tuar zorta zailríon a'r zainb-ríon.
Storm and tempest, fore-runners of famine.
After a famine in the stall,
Comes a famine in the hall.—Somerset.

Tuar fozla, feartainn dian.
Violent rain is the omen of calamity.

Tuibe an áit air an muillionn.
Putting on the mill the straw of the kiln.
Rob Peter to pay Paul.—Eng. Or rather, meeting one necessity by what is immediately required for another.

Tus maic leat na h-oibre.
A good beginning (is) half the work.
Well begun is half done.—Eng.
Dimidium facti qui cœpit habet.—Horat.
Barba bagnata mezza rasa.—Ital.
A beard washed is half shaven.
Αρχὴ δέ τοι ἥμισυ παντος.—Lucian.

Uabar zan tairbe.
Pride without profit.
Profitless pride.—Eng.

Uallac ꜃iolla na leiṛ꜃e.
The sluggard's load.

Uiṁlact b' uaiṗleact.
Obedience (is due) to nobleness.

Uaiṗleact ꜃an ṛubailce.
(No) nobility without virtue.

Uiṛ꜃e a b' ioinċuiṛ a ꜃-criaṫuiṛ.
To carry water in a sieve.

*** For the last ten years the writer of these pages has been forming a collection of Irish proverbs: the number already in his possession would form a neat octavo volume. It is his intention one day to publish them. Those now presented to the public will, he hopes, revive a taste for this species of literary wisdom.

THE CELTIC TONGUE.

Composed, in 1855, by the Rev. Michael Mullin, Professor at St. Brendan's Seminary, Loughrea, while he had been yet a student of Maynooth College.

I.

It is fading! it is fading! like the leaves upon the trees!
It is dying! it is dying! like the Western-ocean breeze!
It is fastly disappearing, as footprints on the shore,
Where the Barrow, and the Erne, and Lough Swilly's waters roar—
Where the parting sunbeam kisses the Corrib in the West,
And the ocean, like a mother, clasps the Shannon to its breast!
The language of old Erin, of her history and name—
Of her monarchs and her heroes, of her glory and her fame—
The sacred shrine where rested, through her sunshine and her gloom,
The spirit of her martyrs, as their bodies in the tomb!
The time-wrought shell where murmured, through centuries of wrong,
The secret voice of freedom in annal and in song—
Is surely, fastly sinking into silent death at last,
To live but in the memories and relics of the Past!

II.

The olden Tongue is sinking, like a Patriarch to rest,
Whose Youthhood saw the Tyrian, on our Irish coasts a guest,*
Ere the Saxon or the Roman—ere the Norman or the Dane
Had first set foot in Britain, or the Visigoth in Spain.

* There is an old tradition to the effect, that during the commerce of the adventurous Tyrians with this country, one of their princes was invited over to Ireland by the king, and got married to one of the Irish princesses. Indeed, the antiquity of the "Celtic Tongue" cannot be traced out at present. Its origin is far within the past, and "loses itself in the night of fable." Some go so far as to assert *it* was the language of Adam and Eve in Paradise. *Satis superque!*

APPENDIX.

Whose Manhood saw the druid rite at forest tree and rock—
The savage tribes of Britain round the shrines of Zernebock;*
And for generations witnessed all the glories of the Gael,
Since our Celtic sires sung war-songs round the warrior-fires of Baal!
The tongues that saw its infancy are ranked among the Dead;
And from their graves have risen those now spoken in their stead.
All the glories of old Erin, with her liberty, have gone,
Yet their halo lingered round her while her olden Tongue l'ved on;
For, 'mid the desert of her woe, a monument more vast
Than all her pillar-towers, it stood—that old Tongue of the Past!

III.

And now 'tis sadly shrinking from the soil that gave it birth,
Like the ebbing tide from shore, or the spring-time from the earth;
O'er the island dimly fading, as a circle o'er the wave—
Still receding, as its people lisp the language of the slave.†
And with it, too, seem fading, as a sunset into night,
All the scattered rays of Freedom, that lingered in its light!
For, ah! though long with filial love it clung to Motherland,
And Irishmen were Irish still, in *tongue*, and heart, and hand!
Before the Saxon tongue, alas! proscribed it soon became;‡
And we are Irishmen to-day, but Irishmen in name!
The Saxon chain our rights and tongue alike doth hold in thrall,
Save where, amid the Connaught wilds, and hills of Donegal,
And by the shores of Munster, like the broad Atlantic blast,
The olden language lingers yet—an echo from the Past!

IV.

Through cold neglect 'tis dying, like a stranger on our shore.
No Teamhore's halls shall vibrate to its thrilling tones e'ermore—
No Laurence fire the Celtic clans round leaguered Athacleith—§
No Shannon waft from Luimneach's towers their war-songs to the sea.
Ah, the pleasant Tongue, whose accents were music to the ear!
Ah, the magic Tongue, that round us wove its spell so soft and dear!
Ah, the glorious Tongue, whose murmur could each Celtic heart enthral!
Ah, the rushing Tongue, that sounded like the rushing torrent's fall!

---

* Odin and Zernebuck were two divinities adored by the inhabitants of Britain.

† Tacitus, in his Germania, says: "The language of the conqueror in the mouth of the conquered, is ever the language of the slave."

‡ Not only have our rulers—especially during the early part of the last century—done everything they could to introduce the English language into those districts in which the Irish was spoken, but even the people seem to have co-operated with them in their endeavours. One fact (for which I can vouch) will show this:—Not many years since, in a certain district of the West, the children were compelled to carry to school, suspended round their necks, pieces of wood, on which were marked a number of "notches" equal to the number of Irish words spoken by the children during their absence from school. A punishment proportionate to the number of Irish words spoken was inflicted on the delinquent. O tempora! O mores!

§ St. Laurence O'Tuathail, Archbishop of Dublin (Athacleith in the Irish), by his eloquence, succeeded in organising the Irish chieftains, under the leadership of Roderick O'Connor, King of Connaught, against the first band of invaders who landed in this country, led by Strongbow and the traitorous Diarmud M'Murtach.

The Tongue that in the senate was the lightning flashing bright,
Whose echo in the battle was the thunder in its might;
The Tongue that once in chieftain's hall swelled loud the minstrel's lay
As chieftain, serf, or minstrel old, is silent there to-day;
Whose password burst upon the foe at Kong and Mullaghmast,*
Like those who nobly perished there, is numbered with the Past!

V.

The Celtic tongue is fading, and we coldly standing by—
Without a pang within the heart, a tear within the eye—
Without one pulse for freedom stirred, one effort made to save
The language of our fathers, lisp the language of the slave!
Sons of Erin! vain your efforts—vain your prayers for freedom's crown
Whilst you crave it in the language of the foe that clove it down.
Know you not that tyrants ever, with an art from darkness sprung,
Strive to make the conquered nation slaves alike in limb and *tongue*.
The Russian Bear ne'er stood secure o'er Poland's shattered frame,
Until he trampled from her breast the tongue that bore her name.†
Oh, be *Irish*, Irishmen, and rally for the dear old Tongue
Which, as ivy to a ruin, to the dear old land has clung;
Oh, snatch this relic from the wreck, the only and the last,
To show what Erin ought to be, by pointing to the Past!

* 'Nothing," says O'Callaghan, "so affrighted the enemy at the *raid* of Mullaghmast, and at a later period, on the field of Fontenoy, as the wild, unintelligible password—in the Irish tongue—with which the Irish troops burst upon the foe."

† Few readers of history can be unacquainted with the implacable hatred which the Russian government manifested towards the Polish tongue after the subjugation of that noble but ill-fated country by the myrmidons of the Empress Catherine. In a leading article on the Irish Language, in one of the numbers of the old *Nation*, the writer adduces the Polish tongue as a proof that, while the language of a country exists, the bulwarks of her liberty—that liberty which ever clings and breathes through the language of the people—can never be shaken in the heart of the country.

Críoċ.

CRITICAL NOTICES.

The following notices are deemed worthy of being re-published, chiefly for the combination of proofs and varied views they exhibit in favour of the language:

From The Nation, June, 28th, 1856.

No one who has not lived in an Irish speaking district can imagine the powerful effect of the language, when used by those who are known to understand English too—it is a magic key to the best affections of the people. We shall not easily forget the fervent blessings we have heard from peasant lips, the tears of loving pride in peasant eyes, at hearing the dear old speech *preferred* by those who had the choice of two; nor their habitual journeys of five or even eight miles on a Sunday morning to hear an Irish sermon.

There can be no question but that the Irish priesthood could do more for the cultivation of the language than any or all other influences. Premising that the present generation of students have zeal enough to set themselves in good earnest to acquire the language, it will be no fault of Mr. Bourke's if they do not succeed. His grammar, less elaborate than Mr. O'Donovan's, is much more complete than Connellan's, which too often assumes an amount of learning in the student that should make him independent of explanation; and, we think, superior to both in the practical clearness of its arrangement—being quite equal, indeed, to the best of the continental grammars, and excellently adapted to popularise the study of Irish among those who have hitherto been deterred by the formidable display of recondite difficulties put before the learner at every step. Spenser had revealed to Elizabeth the subtle influence of language upon nationality, and the severe measures taken in that reign for the suppression of the Irish tongue, though set at nought in the beginning, seem to have at length taken effect in the gradual decay of the language—for our rulers, alas, have ever been more wise and consistent in their oppression than we in our resistance. Other causes, no doubt, contributed to this result; settlement, intermarriage, and forfeiture. The plantation of James and the ruthless ravages of Cromwell, must have sorely deranged the social economy of the Irish-speaking race, and Dublin sufficiently un-Celtic always would naturally be the first to feel the influence of every change.

From The Catholic University Gazette, No. 54.

"The College Irish Grammar" appears to possess two principal excellencies attaching to this kind of composition—namely, brevity and perspicuity. We can turn at once to the declensions of substantives or the conjugations of verbs, drawn out in intelligible order in their respective places, without the need of having painfully to collect them for ourselves, as happens in some grammars, out of the midst of an interminable discussion; and the grammatical rules are simply and distinctly given. Nor, again, is the writer incompetent to illustrate his subject by examples and analogies drawn from the French, Italian, Latin, and Hebrew languages.

From The Cork Examiner, November 3rd, 1856.

And really, truth to speak, it is a decided acquisition to the Irish student. Although we cannot go to the extent of asserting that it is a very considerable improvement on the two latest and best—Connellan's and O'Donovan's grammars, yet, we must say, that it has its certain advantages. We must take it as the substitute for the former, because it is, indeed, fuller; whilst O'Donovan's great grammar—whose value Mr. Burke fully admits, because of its size and expense, is less accessible to the ordinary class of students. The introduction points out, amongst the special objects and tendency of this work, the necessity for its publication, arising from those causes, and observes, that former grammars were more particularly adapted to those who already knew how to *speak* Irish, than to those learners totally unacquainted with the language. For the latter class, therefore, a work such as is now provided, framed for facilitating its acquisition by them, is unquestionably a great advantage.

Our limits will not permit us to enter into details, on many points which we had marked for notice; but at the outset we must express our satisfaction with his directions for spelling, which are highly useful. The absence of a fixed system by the old writers, forms one of the greatest difficulties of our ancient MSS., each writer using a peculiar and arbitrary style of his own, much to the embarrassment of the student, who finds no assistance from his dictionary. We also fully subscribe to his view of the ultility and importance of the rule of Caol ne Caol, &c., that is, a narrow with a narrow and a broad with a broad vowel, which has so much influence in regulating Irish orthography. This rule has been a debatable point with Irish grammarians, being alternately condemned and approved of, but we think the weight of reason and authority is with those who are for maintaining it, as Mr. Burke does. It is indeed only by this rule that we can see any rational probability of reducing the language to any stable form of orthography, an object highly desirable to be kept in view.

We cannot too much commend our author for his observations on writing Irish in the English (or Roman) character which he utterly denounces.

The following observations from this truly excellent journal are truthful and judicious:

Our institutions, habits, and manners were for ages the objects of an incessant aggression. Instead of fostering and encouraging the national resources, spoliation and confiscation seem to have been the sole end and motive of English government. It was made penal to wear the hair in a particular fashion, *or to speak the native language*. The latter was assailed as the preserver and upholder of our distinct nationality, the barrier against subjugation and submission. This hostility has descended to our times. We find it in operation in a variety of ways —the bolt of ridicule has been discharged against it, and, as national pride dies out, it comes to be despised even by ourselves. In producing this calamitous result—this strange phase of opinion—our educational institutes, from the highest to the very lowest, have had an important share. Expelled from the higher schools, its latest injury came from the despicable hedge-school. It is notorious that these wretched seminaries, so long under the ban of the law, became within the last two or three generations the active instruments in the destruction and decay of the old national tongue. The utterance of an Irish sentence at home, or at school, incurred chastisement at the hands of the miserable pedagogue, himself scarcely knowing any other language. This spirit of persecution still lingers amongst us, and has been carried into our "*national* schools." Here love of the language by the master no less than the pupil is regarded as a crime. We have before us the second volume of the 21st report of the Commissioners of national education in Ireland, in which we find Newell reporting against a teacher of one of the schools thus under his inspection, not, be it remarked, for teaching Irish in his school or encouraging its use, but for cultivating it himself, as a literature, and solacing himself with the old language, doubtless, as a relaxation after the severe and ill-paid duties of his school are over. "Whitechurch—an untrained teacher; teacher appears deficient in energy; he is pretty constantly employed in translation of Irish MSS., which may interfere with his proper vocation as a schoolmaster!" The same spirit is *practically* at work in our local Queen's Colleges. In these we have professorships of the "Celtic" language established, it would seem, as sops to Cerberus, to blind a suspicious people, mistrustful of covert objects, with a semblance of nationality. The cultivation of Irish as a literature, and thereby the elucidation of our thousands of manuscript volumes, treating of history, law, medicine, divinity, astronomy, poetry, and romance, the preparation of pupils whose after pursuits would bring them into contact, or intercourse of business, or instruction, with a people speaking principally this language, bringing the landlord and his agent into useful communication with the tenantry, the counsel or attorney with the client and the witness, the trader with the customer, the physician with the patient, the clergyman with his parishioner, these would seem to be the natural and legitimate objects of these " chairs ;" yet no provision whatsoever is made for carrying out the pretended intent.

We fear we have trespassed farther than newspaper limits will permit in these observations, but we cannot conclude without expressing our honest conviction, that the author of this grammar has, by its publication, conferred a substantial benefit on Irish literature, and greatly facilitated the labours of the student by the assistance which this well-timed and well-executed publication must undoubtedly afford him.

From *The Dublin Evening Post*, July 1, 1856.

The young student wishing to add a knowledge of the Irish language—the oldest spoken in Europe—to his acquirements or accomplishments, could not possess a simpler, a safer, or a surer guide than this excellent grammar. The Rev. Author has produced it upon the common sense, and, consequently, the most perfect plan of adapting it in every respect to the capacity of the beginner. We do not know a better guide for students than this, whilst even the more advanced on the road to proficiency will find it a valuable assistant towards the attainment of perfection. The author has taken great pains, and proved very successful, in simplifying and explaining the difficulties of a language which has not had the aid of national cultivation, but which, on the contrary, has struggled for existence since the period of the Anglo-Norman settlement in this country. We have looked through it with care, and our good opinion of its merits is the result of our investigation. Mr. Bourke's work is not as ambitious as Dr. O'Donovan's more elaborate and more learned grammar; but it is equally, if not more useful; and we have, therefore, no hesitation in according it our hearty approval and warm recommendation.

From *The Galway Vindicator*, June 25th, 1856.

This is a most elaborate work, and must prove a perfect treasure not only to the students for the use of whom it is chiefly compiled, but to all those who aspire to a knowledge of the magnificent old Celtic language of Ireland. From the plan of the present work, the learner can nearly in every case, know from the nominative to what gender, and what declension every noun belongs, without wanting to learn first how it forms the genitive or possessive case. The forms of the different conjugation of verbs are given with great clearness and copiousness. Indeed, in this important particular alone, it is far superior to its predecessors.

From *The Freeman's Journal*, 5th July, 1856.

The Rev. Mr Bourke has done a signal service to the progress and spread of the Irish tongue, in supplying at a moderate charge, a clear and concise grammar, fit for the junior as well as the more advanced student. The rules on orthography are very lucid and practical, affording an unerring rule for the pronunciation of the language as now spoken in Connaught.

The declensions in Mr. Bourke's grammar are admirably arranged with as much precision as old Lilly gave those for the variation of Latin nouns. In this particular the work before us fills up a great desideratum.

His mode of conjugating verbs has given us much satisfaction; and we may here say that it is wonderful how few irregular verbs there are in our language as compared with others, especially the Saxon, which abounds in them: they are nearly all irregular.

The rules of syntax laid down in the grammar of the Rev. Mr. Bourke are very plain, easily understood, and are a decided improvement, as being more methodic than previous treatises. The treatise on prosody is highly interesting. He fully enters into the various systems of composition practised by our ancestors.

Some asserted that we had no subjunctive mood in Irish; but the rev. author has clearly dispelled this error. As well might it be said there was no subjunctive in Latin, whereas it is the same as the potential in form, or as the old optative in Lilly's praxis.

Our erudite author tells us there are only two conjugations in Irish. This is a great advantage.

The Kilkenny Journal.

Clearness, simplicity, and systematic arrangement, are the chief characteristics of the volume; and the whole is pervaded by an intense aroma of nationality which will at once win the confidence and secure the attention of the young generation which is now growing up to represent Ireland.

From The Tablet (First notice).

His having consulted, in the first place, for the students of St. Patrick's, Maynooth, does not lessen our obligations; for, if the old language becomes despised or neglected there, all efforts to preserve it are vain. Experience taught him that such a grammar as his was much needed in the *Alma Mater* of the Irish Priesthood.

There is no student of modern Irish, as now spoken and written, no matter how great may have been his proficiency in the study of the language, who will not find in it all that he desires, and much that he will not find in any other Irish grammar extant. In proof of this latter assertion, we need only point to his dissertations on fixing the standard Irish of orthography, on the number of conjugations, and on the subjunctive mood. As to the orthography, he seems to us to have weighed well and to have given its due share of consideration to that famous rule of Irish spelling, "*slender with slender, and broad with broad,*" which may be justly regarded as the anchor of Irish orthography. We have ourselves spent no little time in reading and studying Irish grammars, and we have never seen rules so clear, so concise, and so condensed as in his grammar.

In his prosody he takes up Macaulay's idea of poetry, which was that of Aristotle, and shows how imperious in fettering genius were the absurdly difficult sorts of ancient Irish verse, by which the Irish muse was as cramped in her movements as a Chinese lady.

It is a source of unmixed pleasure to us to see a student of Maynooth publish such a book at such a time; for it affords us a proof of the ardour and success with which some of the students of St. Patrick's (and we trust they are not a few) study the language in which our great Apostle preached to our pagan sires, and in which many a saint and hoary hermit prayed. We rejoice at it, because, as a class, none can do more—we won't say for the revival of the old language, for, thank Heaven, it is not yet dead, but for its wide and successful cultivation—than the Irish Priests. Hence it gave us considerable pain, some months ago, to be informed that nearly all the students of two provinces are exempted by their bishops from the study of Irish in Maynooth.

The Tipperary Free Press and Clonmel General Advertiser, June 17*th,* 1856.

If we mistake not, his Irish Grammar will become a standard authority, appreciated wherever industry, combined with a thorough mastery of his subject, and a facility of giving that knowledge clear expression, are valued as they deserve.

The Castlebar Telegraph, among other things, says:

But, it will be asked, were there not many grammars written before this? Had we not O'Brien's, Halliday's, O'Donovan's? It is true we had, but not one of them was calculated to popularise our venerable tongue, or to render its study agreeable. Dr. O'Donovan's is better adapted to suit the taste of the antiquarian and the erudite than the wants of the mere scholar. But Rev. Mr. Bourke's embraces all the qualities that can render a work written on a dry subject interesting. The style is at once clear, simple, attractive; his views of the subject plain and natural; the arrangement orderly and masterly; and the classification of the nouns and verbs new, original, and striking, enabling the learner at a glance to grasp the whole subject. Tracing Irish orthography to its source, he brings the mind of the reader on from point to point, showing from a few simple principles how easy it is, by keeping them before the mind, to learn the spelling of the Irish language, which, like Greek, abounds so much in primitives of one or two syllables and their combinations. This is a great point gained, as it was one that had not, we beg to observe, up to this been settled. "Every one," as he remarks in his preface, "dealt with the spelling of the language as he thought proper."

From The Anglo-Celt, July 19*th,* 1856.

The scholar, the patriot, the legist, the antiquarian, the historiographer are his debtors for the efforts which he has made to revive a time-honoured literature; and, so far, as our opinion may be judged worthy of being considered in the matter, these efforts may be taken as being eminently successful. The grammatical canons are clear, concise and illustrated in every instance with apposite examples: the arrangement is methodical throughout, and philology is carefully attended to wherever a knowledge of it could be deemed important. We would direct special attention to the rules laid down for writing in Irish and for fixing the orthography of words. Attention to the former will ensure such a knowledge of the tongue as may serve to render it a competent medium of communication; and without the aid of the latter, any knowledge, attained or attainable, must be knowledge of a jargon not of a language. The essays on metrical writing are correct and satisfactory, and the collection of Irish proverbs with the homogeneous ones in English, Greek, Latin, Italian, besides affording in itself a rich treat for the curious, shows the collector to be a gentleman of considerable reading and research.

Kilkenny Moderator, June 25*th,* 1856.

It promises to facilitate largely the study and acquirement of the language of which, as a key to the unlocking of our too long closed up historical records, and a means of elucidating the notable memories of our country in the olden time, we fully recognise the value.

From The Irish Reporter, October 1st, 1856.

" The College Irish Grammar" by obviating both these objections (that elaborate research and dearness of price), supplies a desideratum. Its peculiar and great merit is its simplicity and adaptation to the design of the author—to popularise the study, by supplying a suitable elementary treatise to the student who wishes to know something of the Irish language, as it it spoken at the present day. The whole subject, from the alphabet to the prosodial rhythm, is arranged and argued in a manner and with a view to its simplification and to lighten the labours of the learner.

From The Catholic Institute Magazine, August, 1856.

A glance will show the most uninitiated that the grammatical rules are here full, clear, and well-arranged, and that experience and anxious care are evidenced throughout.

From The American Celt, New York, February, 1857, published by T. D. MacGee, Esq.

It is in the highest degree creditable to the author that he should have conceived and perfected such a work while a divinity student. As an historical agent, as a national inheritance, the cultivation of the Gælic ought to be mainly advocated. These are reasons quite strong enough to sustain its votaries on both those grounds. Every man educated in Ireland, from this forth, ought certainly be held degraded if he neglected the lectures and classes devoted to native studies. Relentless war ought to be proclaimed against those Inspectors and Teachers of "National Schools," who proscribe and ridicule the old national language. Not, we repeat, that we, for our part either expect or desire to see an antique language generally revived in a modern empire, as the language of daily life. But just as the Flemings, who use French for the most part, still cherish their mother tongue along with it; and as the Canadians and Louisianians of the cities use French within doors, and keep English for the streets—so ought every young Irishman, with the greatly increased facilities now offered, be held bound in honor to learn the language of his country, and to use it, per preference, in the family circle.

The Tablet, second notice.

We have received much satisfaction from Mr. Bourke's mode of conjugating verbs. He has two conjugations. His syntax is full of lucidity and his prosody full of interest.

On the language he remarks: A national language is the epitome, the miniature picture of the nation. The dignity of the ancient Spanish character is impressed on the language of Spain, and the Italian tongue reflects the attributes of that music and pleasure-loving people. This seems to have been felt by Charles V. when he said that he should speak to his mistress in Italian, to his horse in German, to his birds in English, while the majesty of the Spanish language rendered it, he hoped, suitable medium for reverent and awful communings with the Deity. A peculiarity of the Hebrew people, ever contemplating the past, or vainly imagining the future, seems to be found in the Hebrew verb which has no present tense; and it is, we think, an illustration of the Irish character that the language of Ireland possesses no *Habeo.* As Father Bourke says, "We have no helping verb answering to the *avoir* of the French." The generosity and disinterestedness of the Irish character is disclosed in this fact, for a covetous people would certainly possess a "*habeo.*" Their mind, stammering out its cravings, would, in its struggles to articulate its greediness, finally give birth to a vocable expressive of "having;" but this effort has never been successfully made by the native Irish; and shall we not find in every page of their history the reflex of this peculiarity. . . . . A more selfish people would have been less unfortunate.

It would seem as if the native Irishman were either too poor or too high-minded to proclaim boldly that he has property. He cannot say it; his language does not supply the apposite verb; he gently states that it is "with him," *ta agam.* It is the "*est pro habeo.* Now, this peculiarity must have some cause, and that cause, we believe, is to be found in the unselfish disposition of the Irish. We can never understand Irish character and history without some knowledge of the Irish language.

It is another peculiarity of the Irish tongue that the imperative mood is invariably the root of all the ramifications of its verb. From this a philosophic mind would inevitably infer that the people who spoke this language were not intended by nature to be slaves. On the contrary, command is the foremost characteristic of the Irish. Their imperative mood is well, clearly, and prominently defined. It is the first thing you learn in studying the verbs. You learn to command when learning Irish. Now this peculiarity, like the former, must originate in some cause, and this cause assuredly is Irish character; it can be no other, for, as a necessary consequence from the nature of language, it harmonises to, and blends with, the nature of the people who speak it. The Irishman is the incarnation of the Irish tongue, and the Irish tongue is the vocalisation of the Irishman.

A people so eminently military as the Irish must employ the imperative mood, and, therefore, their language supplies them with powerful imperatives

REVIEWS OF THE SECOND EDITION OF "THE COLLEGE IRISH GRAMMAR."

The following is from the Dublin "Nation," 20th September, 1862.

THE CELTIC TONGUE.

"The College Irish Grammar;" by the Rev. U. J. Bourke, Professor of Humanity, Natural Philosophy, and Irish, St. Jarlath's College, Tuam. Second Edition. Published by John Mullany, 1, Parliament-street, Dublin.

We could not count many decades of years since we feared that we were destined to witness, in our own day, the total extinction from amongst us of our fine old Celtic language. For ages a proscribed dialect, it was dying away fast and sensibly; or rather, we should say, the hearts that loved and prized it, both for its intrinsic worth and as a distinctive feature of their nationality, were succumbing gradually to the fate which they could not avert, and the generation that succeeded did not seem to inherit their instincts and their sympathies. It began to be esteemed fashionable to ape after all that was English in dress and manners; and numbers, fearing to appear less Saxon than the Saxons themselves, were the foremost in decrying their national language from all polite circles, lest it might be suspected that they belonged to a race and country whose misfortunes they deemed a disgrace, and whose virtues they knew not how to appreciate. There still remained, however, a small section of enlightened Irishmen who disdained to join this vulgar crusade in discarding their country and their country's language, and who bravely endeavoured to stem this tide of anti-national prejudice which was fast sweeping away every vestige of our ancient enlightenment. So far from decrying the national language, as an "uncouth jargon," they adjudged it equal in beauty, strength, and copiousness to the classic tongues of Greece and Rome, and desired to see it largely cultivated, not merely among the peasantry, who always cherished it as a national inheritance, but also among the better educated and the more influential of their countrymen. For a long time the laudable desire of this true-hearted section of Irishmen seemed exceedingly difficult to be realized. Besides the adverse feelings described, there were many other obstacles to impede their noble efforts. The greatest of these arose from the fact, that, although their were many enlightened Irishmen both able and willing to benefit their country by rescuing from oblivion and illustrating its history, its language, and its antiquities, still there were no cheap, popular, elementary works in the Irish character adapted to the use of those who were almost utterly unacquainted with their mother tongue. This obstacle, in itself quite sufficient to deter students, otherwise well inclined to labor, from endeavouring to learn the Irish language, was some time since removed, to a great extent, by the publication of the Rev. Father Bourke's "Irish Grammar," and still further by the circulation of the "Easy Lessons" of *The Nation*—a work which, though of a simple and unpretending character, is nevertheless the very best we could conceive in the hands of any tyro, anxious, by his own unaided industry, to acquire in a short period a thorough knowledge of Gaelic.

With much pleasure, therefore, we peruse the Second Edition of the work, nothing the heavier by the various addenda, and rendered still more lucid than the first by a more precise and methodic arrangement of its parts. This is intended to be the people's edition, and it is, therefore, published at the cheapest possible price—a price that brings it within the reach of all; and it is sufficiently full and finished to enable any student who has mastered its contents to launch forth boldly into the sea of Irish classics—to unlock those sealed tomes which contain the science, the poesy, the history, and romance of our country—or read, in numbers full nigh as bold and sonorous as Homer's own, his masterly descriptions of the battles of the Greeks and Trojans, the debates of hoary octogenarian warriors, and the glowing harangues of god-like men. Or, should he desire to know how those soul-stirring airs, which Moore has rendered immortal, flow on and affect the soul when gushing forth through the medium of the sweet Celtic, he may open Dr. MacHale's translation of the "Irish Melodies," and sing, as Carolan would have sung, the woes of his heart for his afflicted lone land, because, like Sion, her "parent," "fallen from her head is the once regal crown; in her streets in her halls, Desolation hath spoken; and whilst it is day yet, her sun is gone down." Or, should hope inspire his song, he may prophesy in impassioned poetry "that her sun shall shine out when the brightest shall fade." But whatever be the pleasure or advantage he may propose to himself in cultivating his national language—whether to strengthen his claim to scholarship, or enjoy the laudable boast of having learned for her own sake his country's language—it is satisfactory to know that very few, if any, obstacles now remain to damp his energy in the generous pursuit—that, thanks to the learning and patriotism of Rev. U. J. Bourke, we have now an Irish grammar as finished and as cheap as any of the Continental grammars—and that the Irish is as easy of acquisition as any of the Continental dialects. The truth of this assertion may be tested by an examination of the work. The classification of letters and the determining of their proper sounds being the first thing which the learner of a strange language has to start with, and that on which mainly depends the ease and rapidity of his progress, the author has taken great pains to give, besides the names of the letters, their correct sounds, as far as that may be done by the aid of a strange alphabet. These the learner acquires at a glance, by having set before him a table, setting forth in one column the Irish vowels and diphthongs, and in immediate juxta-position another column, illustrating the former, by precisely similar sounds of English or French letters, with which his ear is already familiar; and the sound of the simple vowels and consonants once ascertained and noted, he readily acquires, by the aid of a similar table, containing double consonants and diphthongs, similarly illustrated, the precise sounds of all the combinations of letters that may take place throughout. By this ingenious method the student can easily master that which has been considered most difficult in the learning of Irish—the proper sounds of all the letters, whatever be their combination, being guided by similar sounds of English and French letters, in forming his ear to the correct standard pronunciation. A little farther on "accent" and "aspiration" lend their aid; and for any initial changes which, for euphony's sake, nouns may undergo when influenced, in certain cases, by the article and pronoun, the few simple and concise rules given are quite sufficient. Thus in the pronunciation of certain English and French words, which we articulate with the greatest ease, we equivalently pronounce some Irish words which we deemed above the power of our organs of speech. We know nothing more brief and simple than the few judicious rules for knowing the gender of all Irish nouns, of whatsoever class they be, and the exceptions to the general rules so few that they are remembered without an effort. The same may, in all truth, be affirmed of the " few practical hints" which the author gives for spelling; they contain *multum in parvo*. With such rules before us, we cannot but pronounce the knowledge of Irish spelling easy of acquisition, no matter how beginners may start at what they consider an unsightly array of apparently superfluous consonants, presenting, as they deem, a barrier to the smooth flow of the sound. The use and advantage of those apparently superfluous consonants is, however, soon experienced

If sound afford a clue to spelling, as it certainly should, the foreigner who undertakes to learn the English language will find spelling and pronunciation oftener at variance with each other than he could in learning Irish, and he will be the more perplexed at finding one word, which he is taught to pronounce in a certain manner, differ very widely in spelling from another word of precisely similar pronunciation. Thus, for instance, the words "*plough*," "*now*," "*thou*," and many others, are pronounced similarly, but spelt quite differently. A foreigner, judging from analogy of sound, can see no reason why the first of these words should not be written, " plow," for analogy of sound is the aid to which beginners naturally trust, and in a thousand cases it will deceive them. An Englishman discovers the same difficulty in learning French when he learns that " *vous*" is pronounced as if written " *voo*," the verbal termination "*ent*," as if " *ong*," and in some places not pronounced at all, as in " *dirent*." Seeing such irregularities in those highly cultivated languages, we should not marvel at a few irregularities, if any there be, in the persecuted dialect of Ireland. The rule caol le caol ᴀᴢᴜʀ leaṫan le leaṫan, which, as a general rule, the author advocates, is found to be of very great utility. It requires that a slender vowel comes before a consonant or consonants, a slender vowel also immediately follows, and similarly with regard to a broad vowel preceding a consonant. This rule obviates a great many difficulties in spelling which could not be removed by analogy of sound.

With regard to declension—the most unsettled portion of Irish grammar—the author adopts a system of O'Donovan, fixing the number of declensions at five; and we think his reasons for th; determination are valid. A lesser number of declensions would not certainly exhaust all the distinct classes of Irish nouns; whereas, if with Halliday and Connellan, we admit a greater number, we will have some declensions comprising under them only a few nouns, and even those reducible to some one of the five classes. Thus, we might say, we would have a rule without a subject. The rules for the formation of cases appear to us exceedingly concise and plain. With reference to the characteristic sign of the declensions, there is very little difficulty about it in the three first declensions—a broad vowel before a final consonant marking the first declension; a slender vowel similarly situated, the second; and a peculiar class of verbal and abstract nouns comprising the third declension. But with regard to the fourth and fifth declensions, we perceived in some grammars something like a *circulus vitiosus*, or perhaps an absurdity. Thus in declining nouns of this class, we could not tell to which declension they belonged without first knowing what termination they assumed in the genitive; and how know this, when, *ex hypothesi*, we did not know how to inflect them? The only remedy for this seemed to be, to collect all nouns of the fifth declension, and give them in column; knowing the declension, of course, there was no difficulty in inflecting them. In this manner has Professor Bourke, with much expenditure of time and labor, remedied this defect. We now come to another part of grammar, concerning which there exists a diversity of opinion—the number of conjugations that we should admit. Some admit only one; Professor Bourke is an advocate for two, and argues from a fact which, if true, gives great force to his reasoning. The fact on which his reasoning depends is, that if we admit only one conjugation, we will, in that case, have remaining as exceptions, a class of verbs larger than that class which the conjugation is intended to regulate. And the fact is true, so far as our experience of the language enables us to judge. There is, therefore, to say the least, as much reason for grouping into a class, and regulating by a second conjugation those verbs that would otherwise remain exceptions to the first conjugation, as there was for forming the class comprehended under the first conjugation itself. Besides, this is so much the more convenient for the student, seeing that, if he knows how to inflect one verb throughout, he knows how to inflect every verb in its class; whereas if they remain exceptions to a conjugation, he has no such analogy to guide him, every verb in that case being, so to speak, *sui juris*. Hence the propriety of two conjugations instead of one; the axiom that rules should not be multiplied without utility, affords a reason for having no more than two. In this section Professor Bourke's grammar is perfect. His rules for the formation of tenses are most judicious and plain, and his observations on moods and tenses are very philosophic. A synopsis, showing forth at a glance all the changes of the inflected verbs, still further aids the student, who, in fact, has but to learn the conjugation of two verbs, and he has mastered all. These are the principal sections in Part I. of the "Irish Grammar," and certainly nothing can be more clear, concise, and methodic than the entire of it. There is no confusion of arrangement, no obscurity of diction; everything is neatly mapped and defined in its proper place, and everything is illustrated by example. . . . . . .

It possesses, moreover, another advantage not to be despised by the public in those days of venal scribes—it is published at the cheapest possible price—a price which should make it a household work with all, if not to profit by, at least to extend patronage to those who deserve well of their country. We have at present very few either willing or competent to labor in collecting and illustrating our history and antiquities. And, truth to say, the labors of the few such we have, are too often depreciated. Unwilling though we may be to admit the fact, we are forced to yield to the conviction that the "brave men and true" whose glory it was to fight and toil with hand and brain for their country's weal and glory, are becoming fewer every day, and that the love of country and kindred, which burned strong within them, is disappearing with them.

This is an age of scholarship, in which languages are acquired with a dispatch before unknown, and yet we find numbers laying claims to extensive knowledge quite ignorant of their country's language—nay, worse, determined to be so. If such apathy and indifference to the claims of country be not an index of a generous, noble, and manly spirit, we cannot form too high an estimate of the nobility of soul of a large section of those whom we claim as countrymen. We are not now enthusiastic in the cause we advocate—we do not hope that men will inconvenience themselves in upholding the honor of their country by doing justice to its history and traditions; but we would expect that no Irishman would contemn or despise that which he is incapable of judging. Those who are acquainted with the Irish language cannot but admit its intrinsic worth. If we decry it as uncouth and barbarous, we do it an injustice—nay, we do an injustice to our race, our country, and its claims to enlightenment, to its music and its poetry—for a people's language is the truest test of their enlightenment. If that be barbarous, one will find it difficult to repel the charge of barbarism, should any one at present choose to designate three millions of our people as barbarous, for among them that language still lives and flourishes, and, nevertheless, we would scorn the man who would feel inclined to be ashamed of them. It were as well to speak out and join with our enemies in dooming our language to the same fate that millions of our people have already undergone, as endeavour to degrade it by such contempt. The languages of Greece, and Rome, and Italy, and France flourish in the Irish schools and colleges, and Irish students at home seek and obtain exemption from the duty of learning their own. No enemy of Ireland would desire to see her sons more apathetic than this, and when such apathy prevails it is in vain that a few sincere lovers toil for their country. It might be as well if they abandoned their toils, and sought solace from disappointment in the near prospect of hearing English bucolics chanted in a pastoral country.

From the Dublin " Irishman."
THE PEOPLE'S EDITION.
"The College Irish Grammar;" Second Edition, Part I., price 2s. By the Rev. ULICK J. BOURKE, Professor, St. Jarlath's College, Tuam.

WE hail with much delight this new edition of Father Bourke's valuable Grammar. At any time it would be an immense accession to our fund of Celtic literature; but at present, when the effort to eradicate everything bearing the name of Celt out of this Celtic land is redoubled, it is doubly to be prized, and the zealous and learned reverend author doubly to be thanked for its re-appearance. It is a decided improvement on the first edition, both in matter and arrangement; not that the first was not peculiarly excellent, but that this is, what is saying a good deal, much better still.

Nothing is omitted, and you are led, step by step, from the elementary sounds of the letters of the alphabet, the different declensions simplified, comparison, collocation, conjugation, to the most select elegancies of expression and style. In his manner of dealing with the intricate matter of declension, we much admire Father Bourke's masterly hand. He simplifies the rules, so as to almost entirely eliminate exceptions. In dealing with the vexed and unsettled question of orthography, he adopts the grand rule always practised by his Grace the Archbishop of Tuam—now, perhaps, the only living superior of Father Bourke as an Irish scholar—of caol le caol, &c., a rule which, if generally followed, would vastly smooth the path of the Irish student. . . .

The book is a marvel of cheapness, and we wish it were in the hands of Irish men and women in every clime throughout the globe.

From the " Galway Vindicator," 31st December, 1862.
Now that the task hitherto considered difficult, of learning the written and spoken Irish language, has been, by means of the " College Grammar" and the "Easy Lessons," republished from the pages of the *Nation,* been rendered

comparatively easy, it appears to us the duty of every Irishman to learn his native tongue.

The writer of those lines would say to each of his readers—"begin." Three or four years ago he himself did not know either to speak or write the language of old Ireland. He had not had the opportunity, and he did not learn it before nor along with the English tongue. Still he laboured, and by means of the "Easy Lessons," the "College Grammar," and other helps, he has at length succeeded so far as to be able to speak it fairly—nay, it might be said, fluently, and to write it correctly. Could you not at least endeavour to do the same? Well, then, if you do not learn it yourself do not at least raise, as was the fashion, the voice of disparagement against the speech of your fathers. This was the enemy's game, played, alas! too long. It is their wish to uproot the National Tongue—it ought to be yours to keep it, like the ruined abbeys, an *abiding* relic of the glories of the past. The same policy that waged war with the faith of the people waged war with their language too; the latter has succumbed—the former, like its Founder, has arisen from the grave in which heretical hate had in vain consigned it. Will the language be allowed to moulder, through our own neglect, in the tomb of decay to which it has been sought to consign it?

From the "Castlebar Telegraph," October, 1862.

"The College Irish Grammar;" by the Rev. ULICK J. BOURKE, Second Edition. John Mullany, 1, Parliament-street, Dublin.

ONCE on a time our legislators made it penal to speak the Irish language, That time has passed away, and that law has lost its force; but the spirit that gave it being is still alive and vigorous. It does not work now-a-days so ruthlessly as it did some two centuries ago; yet it is at this moment as determined on carrying out its object—the annihilation of the Irish language—as it has been when an Irish-speaking man was a criminal amenable to English law. No wonder, then, if, under such a blighting influence as this spirit of intolerance has been to everything National in this country, our native tongue should have totally disappeared from many parts of our native land.

Fortunately, many gentlemen of great talents and high standing have arrayed all their energies against this intolerant spirit; they have done, and are still doing, a great deal in the good cause. The Rev. Father Bourke has been enrolled in their ranks, and it is no small praise to him to say, that his labours in defence of the Irish language have gained him a distinguished position amongst his co-operators.

Against the spirit that would destroy our tongue Father Bourke has entered the lists. He saw, as we all must see, that a Nation without a language was an anomaly—he saw a silent but pertinacious effort made to destroy our tongue—he saw the sad consequence to the religion and patriotism of our countrymen that would infallibly attend the success of this endeavour. On all these accounts he has given his assistance to check the progress of destruction. The preservation of a language is, and ever must be, one of the most important means for the preservation of a Nationality. Strange as it may appear at first sight, the Irish language has been proved to be a strong bulwark in defence of the Irish Catholic Church. These two facts have been felt by our rulers, past and present, and therefore they have determined to destroy our language. They have been felt by Father Bourke, and therefore he has given his aid to raise it to its former proud position amongst our people. We believe he has so far done his part well.

On a previous occasion we have given the first edition of his grammar that praise which it has so well merited. In doing so we have no more than echoed the sentiments of the whole Irish Press. Indeed, if we had not this confirmation of our remarks, we might, with some show of reason, be accused of undue impartiality, as possessing a more than usual interest in the author. We have now before us the first part of the second edition. Its greatest advantage over the other appears, at the first glance, to consist in its being issued in a more popular form; and a careful perusal of its contents will show this to have been the writer's object. The great obstacles to the use of O'Donovan's Grammar, was a bulkiness that excluded a general circulation, or an erudition that ignored a want of rudimental knowledge in the learner. The first of these obstacles prevented its reaching the humbler classes of Irishmen; the second rendered it less useful to the rich than it might be. In his first edition Rev. Father Bourke has endeavoured to remove these. The result of his labours was a work, neat, cheap, perspicuous—a work which, whilst discarding the long disquisitions of its predecessors, gave in a few words their conclusions, with a few reasons for those conclusions—a work which recognized the merits of former works, and explained and reduced to system, all that was obscure and ill-arranged in them. His first edition, therefore, has been the most popular Irish Grammar ever presented to the Irish public. The second is a decided improvement on the popularity of the first. It is a small volume, tastefully got up, well printed on good paper. Its size and price would lead us to imagine it a mere abridgement, whilst it, in reality, contains nearly twice as much matter as the other.

Our limits render it imposible for us to attempt an extensive analysis of its contents—we can do no more than mark its general features. When we state that it is a philosophic work, we fear to terrify some of our more indolent readers. But there is such a thing as philosophy without puzzling syllogisms and mysterious technicalities. It is, in fact, no more than the common sense of one man examined by and united to the common sense of a second; this, again, refined by that of a third; and so on, until some master mind reduces this sublimated common sense of many to a fixed and certain form. And so is it with the work before us. In its present form it is evidently the result of great and persevering labour. Points which we imagined sufficiently explained before are again studied over; hence the addition of much useful and interesting knowledge. The information given by preceding writers is examined and, if not found to rest on sound philological principles, condemned. The origin of the facts treated of are investigated, until the ultimate principles regulating the construction of the language are reached. These principles, then, are the foundation upon which the whole structure is raised; from them conclusions are drawn, and from these conclusions easy and simple rules are adduced for arriving at a perfect acquaintance with the language. All this appears to us to be done in such a way as to enable the student in a very short time to gain a high degree of proficiency in the spoken and written tongue; and it is in this method of deducing from first principles that this book lays claim to be framed on a philosophic basis. . . . .

Thirty pages are devoted to Irish Orthography. This very important subject appears to us to be treated in such a way as to remove, as far as possible, all difficulties from the path of the learner. The rules for the pronunciation and spelling are given in the shortest and clearest form. So short and clear, indeed, are they, that a person entirely ignorant of the language could, we believe, pronounce and spell almost every word in Irish after a few hours' application. The importance of this will be readily estimated when we remember, that it is not every educated Englishman that can pronounce and spell every word in his own tongue correctly, even after a school acquaintance with it of many years. Rev. Professor Bourke is, therefore, deserving of praise for having made the nearest approach to what might be called the royal road over the *pons assinorum* of the philologist.

No point, perhaps, in the construction of our native tongue has given rise to such a diversity of opinions as the declension of nouns. Every writer thought his own theory best calculated to mark distinctly the changes of the several classes. The consequence was, that the learner was confounded amidst antagonistic systems if he attempted to consult different authors, and was often exposed to be lost in a labyrinth of divisions and sub-divisions if he confined himself to one. This was by no means the fault of the language itself. Even here, though it admits a great variety in the forms and inflections of its nouns, there can still be traced an analogy that smooths away what appears at first sight to be almost insuperable difficulties. It was the fault of the expounder, who rendered imaginary difficulties real, by endeavouring to simplify what was already sufficiently simple. Such a state of things could not, of course, be permitted to continue. Dr. O'Donovan solved the difficulty by reducing all nouns to five declensions; but, though he solved the difficulty, a clue by which one could at first sight know unerringly the gender and declension, he did not supply. It was reserved for Mr. Bourke to solidify, as it were, by a book within the reach of all, that which has been a moving quicksand with Celtic etymologists.

The classification of verbs under the smallest possible number of conjugations removes one of the greatest obstacles to the acquirement of a language. If, indeed, all verbs could be reduced to a single conjugation, with determinate case-endings admitting no exceptions for the several moods and tenses, it would certainly be a very great advantage; but no language, so far as we are aware, has this simplicity of arrangement. It must remain a desideratum until our philosophers give us what they have long ago promised—the universal language. The Irish has here, admittedly, a great superiority over the other European tongues. Many of them have four or five conjugations, thus heaping difficulty on difficulty in the path of the learner. The Irish, by having only two, removes a great deal of these obstacles; and the peculiarities of these two are so well explained, and their relations to each other, and their analogies and points of difference with foreign tongues so clearly defined, and the rules to guide in their formation so simple, that that which has been hitherto somewhat troublesome is now comparatively plain and easy.

We have compared this little work with others of the same class, and we do not hesitate to affirm that, though great energies have been devoted to the completion of these, and though many of them are proud monuments of what our dear old tongue has been, and may yet be, still this Grammar, taken on the whole, so far from suffering by a comparison with any of its predecessors, will only rise the higher in the estimation of the candid examiner. We hail its appearance, therefore, with a hearty welcome, and have a confident trust that the day will come when success shall crown the labours of our author, and of the other true men of our country, who love to see our dear old Gaelic tongue raised to its former proud position in the land of our fathers.

www.ingramcontent.com/pod-product-compliance
Lightning Source LLC
Chambersburg PA
CBHW030006240426
43672CB00007B/851